Lecture Notes in Computer Science 12073

More information about this series at http://www.springer.com/series/7407

Keisuke Nakano · Konstantinos Sagonas (Eds.)

Functional and Logic Programming

15th International Symposium, FLOPS 2020
Akita, Japan, September 14–16, 2020
Proceedings

 Springer

Editors
Keisuke Nakano (iD)
Tohoku University
Sendai, Japan

Konstantinos Sagonas (iD)
Uppsala University
Uppsala, Sweden

ISSN 0302-9743   ISSN 1611-3349 (electronic)
Lecture Notes in Computer Science
ISBN 978-3-030-59024-6   ISBN 978-3-030-59025-3 (eBook)
https://doi.org/10.1007/978-3-030-59025-3

LNCS Sublibrary: SL1 – Theoretical Computer Science and General Issues

This Springer imprint is published by the registered company Springer Nature Switzerland AG
The registered company address is: Gewerbestrasse 11, 6330 Cham, Switzerland

Preface

This volume contains the papers presented at 15th International Symposium on Functional and Logic Programming (FLOPS 2020) held during September 14–16, 2020, online due to the COVID-19 pandemic, while initially expected to take place in Akita, Japan, during April 23–25, with beautiful cherry blossoms in the best season.

FLOPS aims to bring together practitioners, researchers, and implementors of declarative programming, to discuss mutually interesting results and common problems: theoretical advances, their implementations in language systems and tools, and applications of these systems in practice. The scope includes all aspects of the design, semantics, theory, applications, implementations, and teaching of declarative programming. FLOPS specifically aims to promote cross-fertilization between theory and practice and among different styles of declarative programming.

For the first time, FLOPS 2020 employed a double-blind reviewing process. The call for papers resulted in 31 abstract submissions from which 25 were submitted as full papers. Each submission was reviewed by at least four reviewers, either members of the Program Committee (PC) or external referees. After careful and thorough discussions, the PC accepted 11 papers and a short paper. The program also included three invited talks by Makoto Hamana and Adam Chlipala.

We would like to thank all invited speakers and authors for their contributions. We are grateful to all PC members and external reviewers, for their hard work, and to EasyChair for their conference management system that made our work of organizing FLOPS 2020 much easier. We thank the local co-chairs, Kazuyuki Asada, Ryoma Sin'ya, and Katsuhiro Ueno, who made an invaluable effort in setting up the conference and making sure everything ran smoothly, even online.

Finally, we would like to thank our sponsor, the Japan Society for Software Science and Technology (JSSST) SIGPPL, for their continued support. We acknowledge the cooperation of ACM SIGPLAN, the Asian Association for Foundation of Software (AAFS), and the Association for Logic Programming (ALP).

August 2020

Keisuke Nakano
Konstantinos Sagonas

Organization

Program Chairs

Keisuke Nakano   Tohoku University, Japan
Konstantinos Sagonas   Uppsala University, Sweden

General Chair

Keisuke Nakano   Tohoku University, Japan

Local Chairs

Kazuyuki Asada   Tohoku University, Japan
Ryoma Sin'ya   Akita University, Japan
Katsuhiro Ueno   Tohoku University, Japan

Program Committee

Elvira Albert   Universidad Complutense de Madrid, Spain
María Alpuente   Universitat Politècnica de València, Spain
Edwin Brady   University of St Andrews, UK
Michael Hanus   CAU Kiel, Germany
Nao Hirokawa   JAIST, Japan
Zhenjiang Hu   Peking University, China
John Hughes   Chalmers University of Technology, Sweden
Kazuhiro Inaba   Google, Japan
Shin-Ya Katsumata   National Institute of Informatics, Japan
Ekaterina Komendantskaya   Heriot-Watt University, UK
Leonidas Lampropoulos   University of Maryland, USA
Akimasa Morihata   The University of Tokyo, Japan
Shin-Cheng Mu   Academia Sinica, Taiwan
Koji Nakazawa   Nagoya University, Japan
Enrico Pontelli   New Mexico State University, USA
Didier Remy   Inria, France
Ricardo Rocha   University of Porto, Portugal
Ilya Sergey   Yale-NUS College, Singapore
Kohei Suenaga   Kyoto University, Japan
Tachio Terauchi   Waseda University, Japan
Kazushige Terui   Kyoto University, Japan
Simon Thompson   University of Kent, UK
Philip Wadler   The University of Edinburgh, UK
Nicolas Wu   Imperial College London, UK

External Reviewers

Jacques Garrigue
Miguel Isabel
Oleg Kiselyov
Alicia Merayo
Pedro Vasconcelos

Performance-Scaling Challenges in Formal Verification with Proof Assistants (Abstract)

Adam Chlipala

MIT CSAIL, Cambridge MA 02139, USA
adamc@csail.mit.edu

Abstract. The twenty-first century has seen an exciting uptick in the use of proof assistants for mechanized correctness proof of realistic computer systems. That is, developers are not just writing code but also using software tools for writing and checking proofs, establishing that code behaves as it should, increasing assurance dramatically compared to alternatives like testing. These developments, using proof assistants like Isabelle and Coq, exhibit widely varying levels of *proof automation*. That is, the individual steps of logical arguments come at very different levels of detail, from "now apply modus ponens" to "now establish the correctness of this whole phase of my compiler, through the following several pages of heuristic scripting." Increased levels of automation seem important for more widespread adoption for proof of real-world systems, to overcome doubts that mechanized proof adds too much developer effort.

This talk will give my reections on trying to scale up automation in the Coq proof assistant, and I hope, also provide lessons relevant to other proof assistants. My collaborators and I have found that almost any serious effort of this kind is likely to hit a performance wall, with Coq as it stands today. The existence of such a wall may surprise Coq users who are accustomed to writing more manual proofs, roughly at the level of careful paper proofs; and it may be all the more surprising to those who think of any kind of "proof" as inherently theoretical and thus disconnected from concerns of performance optimization. I will give examples in proof of functional correctness for software and hardware systems.

What are the key challenges? In the tradition of dependent type theory that Coq builds on, *term reduction* is a central operation of proof checking, and reduction strategies matter a lot for performance. Coq users can learn about the intricacies of how the proof checker chooses strategies, or they can be more explicit through methods like *proof by reflection*, one successful example of which I will describe. On top of the core mechanics of proof checking, a proof assistant will typically provide a *proof engine* that exports higher-level operations managing subgoals and unification variables. We have been studying the fundamental determinants of poor performance scaling by Coq's proof engine, and I will sketch preliminary results on bottlenecks in key operations.

My overall goal in the talk is to make clear that these performance issues are underappreciated but crucial to scaling proofs. As a community, we are evolving proof assistants and their applications in tandem, learning lessons about the design of both. No doubt today's performance bottle-necks will be addressed by a mix of "mere engineering" and new scientific contributions, and I would like to encourage the audience to consider looking into both!

Keywords: Proof assistants · Dependent types · Proof engines · Program verification · Coq

Contents

Invited Talk

Theory and Practice of Second-Order Rewriting: Foundation, Evolution, and SOL

Makoto Hamana$^{(\boxtimes)}$

Department of Computer Science, Gunma University, Kiryu, Japan
`hamana@gunma-u.ac.jp`

Abstract. We give an overview of the theory and practice of second-order rewriting. Second-order rewriting methods have been demonstrated as useful that is applicable to important notions of programming languages such as logic programming, algebraic effects, quantum computation, and cyclic computation. We explain foundation and evolution of second-order rewriting by presenting the framework of second-order computation systems. We also demonstrate our system SOL of second-order laboratory through various programming language examples.

1 Introduction

Computation rules such as the β-reduction of the λ-calculus and arrangement of let-expressions are fundamental mechanisms of functional programming. Computation rules for modern functional programming are necessarily higher-order and are presented as a λ-calculus extended with extra rules such as rules of let-expressions or first-order algebraic rules like "$0 + x \to x$".

Because of ubiquity of computation rules, a general framework to describe and reason about them is necessary. **Second-order computation systems** are a framework of second-order rewriting the present author has developed for recent years [Ham17b, Ham18, Ham19, HAK20]. A second-order computation system consists of rewrite rules that may involve second-order typed terms.

2 Foundation: Second-Order Computation Systems

We give the definition of monomorphic second-order computation systems. We assume that $\mathcal{A}$ is a set of *atomic types* (e.g.. Bool, Nat, etc.). We assume that the set of *molecular types* (or *mol types* for short) $\mathcal{T}$ is generated by atomic types, and type constructors is the least set satisfying $\mathcal{T} = \mathcal{A} \cup \{T(a_1, \ldots, a_n) \mid a_1, \ldots, a_n \in \mathcal{T}, T \text{ is an } n\text{-ary type constructor}\}$. By a *type constructor* T of arity n, we mean that it takes n-mol types $a_1, \ldots, a_n$ and gives a mol type $T(a_1, \ldots, a_n)$. A *signature* Σ is a set of function symbols of the form

$$f : (\overline{a_1} \to b_1), \ldots, (\overline{a_m} \to b_m) \to c$$

© Springer Nature Switzerland AG 2020
K. Nakano and K. Sagonas (Eds.): FLOPS 2020, LNCS 12073, pp. 3–9, 2020.
https://doi.org/10.1007/978-3-030-59025-3_1

where all a_i, b_i, c are mol types (thus any function symbol is of up to second-order type).

$$\frac{y : b \in \Gamma}{\Theta \rhd \Gamma \vdash y : b} \qquad \frac{(M : a_1, \ldots, a_m \to b) \in \Theta \qquad \Theta \rhd \Gamma \vdash t_i : a_i \quad (1 \leq i \leq m)}{\Theta \rhd \Gamma \vdash M[t_1, \ldots, t_m] : b}$$

$$\frac{f : (\overline{a_1} \to b_1), \cdots, (\overline{a_m} \to b_m) \to c \in \Sigma \qquad \Theta \rhd \Gamma, \overline{x_i : a_i} \vdash t_i : b_i \quad (1 \leq i \leq m)}{\Theta \rhd \Gamma \vdash f(\overline{x_1^{a_1}.t_1}, \ldots \overline{x_m^{a_m}.t_m}) : c}$$

Fig. 1. Typing rules of meta-terms

A *metavariable* is a variable of (at most) first-order function type, declared as $M : \overline{a} \to b$ (written as capital letters $M, n, K, \ldots$). A *variable* of a molecular type is merely called variable (written usually $x, y, \ldots$, or sometimes written x^b when it is of type b). The raw syntax is given as follows.

- *Terms* have the form $t ::= x \mid x.t \mid f(t_1, \ldots, t_n)$.
- *Meta-terms* extend terms to $t ::= x \mid x.t \mid f(t_1, \ldots, t_n) \mid M[t_1, \ldots, t_n]$.

The last form $M[t_1, \ldots, t_n]$ is called a *meta-application*, meaning that when we instantiate $M : \overline{a} \to b$ with a term s, free variables of s (which are of types $\overline{a}$) are replaced with (meta-)terms $t_1, \ldots, t_n$.

A metavariable context Θ is a sequence of (metavariable:type)-pairs, and a context Γ is a sequence of (variable:mol type)-pairs. A judgment is of the form $\Theta \rhd \Gamma \vdash t : b$. A meta-term t is *well-typed* by the typing rules Fig. 1.

For meta-terms $\Theta \rhd \Gamma \vdash \ell : b$ and $\Theta \rhd \Gamma \vdash r : b$, a *computation rule* is of the form $\Theta \rhd \Gamma \vdash \ell \Rightarrow r : b$ satisfying: (i) ℓ is a deterministic second-order pattern [YHT04]. (ii) all metavariables in r appear in ℓ. We usually omit the context and type and simply write $\ell \Rightarrow r$.

A **computation system** is a set $\mathcal{C}$ of computation rules. We write $s \Rightarrow_{\mathcal{C}} t$ to be one-step computation using $\mathcal{C}$ obtained by the inference system in Fig. 2.

Example 1. The simply typed λ-terms on base types Ty are modelled in our setting as follows. Suppose that Arr is a type constructor. The set $\mathcal{T}$ of all mol types is the least set satisfying $\mathcal{T} = \text{Ty} \cup \{\text{Arr}(a, b) \mid a, b \in \mathcal{T}\}$, i.e., the set of all simple types in our encoding. The λ-terms are given by a signature

$$\Sigma_{\text{lam}} = \left\{ \begin{array}{l} \text{lam}_{a,b} : (a \to b) \to \text{Arr}(a, b) \\ \text{app}_{a,b} : \text{Arr}(a, b), a \to b \end{array} \middle| \; a, b \in \mathcal{T} \right\}$$

The β-reduction law is presented as for each $a, b \in \mathcal{T}$,

(beta) $M : a \to b, \; N : a \; \rhd \; \vdash \text{app}_{a,b}(\text{lam}_{a,b}(x^a. M[x]), N) \; \Rightarrow \; M[N] : b$

Note that $\text{Arr}(a, b)$ is a mol type, but function types $a \to b$ are not mol types.

3 Evolution of Second-Order Computation

Using the second-order computation systems, we have formulated various higher-order calculi and have checked their decidability [Ham17b, Ham18, Ham19, HAK20]. The framework of second-order computation systems is founded on foundational studies on second-order computation. We describe below the foundations and succeeding developments how the theory of second-order computation systems is evolved.

$$
\text{(Rule)} \frac{\Theta \triangleright \Gamma', \overline{x_i : a_i} \vdash s_i : b_i \quad (1 \le i \le k) \quad \theta = [\overline{M \mapsto \overline{x}.s}] \\ (M_1 : (\overline{a_1} \to b_1), \dots, M_k : (\overline{a_k} \to b_k)) \triangleright \ \vdash \ \ell \Rightarrow r \ : c) \in \mathcal{C}}{\Theta \triangleright \Gamma' \vdash \ \ell[\overline{M \mapsto \overline{x}.s}] \Rightarrow_\mathcal{C} r[\overline{M \mapsto \overline{x}.s}] \ : c}
$$

$$
\text{(Fun)} \frac{f : (\overline{a_1} \to b_1), \cdots, (\overline{a_k} \to b_k) \to c \in \Sigma \\ \Theta \triangleright \Gamma, \overline{x_i : a_i} \vdash \ t_i \Rightarrow_\mathcal{C} t'_i : b_i \quad (\text{some } i \text{ s.t. } 1 \le i \le k)}{\Theta \triangleright \Gamma \vdash \ f(\overline{x_1^{a_1}}.t_1, \dots, \overline{x_i^{a_i}}.t_i \dots, \overline{x_1^{a_1}}.t_k) \Rightarrow_\mathcal{C} f(\overline{x_1^{a_1}}.t_1, \dots, \overline{x_i^{a_i}}.t'_i \dots, \overline{x_1^{a_1}}.t_k) \ : c}
$$

Fig. 2. Second-order computation (one-step)

Second-Order Abstract Syntax. The syntactic structure of meta-terms and substitution for abstract syntax with variable binding was introduced by Aczel [Acz78] for his general framework of rewrite rules. Fiore, Plotkin, and Turi formulated *second-order abstract syntax* [FPT99, Fio08] as a mathematical structure of syntax with variable binding using algebras on presheaves. The abstract syntax and the associated algebraic structure have extended to second-order abstract syntax with extra feature or type discipline: having metavariables [Ham04], simple types [Fio02, Ham07], dependent types [Fio08], and polymorphic types [Ham11].

Second-Order Algebraic Theories. Ordinary equational logic is logic for equations on first-order algebraic terms. Second-order algebraic theories and equational logic [FM10, FH10] are second-order extensions, which provide mathematical models of second-order equations and deduction based on second-order abstract syntax and its algebraic models. This algebraic modelling of syntax, theory, type system, or programming laguage has been actively investigated. Staton demonstrated that second-order algebraic theories are a useful framework that models various important notions of programming languages such as logic programming [Sta13a], algebraic effects [Sta13b, FS14], and quantum computation [Sta15]. We have also applied it to modelling cyclic structures [Ham10a] and cyclic datatypes modulo bisimulation [Ham17a]. This line of algebraic modelling is still active. Recently, Arkor and Fiore [AF20] gave algebraic models of simple type theories.

Second-Order Computation Systems. Based on the structures of second-order abstract syntax and algebraic theories, the present author developed the

framework of **second-order computation systems** and its algebraic semantics [Ham05]. Notably, the semantics established the first *sound and complete*
model of second-order rewriting systems. It has been extended to *simply-typed*
second-order computation systems and its algebraic semantics [Ham07]. This is
the basis of our SOL system described below. We also applied the semantical
structures to develop termination proof techniques: the interpretation method
[Ham05], higher-order semantic labelling [Ham07,Ham10b], and modular termination [Ham20].

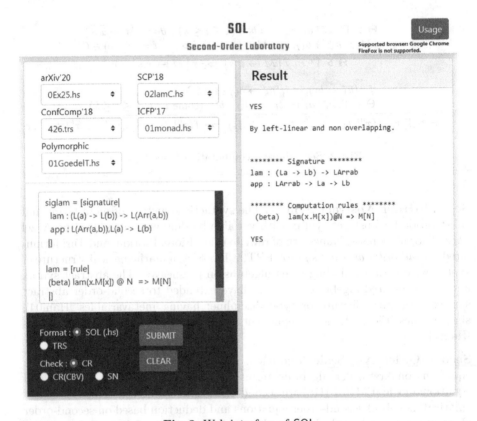

Fig. 3. Web interface of SOL

Second-Order Rewriting. As the rewriting theoretic side, Aczel's formal
language allowed him to consider a general framework of rewrite rules for
calculi with variable binding, which influenced Klop's rewriting framework of
combinatory reduction systems [Klo80]. Blanqui introduced a typed version of
Klop's framework and provided a termination criterion of the General Schema
[Bla00,Bla16]. SOL implemented the General Schema criterion for termination
checking.

Polymorphic Computation Systems with Call-by-Value. We have developed a general framework of *multiversal polymorphic algebraic theories* [FH13]

based on polymorphic abstract syntax [Ham11]. It admits multiple type universes and higher-kinded polymorphic types. Based on it, we presented a new framework of polymorphic second-order computation systems [Ham18] that can accommodate a distinction between values and non-values [HAK20]. It is suitable for analysing fundamental calculi of programming languages. We developed a type inference algorithm and new criteria to check the confluence property.

4   SOL: Second-Order Laboratory

Based on the above foundations and evolution, we have implemented the system SOL (Fig. 3) [Ham17b, Ham18, Ham19, HAK20]. SOL is a tool to check confluence and termination of polymorphic second-order computation systems. The system works on top of the interpreter of Glasgow Haskell Compiler. SOL uses the feature of quasi-quotation (i.e. [signature|..] and [rule|..] are quasi-quotations) of Template Haskell, with a custom parser which provides a readable notation for signature, terms and rules. It makes the language of our formal computation rules available within a Haskell script. For example, the computation system of λ-calculus in Example 1 is described as

```
siglam = [signature| lam : (a -> b) -> Arr(a,b)
                     app : Arr(a,b),a -> b       |]

lambdaCal = [rule|  (beta) lam(x.M[x])@N => M[N] |]
```

The web interface for SOL is available at the author's homepage: http://www.cs.gunma-u.ac.jp/hamana/sol/.

References

[Acz78] Aczel, P.: A general Church-Rosser theorem. Technical report, University of Manchester (1978)

[AF20]   Arkor, N., Fiore, M.: Algebraic models of simple type theories: a polynomial approach. In: Proceedings of LICS 2020, pp. 88–101. ACM (2020)

[Bla00] Blanqui, F.: Termination and confluence of higher-order rewrite systems. In: Bachmair, L. (ed.) RTA 2000. LNCS, vol. 1833, pp. 47–61. Springer, Heidelberg (2000). https://doi.org/10.1007/10721975_4

[Bla16] Blanqui, F.: Termination of rewrite relations on λ-terms based on Girard's notion of reducibility. Theor. Comput. Sci. **611**, 50–86 (2016)

[FH10]   Fiore, M., Hur, C.-K.: Second-order equational logic (extended abstract). In: Dawar, A., Veith, H. (eds.) CSL 2010. LNCS, vol. 6247, pp. 320–335. Springer, Heidelberg (2010). https://doi.org/10.1007/978-3-642-15205-4_26

[FH13]   Fiore, M., Hamana, M.: Multiversal polymorphic algebraic theories: syntax, semantics, translations, and equational logic. In: 28th Annual ACM/IEEE Symposium on Logic in Computer Science, LICS 2013, pp. 520–529 (2013)

[Fio02] Fiore, M.: Semantic analysis of normalisation by evaluation for typed lambda calculus. In: Proceedings of PPDP 2002, pp. 26–37. ACM Press (2002)

[Fio08]   Fiore, M.: Second-order and dependently-sorted abstract syntax. In: Proceedings of LICS 2008, pp. 57–68 (2008)

[FM10]   Fiore, M., Mahmoud, O.: Second-order algebraic theories. In: Hlinený, P., Kucera, A. (eds.) MFCS 2010. LNCS, vol. 6281, pp. 368–380. Springer, Heidelberg (2010). https://doi.org/10.1007/978-3-642-15155-2_33

[FPT99]   Fiore, M., Plotkin, G., Turi, D.: Abstract syntax and variable binding. In: Proceedings of LICS 1999, pp. 193–202 (1999)

[FS14]   Fiore, M., Staton, S.: Substitution, jumps, and algebraic effects. In: Proceedings of the CSL-LICS 2014, pp. 41:1–41:10 (2014)

[HAK20]   Hamana, M., Abe, T., Kikuchi, K.: Polymorphic computation systems: theory and practice of confluence with call-by-value. Sci. Comput. Program. **187**(102322) (2020)

[Ham04]   Hamana, M.: Free Σ-monoids: a higher-order syntax with metavariables. In: Chin, W.-N. (ed.) APLAS 2004. LNCS, vol. 3302, pp. 348–363. Springer, Heidelberg (2004). https://doi.org/10.1007/978-3-540-30477-7_23

[Ham05]   Hamana, M.: Universal algebra for termination of higher-order rewriting. In: Giesl, J. (ed.) RTA 2005. LNCS, vol. 3467, pp. 135–149. Springer, Heidelberg (2005). https://doi.org/10.1007/978-3-540-32033-3_11

[Ham07]   Hamana, M.: Higher-order semantic labelling for inductive datatype systems. In: Proceedings of PPDP 2007, pp. 97–108. ACM Press (2007)

[Ham10a] Hamana, M.: Initial algebra semantics for cyclic sharing tree structures. Log. Methods Comput. Sci. **6**(3(15)), 1–1–23 (2010)

[Ham10b] Hamana, M.: Semantic labelling for proving termination of combinatory reduction systems. In: Escobar, S. (ed.) WFLP 2009. LNCS, vol. 5979, pp. 62–78. Springer, Heidelberg (2010). https://doi.org/10.1007/978-3-642-11999-6_5

[Ham11]   Hamana, M.: Polymorphic abstract syntax via Grothendieck construction. In: Hofmann, M. (ed.) FoSSaCS 2011. LNCS, vol. 6604, pp. 381–395. Springer, Heidelberg (2011). https://doi.org/10.1007/978-3-642-19805-2_26

[Ham17a] Hamana, M.: Cyclic datatypes modulo bisimulation based on second-order algebraic theories. Log. Methods Comput. Sci. **13**, 1–38 (2017)

[Ham17b] Hamana, M.: How to prove your calculus is decidable: practical applications of second-order algebraic theories and computation. Proc. ACM Program. Lang. **1**(22), 1–28 (2017)

[Ham18]   Hamana, M.: Polymorphic rewrite rules: confluence, type inference, and instance validation. In: Gallagher, J.P., Sulzmann, M. (eds.) FLOPS 2018. LNCS, vol. 10818, pp. 99–115. Springer, Cham (2018). https://doi.org/10.1007/978-3-319-90686-7_7

[Ham19]   Hamana, M.: How to prove decidability of equational theories with second-order computation analyser SOL. J. Funct. Program. **29**(e20) (2019)

[Ham20]   Hamana, M.: Modular termination for second-order computation rules and application to algebraic effect handlers. arXiv:1912.03434 (2020)

[Klo80]   Klop, J.W.: Combinatory reduction systems. Ph.D. thesis, CWI. Mathematical Centre Tracts, vol. 127, Amsterdam (1980)

[Sta13a] Staton, S.: An algebraic presentation of predicate logic. In: Proceedings of FOSSACS 201, pp. 401–417 (2013)

[Sta13b] Staton, S.: Instances of computational effects: an algebraic perspective. In: Proceedings of LICS 2013, p. 519 (2013)

[Sta15] Staton, S.: Algebraic effects, linearity, and quantum programming languages. In: Proceedings of POPL 2015, pp. 395–406 (2015)

[YHT04] Yokoyama, T., Hu, Z., Takeichi, M.: Deterministic second-order patterns. Inf. Process. Lett. **89**(6), 309–314 (2004)

Contributed Papers

The Bang Calculus Revisited

Antonio Bucciarelli[1], Delia Kesner[1,2], Alejandro Ríos[3], and Andrés Viso[3,4(✉)]

[1] Université de Paris, CNRS, IRIF, Paris, France
kesner@irif.fr
[2] Institut Universitaire de France, Paris, France
[3] Universidad de Buenos Aires, Buenos Aires, Argentina
aeviso@dc.uba.ar
[4] Universidad Nacional de Quilmes, Bernal, Argentina

Abstract. Call-by-Push-Value (CBPV) is a programming paradigm subsuming both Call-by-Name (CBN) and Call-by-Value (CBV) semantics. The paradigm was recently modelled by means of the Bang Calculus, a term language connecting CBPV and Linear Logic.

This paper presents a revisited version of the Bang Calculus, called $\lambda!$, enjoying some important properties missing in the original system. Indeed, the new calculus integrates commutative conversions to unblock value redexes while being confluent at the same time. A second contribution is related to non-idempotent types. We provide a quantitative type system for our $\lambda!$-calculus, and we show that the length of the (weak) reduction of a typed term to its normal form *plus* the size of this normal form is bounded by the size of its type derivation. We also explore the properties of this type system with respect to CBN/CBV translations. We keep the original CBN translation from λ-calculus to the Bang Calculus, which preserves normal forms and is sound and complete with respect to the (quantitative) type system for CBN. However, in the case of CBV, we reformulate both the translation and the type system to restore two main properties: preservation of normal forms and completeness. Last but not least, the quantitative system is refined to a *tight* one, which transforms the previous upper bound on the length of reduction to normal form plus its size into two independent *exact* measures for them.

1 Introduction

Call-by-Push-Value. The Call-by-Push-Value (CBPV) paradigm, introduced by P.B. Levy [37,38], distinguishes between values and computations under the slogan *"a value is, a computation does"*. It subsumes the λ-calculus by adding some primitives that allow to capture both the Call-by-Name (CBN) and Call-by-Value (CBV) semantics. CBN is a lazy strategy that consumes arguments without any preliminary evaluation, potentially duplicating work, while CBV is greedy, always computing arguments disregarding whether they are used or not, which may prevent a normalising term from terminating, *e.g.* $(\lambda x.I)\,\Omega$, where $I = \lambda x.x$ and $\Omega = (\lambda x.x\,x)\,(\lambda x.x\,x)$.

© Springer Nature Switzerland AG 2020
K. Nakano and K. Sagonas (Eds.): FLOPS 2020, LNCS 12073, pp. 13–32, 2020.
https://doi.org/10.1007/978-3-030-59025-3_2

Essentially, CBPV introduces unary primitives thunk and force. The former freezes the execution of a term (*i.e.* it is not allowed to compute under a thunk) while the latter fires again a frozen term. Informally, force (thunk t) is semantically equivalent to t. Resorting to the paradigm slogan, thunk turns a computation into a value, while force does the opposite. Thus, CBN and CBV are captured by conveniently labelling a λ-term using force and thunk to pause/resume the evaluation of a subterm depending on whether it is an argument (CBN) or a function (CBV). In doing so, CBPV provides a unique formalism capturing two distinct λ-calculi strategies, thus allowing to study operational and denotational semantics of CBN and CBV in a unified framework.

Bang Calculus. T. Ehrhard [25] introduces a typed calculus, that can be seen as a variation of CBPV, to establish a relation between this paradigm and Linear Logic (LL). A simplified version of this formalism is later dubbed Bang calculus [26], showing in particular how CBPV captures the CBN and CBV semantics of λ-calculus via Girard's translations of intuitionistic logic into LL. A further step in this direction [15] uses Taylor expansion [27] in the Bang Calculus to approximate terms in CBPV. The Bang calculus is essentially an extension of λ-calculus with two new constructors, namely *bang* (!) and *dereliction* (der), together with the reduction rule der $(!t) \mapsto t$. There are two notions of reduction for the Bang calculus, depending on whether it is allowed to reduce under a bang constructor or not. They are called *strong* and *weak reduction* respectively. Indeed, it is weak reduction that makes bang/dereliction play the role of the primitives thunk/force. Hence, these modalities are essential to capture the essence behind the CBN–CBV duality. A similar approach appears in [42], studying (simply typed) CBN and CBV translations into a fragment of IS4, recast as a very simple λ-calculus equipped with an indeterminate lax monoidal comonad.

Non-idempotent Types. Intersection types, pioneered by [16,17], can be seen as a syntactical tool to denote programs. They are invariant under the equality generated by the evaluation rules, and type all and only all normalising terms. They are originally defined as *idempotent* types, so that the equation $\sigma \cap \sigma = \sigma$ holds, thus preventing any use of the intersection constructor to count resources. On the other hand, *non-idempotent* types, pioneered by [28], are inspired from LL, they can be seen as a syntactical formulation of its relational model [11,30]. This connection suggests a *quantitative* typing tool, being able to specify properties related to the consumption of resources, a remarkable investigation pioneered by the seminal de Carvalho's PhD thesis [18] (see also [20]). Non-idempotent types have also been used to provide characterisations of complexity classes [8]. Several papers explore the qualitative and quantitative aspects of non-idempotent types for different higher order languages, as for example Call-by-Name, Call-by-Need and Call-by-Value λ-calculi, as well as extensions to Classical Logic. Some references are [3,4,13,24,36]. Other relational models were directly defined in the more general context of LL, rather than in the λ-calculus [19,21,22,33].

An interesting recent research topic concerns the use of non-idempotent types to provide *bounds* of reduction lengths. More precisely, the size of type derivations has often been used as an *upper bound* to the length of different evaluation strategies [13, 24, 34–36, 40]. A key notion behind these works is that when t evaluates to t', then the size of the type derivation of t' is smaller than the one of t, thus the size of type derivations provides an upper bound for the *length* of the reduction to a normal form as well as for the *size* of this normal form.

A crucial point to obtain *exact bounds*, instead of upper bounds, is to consider only *minimal* type derivations, as the ones in [9, 18, 22]. Another approach was taken in [1], which uses an appropriate notion of *tightness* to implement minimality, a technical tool adapted to Call-by-Value [3, 31] and Call-by-Need [4].

1.1   Contributions and Related Works

This paper presents a reformulation of the untyped Bang calculus, and proposes a quantitative study of it by means of non-idempotent types.

The Untyped Reduction. The Bang calculus in [25] suffers from the absence of *commutative conversions* [14, 41], making some redexes to be syntactically blocked when open terms are considered. A consequence of this approach is that there are some normal forms that are semantically equivalent to non-terminating programs, a situation which is clearly unsound. This is repaired in [26] by adding commutative conversions specified by means of σ-reduction rules, which are crucial to unveil hidden (value) redexes. However, this approach presents a major drawback since the resulting combined reduction relation is not confluent.

Our revisited Bang calculus, called $\lambda!$, fixes these two problems at the same time. Indeed, the syntax is enriched with explicit substitutions, and σ-equivalence is integrated in the primary reduction system by using the *distance* paradigm [5], without any need to unveil hidden redexes by means of an independent relation. This approach restores *confluence*.

The Untyped CBN and CBV Encodings. CBN and CBV (untyped) translations are extensively studied in [23, 32, 39]. The authors establish two encodings *cbn* and *cbv*, from untyped λ-terms into untyped terms of the Bang calculus, such that when t reduces to u in CBN (resp. CBV), $cbn(t)$ reduces to $cbn(u)$ (resp. $cbv(t)$ reduces to $cbv(u)$) in the Bang calculus. However, CBV normal forms in λ-calculus are not necessarily translated to normal forms in the Bang calculus.

Our revisited notion of reduction naturally encodes (weak) CBN as well as (open) CBV. More precisely, the $\lambda!$-calculus encodes weak CBN and open CBV specified by means of explicit substitutions, which in turn encode the corresponding well-known notions of weak CBN and open CBV (see for example [6]). These two notions are dual: weak CBN forbids reduction inside arguments, which are translated to bang terms, while open CBV forbids reduction under λ-abstractions, also translated to bang terms. More precisely, we simply extend to explicit substitutions the original CBN translation from λ-calculus to the Bang calculus, which preserves normal forms, but we subtly reformulate the CBV one. In contrast to [32], our CBV translation does preserve normal forms.

The Typed System. Starting from the relational model for the Bang calculus proposed in [32], we propose a type system for the $\lambda!$-calculus, called $\mathcal{U}$, based on non-idempotent intersection types. System $\mathcal{U}$ is able to fully *characterise* normalisation, in the sense that a term t is $\mathcal{U}$-typable if and only if t is normalising. More interestingly, we show that system $\mathcal{U}$ has also a quantitative flavour, in the sense that the length of any reduction sequence from t to normal form *plus* the size of this normal form is *bounded* by the size of the type derivation of t. We show that system $\mathcal{U}$ also captures the standard non-idempotent intersection type system for CBN, as well as a new type system $\mathcal{V}$ that we define in this paper for CBV. System $\mathcal{V}$ characterises termination of open CBV, in the sense that t is typable in $\mathcal{V}$ if and only if t is terminating in open CBV. This can be seen as another (collateral) contribution of this paper. Moreover, the CBV embedding in [32] is not complete with respect to their type system for CBV. System $\mathcal{V}$ recovers completeness (left as an open question in [32]). Finally, an alternative CBV encoding of typed terms is proposed. This encoding is not only sound and complete, but now enjoys preservation of normal-forms.

A Refinement of the Type System Based on Tightness. A major observation concerning β-reduction in λ-calculus (and therefore in the Bang calculus) is that the size of normal forms can be exponentially bigger than the number of steps to these normal forms. This means that bounding the sum of these two integers *at the same* time is too rough, not very relevant from a quantitative point of view. Following ideas in [1,9,18], we go beyond upper bounds. Indeed, another major contribution of this paper is the refinement of the non-idempotent type system $\mathcal{U}$ to another type system $\mathcal{E}$, equipped with constants and counters, together with an appropriate notion of *tightness* (*i.e.* minimality). This new formulation fully exploits the quantitative aspect of the system, in such a way that *upper bounds* provided by system $\mathcal{U}$ are refined now into *independent exact bounds* for time and space. More precisely, given a tight type derivation Φ with counters (b, e, s) for a term t, we can show that t is normalisable in $(b + e)$-steps and its normal form has *size* s. The opposite direction also holds. Therefore, exact measures concerning the *dynamic* behaviour of t, are extracted from a *static* (tight) typing property of t.

Road-Map. Section 2 introduces the $\lambda!$-calculus. Section 3 presents the sound and complete type system $\mathcal{U}$. Section 4 discusses (untyped and typed) CBN/CBV translations. In Sect. 5 we refine system $\mathcal{U}$ into system $\mathcal{E}$, and we prove soundness and completeness. Conclusions and future work are discussed in Sect. 6. Most of the proofs are omitted and can be found in [12].

2   The Bang Calculus Revisited

This section presents a revisited (conservative) extension of the original Bang calculi [25,26], called $\lambda!$. From a syntactical point of view, we just add explicit substitutions operators. From an operational point of view, we use *reduction at a distance* [5], thus integrating commutative conversions without jeopardising confluence (see the discussion below).

Given a countably infinite set $\mathcal{X}$ of variables $x, y, z, \ldots$ we consider the following grammar for terms (denoted by $\mathcal{T}$) and contexts:

$$\begin{aligned}
\textbf{(Terms)} \quad & t, u ::= x \in \mathcal{X} \mid t\,u \mid \lambda x.t \mid !\,t \mid \mathtt{der}\,t \mid t[x \backslash u] \\
\textbf{(List contexts)} \quad & \mathtt{L} ::= \square \mid \mathtt{L}[x \backslash t] \\
\textbf{(Contexts)} \quad & \mathtt{C} ::= \square \mid \mathtt{C}\,t \mid t\,\mathtt{C} \mid \lambda x.\mathtt{C} \mid !\,\mathtt{C} \mid \mathtt{der}\,\mathtt{C} \mid \mathtt{C}[x \backslash u] \mid t[x \backslash \mathtt{C}] \\
\textbf{(Weak contexts)} \quad & \mathtt{W} ::= \square \mid \mathtt{W}\,t \mid t\,\mathtt{W} \mid \lambda x.\mathtt{W} \mid \mathtt{der}\,\mathtt{W} \mid \mathtt{W}[x \backslash u] \mid t[x \backslash \mathtt{W}]
\end{aligned}$$

Terms of the form $t[x \backslash u]$ are **closures**, and $[x \backslash u]$ is called an **explicit substitution** (ES). Special terms are $\mathtt{I} = \lambda z.z$, $\mathtt{K} = \lambda x.\lambda y.x$, $\Delta = \lambda x.x\,!\,x$, and $\Omega = \Delta\,!\,\Delta$. Weak contexts do not allow the symbol $\square$ to occur inside the bang construct. This is similar to weak contexts in λ-calculus, where $\square$ cannot occur inside λ-abstractions. We will see in Sect. 4 that weak reduction in the $\lambda!$-calculus perfectly captures head reduction in CBN, disallowing reduction inside arguments, as well as open CBV, disallowing reduction inside abstractions. We use $\mathtt{C}\langle t \rangle$ (resp. $\mathtt{W}\langle t \rangle$ and $\mathtt{L}\langle t \rangle$) for the term obtained by replacing the hole $\square$ of $\mathtt{C}$ (resp. $\mathtt{W}$ and $\mathtt{L}$) by t. The notions of **free** and **bound** variables are defined as expected, in particular, $\mathtt{fv}(t[x \backslash u]) \stackrel{def}{=} \mathtt{fv}(t) \setminus \{x\} \cup \mathtt{fv}(u)$, $\mathtt{fv}(\lambda x.t) \stackrel{def}{=} \mathtt{fv}(t) \setminus \{x\}$, $\mathtt{bv}(t[x \backslash u]) \stackrel{def}{=} \mathtt{bv}(t) \cup \{x\} \cup \mathtt{bv}(u)$ and $\mathtt{bv}(\lambda x.t) \stackrel{def}{=} \mathtt{bv}(t) \cup \{x\}$. We extend the standard notion of α-**conversion** [7] to ES, as expected. We use $t\,\{x \backslash u\}$ to denote the **meta-level** substitution operation, *i.e.* all the free occurrences of the variable x in the term t are replaced by u. This operation is defined, as usual, modulo α-conversion. We use two special predicates to distinguish abstractions and bang terms possibly affected by a list of explicit substitutions. Indeed, $\mathtt{abs}(t)$ iff $t = \mathtt{L}\langle \lambda x.t' \rangle$ and $\mathtt{bang}(t)$ iff $t = \mathtt{L}\langle !\,t' \rangle$. Finally, we define the **w-size** of terms as follows: $|x|_w := 0$, $|t\,u|_w := 1 + |t|_w + |u|_w$, $|\lambda x.t|_w := 1 + |t|_w$, $|!\,t|_w := 0$, $|\mathtt{der}\,t|_w := 1 + |t|_w$, and $|t[x \backslash u]|_w := |t|_w + |u|_w$.

The $\lambda!$-**calculus** is given by the set of terms $\mathcal{T}$ and the **(weak) reduction relation** $\to_{\mathtt{w}}$, which is defined as the *union* of $\to_{\mathtt{dB}}$ (distant Beta), $\to_{\mathtt{s!}}$ (substitute bang) and $\to_{\mathtt{d!}}$ (distant bang), defined respectively as the closure by contexts $\mathtt{W}$ of the following rewriting rules:

$$\begin{aligned}
\mathtt{L}\langle \lambda x.t \rangle\,u &\mapsto_{\mathtt{dB}} \mathtt{L}\langle t[x \backslash u] \rangle \\
t[x \backslash \mathtt{L}\langle !\,u \rangle] &\mapsto_{\mathtt{s!}} \mathtt{L}\langle t\,\{x \backslash u\} \rangle \\
\mathtt{der}\,(\mathtt{L}\langle !\,t \rangle) &\mapsto_{\mathtt{d!}} \mathtt{L}\langle t \rangle
\end{aligned}$$

We assume that all these rules avoid capture of free variables.

Example 1. Let $t_0 = \mathtt{der}\,(!\,\mathtt{K})\,(!\,\mathtt{I})\,(!\,\Omega)$. Then,

$$t_0 \to_{\mathtt{d!}} \mathtt{K}\,(!\,\mathtt{I})\,(!\,\Omega) \to_{\mathtt{dB}} (\lambda y.x)[x \backslash !\,\mathtt{I}]\,(!\,\Omega) \to_{\mathtt{dB}} x[y \backslash !\,\Omega][x \backslash !\,\mathtt{I}] \to_{\mathtt{s!}} x[x \backslash !\,\mathtt{I}] \to_{\mathtt{s!}} \mathtt{I}$$

Remark that the second dB-step uses action at a distance, where $\mathtt{L}$ is $\square[x \backslash !\,\mathtt{I}]$.

Given the translation of the Bang Calculus into LL proof-nets [25], we refer to dB-steps as m-steps (multiplicative) and (s!, d!)-steps as e-steps (exponential).

Remark that reduction is *at a distance*, in the sense that the list context $\mathtt{L}$ in the rewriting rules allows the main constructors involved in these rules to be separated by an arbitrary finite list of substitutions. This new formulation integrates commutative conversions inside the main (logical) reduction rules of the calculus, in contrast to [26] which treats these conversions by means of a set of independent σ-rewriting rules, thus inheriting many drawbacks. More precisely, in the first formulation of the Bang calculus [25], there are hidden (value) redexes that block reduction, thus creating a mismatch between normal terms that are semantically non-terminating. The second formulation in [26] recovers soundness, by integrating a notion of σ-equivalence which is crucial to unveil hidden redexes and ill-formed terms (called *clashes*)[1]. However, adding σ-reduction to the logical reduction rules does not preserve confluence. Our notion of reduction addresses this two issues at the same time[2]: it integrates commutative conversions and is confluent (Theorem 1).

We write $\twoheadrightarrow_{\mathsf{w}}$ for the reflexive-transitive closure of $\rightarrow_{\mathsf{w}}$. We write $t \twoheadrightarrow_{\mathsf{w}}^{(b,e)} u$ if $t \twoheadrightarrow_{\mathsf{w}} u$ using b dB steps and e (s!, d!)-steps.

The reduction relation $\rightarrow_{\mathsf{w}}$ enjoys a weak diamond property, *i.e.* one-step divergence can be closed in one step if the diverging terms are different, since $\rightarrow_{\mathsf{w}}$ is not reflexive. Otherwise stated, the reflexive closure of $\rightarrow_{\mathsf{w}}$ enjoys the strong diamond property.

Lemma 1. *If $t \rightarrow_{p_1} t_1$ and $t \rightarrow_{p_2} t_2$ where $t_1 \neq t_2$ and $p_1, p_2 \in \{\mathsf{dB}, \mathsf{s!}, \mathsf{d!}\}$, then there exists t_3 such that $t_1 \rightarrow_{p_2} t_3$ and $t_2 \rightarrow_{p_1} t_3$.*

The result above does not hold if reductions are allowed inside arbitrary contexts. Consider for instance the term $t = (x\,!\,x)[x\backslash!\,(\mathtt{I}\,!\,\mathtt{I})]$. We have $t \rightarrow_{\mathsf{s!}} (\mathtt{I}\,!\,\mathtt{I})\,!\,(\mathtt{I}\,!\,\mathtt{I})$ and, if we allow the reduction of the dB-redex $\mathtt{I}\,!\,\mathtt{I}$ appearing banged inside the explicit substitution, we get $t \rightarrow_{\mathsf{dB}} (x\,!\,x)[x\backslash!\,z[z\backslash!\,\mathtt{I}]]$. Now, the term $(x\,!\,x)[x\backslash!\,z[z\backslash!\,\mathtt{I}]]$ s!-reduces to $z[z\backslash!\,\mathtt{I}]\,!\,(z[z\backslash!\,\mathtt{I}])$, whereas two dB-reductions are needed in order to close the diamond, *i.e.* to rewrite $(\mathtt{I}\,!\,\mathtt{I})\,!\,(\mathtt{I}\,!\,\mathtt{I})$ into $z[z\backslash!\,\mathtt{I}]\,!\,(z[z\backslash!\,\mathtt{I}])$.

This gives the following two major results (see [12] for details).

Theorem 1.

- *The reduction relation $\rightarrow_{\mathsf{w}}$ is confluent.*
- *Any two different reduction paths to normal form have the same length.*

As explained above, the strong property expressed in the second item of Theorem 1 relies essentially on the fact that reductions are disallowed under bangs.

Normal Forms and Neutral Terms. A term is said to be **w-*normal*** if there is no t' such that $t \rightarrow_{\mathsf{w}} t'$, in which case we write $t \not\rightarrow_{\mathsf{w}}$. This notion can be characterised by means of the following inductive grammars:

$$
\begin{aligned}
\textbf{(Neutral)} \quad & \mathsf{ne_w} ::= x \in \mathcal{X} \mid \mathsf{na_w}\,\mathsf{no_w} \mid \mathsf{der}\,(\mathsf{nb_w}) \mid \mathsf{ne_w}[x\backslash\mathsf{nb_w}] \\
\textbf{(Neutral-Abs)} \quad & \mathsf{na_w} ::= \,!\,t \mid \mathsf{ne_w} \mid \mathsf{na_w}[x\backslash\mathsf{nb_w}] \\
\textbf{(Neutral-Bang)} \quad & \mathsf{nb_w} ::= \mathsf{ne_w} \mid \lambda x.\mathsf{no_w} \mid \mathsf{nb_w}[x\backslash\mathsf{nb_w}] \\
\textbf{(Normal)} \quad & \mathsf{no_w} ::= \mathsf{na_w} \mid \mathsf{nb_w}
\end{aligned}
$$

---

[1] Indeed, there exist clash-free terms in normal form that are σ-reducible to normal terms with clashes, *e.g.* $R = \mathsf{der}\,((\lambda y.\lambda x.z)\,(\mathsf{der}\,(y)\,y)) \equiv_\sigma \mathsf{der}\,(\lambda x.(\lambda y.z)\,(\mathsf{der}\,(y)\,y))$.

[2] In particular, the term R is not in normal form in our framework, and it reduces to a clash term in normal form which is filtered by the type system.

All these terms are w-normal. Moreover, **neutral** terms do not produce any kind of redexes when inserted into a context, while **neutral-abs** terms (resp. **neutral-bang**) may only produce s! or d! redexes (resp. dB redexes) when inserted into a context.

The intended meaning of the sets of terms defined above may be summarised as follows:

$$\mathsf{ne_w} \ = \ \mathsf{na_w} \cap \mathsf{nb_w} \ \subset \ \mathsf{na_w} \cup \mathsf{nb_w} \ = \ \mathsf{no_w}$$

Remark 1. Consider $t \in \mathcal{T}$. Then $t \in \mathsf{na_w}$ and $t \in \mathsf{nb_w}$ iff $t \in \mathsf{ne_w}$, $t \in \mathsf{na_w}$ and $t \notin \mathsf{nb_w}$ implies $\mathsf{bang}(t)$, and $t \in \mathsf{nb_w}$ and $t \notin \mathsf{na_w}$ implies $\mathsf{abs}(t)$.

Proposition 1 (Normal Forms). *Let $t \in \mathcal{T}$. Then $t \not\rightarrow_w$ iff $t \in \mathsf{no_w}$.*

Clashes. Some ill-formed terms are not redexes but they don't represent a desired result for a computation either. They are called **clashes** (meta-variable c), and defined as follows:

$$\mathsf{L}\langle !\, t \rangle\, u \qquad t[y \backslash \mathsf{L}\langle \lambda x.u \rangle] \qquad \mathsf{der}\,(\mathsf{L}\langle \lambda x.u \rangle) \qquad t\,(\mathsf{L}\langle \lambda x.u \rangle)$$

Remark that in the three first kind of clashes, replacing $\lambda x.$ by !, and inversely, creates a (root) redex, namely $(\mathsf{L}\langle \lambda x.t \rangle)\, u$, $t[x \backslash \mathsf{L}\langle !\, t \rangle]$ and $\mathsf{der}\,(\mathsf{L}\langle !\, t \rangle)$, respectively. In the fourth kind of clash, however, this is not the case since $t\,(\mathsf{L}\langle !\, u \rangle)$ is not a redex in general.

A term is **clash free** if it does not reduce to a term containing a clash, it is **weak clash free**, written wcf, if it does not reduce to a term containing a clash outside the scope of any constructor !. In other words, t is not wcf if and only if there exist a weak context W and a clash c such that $t \twoheadrightarrow_w \mathsf{W}\langle c \rangle$.

Weak clash-free normal terms can be characterised as follows:

$$\begin{aligned}
\textbf{(Neutral wcf)} \ \ \mathsf{ne_{wcf}} &::= x \in \mathcal{X} \mid \mathsf{ne_{wcf}}\, \mathsf{na_{wcf}} \mid \mathsf{der}\,(\mathsf{ne_{wcf}}) \mid \mathsf{ne_{wcf}}[x \backslash \mathsf{ne_{wcf}}]\\
\textbf{(Neutral-Abs wcf)} \ \ \mathsf{na_{wcf}} &::= !\,t \mid \mathsf{ne_{wcf}} \mid \mathsf{na_{wcf}}[x \backslash \mathsf{ne_{wcf}}]\\
\textbf{(Neutral-Bang wcf)} \ \ \mathsf{nb_{wcf}} &::= \mathsf{ne_{wcf}} \mid \lambda x.\mathsf{no_{wcf}} \mid \mathsf{nb_{wcf}}[x \backslash \mathsf{ne_{wcf}}]\\
\textbf{(Normal wcf)} \ \ \mathsf{no_{wcf}} &::= \mathsf{na_{wcf}} \mid \mathsf{nb_{wcf}}
\end{aligned}$$

Intuitively, $\mathsf{no_{wcf}}$ denotes $\mathsf{no_w} \cap \mathsf{wcf}$ (respectively for $\mathsf{ne_{wcf}}$, $\mathsf{na_{wcf}}$ and $\mathsf{nb_{wcf}}$).

Proposition 2 (Clash-free). *Let $t \in \mathcal{T}$. Then t is a weak clash-free normal form iff $t \in \mathsf{no_{wcf}}$.*

3 The Type System $\mathcal{U}$

This section introduces a first type system $\mathcal{U}$ for our revisited version of the Bang calculus, which extends the one in [32] to explicit substitutions. We show in this paper that $\mathcal{U}$ does not only qualitatively characterise normalisation, but is also *quantitative*, in the sense that the length of the (weak) reduction of a typed term to its normal form plus the size of this normal form is bounded by the size of its type derivation. We also explore in Sect. 4 the properties of this type system with respect to the CBN and CBV translations.

Given a countable infinite set $\mathcal{TV}$ of base type variables $\alpha, \beta, \gamma, \ldots$, we define the following sets of types:

$$\textbf{(Types)}\ \sigma, \tau ::= \alpha \in \mathcal{TV} \mid \mathcal{M} \mid \mathcal{M} \to \sigma$$
$$\textbf{(Multiset types)}\ \mathcal{M} ::= [\sigma_i]_{i \in I} \text{ where } I \text{ is a finite set}$$

The empty multiset is denoted by $[\,]$. Also, $|\mathcal{M}|$ denotes the size of the multiset, thus if $\mathcal{M} = [\sigma_i]_{i \in I}$ then $|\mathcal{M}| = \#(I)$.

Typing contexts (or just **contexts**), written Γ, Δ, are functions from variables to multiset types, assigning the empty multiset to all but a finite set of variables. The domain of Γ is given by $\text{dom}(\Gamma) \stackrel{def}{=} \{x \mid \Gamma(x) \neq [\,]\}$. The **union of contexts**, written $\Gamma + \Delta$, is defined by $(\Gamma + \Delta)(x) \stackrel{def}{=} \Gamma(x) \sqcup \Delta(x)$, where $\sqcup$ denotes multiset union. An example is $(x : [\sigma], y : [\tau]) + (x : [\sigma], z : [\tau]) = (x : [\sigma, \sigma], y : [\tau], z : [\tau])$. This notion is extended to several contexts as expected, so that $+_{i \in I} \Gamma_i$ denotes a finite union of contexts (when $I = \emptyset$ the notation is to be understood as the empty context). We write $\Gamma \setminus\!\setminus x$ for the context $(\Gamma \setminus\!\setminus x)(x) = [\,]$ and $(\Gamma \setminus\!\setminus x)(y) = \Gamma(y)$ if $y \neq x$.

Type judgements have the form $\Gamma \vdash t : \sigma$, where Γ is a typing context, t is a term and σ is a type. The type system $\mathcal{U}$ for the $\lambda!$-calculus is given in Fig. 1.

$$\frac{}{x : [\sigma] \vdash x : \sigma}\ (\textbf{ax}) \qquad \frac{\Gamma \vdash t : \sigma \quad \Delta \vdash u : \Gamma(x)}{(\Gamma \setminus\!\setminus x) + \Delta \vdash t[x\backslash u] : \sigma}\ (\textbf{es}) \qquad \frac{\Gamma \vdash t : \tau}{\Gamma \setminus\!\setminus x \vdash \lambda x.t : \Gamma(x) \to \tau}\ (\textbf{abs})$$

$$\frac{\Gamma \vdash t : \mathcal{M} \to \tau \quad \Delta \vdash u : \mathcal{M}}{\Gamma + \Delta \vdash tu : \tau}\ (\textbf{app}) \qquad \frac{(\Gamma_i \vdash t : \sigma_i)_{i \in I}}{+_{i \in I} \Gamma_i \vdash\ !t : [\sigma_i]_{i \in I}}\ (\textbf{bg}) \qquad \frac{\Gamma \vdash t : [\sigma]}{\Gamma \vdash \text{der}\, t : \sigma}\ (\textbf{dr})$$

Fig. 1. System $\mathcal{U}$ for the $\lambda!$-calculus.

The axiom (**ax**) is relevant (there is no weakening) and the rules (**app**) and (**es**) are multiplicative. Note that the argument of a bang is typed $\#(I)$ times by the premises of rule (**bg**). A particular case is when $I = \emptyset$: the subterm t occurring in the typed term $!t$ turns out to be untyped.

A **(type) derivation** is a tree obtained by applying the (inductive) typing rules of system $\mathcal{U}$. The notation $\rhd_{\mathcal{U}} \Gamma \vdash t : \sigma$ means there is a derivation of the judgement $\Gamma \vdash t : \sigma$ in system $\mathcal{U}$. The term t is typable in system $\mathcal{U}$, or $\mathcal{U}$-typable, iff there are Γ and σ such that $\rhd_{\mathcal{U}} \Gamma \vdash t : \sigma$. We use the capital Greek letters $\Phi, \Psi, \ldots$ to name type derivations, by writing for example $\Phi \rhd_{\mathcal{U}} \Gamma \vdash t : \sigma$. The **size of the derivation** Φ, denoted by $\text{sz}(\Phi)$, is defined as the number of rules in the type derivation Φ except rules (**bg**) and (**es**). Note in particular that given a derivation Φ_t for a term t we always have $\text{sz}(\Phi_t) \geq |t|_w$.

Example 2. The following tree Φ_0 is a type derivation for term t_0 of Example 1.

$$\dfrac{\dfrac{\dfrac{\dfrac{\dfrac{\dfrac{\overline{x : [[\tau] \to \tau] \vdash x : [\tau] \to \tau}\ (\mathtt{ax})}{x : [[\tau] \to \tau] \vdash \lambda y.x : [\,] \to [\tau] \to \tau}\ (\mathtt{abs})}{\vdash \lambda x.\lambda y.x : [[\tau] \to \tau] \to [\,] \to [\tau] \to \tau}\ (\mathtt{abs})}{\vdash\, !\,\mathtt{K} : [[[\tau] \to \tau] \to [\,] \to [\tau] \to \tau]}\ (\mathtt{bg})}{\vdash \mathrm{der}\,(!\,\mathtt{K}) : [[\tau] \to \tau] \to [\,] \to [\tau] \to \tau}\ (\mathtt{dr})\qquad \dfrac{\dfrac{\dfrac{\overline{x : [\tau] \vdash x : \tau}\ (\mathtt{ax})}{\vdash \lambda x.x : [\tau] \to \tau}\ (\mathtt{abs})}{\vdash\, !\,\mathtt{I} : [[\tau] \to \tau]}\ (\mathtt{bg})}{}}{\vdash \mathrm{der}\,(!\,\mathtt{K})\,(!\,\mathtt{I}) : [\,] \to [\tau] \to \tau}\ (\mathtt{app})\qquad \dfrac{}{\vdash\, !\,\Omega : [\,]}\ (\mathtt{bg})}{\vdash \mathrm{der}\,(!\,\mathtt{K})\,(!\,\mathtt{I})\,(!\,\Omega) : [\tau] \to \tau}\ (\mathtt{app})$$

Note that $\mathtt{sz}(\Phi_0) = 8$ since (bg) nodes are not counted by definition.

Typable terms are necessarily weak clash-free:

Lemma 2. *If* $\rhd_{\mathcal{U}} \Gamma \vdash t : \sigma$, *then* t *is* wcf.

Proof. Assume towards a contradiction that t is not wcf, *i.e.* there exists a weak context W and a clash c such that $t \to_{\mathtt{w}} \mathtt{W}\langle c \rangle$. Then, Lemma 3 (WSR) gives $\Phi' \rhd_{\mathcal{U}} \Gamma \vdash \mathtt{W}\langle c \rangle : \sigma$. If we show that a term of the form $\mathtt{W}\langle c \rangle$ cannot be typed in system $\mathcal{U}$, we are done. This follows by straightforward induction on W. The base case is when $\mathtt{W} = \square$. For every possible c, it is immediate to see that there is a mismatch between its syntactical form and the typing rules of system $\mathcal{U}$. For instance, if $c = \mathtt{L}\langle !\,t \rangle\,u$, then $\mathtt{L}\langle !\,t \rangle$ should have a functional type by rule (app) but it can only be assigned a multiset type by rules (es) and (bg). As for the inductive case, an easy inspection of the typing rules shows for all terms t and weak contexts W, t must be typed in order to type $\mathtt{W}\langle t \rangle$. □

However, normal terms are not necessarily clash-free, but the type system captures clash-freeness of normal terms. Said differently, when restricted to $\mathtt{no}_{\mathtt{w}}$, typability exactly corresponds to weak clash-freeness.

Theorem 2. *Let* $t \in \mathcal{T}$. *Then,* $t \in \mathtt{no}_{\mathtt{wcf}}$ *iff* $t \in \mathtt{no}_{\mathtt{w}}$ *and is* $\mathcal{U}$-*typable*.

The quantitative aspect of system $\mathcal{U}$ is materialised in the following weighted subject reduction (WSR) and expansion (WSE) properties.

Lemma 3. *Let* $\Phi \rhd_{\mathcal{U}} \Gamma \vdash t : \tau$.

(WSR) *If* $t \to_{\mathtt{w}} t'$, *then there is* $\Phi' \rhd_{\mathcal{U}} \Gamma \vdash t' : \tau$ *such that* $\mathtt{sz}(\Phi) > \mathtt{sz}(\Phi')$.
(WSE) *If* $t' \to_{\mathtt{w}} t$, *then there is* $\Phi' \rhd_{\mathcal{U}} \Gamma \vdash t' : \tau$ *such that* $\mathtt{sz}(\Phi') > \mathtt{sz}(\Phi)$.

Erasing steps like $y[x\backslash !\,z] \to_{\mathtt{s!}} y$ may seem problematic for subject reduction and expansion, but they are not: the variable x, as well as $!\,z$ are necessarily both typed with $[\,]$, so there is no loss of information since the contexts allowing to type the redex and the reduced term are the same.

Typability can then be shown to (qualitatively and quantitatively) characterise normalisation.

Theorem 3 (Soundness and Completeness). *The term t is $\mathcal{U}$-typable iff t w-normalises to a term $p \in \mathsf{no}_{\mathsf{wcf}}$. Moreover, if $\Phi \triangleright_{\mathcal{U}} \Gamma \vdash t : \tau$, then $t \rightarrow_{\mathsf{w}}^{(b,e)} p$ and $\mathsf{sz}(\Phi) \geq b + e + |p|_w$.*

Proof. The soundness proof is straightforward by Lemma 3 (WSR) and Theorem 2. Remark that the argument is simply combinatorial, no reducibility argument is needed. Moreover, unlike [26,32], there is no need to reason through any intermediate *resource* Bang calculus. For the completeness proof, we reason by induction on the length of the w-normalising sequence. For the base case, we use Theorem 2 which states that $p \in \mathsf{no}_{\mathsf{wcf}}$ implies p is $\mathcal{U}$-typable. For the inductive case we use Lemma 3 (WSE). The *moreover* statement holds by Lemma 3 and the fact that the size of the type derivation of p is greater than or equal to $|p|_w$.   □

The previous theorem can be illustrated by the term $t_0 = \mathsf{der}\,(!\,\mathsf{K})\,(!\,\mathsf{I})\,(!\,\Omega)$ defined in Example 1, which normalises in 5 steps to a normal form of w-size 1, the sum of the two being bounded by the size 8 of its type derivation Φ_0 given in Example 2.

4   Capturing Call-by-Name and Call-by-Value

This section explores the CBN/CBV embeddings into the $\lambda!$-calculus. For CBN, we slightly adapt Girard's translation into LL [29], which preserves normal forms and is sound and complete with respect to the standard (quantitative) type system [28]. For CBV, however, we reformulate both the translation and the type system, so that preservation of normal forms and completeness are restored. In both cases, we specify the operational semantics of CBN and CBV by means of a very simple notion of explicit substitution, see for example [6].

Terms ($\mathcal{T}_\lambda$), values and contexts are defined as follows:

$$
\begin{array}{rl}
\textbf{(Terms)} & t, u ::= v \mid t\,u \mid t[x\backslash u] \\
\textbf{(Values)} & v ::= x \in \mathcal{X} \mid \lambda x.t \\
\textbf{(List Contexts)} & \mathtt{L} ::= \Box \mid \mathtt{L}[x\backslash t] \\
\textbf{(Call-by-Name Contexts)} & \mathtt{N} ::= \Box \mid \mathtt{N}\,t \mid \lambda x.\mathtt{N} \mid \mathtt{N}[x\backslash u] \\
\textbf{(Call-by-Value Contexts)} & \mathtt{V} ::= \Box \mid \mathtt{V}\,t \mid t\,\mathtt{V} \mid \mathtt{V}[x\backslash u] \mid t[x\backslash\mathtt{V}]
\end{array}
$$

As in Sect. 2 we use the predicate $\mathsf{abs}(t)$ iff $t = \mathtt{L}\langle\lambda x.t'\rangle$. We also use the predicates $\mathsf{app}(t)$ iff $t = \mathtt{L}\langle t'\,t''\rangle$ and $\mathsf{var}(t)$ iff $t = \mathtt{L}\langle x\rangle$.

The **Call-by-Name** reduction relation $\rightarrow_{\mathsf{n}}$ is defined as the closure of contexts $\mathtt{N}$ of the rules dB and s presented below, while the **Call-by-Value** reduction relation $\rightarrow_{\mathsf{v}}$ is defined as the closure of contexts $\mathtt{V}$ of the rules dB and sv below. Equivalently, $\rightarrow_{\mathsf{n}} := \mathtt{N}(\mapsto_{\mathsf{dB}} \cup \mapsto_{\mathsf{s}})$ and $\rightarrow_{\mathsf{v}} := \mathtt{V}(\mapsto_{\mathsf{dB}} \cup \mapsto_{\mathsf{sv}})$ and

$$
\begin{array}{rl}
\mathtt{L}\langle\lambda x.t\rangle\,u & \mapsto_{\mathsf{dB}} \mathtt{L}\langle t[x\backslash u]\rangle \\
t[x\backslash u] & \mapsto_{\mathsf{s}} t\,\{x\backslash u\} \\
t[x\backslash\mathtt{L}\langle v\rangle] & \mapsto_{\mathsf{sv}} \mathtt{L}\langle t\,\{x\backslash v\}\rangle
\end{array}
$$

We write $t \not\rightarrow_n$ (resp. $t \not\rightarrow_v$), and call t an **n-*normal form*** (resp. **n-*normal form***), if t cannot be reduced by means of $\rightarrow_n$ (resp. $\rightarrow_v$).

Remark that we use CBN and CBV formulations based on distinguished multiplicative (*cf.* dB) and exponential (*cf.* s and sv) rules, inheriting the nature of cut elimination rules in LL. Moreover, CBN is to be understood as *head* CBN reduction [7], *i.e.* reduction does not take place in arguments of applications, while CBV corresponds to *open* CBV reduction [2,6], *i.e.* reduction does not take place inside abstractions.

Embeddings. The CBN and CBV embeddings into the λ!-calculus, written $\_^{\mathsf{cbn}}$ and $\_^{\mathsf{cbv}}$ resp., are inductively defined as:

$$
\begin{aligned}
x^{\mathsf{cbn}} &\overset{def}{=} x \\
(\lambda x.t)^{\mathsf{cbn}} &\overset{def}{=} \lambda x.t^{\mathsf{cbn}} \\
(t\,u)^{\mathsf{cbn}} &\overset{def}{=} t^{\mathsf{cbn}} \,!\, u^{\mathsf{cbn}} \\
(t[x\backslash u])^{\mathsf{cbn}} &\overset{def}{=} t^{\mathsf{cbn}}[x\backslash \,!\, u^{\mathsf{cbn}}]
\end{aligned}
\qquad
\begin{aligned}
x^{\mathsf{cbv}} &\overset{def}{=} \,!\,x \\
(\lambda x.t)^{\mathsf{cbv}} &\overset{def}{=} \,!\,\lambda x.t^{\mathsf{cbv}} \\
(t\,u)^{\mathsf{cbv}} &\overset{def}{=} \begin{cases} \mathsf{L}\langle s\rangle\, u^{\mathsf{cbv}} & \text{if } t^{\mathsf{cbv}} = \mathsf{L}\langle \,!\, s\rangle \\ \mathsf{der}\,(t^{\mathsf{cbv}})\, u^{\mathsf{cbv}} & \text{otherwise} \end{cases} \\
(t[x\backslash u])^{\mathsf{cbv}} &\overset{def}{=} t^{\mathsf{cbv}}[x\backslash u^{\mathsf{cbv}}]
\end{aligned}
$$

Remark that there are no two consecutive ! constructors in the image of the translations. The CBN embedding extends Girard's translation to explicit substitutions, while the CBV one is different. Indeed, the translation of an application $t\,u$ is usually defined as $\mathsf{der}\,(t^{\mathsf{cbv}})\, u^{\mathsf{cbv}}$ (see for example [26]). This definition does not preserve normal forms, *i.e.* $x\,y$ is a v-normal form but its translated version $\mathsf{der}\,(!\,x)\,!\,y$ is not a w-normal form. We restore this fundamental property by using the well-known notion of superdevelopment [10], so that d!-reductions are applied by the translation on the fly.

Lemma 4. *Let* $t \in \mathcal{T}_\lambda$. *If* $t \not\rightarrow_n$, *then* $t^{\mathsf{cbn}} \not\rightarrow_w$. *If* $t \not\rightarrow_v$, *then* $t^{\mathsf{cbv}} \not\rightarrow_w$.

Simulation of CBN and CBV reductions in the λ!-calculus can be shown by induction on the reduction relations.

Lemma 5. *Let* $t \in \mathcal{T}_\lambda$. *If* $t \rightarrow_n s$, *then* $t^{\mathsf{cbn}} \twoheadrightarrow_w s^{\mathsf{cbn}}$. *If* $t \rightarrow_v s$, *then* $t^{\mathsf{cbv}} \twoheadrightarrow_w s^{\mathsf{cbv}}$.

Note that the CBV case may require many reduction steps between t^{cbv} and s^{cbv} and not just one. For instance, if $t = \mathsf{I}\,y\,z \rightarrow_v w[w\backslash y]\,z = s$, then $t^{\mathsf{cbv}} = \mathsf{der}\,((\lambda w.!\,w)\,!\,y)\,!\,z \rightarrow_w \mathsf{der}\,(!\,w[w\backslash !\,y])\,!\,z \rightarrow_w w[w\backslash !\,y]\,!\,z = s^{\mathsf{cbv}}$.

Non-idempotent Types for Call-by-Name and Call-by-Value. For CBN we use the non-idempotent type system defined in [35] for explicit substitutions, that we present in Fig. 2 (top), and which is an extension of that in [28]. For CBV we slightly reformulate the non-idempotent system in [32], as presented in Fig. 2 (bottom), in order to recover completeness of the (typed) CBV translation.

We write $\Phi \triangleright_\mathcal{N} \Gamma \vdash t : \sigma$ (resp. $\Phi \triangleright_\mathcal{V} \Gamma \vdash t : \sigma$) for a type derivation Φ in system $\mathcal{N}$ (resp. $\mathcal{V}$). Remark that potential erasable terms are typed with multiple premises: this is the case for the arguments of applications and the arguments of substitutions in CBN, as well as the values in CBV. A key point in rule (app_v) is

System $\mathcal{N}$ for Call-by-Name

$$\frac{}{x : [\sigma] \vdash x : \sigma} \ (\text{ax}_n)$$

$$\frac{\Gamma ; x : [\sigma_i]_{i \in I} \vdash t : \tau \quad (\Delta_i \vdash u : \sigma_i)_{i \in I}}{\Gamma +_{i \in I} \Delta_i \vdash t[x \backslash u] : \tau} \ (\text{es}_n)$$

$$\frac{\Gamma \vdash t : \tau}{\Gamma \backslash\!\backslash x \vdash \lambda x.t : \Gamma(x) \to \tau} \ (\text{abs}_n)$$

$$\frac{\Gamma \vdash t : [\sigma_i]_{i \in I} \to \tau \quad (\Delta_i \vdash u : \sigma_i)_{i \in I}}{\Gamma +_{i \in I} \Delta_i \vdash tu : \tau} \ (\text{app}_n)$$

System $\mathcal{V}$ for Call-by-Value

$$\frac{}{x : \mathcal{M} \vdash x : \mathcal{M}} \ (\text{ax}_v)$$

$$\frac{\Gamma \vdash t : \sigma \quad \Delta \vdash u : \Gamma(x)}{(\Gamma \backslash\!\backslash x) + \Delta \vdash t[x \backslash u] : \sigma} \ (\text{es}_v)$$

$$\frac{(\Gamma_i \vdash t : \tau_i)_{i \in I}}{+_{i \in I} \Gamma_i \backslash\!\backslash x \vdash \lambda x.t : [\Gamma_i(x) \to \tau_i]_{i \in I}} \ (\text{abs}_v)$$

$$\frac{\Gamma \vdash t : [\mathcal{M} \to \tau] \quad \Delta \vdash u : \mathcal{M}}{\Gamma + \Delta \vdash tu : \tau} \ (\text{app}_v)$$

Fig. 2. Typing schemes for CBN/CBV.

that left hand sides of applications are typed with multisets of the form $[\mathcal{M} \to \tau]$, where τ is any type, potentially a base one, while [32] necessarily requires a multiset of the form $[\mathcal{M} \to \mathcal{M}']$, a subtle difference which breaks completeness. System $\mathcal{N}$ (resp. $\mathcal{V}$) can be understood as a relational model of the Call-by-Name (resp. Call-by-Value) calculus, in the sense that typing is stable by reduction and expansion [12].

The CBV translation is not complete for the system in [32], *i.e.* there exist a λ-term t such that $\Gamma \vdash t^{\text{cbv}} : \sigma$ is derivable in $\mathcal{U}$ but $\Gamma \vdash t : \sigma$ is not derivable in their system. This is restored in this paper. More precisely, our two embeddings are sound and complete w.r.t. system $\mathcal{U}$:

Theorem 4 (Soundness/Completeness of the Embeddings). *Let* $t \in \mathcal{T}_\lambda$.

1. $\triangleright_{\mathcal{N}} \Gamma \vdash t : \sigma$ *iff* $\triangleright_{\mathcal{U}} \Gamma \vdash t^{\text{cbn}} : \sigma$.
2. $\triangleright_{\mathcal{V}} \Gamma \vdash t : \sigma$ *iff* $\triangleright_{\mathcal{U}} \Gamma \vdash t^{\text{cbv}} : \sigma$.

The type system $\mathcal{N}$ (resp. $\mathcal{V}$) characterises n-normalisation (resp. v-normalisation). More precisely:

Theorem 5 (Characterisation of CBN/CBV Normalisation). *Let* $t \in \mathcal{T}_\lambda$.

- t *is* $\mathcal{N}$-*typable iff* t *is* n-*normalising*.
- t *is* $\mathcal{V}$-*typable iff* t *is* v-*normalising*.

5   A Tight Type System Giving Exact Bounds

In order to count exactly the length of w-reduction sequences to normal forms, we first fix a *deterministic* strategy for the $\lambda!$-calculus, called dw, which computes the *same* w-normal forms. We then define the *tight* type system $\mathcal{E}$, being able to count exactly the length of dw-reduction sequences. Theorem 1, stating that any two different reductions paths to normal form have the same length, guarantees that *any* w-reduction sequence to normal form can be exactly measured.

A Deterministic Strategy for the $\lambda!$-Calculus. The reduction relation $\to_{dw}$ defined below is a deterministic version of $\to_w$ and is used, as explained, as a technical tool of our development.

$$\overline{\mathsf{L}\langle \lambda x.t\rangle\, u \to_{dw} \mathsf{L}\langle t[x\backslash u]\rangle} \qquad \overline{t[x\backslash \mathsf{L}\langle !\, u\rangle] \to_{dw} \mathsf{L}\langle t\,\{x\backslash u\}\rangle} \qquad \overline{\mathrm{der}\,(\mathsf{L}\langle !\, t\rangle) \to_{dw} \mathsf{L}\langle t\rangle}$$

$$\frac{t \to_{dw} u}{\lambda x.t \to_{dw} \lambda x.u} \qquad \frac{t \to_{dw} u \quad \neg\mathsf{bang}(t)}{r[x\backslash t] \to_{dw} r[x\backslash u]} \qquad \frac{t \to_{dw} u \quad \neg\mathsf{bang}(t)}{\mathrm{der}\,t \to_{dw} \mathrm{der}\,u}$$

$$\frac{t \to_{dw} u \quad \neg\mathsf{abs}(t)}{t\,r \to_{dw} u\,r} \qquad \frac{t \to_{dw} u \quad r \in \mathsf{na_w}}{r\,t \to_{dw} r\,u} \qquad \frac{t \to_{dw} u \quad r \in \mathsf{nb_w}}{t[x\backslash r] \to_{dw} u[x\backslash r]}$$

Normal forms of $\to_w$ and $\to_{dw}$ are the same, both characterised by the set $\mathsf{no_w}$.

Proposition 3. *Let $t \in \mathcal{T}$. Then, (1) $t \not\to_w$ iff (2) $t \not\to_{dw}$ iff (3) $t \in \mathsf{no_w}$.*

Proof. Notice that (1) $\implies$ (2) follows from $\to_{dw} \subseteq \to_w$. Moreover, (1) iff (3) holds by Proposition 1. The proof of (2) $\implies$ (3) follows from a straightforward adaptation of this same proposition.   □

The Type System $\mathcal{E}$. We now extend the type system $\mathcal{U}$ to a *tight* one, called $\mathcal{E}$, being able to provide *exact* bounds for dw-normalising sequences and size of normal forms. The technique is based on [1], which defines type systems to count reduction lengths for different strategies in the λ-calculus. The notion of tight derivation turns out to be a particular implementation of *minimal derivation*, pioneered by de Carvalho in [18], where exact bounds for CBN abstract machines are inferred from minimal type derivations.

We define the following sets of types:

$$\begin{array}{ll} \textbf{(Tight types)} & \mathsf{tt} ::= \mathsf{a} \mid \mathsf{b} \mid \mathsf{n} \\ \textbf{(Types)} & \sigma,\tau ::= \mathsf{tt} \mid \mathcal{M} \mid \mathcal{M} \to \sigma \\ \textbf{(Multiset types)} & \mathcal{M} ::= [\sigma_i]_{i\in I} \text{ where } I \text{ is a finite set} \end{array}$$

Inspired by [1], which only uses two constant types a and n for abstractions and neutral terms respectively, we now use three base types. Indeed, the constant a (resp. b) types terms whose normal form has the shape $\mathsf{L}\langle \lambda x.t\rangle$ (resp. $\mathsf{L}\langle !\, t\rangle$), and the constant n types terms whose normal form is in $\mathtt{ne_{wcf}}$. As a matter of notation, given a tight type $\mathtt{tt_0}$ we write $\overline{\mathtt{tt_0}}$ to denote a tight type different from $\mathtt{tt_0}$. Thus for instance, $\overline{\mathtt{a}} \in \{\mathtt{b}, \mathtt{n}\}$.

Typing contexts are functions from variables to multiset types, assigning the empty multiset to all but a finite number of variables. Sequents are of the form $\Gamma \vdash^{(b,e,s)} t : \sigma$, where the natural numbers b, e and s provide information on the reduction of t to normal form, and on the size of its normal form. More precisely, b (resp. e) indicates the number of multiplicative (resp. exponential) steps to normal form, while s indicates the w-size of this normal form. Remark that we do not count s! and d! steps separately, because both of them are exponential steps of the same nature. It is also worth noticing that only two counters suffice in the case of the λ-calculus [1], one to count β-reduction steps, and another to count the size of normal forms. The difficulty in the case of the λ!-calculus is to statically discriminate between multiplicative and exponential steps. Typing rules (Fig. 3) are split in two groups: the *persistent* and the *consuming* ones. A constructor is consuming (resp. persistent) if it is consumed (resp. not consumed) during w-reduction. For instance, in der $(!\mathtt{K})(!\mathtt{I})(!\Omega)$ the two abstractions of K are consuming, while the abstraction of I is persistent, and all the other constructors are also consuming, except those of Ω that turns out to be an untyped subterm. This dichotomy between consuming/persistent constructors has been used in [1] for the λ-calculus, and adapted here for the λ!-calculus.

The persistent rules are those typing persistent constructors, so that none of them increases the first two counters, but only possibly the third one, which contributes to the size of the normal form. The consuming rules type consuming constructors, so that they increase the first two counters, contributing to the length of the normalisation sequence. More precisely, rules $(\mathtt{ae_{c1}})$ and $(\mathtt{ae_{c2}})$ increments the first counter because the (consuming) application will be used to perform a dB-step, while rule $(\mathtt{bg_c})$ increments the second counter because the (consuming) bang will be used to perform either a s! or a d!-step. Rule $(\mathtt{ae_{c2}})$ is particularly useful to type dB-redexes whose reduction does not create an exponential redex, because the argument of the substitution created by the dB-step does not reduce to a bang.

A multiset type $[\sigma_i]_{i \in I}$ is **tight**, written $\mathsf{tight}([\sigma_i]_{i \in I})$, if $\sigma_i \in \mathtt{tt}$ for all $i \in I$. A context Γ is said to be **tight** if it assigns tight multisets to all variables. A type derivation $\Phi \rhd_{\mathcal{E}} \Gamma \vdash^{(b,e,s)} t : \sigma$ is **tight** if Γ is tight and $\sigma \in \mathtt{tt}$.

Persistent Typing Rules

$$\frac{\Gamma \vdash^{(b,e,s)} t : \mathtt{n} \quad \Delta \vdash^{(b',e',s')} u : \overline{\mathtt{a}}}{\Gamma + \Delta \vdash^{(b+b',e+e',s+s'+1)} t\,u : \mathtt{n}} \ (\mathsf{ae_p}) \qquad \frac{\Gamma \vdash^{(b,e,s)} t : \mathtt{tt} \quad \mathrm{tight}(\Gamma(x))}{\Gamma \setminus\!\setminus x \vdash^{(b,e,s+1)} \lambda x.t : \mathtt{a}} \ (\mathsf{ai_p})$$

$$\frac{}{\vdash^{(0,0,0)} \,!\,t : \mathtt{b}} \ (\mathsf{bg_p}) \qquad \frac{\Gamma \vdash^{(b,e,s)} t : \mathtt{n}}{\Gamma \vdash^{(b,e,s+1)} \mathrm{der}\, t : \mathtt{n}} \ (\mathsf{dr_p})$$

$$\frac{\Gamma \vdash^{(b,e,s)} t : \mathtt{tt} \quad \Delta \vdash^{(b',e',s')} u : \mathtt{n} \quad \mathrm{tight}(\Gamma(x))}{(\Gamma \setminus\!\setminus x) + \Delta \vdash^{(b+b',e+e',s+s')} t[x\backslash u] : \mathtt{tt}} \ (\mathsf{es_p})$$

Consuming Typing Rules

$$\frac{}{x : [\sigma] \vdash^{(0,0,0)} x : \sigma} \ (\mathsf{ax_c}) \qquad \frac{\Gamma \vdash^{(b,e,s)} t : \mathcal{M} \to \tau \quad \Delta \vdash^{(b',e',s')} u : \mathcal{M}}{\Gamma + \Delta \vdash^{(b+b'+1,e+e',s+s')} t\,u : \tau} \ (\mathsf{ae_{c1}})$$

$$\frac{\Gamma \vdash^{(b,e,s)} t : \mathcal{M} \to \mathtt{tt} \quad \Delta \vdash^{(b',e',s')} u : \mathtt{n} \quad \mathrm{tight}(\mathcal{M})}{\Gamma + \Delta \vdash^{(b+b'+1,e+e',s+s')} t\,u : \mathtt{tt}} \ (\mathsf{ae_{c2}})$$

$$\frac{\Gamma \vdash^{(b,e,s)} t : \tau}{\Gamma \setminus\!\setminus x \vdash^{(b,e,s)} \lambda x.t : \Gamma(x) \to \tau} \ (\mathsf{ai_c}) \qquad \frac{(\Gamma_i \vdash^{(b_i,e_i,s_i)} t : \sigma_i)_{i \in I}}{+_{i \in I} \Gamma_i \vdash^{(+_{i \in I} b_i, 1 +_{i \in I} e_i, +_{i \in I} s_i)} \,!\,t : [\sigma_i]_{i \in I}} \ (\mathsf{bg_c})$$

$$\frac{\Gamma \vdash^{(b,e,s)} t : [\sigma]}{\Gamma \vdash^{(b,e,s)} \mathrm{der}\, t : \sigma} \ (\mathsf{dr_c}) \qquad \frac{\Gamma \vdash^{(b,e,s)} t : \sigma \quad \Delta \vdash^{(b',e',s')} u : \Gamma(x)}{(\Gamma \setminus\!\setminus x) + \Delta \vdash^{(b+b',e+e',s+s')} t[x\backslash u] : \sigma} \ (\mathsf{es_c})$$

Fig. 3. System $\mathcal{E}$ for the $\lambda!$-Calculus.

Example 3. The following tight typing can be derived for term t_0 of Example 1:

$$\cfrac{\cfrac{\cfrac{\cfrac{\cfrac{\cfrac{\cfrac{}{x : [\mathtt{a}] \vdash^{(0,0,0)} x : \mathtt{a}} \ (\mathsf{ax_c})}{x : [\mathtt{a}] \vdash^{(0,0,0)} \lambda y.x : [] \to \mathtt{a}} \ (\mathsf{ai_c})}{\vdash^{(0,0,0)} \lambda x.\lambda y.x : [\mathtt{a}] \to [] \to \mathtt{a}} \ (\mathsf{ai_c})}{\vdash^{(0,1,0)} \,!\,\mathtt{K} : [[\mathtt{a}] \to [] \to \mathtt{a}]} \ (\mathsf{bg_c})}{\vdash^{(0,1,0)} \mathrm{der}\,(!\mathtt{K}) : [\mathtt{a}] \to [] \to \mathtt{a}} \ (\mathsf{dr_c}) \qquad \cfrac{\cfrac{\cfrac{\cfrac{}{x : [\mathtt{n}] \vdash^{(0,0,0)} x : \mathtt{n}} \ (\mathsf{ax_c})}{\vdash^{(0,0,1)} \lambda x.x : \mathtt{a}} \ (\mathsf{ai_p})}{\vdash^{(0,1,1)} \,!\,\mathtt{I} : [\mathtt{a}]} \ (\mathsf{bg_c})}{}}{\vdash^{(1,2,1)} \mathrm{der}\,(!\mathtt{K})\,(!\mathtt{I}) : [] \to \mathtt{a}} \ (\mathsf{ae_{c1}}) \qquad \cfrac{}{\vdash^{(0,1,0)} \,!\,\Omega : []} \ (\mathsf{bg_c})}{\vdash^{(2,3,1)} \mathrm{der}\,(!\mathtt{K})\,(!\mathtt{I})\,(!\Omega) : \mathtt{a}} \ (\mathsf{ae_{c1}})$$

Note that the only persistent rule used is $(\mathsf{ai_p})$ when typing $\mathtt{I}$, thus contributing to count the w-size of the w-normal form of t_0, which is $\mathtt{I}$.

Soundness. We now study soundness of the type system $\mathcal{E}$, which does not only guarantee that typable terms are normalising –a qualitative property– but also provides quantitative (exact) information for normalising sequences. More precisely, given a tight type derivation Φ with counters (b, e, s) for a term t, t is w-normalisable in $(b + e)$-steps and its w-normal form has size s. Therefore, information about a *dynamic* behaviour of t, is extracted from a static typing property of t. The soundness proof is mainly based on a subject reduction property (Lemma 9), as well as on some auxiliary lemmas.

As in system $\mathcal{U}$, typable terms are weak clash-free:

Lemma 6. *If* $\Phi \rhd_{\mathcal{E}} \Gamma \vdash^{(b,e,s)} t : \sigma$, *then* t *is* wcf.

The following properties can be shown by induction on the derivations.

Lemma 7. *If* $\Phi \rhd_{\mathcal{E}} \Gamma \vdash^{(b,e,s)} t : \sigma$ *is tight, then* $b = e = 0$ *iff* $t \in$ no$_{w}$.

Lemma 8. *If* $\Phi \rhd_{\mathcal{E}} \Gamma \vdash^{(0,0,s)} t : \sigma$ *is tight, then* $s = |t|_{w}$.

The type system $\mathcal{E}$ also captures clash-freeness of normal terms:

Theorem 6. *Let* $t \in \mathcal{T}$. *Then* $t \in$ no$_{w}$ *and* t *is* $\mathcal{E}$-*typable iff* $t \in$ no$_{\text{wcf}}$.

To conclude soundness, the key property is subject reduction, stating that every reduction step decreases the counters of tight derivations by exactly one.

Lemma 9 (Exact Subject Reduction). *Let* $\Phi \rhd_{\mathcal{E}} \Gamma \vdash^{(b,e,s)} t : \sigma$ *such that* Γ *is tight, and either* $\sigma \in$ tt *or* $\neg$abs(t). *If* $t \to_{\text{dw}} t'$, *then there is* $\Phi' \rhd_{\mathcal{E}}$ $\Gamma \vdash^{(b',e',s)} t' : \sigma$ *such that*

- $b' = b - 1$ *and* $e' = e$ *if* $t \to_{\text{dw}} t'$ *is an* m-*step.*
- $e' = e - 1$ *and* $b' = b$ *if* $t \to_{\text{dw}} t'$ *is an* e-*step.*

Theorem 7 (Soundness). *If* $\Phi \rhd_{\mathcal{E}} \Gamma \vdash^{(b,e,s)} t : \sigma$ *is tight, then there exists* p *such that* $p \in$ no$_{\text{wcf}}$ *and* $t \twoheadrightarrow_{w}^{(b,e)} p$ *with* b m-*steps,* e e-*steps, and* $|p|_{w} = s$.

Proof. We prove the statement by showing that $t \twoheadrightarrow_{\text{dw}}^{(b,e)} p$ holds for the deterministic strategy, then we conclude since $\to_{\text{dw}} \subseteq \to_{w}$. Let $\Phi \rhd_{\mathcal{E}} \Gamma \vdash^{(b,e,s)} t : \sigma$. We reason by induction on $b + e$.

If $b + e = 0$, then $b = e = 0$ and Lemma 7 gives $t \in$ no$_{w}$. Moreover, by Lemma 8 and Theorem 6, we get both $|t|_{w} = s$ and $t \in$ no$_{\text{wcf}}$. Thus, we conclude with $p = t$.

If $b + e > 0$, then $t \notin$ no$_{w}$ holds by Lemma 7 and thus there exists t' such that $t \twoheadrightarrow_{\text{dw}}^{(1,0)} t'$ or $t \twoheadrightarrow_{\text{dw}}^{(0,1)} t'$ by Proposition 3. By Lemma 9 there is $\Phi' \rhd_{\mathcal{E}}$ $\Gamma \vdash^{(b',e',s)} t' : \sigma$ such that $1 + b' + e' = b + e$. By the *i.h.* there is p such that $p \in$ no$_{\text{wcf}}$ and $t' \twoheadrightarrow_{\text{dw}}^{(b',e')} p$ with $s = |p|_{w}$. Then $t \twoheadrightarrow_{\text{dw}}^{(1,0)} t' \twoheadrightarrow_{\text{dw}}^{(b',e')} p$ (resp. $t \twoheadrightarrow_{\text{dw}}^{(0,1)} t' \ldots$) which means $t \twoheadrightarrow_{\text{dw}}^{(b,e)} p$, as expected. $\square$

Completeness. We now study completeness of the type system $\mathcal{E}$, which does not only guarantee that normalising terms are typable –a qualitative property– but also provides a tight type derivation having appropriate counters. More precisely, given a term t which is w-normalisable by means of b dB-steps and e (s!, d!)-steps, and having a w-normal form of size s, there is a tight derivation Φ for t with counters (b, e, s). The completeness proof is mainly based on a subject expansion property (Lemma 11), as well as on an auxiliary lemma providing tight derivations with appropriate counters for w-normal weak clash-free terms.

Lemma 10. *If $t \in \mathsf{no_{wcf}}$, then there is a tight derivation $\Phi \triangleright_{\mathcal{E}} \Gamma \vdash^{(0,0,|t|_w)} t : \sigma$.*

Lemma 11 (Exact Subject Expansion). *Let $\Phi' \triangleright_{\mathcal{E}} \Gamma \vdash^{(b',e',s)} t' : \sigma$ be a tight derivation. If $t \to_{\mathsf{dw}} t'$, then there is $\Phi \triangleright_{\mathcal{E}} \Gamma \vdash^{(b,e,s)} t : \sigma$ such that*

- *$b' = b - 1$ and $e' = e$ if $t \to_{\mathsf{dw}} t'$ is an m-step.*
- *$e' = e - 1$ and $b' = b$ if $t \to_{\mathsf{dw}} t'$ is an e-step.*

Theorem 8 (Completeness). *If $t \twoheadrightarrow_{\mathsf{w}}^{(b,e)} p$ with $p \in \mathsf{no_{wcf}}$, then there exists a tight type derivation $\Phi \triangleright_{\mathcal{E}} \Gamma \vdash^{(b,e,|p|_w)} t : \sigma$.*

Proof. We prove the statement for $\to_{\mathsf{dw}}$ and then conclude for the general notion of reduction $\to_{\mathsf{w}}$ by Theorem 1. Let $t \twoheadrightarrow_{\mathsf{dw}}^{(b,e)} p$. We proceed by induction on $b + e$.

If $b + e = 0$, then $b = e = 0$ and thus $t = p$, which implies $t \in \mathsf{no_{wcf}}$. Lemma 10 allows to conclude.

If $b + e > 0$, then there is t' such that $t \to_{\mathsf{dw}}^{(1,0)} t' \twoheadrightarrow_{\mathsf{dw}}^{(b-1,e)} p$ or $t \to_{\mathsf{dw}}^{(0,1)} t' \twoheadrightarrow_{\mathsf{dw}}^{(b,e-1)} p$. By the *i.h.* there is a tight derivation $\Phi' \triangleright_{\mathcal{E}} \Gamma \vdash^{(b',e',|p|_w)} t' : \sigma$ such $b' + e' = b + e - 1$. Lemma 11 gives a tight derivation $\Phi \triangleright_{\mathcal{E}} \Gamma \vdash^{(b'',e'',|p|_w)} t : \sigma$ such $b'' + e'' = b' + e' + 1$. We then have $b'' + e'' = b + e$. The fact that $b'' = b$ and $e'' = e$ holds by a simple case analysis. □

The main results can be illustrated by the term $t_0 = \mathsf{der}\,(!\mathsf{K})\,(!\mathsf{I})\,(!\Omega)$ in Sect. 2, which normalises in 2 multiplicative steps and 3 exponential steps to a normal form of w-size 1. A tight derivation for t_0 with appropriate counters $(2, 3, 1)$ is given in Example 3.

6   Conclusion

This paper gives a fresh view of the Bang Calculus, a formalism introduced by T. Ehrhard to study the relation between CBPV and Linear Logic.

Our reduction relation integrates commutative conversions inside the logical original formulation of [25], thus recovering soundness, *i.e.* avoiding mismatches between terms in normal form that are semantically non-terminating. In contrast to [26], which models commutative conversions as σ-reduction rules by paying the cost of loosing confluence, our *at a distance* formulation yields a confluent reduction system.

We then define two non-idempotent type systems for our calculus. System $\mathcal{U}$ provides upper bounds for the length of normalising sequences plus the size of normal forms. Moreover, it captures typed CBN and CBV. In particular, we reformulate the translation and the type system of CBV to restore two major properties missing in [32]: preservation of normal forms and completeness. Last but not least, the quantitative system $\mathcal{U}$ is further refined into system $\mathcal{E}$, being able to provide *exact* bounds for normalising sequences and size of normal forms, independently. Moreover, our tight system $\mathcal{E}$ is able to *discriminate* between different kind of steps performed to normalise terms.

Different topics deserve future attention. One of them is the study of *strong* reduction for the $\lambda!$-calculus, which allows to reduce terms under *all* the constructors, including !. Another challenging problem is to relate *tight* typing in CBN/CBV with *tight* typing in our calculus, thus providing an exact correspondence between (CBN/CBV) reduction steps and $\lambda!$-reduction steps.

Acknowledgments. We are grateful to Giulio Guerrieri and Giulio Manzonetto for fruitful discussions. This work has been partially supported by LIA INFINIS/IRP SINFIN, the ECOS-Sud program PA17C01, and the ANR COCA HOLA.

References

1. Accattoli, B., Graham-Lengrand, S., Kesner, D.: Tight typings and split bounds. In: PACMPL, 2 (ICFP), pp. 94:1–94:30 (2018)
2. Accattoli, B., Guerrieri, G.: Open call-by-value. In: Igarashi, A. (ed.) APLAS 2016. LNCS, vol. 10017, pp. 206–226. Springer, Cham (2016). https://doi.org/10.1007/978-3-319-47958-3_12
3. Accattoli, B., Guerrieri, G.: Types of fireballs. In: Ryu, S. (ed.) APLAS 2018. LNCS, vol. 11275, pp. 45–66. Springer, Cham (2018). https://doi.org/10.1007/978-3-030-02768-1_3
4. Accattoli, B., Guerrieri, G., Leberle, M.: Types by need. In: Caires, L. (ed.) ESOP 2019. LNCS, vol. 11423, pp. 410–439. Springer, Cham (2019). https://doi.org/10.1007/978-3-030-17184-1_15
5. Accattoli, B., Kesner, D.: The structural λ-calculus. In: Dawar, A., Veith, H. (eds.) CSL 2010. LNCS, vol. 6247, pp. 381–395. Springer, Heidelberg (2010). https://doi.org/10.1007/978-3-642-15205-4_30
6. Accattoli, B., Paolini, L.: Call-by-value solvability, revisited. In: Schrijvers, T., Thiemann, P. (eds.) FLOPS 2012. LNCS, vol. 7294, pp. 4–16. Springer, Heidelberg (2012). https://doi.org/10.1007/978-3-642-29822-6_4
7. Barendregt, H.P.: The Lambda Calculus Its Syntax and Semantics, vol. 103, revised edition. Amsterdam, North Holland (1984)
8. De Benedetti, E., Rocca, S.R.D.: A type assignment for λ-calculus complete both for FPTIME and strong normalization. Inf. Comput. **248**, 195–214 (2016)
9. Bernadet, A., Lengrand, S.: Non-idempotent intersection types and strong normalisation. Log. Methods Comput. Sci. **9**(4), 1–46 (2013)
10. Bezem, M., Klop, J.W., van Oostrom, V.: Term Rewriting Systems (TeReSe). Cambridge University Press, Cambridge (2003)
11. Bucciarelli, A., Ehrhard, T.: On phase semantics and denotational semantics: the exponentials. Ann. Pure Appl. Log. **109**(3), 205–241 (2001)
12. Bucciarelli, A., Kesner, D., Ríos, A., Viso, A.: The bang calculus revisited. Extended report (2020). https://arxiv.org/abs/2002.04011
13. Bucciarelli, A., Kesner, D., Ventura, D.: Non-idempotent intersection types for the lambda-calculus. Log. J. IGPL **25**(4), 431–464 (2017)

14. Carraro, A., Guerrieri, G.: A semantical and operational account of call-by-value solvability. In: Muscholl, A. (ed.) FoSSaCS 2014. LNCS, vol. 8412, pp. 103–118. Springer, Heidelberg (2014). https://doi.org/10.1007/978-3-642-54830-7_7

15. Chouquet, J., Tasson, C.: Taylor expansion for Call-By-Push-Value. In: International Conference on Computer Science Logic (CSL), Barcelona, Spain. LIPIcs, vol. 152, pp. 16:1–16:16. Schloss Dagstuhl - Leibniz-Zentrum fuer Informatik (2020)

16. Coppo, M., Dezani-Ciancaglini, M.: A new type assignment for λ-terms. Arch. Math. Log. **19**(1), 139–156 (1978)

17. Coppo, M., Dezani-Ciancaglini, M.: An extension of the basic functionality theory for the λ-calculus. Notre Dame J. Form. Log. **21**(4), 685–693 (1980)

18. de Carvalho, D.: Sémantiques de la logique linéaire et temps de calcul. Ph.D. thesis, Université Aix-Marseille II (2007)

19. de Carvalho, D.: The relational model is injective for multiplicative exponential linear logic. In: International Conference on Computer Science Logic (CSL), Marseille, France. LIPIcs, vol. 62, pages 41:1–41:19. Schloss Dagstuhl - Leibniz-Zentrum fuer Informatik (2016)

20. de Carvalho, D.: Execution time of λ-terms via denotational semantics and intersection types. Math. Struct. Comput. Sci. **28**(7), 1169–1203 (2018)

21. de Carvalho, D., dede Falco, L.T.: A semantic account of strong normalization in linear logic. Inf. Comput. **248**, 104–129 (2016)

22. de Carvalho, D., Pagani, M., de Falco, L.T.: A semantic measure of the execution time in linear logic. Theor. Comput. Sci. **412**(20), 1884–1902 (2011)

23. Danos, V.: La Logique Linéaire appliquée à l'étude de divers processus de normalisation (principalement du lambda-calcul). PhD thesis, Université Paris 7 (1990)

24. Ehrhard, T.: Collapsing non-idempotent intersection types. In: International Conference on Computer Science Logic (CSL), Fontainebleau, France. LIPIcs, vol. 16, pp. 259–273. Schloss Dagstuhl - Leibniz-Zentrum fuer Informatik (2012)

25. Ehrhard, T.: Call-by-push-value from a linear logic point of view. In: Thiemann, P. (ed.) ESOP 2016. LNCS, vol. 9632, pp. 202–228. Springer, Heidelberg (2016). https://doi.org/10.1007/978-3-662-49498-1_9

26. Ehrhard, T., Guerrieri, G.: The bang calculus: an untyped lambda-calculus generalizing call-by-name and call-by-value. In: International Symposium on Principles and Practice of Declarative Programming (PPDP), Edinburgh, United Kingdom, pp. 174–187. ACM (2016)

27. Ehrhard, T., Regnier, L.: Uniformity and the Taylor expansion of ordinary lambdaterms. TCS **403**(2–3), 347–372 (2008)

28. Gardner, P.: Discovering needed reductions using type theory. In: Hagiya, M., Mitchell, J.C. (eds.) TACS 1994. LNCS, vol. 789, pp. 555–574. Springer, Heidelberg (1994). https://doi.org/10.1007/3-540-57887-0_115

29. Girard, J.-Y.: Linear logic. Theor. Comput. Sci. **50**, 1–102 (1987)

30. Girard, J.-Y.: Normal functors, power series and λ-calculus. Ann. Pure Appl. Log. **37**(2), 129–177 (1988)

31. Guerrieri, G.: Towards a semantic measure of the execution time in call-by-value lambda-calculus. In: Joint International Workshops on Developments in Computational Models and Intersection Types and Related Systems (DCM/ITRS), Oxford, UK, EPTCS 283, pp. 57–72 (2018)

32. Guerrieri, G., Manzonetto, G.: The bang calculus and the two Girard's translations. In: Joint International Workshops on Linearity & Trends in Linear Logic and Applications (Linearity-TLLA), Oxford, UK, EPTCS, pp. 15–30 (2019)

33. Guerrieri, G., Pellissier, L., de Falco, L.T.: Computing connected proof(-structure)s from their taylor expansion. In: International Conference on Formal Structures for Computation and Deduction (FSCD), Porto, Portugal. LIPIcs, vol. 52, pp. 20:1–20:18. Schloss Dagstuhl - Leibniz-Zentrum fuer Informatik (2016)

34. Kesner, D.: Reasoning about call-by-need by means of types. In: Jacobs, B., Löding, C. (eds.) FoSSaCS 2016. LNCS, vol. 9634, pp. 424–441. Springer, Heidelberg (2016). https://doi.org/10.1007/978-3-662-49630-5_25

35. Kesner, D., Ventura, D.: Quantitative types for the linear substitution calculus. In: Diaz, J., Lanese, I., Sangiorgi, D. (eds.) TCS 2014. LNCS, vol. 8705, pp. 296–310. Springer, Heidelberg (2014). https://doi.org/10.1007/978-3-662-44602-7_23

36. Kesner, D., Vial, P.: Types as resources for classical natural deduction. In: International Conference on Formal Structures for Computation and Deduction (FSCD), Oxford, UK. LIPIcs, vol. 84, pp. 24:1–24:17. Schloss Dagstuhl - Leibniz-Zentrum fuer Informatik (2017)

37. Levy, P.B.: Call-By-Push-Value: A Functional/Imperative Synthesis. Semantics Structures in Computation, vol. 2. Springer, Dordrecht (2004). https://doi.org/10.1007/978-94-007-0954-6

38. Levy, P.B.: Call-by-push-value: decomposing call-by-value and call-by-name. High. Order Symb. Comput. **19**(4), 377–414 (2006)

39. Maraist, J., Odersky, M., Turner, D.N., Wadler, P.: Call-by-name, call-by-value, call-by-need and the linear lambda calculus. Theor. Comput. Sci. **228**(1–2), 175–210 (1999)

40. Pagani, M., della Rocca, S.R.: Solvability in resource lambda-calculus. In: Ong, L. (ed.) FoSSaCS 2010. LNCS, vol. 6014, pp. 358–373. Springer, Heidelberg (2010). https://doi.org/10.1007/978-3-642-12032-9_25

41. Regnier, L.: Une équivalence sur les lambda-termes. TCS **126**(2), 281–292 (1994)

42. Santo, J.E., Pinto, L., Uustalu, T.: Modal embeddings and calling paradigms. In: International Conference on Formal Structures for Computation and Deduction (FSCD), Dortmund, Germany. LIPIcs, vol. 131, pp. 18:1–18:20. Schloss Dagstuhl - Leibniz-Zentrum fuer Informatik (2019)

Functional Pearl: The Distributive λ-Calculus

Beniamino Accattoli[1] and Alejandro Díaz-Caro[2,3(✉)]

[1] Inria & LIX, École Polytechnique, UMR 7161, Palaiseau, France
beniamino.accattoli@inria.fr
[2] CONICET-Universidad de Buenos Aires, Instituto de Ciencias de la Computación,
Buenos Aires, Argentina
adiazcaro@icc.fcen.uba.ar
[3] Departamento de Ciencia y Tecnología, Universidad Nacional de Quilmes,
Bernal, BA, Argentina

Abstract. We introduce a simple extension of the λ-calculus with pairs—called the distributive λ-calculus—obtained by adding a computational interpretation of the valid distributivity isomorphism $A \Rightarrow (B \wedge C) \equiv (A \Rightarrow B) \wedge (A \Rightarrow C)$ of simple types. We study the calculus both as an untyped and as a simply typed setting. Key features of the untyped calculus are confluence, the absence of clashes of constructs, that is, evaluation never gets stuck, and a leftmost-outermost normalization theorem, obtained with straightforward proofs. With respect to simple types, we show that the new rules satisfy subject reduction if types are considered up to the distributivity isomorphism. The main result is strong normalization for simple types up to distributivity. The proof is a smooth variation over the one for the λ-calculus with pairs and simple types.

Keywords: λ-calculus · Type isomorphisms · Rewriting · Normalization

1 Introduction

The topic of this paper is an extension of the λ-calculus with pairs, deemed the *distributive λ-calculus*, obtained by adding a natural computational interpretation of the distributivity isomorphism of simple types:

$$A \Rightarrow (B \wedge C) \quad \equiv \quad (A \Rightarrow B) \wedge (A \Rightarrow C) \tag{1}$$

Namely, one extends the calculus with the following commutation rules:

$$\langle t, s \rangle u \to \langle tu, su \rangle \qquad \pi_i(\lambda x.t) \to \lambda x.\pi_i t \quad i = 1, 2$$

The aim of this paper is showing that the distributive λ-calculus is a natural system, and contributions are in both the typed and untyped settings.

We study the untyped setting to show that our calculus makes perfect sense also without types. This is to contrast with System I, another calculus providing

© Springer Nature Switzerland AG 2020
K. Nakano and K. Sagonas (Eds.): FLOPS 2020, LNCS 12073, pp. 33–49, 2020.
https://doi.org/10.1007/978-3-030-59025-3_3

computational interpretations of type isomorphisms recently introduced by Díaz-Caro and Dowek [8], that does not admit an untyped version—the relationship between the two is discussed below.

Typing up to Distributivity and Subject Reduction. At the typed level, the key point is that simple types are here considered *up to distributivity*. In this way, the apparently ad-hoc new rules do satisfy the subject reduction property.

Consider for instance $\pi_1(\lambda x.t)$: working up to the distributivity isomorphism—so that isomorphic types type the same terms—the subterm $\lambda x.t$ may now have both the arrow type $A \Rightarrow (B \wedge C)$ and the conjunctive type $(A \Rightarrow B) \wedge (A \Rightarrow C)$, so that $\pi_1(\lambda x.t)$ can be typed with $A \Rightarrow B$. Distributivity also allows for the type to be preserved—that is, subject reduction holds. According to the arrow type, indeed, the body t of the abstraction has type $B \wedge C$ and thus the reduct of the commutation rule $\pi_1(\lambda x.t) \rightarrow \lambda x.\pi_1 t$ can also be typed with $A \Rightarrow B$. The other commutation rule can be typed similarly.

Overview of the Paper. For the untyped setting, we show that the distributive λ-calculus is confluent, its closed normal forms are values, and it has a leftmost-outermost normalization theorem, exactly as for the λ-calculus (without pairs).

With respect to types, we show subject reduction and strong normalization of the distributive λ-calculus with simple types up to distributivity.

The Pearl. The proofs in the paper are remarkably smooth. The properties for the untyped calculus are immediate. Confluence follows by the fact that the calculus is an orthogonal higher-order rewriting system [1,9,10]. The leftmost-outermost normalization theorem, similarly, follows by an abstract result by van Ramsdonk [12], because the calculus verifies two additional properties of orthogonal higher-order rewriting system from which leftmost-outermost normalization follows. Finally, the fact that closed normal forms are values—what we call *progress*—is obtained via a straightforward induction.

For the typed setting, the given argument for subject reduction goes smoothly through. The main result of the paper is that the simply typed distributive λ-calculus is strongly normalizing. The proof follows Tait's reducibility method. In particular, the interpretation of types is the same at work for the λ-calculus with pairs and projections (that is, without distributive rules). The key point is to prove that the two sides of the distributivity isomorphism have the same interpretation. This can be proved with two easy lemmas. Everything else is as in the case without distributive rules.

Type Isomorphisms and System I. As shown by Bruce, Di Cosmo and Longo [4] the isomorphisms of simple types can be completely characterized by distributivity (that is, Eq. (1)) plus the following three (for more about type isomorphisms see Di Cosmo's short survey [6] or book [5]):

$$
\begin{array}{ll}
\text{Commutativity} & A \wedge B \equiv B \wedge A \\
\text{Associativity} & (A \wedge B) \wedge C \equiv A \wedge (B \wedge C) \\
\text{Currying} & (A \wedge B) \Rightarrow C \equiv A \Rightarrow (B \Rightarrow C)
\end{array}
$$

At the inception of Díaz-Caro and Dowek's System I [8], there is the idea of turning all these type isomorphisms into computational principles. Precisely, these isomorphisms give rise to some equations $t \sim s$ between terms, such as $\langle t, s \rangle \sim \langle s, t \rangle$ for the commutativity of conjunctions, for instance. The result of Díaz-Caro and Dowek is that the λ-calculus with pairs extended with 5 such equations (distributivity induces 2 equations) is strongly normalizing modulo.

System I Rests on Types. The equations of System I, while well behaved with respect to termination, come with two drawbacks. First, the calculus is not confluent. Second, the definitions of the rewriting rules and of the equations depend on types, so that it is not possible to consider an untyped version. Both issues are easily seen considering the commutativity equation. Consider $t = \pi_1 \langle s, u \rangle$. If pairs are commutative, t can rewrite to both s and u:

$$s \leftarrow \pi_1 \langle s, u \rangle \sim \pi_1 \langle u, s \rangle \rightarrow u$$

which breaks both confluence and subject reduction (if s has type A and u has type B). To recover subject reduction, one uses a projection π_A indexed by a type rather than a coordinate so that (if s has type A and u has type B):

$$s \leftarrow \pi_A \langle s, u \rangle \sim \pi_A \langle u, s \rangle \rightarrow s$$

note that in order to apply the rule we need to know the type of s. Moreover, confluence is not recovered—if both s and u have type A then the result may non-deterministically be s or u, according to System I. Díaz-Caro and Dowek in [8] indeed adopt a sort of *proof-irrelevant* point of view, for which subject reduction is more important than confluence for normalization: types guarantee the existence of a result (strong normalization), and this guarantee is stable by evaluation (subject reduction), while uniqueness of the result is abandoned (no confluence).

System I and the Distributive λ-Calculus. The two issues of System I are not due only to the commutativity isomorphism, as the currying and associativity isomorphisms also contribute to them. The distributive λ-calculus essentially restricts System I by keeping only the distributive isomorphism, which is the only one not hindering confluence and the possibility of defining the calculus independently from the type system.

To be precise, we do not simply restrict to distributivity, but we also change its computational interpretation. First, we do not consider equations, but rewriting rules, and also we consider the rule $\pi_i(\lambda x.t) \rightarrow \lambda x.\pi_i t$ that was not part of System I[1], while we remove both equations:

$$\lambda x.\langle t, s \rangle \sim \langle \lambda x.t, \lambda x.s \rangle \qquad \pi_i(ts) \sim \lambda x.(\pi_i t)s \quad i = 1, 2$$

The main reason is that they would make much harder to establish confluence of the calculus, because they introduce various critical pairs—the distributive

---

[1] Such a rule was however present in an early version of System I, see [7].

λ-calculus is instead trivially confluent, because it is an orthogonal higher-order rewriting system, and all such systems are confluent.

To sum up, System I aims at being a maximal enrichment of the λ-calculus with computation principles induced by type isomorphisms, while the distributive λ-calculus rather is a minimal extension aiming at being as conservative as possible with respect to the λ-calculus, and in particular at being definable without types.

Clashes. Let us point out a pleasant by-product of the distributive rewriting rules that we adopt. A nice property of the λ-calculus is that there can never be *clashes* of constructors. In logical terms, there is only one introduction rule (corresponding to the abstraction constructor) and only one elimination rule (application) and they are duals, that is, they interact via β-reduction. Extensions of the λ-calculus usually lack this property. Typically, extending the λ-calculus with pairs $\langle t, s \rangle$ (and of course projections $\pi_1 t$ and $\pi_2 t$) introduces the following two clashes: $\langle t, s \rangle u$ and $\pi_i(\lambda x.t)$, for $i = 1, 2$, where an elimination constructor (application or projection) is applied to the wrong introduction rule (pair or abstraction). These clashes are stuck, as there are no rules to remove them, and it is not clear whether it makes any sense to consider such an unrestricted λ-calculus with pairs.

Our distributive rules deal exactly with these clashes, removing them by commuting constructors. Concretely, the absence of clashes materializes as a *progress* property: all closed normal forms are values, that is, their outermost constructor corresponds to an introduction rule.

Related Work. Beyond Díaz-Caro and Dowek's System I, we are aware of only three works bearing some analogies to ours. The first one is Arbiser, Miquel, and Ríos' λ-calculus with constructors [3], where the λ-calculus is extended with constructors and a pattern matching construct that commutes with applications. They show it to be confluent and even having a separation theorem akin to Bohm's. The calculus has been further studied in a typed setting by Petit [11], but type isomorphisms play no role in this case.

The second related work is Aït-Kaci and Garrigue's label-selective λ-calculus [2], which considers the λ-calculus plus the only type isomorphism for the implication: $A \Rightarrow B \Rightarrow C \equiv B \Rightarrow A \Rightarrow C$[2]. In order to avoid losing confluence and subject reduction, they introduce a labeling system to the arguments, so that the application order becomes irrelevant.

Last, the untyped distributive λ-calculus coincides with the extensionality-free fragment of Støvring's λ_{FP} [13]. Støvring uses it as a technical tool to study confluence and conservativity of surjective pairing. He points out—as we do—that the calculus is confluent because it is an orthogonal higher-order rewriting system, but then he gives nonetheless a proof using Tait-Martin Löf's technique.

---

[2] With conjunction, this isomorphism is a consequence of currying and commutativity.

2 The Untyped Distributive λ-Calculus

The language of the distributive λ-calculus λ_{dist} is given by the following grammar:

$$\text{Terms}\quad t, s, u \quad ::= \quad x \mid \lambda x.t \mid ts \mid \langle t, s \rangle \mid \pi_1 t \mid \pi_2 t$$

The rewriting rules are first given at top level:

RULES AT TOP LEVEL

| Standard rules | $(\lambda x.t)s \;\mapsto_\beta\; t\{x \leftarrow s\}$ | |
| | $\pi_i \langle t_1, t_2 \rangle \;\mapsto_{\pi_i}\; t_i$ | $i = 1, 2$ |

| Distributive rules | $\langle t, s \rangle u \;\mapsto_{@_\times}\; \langle tu, su \rangle$ | |
| | $\pi_i(\lambda x.t) \;\mapsto_{\pi_\lambda}\; \lambda x.\pi_i t$ | $i = 1, 2$ |

Then, we extend them to be applied wherever in a term. We formulate such an extension using contexts, that are terms where exactly one subterm has been replaced with a hole $\langle \cdot \rangle$:

$$\text{Contexts}\quad C, D, E \;::=\; \langle \cdot \rangle \mid \lambda x.C \mid Ct \mid tC \mid \langle C, t \rangle \mid \langle t, C \rangle \mid \pi_1 C \mid \pi_2 C$$

The operation of replacing the hole $\langle \cdot \rangle$ of a context C with a given term t is called *plugging* and it is noted $C\langle t \rangle$. As usual, plugging can capture variables. Now we can define the contextual closure of the top level rules.

CONTEXTUAL CLOSURE

$$\frac{t \mapsto_a s}{C\langle t \rangle \to_a C\langle s \rangle} \quad a \in \{\beta, \pi_1, \pi_2, @_\times, \pi_\lambda\}$$

The contextual closure is given with contexts as a compact way of expressing the closure of all rules by all constructors, in the proofs sometimes we consider the closure by a single constructor. We use $\to_{\mathsf{dist}}$ for the union of all the rewriting rules defined above.

Values and Neutral Terms. Two subsets of terms play a special role in the following, terms whose outermost constructor corresponds to a logical introduction rule (values) and elimination rule (neutral terms), plus—in both cases—variables.

Definition 2.1 (Values and neutral terms).

- Values: *a term is* value *if it is either a variable* x, *an abstraction* $\lambda x.t$, *or a pair* $\langle t, s \rangle$.
- Neutral terms: *a term is* neutral *if it is either a variable* x, *an application* ts, *or a projection* $\pi_i t$.

Sometimes, neutral terms are also required to be normal. Here they are not.

Progress. The first property that we show is that all closed normal forms are *values.* Please note that evaluation is not call-by-value, here the aim is simply to stress that in the distributive λ-calculus there are no clashes, *i.e.* closed-normal neutral terms.

Proposition 2.2 (Progress). *If t is a closed normal form then it is a value.*

Proof. By induction on t. Cases:

- *Variable*: impossible, since t is closed.
- *Abstraction or pair*: then the statement holds.
- *Application, i.e. $t = su$.* Since t is normal and closed, so is s. Then, by *i.h.* s is a value, that is, either an abstraction or a pair. In the first case, rule β applies and in the second case rule $@_\times$ applies. Hence, in any case t is not in normal form, absurd. Therefore, t cannot be an application in normal form.
- *Projection, i.e. $t = \pi_i s$.* Since t is normal and closed, so is s. Then, by *i.h.* s is a value, that is, either an abstraction or a pair. In the first case, rule π_λ applies and in the second case rule π_i applies. Therefore, t cannot be a projection in normal form.   □

Substitution. For the proof of strong normalization we shall need a basic property of substitution with respect to rewriting steps.

Lemma 2.3 (Substitutivity of $\rightarrow_{\text{dist}}$).

1. Left substitutivity: *if $t \rightarrow_{\text{dist}} t'$ then $t\{x{\leftarrow}s\} \rightarrow_{\text{dist}} t'\{x{\leftarrow}s\}$.*
2. Right substitutivity: *if $s \rightarrow_{\text{dist}} s'$ then $t\{x{\leftarrow}s\} \rightarrow^*_{\text{dist}} t\{x{\leftarrow}s'\}$.*

Proof. The first point is an easy induction on the relation $\rightarrow_{\text{dist}}$, the second one on t. Details in the Appendix.   □

Confluence. The distributive λ-calculus is an example of orthogonal higher-order rewriting system [1,9,10], that is a class of rewriting systems for which confluence always holds, because of the good shape of its rewriting rules.

Theorem 2.4 (Confluence). *The distributive λ-calculus is confluent, that is, if $s_1 \;{}^*_{\text{dist}}{\leftarrow}\; t \rightarrow^*_{\text{dist}} s_2$ then there exists u such that $s_1 \rightarrow^*_{\text{dist}} u \;{}^*_{\text{dist}}{\leftarrow}\; s_2$.*   □

Leftmost-Outermost Normalization. A classic property of the ordinary λ-calculus is the (untyped) normalization theorem for leftmost-outermost (shortened to LO) reduction. The theorem states that LO reduction $\rightarrow_{LO}$ is *normalizing*, that is, $\rightarrow_{LO}$ reaches a normal form from t whenever t has a β reduction sequence to a normal form. The definition of LO reduction $\rightarrow_{LO}$ on ordinary λ-terms is given by:

LO REDUCTION FOR THE ORDINARY λ-CALCULUS

$$\frac{}{(\lambda x.t)s \rightarrow_{LO} t\{x{\leftarrow}s\}} \qquad \frac{t \rightarrow_{LO} s \qquad t \text{ is neutral}}{tu \rightarrow_{LO} su}$$

$$\frac{t \rightarrow_{LO} s}{\lambda x.t \rightarrow_{LO} \lambda x.s} \qquad \frac{u \text{ is neutral and normal} \qquad t \rightarrow_{LO} s}{ut \rightarrow_{LO} us}$$

By exploiting an abstract result by van Ramsdonk, we obtain a LO normalization theorem for λ_{dist} for free. Leftmost-outermost reduction $\to_{LO}$ can indeed be defined uniformly for every orthogonal rewriting system. For the distributive λ-calculus we simply consider the previous rules with respect to terms in λ_{dist}, and add the following clauses:

LO REDUCTION CLAUSES FOR PAIRS AND PROJECTIONS

$$\overline{\pi_i\langle t_1, t_2\rangle \to_{LO} t_i} \qquad \overline{\langle t, s\rangle u \to_{LO} \langle tu, su\rangle} \qquad \overline{\pi_i(\lambda x.t) \to_{LO} \lambda x.\pi_i t}$$

$$\frac{t \to_{LO} s}{\pi_i t \to_{LO} \pi_i s} \qquad \frac{t \to_{LO} s}{\langle t, u\rangle \to_{LO} \langle s, u\rangle} \qquad \frac{u \text{ is normal} \qquad t \to_{LO} s}{\langle u, t\rangle \to_{LO} \langle u, s\rangle}$$

In [12], van Ramsdonk shows that every orthogonal higher-order rewriting system that is *fully extended* and *left normal* has a LO normalization theorem[3]. These requirements, similarly to orthogonality, concern the shape of the rewriting rules—see [12] for exact definitions. Verifying that the distributive λ-calculus is fully extended and left normal is a routine check, omitted here to avoid defining formally higher-order rewriting systems. The theorem then follows.

Theorem 2.5 (Leftmost-outermost normalization). *If* $t \to_{\text{dist}}^* s$ *and* s *is* $\to_{\text{dist}}$*-normal then* $t \to_{LO}^* s$. $\qquad\qquad\square$

3 Simple Types up to Distributivity

In this section we define the simply typed distributive λ-calculus and prove subject reduction.

The Type System. The grammar of types is given by

$$A \quad ::= \quad \tau \mid A \Rightarrow A \mid A \wedge A$$

where τ is a given atomic type.

The relation $\equiv$ denoting type isomorphism is defined by

$$\frac{}{A \equiv A} \qquad \frac{B \equiv A}{A \equiv B} \qquad \frac{A \equiv B \quad B \equiv C}{A \equiv C} \qquad \frac{}{A \Rightarrow B \wedge C \equiv (A \Rightarrow B) \wedge (A \Rightarrow C)}$$

$$\frac{A \equiv C}{A \Rightarrow B \equiv C \Rightarrow B} \qquad \frac{B \equiv C}{A \Rightarrow B \equiv A \Rightarrow C} \qquad \frac{A \equiv C}{A \wedge B \equiv C \wedge B} \qquad \frac{B \equiv C}{A \wedge B \equiv A \wedge C}$$

---

[3] Precisely, on the one hand van Ramsdonk in [12] shows that full extendedness implies that outermost-fair strategies are normalizing. On the other hand, left-normality implies that leftmost-fair rewriting is normalizing. Then, the LO strategy is normalizing.

The typing rules are:

$$\frac{}{\Gamma, x : A \vdash x : A} \ (ax) \qquad \frac{\Gamma \vdash t : A \quad A \equiv B}{\Gamma \vdash t : B} \ (\equiv)$$

$$\frac{\Gamma, x : A \vdash t : B}{\Gamma \vdash \lambda x.t : A \Rightarrow B} \ (\Rightarrow_i) \qquad \frac{\Gamma \vdash t : A \Rightarrow B \quad \Gamma \vdash s : B}{\Gamma \vdash ts : B} \ (\Rightarrow_e)$$

$$\frac{\Gamma \vdash t : A \quad \Gamma \vdash s : B}{\Gamma \vdash \langle t, s \rangle : A \wedge B} \ (\wedge_i) \quad \frac{\Gamma \vdash t : A \wedge B}{\Gamma \vdash \pi_1 t : A} \ (\wedge_{e_1}) \quad \frac{\Gamma \vdash t : A \wedge B}{\Gamma \vdash \pi_2 t : B} \ (\wedge_{e_2})$$

Note rule $\equiv$: it states that if t is typable with A then it is also typable with B for any type $B \equiv A$. It is the key rule for having subject reduction for the distributive λ-calculus.

Subject Reduction. The proof of subject reduction is built in a standard way, from a generation and a substitution lemma, plus a straightforward lemma on the shape of isomorphic types.

Lemma 3.1 (Generation). *Let* $\Gamma \vdash t : A$. *Then,*

1. *If* $t = x$, *then* $\Gamma = \Gamma', x : B$ *and* $B \equiv A$.
2. *If* $t = \lambda x.s$, *then* $\Gamma, x : B \vdash s : C$ *and* $B \Rightarrow C \equiv A$.
3. *If* $t = \langle s_1, s_2 \rangle$, *then* $\Gamma \vdash s_i : B_i$, *for* $i = 1, 2$, *and* $B_1 \wedge B_2 \equiv A$.
4. *If* $t = su$, *then* $\Gamma \vdash s : B \Rightarrow A$, $\Gamma \vdash u : A$.
5. *If* $t = \pi_i s$, *then* $\Gamma \vdash s : B_1 \wedge B_2$ *and* $B_i = A$.

Proof. Formally, the proof is by induction on $\Gamma \vdash t : A$, but we rather give an informal explanation. If t is a value (x, $\lambda x.s$, or $\langle s_1, s_2 \rangle$) then the last rule may be either the corresponding introduction rule or $\equiv$, and the statement follows. If t is not a value there are two similar cases. If $t = su$ what said for values still holds, but we can say something more. Note indeed that if $A \equiv C$ and $\Gamma \vdash s : B \Rightarrow C$ then since C is a sub-formula of $B \Rightarrow C$ we can permute the $\equiv$ rule upwards and obtain $\Gamma \vdash s : B \Rightarrow A$. Similarly if $t = \pi_i s$, which is also an elimination rule. $\square$

Lemma 3.2 (Substitution). *If* $\Gamma, x : A \vdash t : B$ *and* $\Gamma \vdash s : A$, *then* $\Gamma \vdash t\{x \leftarrow s\} : B$.

Proof. Easy induction on the derivation of $\Gamma, x : A \vdash t : B$. Details in the Appendix. $\square$

Lemma 3.3 (Equivalence of types).

1. *If* $A \wedge B \equiv C \wedge D$ *then* $A \equiv C$ *and* $B \equiv D$.
2. *If* $A \Rightarrow B \equiv C \Rightarrow D$ *then* $A \equiv C$ *and* $B \equiv C$.
3. *If* $A \wedge B \equiv C \Rightarrow D$ *then* $D \equiv D_1 \wedge D_2$, $A \equiv C \Rightarrow D_1$ *and* $B \equiv C \Rightarrow D_2$.

Proof. By induction on the definition of $\equiv$. $\square$

Theorem 3.4 (Subject reduction). *If $\Gamma \vdash t : A$ and $t \to_{\mathsf{dist}} s$, then $\Gamma \vdash s : A$.*

Proof. By induction on $t \to_{\mathsf{dist}} s$ using the generation lemma (Lemma 3.1). We first deal with the cases of the rules applied at top level:

- *β-rule*: $(\lambda x.t)s \mapsto_\beta t\{x\leftarrow s\}$. By generation, $\Gamma \vdash \lambda x.t : B \Rightarrow A$, $\Gamma \vdash s : B$. Again by generation, $\Gamma, x : C \vdash t : D$, with $C \Rightarrow D \equiv B \Rightarrow A$, so by Lemma 3.3, $C \equiv B$ and $D \equiv A$. Then, by rule ($\equiv$) we have $\Gamma \vdash s : C$, and so, by the substitution lemma (Lemma 3.2) we have $\Gamma \vdash t\{x\leftarrow s\} : D$, therefore, by rule ($\equiv$), $\Gamma \vdash t\{x\leftarrow s\} : A$.
- *Projection*: $\pi_i\langle t_1, t_2\rangle \mapsto_{\pi_i} t_i$. By generation, $\Gamma \vdash \langle t_1, t_2\rangle : B_1 \wedge B_2$ with $B_i = A$. By generation again, $\Gamma \vdash t_i : C_i$ with $C_1 \wedge C_2 \equiv B_1 \wedge B_2$. Therefore, by rule ($\equiv$), $\Gamma \vdash t_i : A$.
- *Pair-application*: $\langle t, s\rangle u \mapsto_{@_\times} \langle tu, su\rangle$. By generation, $\Gamma \vdash \langle t, s\rangle : B \Rightarrow A$ and $\Gamma \vdash u : B$. By generation again, $\Gamma \vdash t : C$ and $\Gamma \vdash s : D$ with $C \wedge D \equiv B \Rightarrow A$. By Lemma 3.3, $A \equiv A_1 \wedge A_2$, $C \equiv B \Rightarrow A_1$ and $D \equiv B \Rightarrow A_2$. Then,

$$
\cfrac{
\cfrac{
\cfrac{\Gamma \vdash t : C}{\Gamma \vdash t : B \Rightarrow A_1}\ (\equiv) \quad \Gamma \vdash u : B
}{\Gamma \vdash tu : A_1}\ (\Rightarrow_e)
\quad
\cfrac{
\cfrac{\Gamma \vdash s : D}{\Gamma \vdash s : B \Rightarrow A_2}\ (\equiv) \quad \Gamma \vdash u : B
}{\Gamma \vdash su : A_2}\ (\Rightarrow_e)
}{
\cfrac{\Gamma \vdash \langle tu, su\rangle : A_1 \wedge A_2}{\Gamma \vdash \langle tu, su\rangle : A}\ (\equiv)
}\ (\wedge_i)
$$

- *Projection-abstraction*: $\pi_i(\lambda x.t) \mapsto_{\pi_\lambda} \lambda x.\pi_i t$. By generation, $\Gamma \vdash \lambda x.t : B_1 \wedge B_2$ with $B_i = A$. By generation again, $\Gamma, x : C \vdash t : D$, with $C \Rightarrow D \equiv B_1 \wedge B_2$. Then, by Lemma 3.3, $D \equiv D_1 \wedge D_2$, $B_1 \equiv C \Rightarrow D_1$, and $B_2 \equiv C \Rightarrow D_2$. Then, $A = C \Rightarrow D_i$, and so,

$$
\cfrac{
\cfrac{
\cfrac{\Gamma, x : C \vdash t : D}{\Gamma, x : C \vdash t : D_1 \wedge D_2}\ (\equiv)
}{\Gamma, x : C \vdash \pi_i t : D_i}\ (\wedge_{e_i})
}{\Gamma \vdash \lambda x.\pi_i t : C \Rightarrow D_i}\ (\Rightarrow_i)
$$

The inductive cases are all straightforward. We give one of them, the others are along the same lines. Let $\lambda x.t \to_{\mathsf{dist}} \lambda x.s$ because $t \to_{\mathsf{dist}} s$. By generation, $\Gamma, x : B \vdash t : C$, with $B \Rightarrow C \equiv A$. By i.h., $\Gamma, x : B \vdash s : C$, so, by rules ($\Rightarrow_i$) and ($\equiv$), $\Gamma \vdash \lambda x.s : A$. □

4   Strong Normalisation

Here we prove strong normalization using Tait's reducibility technique. The key point shall be proving that the interpretation of types is stable by distributivity.

Definition 4.1 (Basic definitions and notations).

- SN terms: *we write* SN *for the set of strongly normalising terms.*
- One-step reducts: *the set* $\{s \mid t \to_{\mathsf{dist}} s\}$ *of all the one-step reducts of a term t is noted* Red(t).
- Evaluation length: eval(t) *is the length of the longest path starting from t to arrive to a normal form*
- Size: size(t) *is the size of the term t defined in the usual way.*

The Interpretation of Types. The starting point of the reducibility technique is the definition of the interpretation of types, which is the standard one.

Definition 4.2 (Interpretation of types).

$$\begin{aligned}
[\![\tau]\!] &:= \mathsf{SN} \\
[\![A \Rightarrow B]\!] &:= \{t \mid \forall s \in [\![A]\!], ts \in [\![B]\!]\} \\
[\![A \wedge B]\!] &:= \{t \mid \pi_1 t \in [\![A]\!] \text{ and } \pi_2 t \in [\![B]\!]\}
\end{aligned}$$

The Reducibility Properties. The next step is to prove the standard three properties of reducibility. The proof is standard, that is, the distributive rules do not play a role here.

Lemma 4.3 (Properties of the interpretation). *For any type A the following properties of its interpretation are valid.*

CR1 $[\![A]\!] \subseteq \mathsf{SN}$.
CR2 *If* $t \in [\![A]\!]$ *and* $t \to_{\mathsf{dist}} s$, *then* $s \in [\![A]\!]$.
CR3 *If* t *is neutral and* $\mathsf{Red}(t) \subseteq [\![A]\!]$, *then* $t \in [\![A]\!]$.

Proof.

CR1 By induction on A. Cases:
- $[\![\tau]\!] = \mathsf{SN}$.
- Let $t \in [\![A \Rightarrow B]\!]$. Then, for all $s \in [\![A]\!]$, we have $ts \in [\![B]\!]$. By *i.h.*, $[\![B]\!] \subseteq \mathsf{SN}$, so $ts \in \mathsf{SN}$, and hence, $t \in \mathsf{SN}$.
- Let $t \in [\![A \wedge B]\!]$. Then, in particular, $\pi_1 t \in [\![A]\!]$. By *i.h.*, $[\![A]\!] \subseteq \mathsf{SN}$, so $\pi_1 t \in \mathsf{SN}$, and hence, $t \in \mathsf{SN}$.

CR2 By induction on A. Cases:
- Let $t \in [\![\tau]\!] = \mathsf{SN}$. Then if $t \to_{\mathsf{dist}} s$, we have $s \in \mathsf{SN} = [\![\tau]\!]$.
- Let $t \in [\![A \Rightarrow B]\!]$. Then, for all $u \in [\![A]\!]$, we have $tu \in [\![B]\!]$. By *i.h.* on B, since $tu \to_{\mathsf{dist}} su$, we have $su \in [\![B]\!]$ and so $s \in [\![A \Rightarrow B]\!]$.
- Let $t \in [\![A_1 \wedge A_2]\!]$. Then, $\pi_i t \in [\![A_i]\!]$, for $i = 1, 2$. By *i.h.* on A_i, since $\pi_i t \to_{\mathsf{dist}} \pi_i s$, we have $\pi_i s \in [\![A_i]\!]$ and so $s \in [\![A_1 \wedge A_2]\!]$.

CR3 By induction on A. Let t be neutral. Cases:
- Let $\mathsf{Red}(t) \subseteq [\![\tau]\!] = \mathsf{SN}$. Then $t \in \mathsf{SN} = [\![\tau]\!]$.
- Let $\mathsf{Red}(t) \subseteq [\![A \Rightarrow B]\!]$. Then for each $t' \in \mathsf{Red}(t)$, we have that for all $s \in [\![A]\!]$, $t's \in [\![B]\!]$. Since ts is neutral, if we show that $\mathsf{Red}(ts) \subseteq [\![B]\!]$ then the *i.h.* on B gives $ts \in [\![B]\!]$ and so $t \in [\![A \Rightarrow B]\!]$.
  Since, by CR1 on $[\![A]\!]$, we have $s \in \mathsf{SN}$, we show that $\mathsf{Red}(ts) \subseteq [\![B]\!]$ by a second induction on $\mathsf{size}(s)$. The possible reducts of ts are:
    - $t's$, with $t \to_{\mathsf{dist}} t'$, which is in $[\![B]\!]$ by hypothesis,
    - ts', with $s \to_{\mathsf{dist}} s'$, then by the second induction hypothesis $\mathsf{Red}(ts') \subseteq [\![B]\!]$ and by *i.h.* $ts' \in [\![B]\!]$.
  Note that since t is neutral there are no other reductions from ts.
- Let $\mathsf{Red}(t) \subseteq [\![A_1 \wedge A_2]\!]$. Then for each $t' \in \mathsf{Red}(t)$, we have that $\pi_i t' \in [\![A_i]\!]$, for $i = 1, 2$. We show that $\mathsf{Red}(\pi_i t) \subseteq [\![A_i]\!]$, which—since $\pi_i t$ is neutral—by *i.h.* implies $\pi_i t \in [\![A_i]\!]$, and so $t \in [\![A_1 \wedge A_2]\!]$.
  Since t is neutral, its only possible reducts have the form $\pi_i t'$, with $t \to_{\mathsf{dist}} t'$, which are in $[\![A_i]\!]$ by hypothesis. $\qquad\square$

Stability of the Interpretation by Isomorphism. Finally, we come to the point where distributivity plays a role. Here we prove that the interpretation of types is stable by $\equiv$, that is, if $A \equiv B$ then $[\![A]\!] = [\![B]\!]$. We need an auxiliary lemma stating a sort of stability by anti-reduction of $[\![A]\!]$ with respect to the standard rewriting rules of β and projection.

Lemma 4.4

1. *If $t, s \in \mathsf{SN}$ and $t\{x\!\leftarrow\!s\} \in [\![A]\!]$ then $(\lambda x.t)s \in [\![A]\!]$.*
2. *If $t_i \in [\![A_i]\!]$ then $\pi_i\langle t_1, t_2 \rangle \in [\![A_i]\!]$, for $i = 1, 2$.*

Proof.

1. By induction on $\mathsf{eval}(t) + \mathsf{eval}(s)$. We show that $\mathsf{Red}((\lambda x.t)s) \subseteq [\![A]\!]$, and obtain the statement by CR3. Cases:
   - $(\lambda x.t)s \to_{\mathsf{dist}} (\lambda x.t')s$ with $t \to_{\mathsf{dist}} t'$. We can apply the *i.h.* because if $t \to_{\mathsf{dist}} t'$ then $t\{x\!\leftarrow\!s\} \to_{\mathsf{dist}} t'\{x\!\leftarrow\!s\}$ by left substitutivity of $\to_{\mathsf{dist}}$ (Lemma 2.3.1), and $t'\{x\!\leftarrow\!s\} \in [\![A]\!]$ by CR2. By *i.h.*, $(\lambda x.t')s \in [\![A]\!]$.
   - $(\lambda x.t)s \to_{\mathsf{dist}} (\lambda x.t)s'$ with $s \to_{\mathsf{dist}} s'$. We can apply the *i.h.* because if $s \to_{\mathsf{dist}} s'$ then $t\{x\!\leftarrow\!s\} \to^*_{\mathsf{dist}} t\{x\!\leftarrow\!s'\}$ by right substitutivity of $\to_{\mathsf{dist}}$ (Lemma 2.3.2), and $t\{x\!\leftarrow\!s'\} \in [\![A]\!]$ by CR2. By *i.h.*, $(\lambda x.t)s' \in [\![A]\!]$.
   - $(\lambda x.t)s \to_\beta t\{x\!\leftarrow\!s\}$, which is in $[\![A]\!]$ by hypothesis.
2. By CR1 we have $t_i \in \mathsf{SN}$. By induction on $\mathsf{eval}(t_1) + \mathsf{eval}(t_2)$. The possible reducts of $\pi_i\langle t_1, t_2 \rangle$ are:
   - t_i, because of a $\to_{\pi_i}$ step. Then $t_i \in [\![A_i]\!]$ by hypothesis.
   - $\pi_i\langle t'_1, t_2 \rangle$, with $t_1 \to_{\mathsf{dist}} t'_1$. We can apply the *i.h.* because $[\![A_1]\!] \ni t_1 \to_{\mathsf{dist}} t'_1$ which is in $[\![A_1]\!]$ by CR2. Then $\pi_i\langle t'_1, t_2 \rangle \in [\![A_1]\!]$ by *i.h.*
   - $\pi_i\langle t_1, t'_2 \rangle$, with $t_2 \to_{\mathsf{dist}} t'_2$. As the previous case, just switching coordinate of the pair. $\qquad\qquad\square$

Lemma 4.5 (Stability by isomorphism). *If $A \equiv B$, then $[\![A]\!] = [\![B]\!]$.*

Proof. By induction on $A \equiv B$. The only interesting case is the base case $A \Rightarrow B_1 \wedge B_2 \equiv (A \Rightarrow B_1) \wedge (A \Rightarrow B_2)$. The inductive cases follow immediately from the *i.h.*

We prove $[\![A \Rightarrow B_1 \wedge B_2]\!] = [\![(A \Rightarrow B_1) \wedge (A \Rightarrow B_2)]\!]$ by proving the double inclusion.

- Let $t \in [\![A \Rightarrow B_1 \wedge B_2]\!]$. Then for all $s \in [\![A]\!]$ we have $ts \in [\![B_1 \wedge B_2]\!]$, so

$$\pi_i(ts) \in [\![B_i]\!] \qquad\qquad (2)$$

We need to prove that $(\pi_i t)s \in [\![B_i]\!]$. Since this term is neutral, we prove that $\mathsf{Red}((\pi_i t)s) \subseteq [\![B_i]\!]$ and conclude by CR3. By CR1 and (2), t and s are in SN, so we proceed by induction on $\mathsf{eval}(t) + \mathsf{eval}(s)$. The possible one-step reducts fired from $(\pi_i t)s$ are:
  - $(\pi_i t')s$, with $t \to_{\mathsf{dist}} t'$, then *i.h.* applies.
  - $(\pi_i t)s'$, with $s \to_{\mathsf{dist}} s'$, then *i.h.* applies.

- $t_i s$, if $t = \langle t_1, t_2 \rangle$. Since $\pi_i(ts) = \pi_i(\langle t_1, t_2 \rangle s) \to_{\text{dist}} \pi_i \langle t_1 s, t_2 s \rangle \to_{\text{dist}} t_1 s$, by (2) and CR2 we have $t_i s \in [\![B_i]\!]$.
- $(\lambda x.\pi_i u)s$ if $t = \lambda x.u$. Then we can apply Lemma 4.4.1, since we know that u and s are SN and that $\pi_i(ts) = \pi_i((\lambda x.u)s) \to_\beta \pi_i u\{x \leftarrow s\}$ which by (2) and CR2 is in $[\![B_i]\!]$. We obtain $(\lambda x.\pi_i u)s \in [\![B_i]\!]$

– Let $t \in [\![(A \Rightarrow B_1) \wedge (A \Rightarrow B_2)]\!]$. Then $\pi_i t \in [\![A \Rightarrow B_i]\!]$, and so for all $s \in [\![A]\!]$, we have $(\pi_i t)s \in [\![B_i]\!]$. By CR1 we have $t, s \in$ SN, so we proceed by induction on $\text{eval}(t) + \text{eval}(s)$ to show that $\text{Red}(\pi_i(ts)) \subseteq [\![B_i]\!]$, which implies $\pi_i(ts) \in [\![B_i]\!]$ and so $ts \in [\![B_1 \wedge B_2]\!]$, and then $t \in [\![A \Rightarrow B_1 \wedge B_2]\!]$. The possible reducts of $\pi_i(ts)$ are:
  - $\pi_i(t's)$ with $t \to_{\text{dist}} t'$, then the *i.h.* applies.
  - $\pi_i(ts')$ with $s \to_{\text{dist}} s'$, then the *i.h.* applies.
  - $\pi_i(u\{x \leftarrow s\})$ if $t = \lambda x.u$. Then since $(\pi_i t)s \in [\![B_i]\!]$, we have $(\pi_i \lambda x.u)s \in [\![B_i]\!]$ and $(\pi_i \lambda x.u)s \to_{\pi_\lambda} (\lambda x.\pi_i u)s \to_\beta \pi_i(u\{x \leftarrow s\})$, so, by CR2, $\pi_i(u\{x \leftarrow s\}) \in [\![B_i]\!]$.
  - $\pi_i \langle t_1 s, t_2 s \rangle$ if $t = \langle t_1, t_2 \rangle$. We apply Lemma 4.4.2, since we have $(\pi_i \langle t_1, t_2 \rangle)s \in [\![B_i]\!]$ and $(\pi_i \langle t_1, t_2 \rangle)s \to_{\pi_i} t_i s$, so, by CR2, $t_i s \in [\![B_i]\!]$. We then obtain $\pi_i \langle t_1 s, t_2 s \rangle \in [\![B_i]\!]$. $\qquad\square$

Adequacy. The last step is to prove what is usually called *adequacy*, that is, that typability of t with A implies that $t \in [\![A]\!]$, up to a substitution θ playing the role of the typing context Γ. The proof is standard, the distributive rules do not play any role.

Definition 4.6 (Valid substitution). *We say that a substitution θ is valid with respect to a context Γ (notation $\theta \vDash \Gamma$) if for all $x : A \in \Gamma$, we have $\theta x \in [\![A]\!]$.*

Lemma 4.7 (Adequacy). *If $\Gamma \vdash t : A$ and $\theta \vDash \Gamma$, then $\theta t \in [\![A]\!]$.*

Proof. By induction on the derivation of $\Gamma \vdash t : A$.

–
$$\frac{}{\Gamma, x : A \vdash x : A} \ (ax) \qquad \text{Since } \theta \vDash \Gamma, x : A, \text{ we have } \theta x \in [\![A]\!].$$

–
$$\frac{\Gamma, x : A \vdash t : B}{\Gamma \vdash \lambda x.t : A \Rightarrow B} \ (\Rightarrow_i)$$

By *i.h.*, if $\theta' \vDash \Gamma, x : A$, then $\theta' t \in [\![B]\!]$. Let $s \in [\![A]\!]$, we have to prove that $\theta(\lambda x.t)s = (\lambda x.\theta t)s \in [\![B]\!]$. By CR1, $s, \theta t \in$ SN, so we proceed by a second induction on $\text{size}(s) + \text{size}(\theta t)$ to show that $\text{Red}((\lambda x.\theta t)s) \subseteq [\![B]\!]$, which implies $(\lambda x.\theta t)s \in [\![B]\!]$. The possible reducts of $(\lambda x.\theta t)s$ are:
  - $(\lambda x.t')s$, with $\theta t \to_{\text{dist}} t'$, then the second *i.h.* applies.
  - $(\lambda x.\theta t)s'$, with $s \to_{\text{dist}} s'$, then the second *i.h.* applies.
  - $\theta t\{x \leftarrow s\}$, then take $\theta' = \theta, x \mapsto s$ and notice that $\theta' \vDash \Gamma, x : A$, so $\theta t\{x \leftarrow s\} \in [\![B]\!]$.

–
$$\frac{\Gamma \vdash t : A \Rightarrow B \quad \Gamma \vdash s : B}{\Gamma \vdash ts : B} \ (\Rightarrow_e)$$

By *i.h.*, $\theta t \in [\![A \Rightarrow B]\!]$ and $\theta s \in [\![B]\!]$, so, by definition, $\theta t \theta s = \theta(ts) \in [\![B]\!]$.

$$- \frac{\Gamma \vdash t_1 : A_1 \quad \Gamma \vdash t_2 : A_2}{\Gamma \vdash \langle t_1, t_2 \rangle : A_1 \wedge A_2} \; (\wedge_i)$$

By *i.h.*, $\theta t_i \in [\![A_i]\!]$, for $i = 1, 2$. By CR1 we have $\theta t_i \in \mathsf{SN}$, hence we proceed by a second induction on $\mathsf{size}(\theta t_1) + \mathsf{size}(\theta t_2)$ to show that $\mathsf{Red}(\pi_i \langle \theta t_1, \theta t_2 \rangle) \subseteq [\![A_1]\!]$, which, by CR3 implies $\pi_i \langle \theta t_1, \theta t_2 \rangle \in [\![A_i]\!]$ and so $\langle \theta t_1, \theta t_2 \rangle \in [\![A_1 \wedge A_2]\!]$. The possible one-step reducts of $\pi_i \langle \theta t_1, \theta t_2 \rangle$ are:

- $\pi_i \langle t', \theta t_2 \rangle$, with $\theta t_1 \to_{\mathsf{dist}} t'$, then the second *i.h.* applies.
- $\pi_i \langle \theta t_1, t' \rangle$, with $\theta t_2 \to_{\mathsf{dist}} t'$, then the second *i.h.* applies.
- $\theta t_i \in [\![A_i]\!]$.

$-\dfrac{\Gamma \vdash t : A_1 \wedge A_2}{\Gamma \vdash \pi_i t : A_i} \; (\wedge_{e_i})$ By *i.h.*, $\theta t \in [\![A_1 \wedge A_2]\!]$, so, by definition, $\pi_i(\theta t) = \theta \pi_i t \in [\![A_i]\!]$.

$-\dfrac{\Gamma \vdash t : A \quad A \equiv B}{\Gamma \vdash t : B} \; (\equiv)$ By *i.h.*, $\theta t \in [\![A]\!]$, so, by Lemma 4.5, $\theta t \in [\![B]\!]$. $\qquad \square$

Theorem 4.8 (Strong normalisation). *If $\Gamma \vdash t : A$, then $t \in \mathsf{SN}$.*

Proof. By Lemma 4.7, if $\theta \vDash \Gamma$, $\theta t \in [\![A]\!]$. By CR3, variables—which are neutral terms—are in all the interpretations, and so the identity substitution is valid in any context, in particular, in Γ. Hence, $t \in [\![A]\!]$. By CR1, $[\![A]\!] \subseteq \mathsf{SN}$. Hence, $t \in \mathsf{SN}$. $\qquad \square$

5   Discussion and Conclusions

The Unit Type. The point of the paper is the fact that the distributive rewriting rules and typing up to distributivity perfectly marry together. The elimination of clashes, on the other hand, is a nice consequence of our approach that should not be taken too seriously, because it does not scale up, as we now show.

Let's consider the extension of the distributive λ-calculus with the unit type $\top$ and a construct $\star$ of type $\top$. In this extended setting it is still possible to interpret distributivity as in the previous sections, and all our results still holds. There are however two new clashes, namely $\star u$ and $\pi_i \star$. If one makes the further step of eliminating them via new rules and type them up to new isomorphisms, then unfortunately normalization breaks, as we now show.

Consider their natural commutation rules:

$$\star u \to \star \qquad \pi_i \star \to \star \qquad i = 1, 2$$

To have subject reduction along the same lines of what we did, one needs to work up to the following two isomorphisms:

$$A \Rightarrow \top \equiv \top \qquad \top \wedge \top \equiv \top$$

Note that $A \Rightarrow \top \equiv \top$ has to be valid for any type A, therefore in particular it is true for $\top$, giving $\top \Rightarrow \top \equiv \top$. Now, unfortunately, one can type the diverging term $\Omega := (\lambda x.xx)(\lambda x.xx)$, as the following derivation shows, and in fact all the terms of the ordinary λ-calculus—said differently strong normalization breaks.

$$\dfrac{\dfrac{\dfrac{\dfrac{x:\mathsf{T}\vdash x:\mathsf{T}}{x:\mathsf{T}\vdash x:\mathsf{T}\Rightarrow\mathsf{T}}\,(ax)}{x:\mathsf{T}\vdash xx:\mathsf{T}}\,(\equiv)\quad\dfrac{x:\mathsf{T}\vdash x:\mathsf{T}}{}\,(ax)}{\dfrac{x:\mathsf{T}\vdash xx:\mathsf{T}}{\vdash\lambda x.x:\mathsf{T}\Rightarrow\mathsf{T}}\,(\Rightarrow_i)}\,(\Rightarrow_e)\quad\dfrac{\dfrac{\dfrac{\dfrac{x:\mathsf{T}\vdash x:\mathsf{T}}{x:\mathsf{T}\vdash x:\mathsf{T}\Rightarrow\mathsf{T}}\,(\equiv)\quad\dfrac{x:\mathsf{T}\vdash x:\mathsf{T}}{}\,(ax)}{\dfrac{x:\mathsf{T}\vdash xx:\mathsf{T}}{\vdash\lambda x.x:\mathsf{T}\Rightarrow\mathsf{T}}\,(\Rightarrow_i)}\,(\Rightarrow_e)}{\vdash\lambda x.xx:\mathsf{T}}\,(\equiv)}{\vdash(\lambda x.xx)(\lambda x.xx):\mathsf{T}}\,(\Rightarrow_e)$$

This example also reinforces the fact, already stressed in the introduction, that interpretations of type isomorphisms tend to break key properties. Distributivity, instead, is somewhat special, as it admits an interpretation that is conservative with respect to the properties of the underlying calculus.

Additional Distributivity Rules. It is possible to add the two following distributive rewriting rules:

$$\lambda x.\langle t,s\rangle \rightarrow \langle \lambda x.t,\lambda x.s\rangle \qquad \pi_i(ts)\rightarrow(\pi_i t)s \quad i=1,2$$

Subject reduction and strong normalization still hold. The problem is that the rewriting system is no longer orthogonal, since the following critical pairs are now possible:

$$\begin{array}{ccc}\pi_i(\lambda x.\langle t_1,t_2\rangle) & \longrightarrow & \pi_i\langle\lambda x.t_1,\lambda x.t_2\rangle\\ \downarrow & & \vdots\\ \lambda x.\pi_i\langle t_1,t_2\rangle & \dashrightarrow & \lambda x.t_i\end{array}\qquad\begin{array}{ccc}(\lambda x.\langle t,s\rangle)u & \longrightarrow & \langle t\{x\leftarrow u\},s\{x\leftarrow u\}\rangle\\ \downarrow & & \vdots\,2\\ \langle\lambda x.t,\lambda x.s\rangle u & \dashrightarrow & \langle(\lambda x.t)u,(\lambda x.s)u\rangle\end{array}$$

$$\begin{array}{ccc}\pi_i(\langle t_1,t_2\rangle s) & \longrightarrow & (\pi_i\langle t_1,t_2\rangle)s\\ \downarrow & & \vdots\\ \pi_i\langle t_1 s,t_2 s\rangle & \dashrightarrow & t_i s\end{array}\qquad\begin{array}{ccc}\pi_i((\lambda x.t)s) & \longrightarrow & \pi_i(t\{x\leftarrow s\})\\ \downarrow & & \uparrow\\ (\pi_i(\lambda x.t))s & \dashrightarrow & (\lambda x.\pi_i t)s\end{array}$$

While the pairs on the left side are easy to deal with, those on the right side have an unpleasant closing diagram and make the rewriting system much harder to study.

Conclusions. We have extended the λ-calculus with pairs with two additional commutation rules inspired by the distributivity isomorphism of simple types, and showed that it is a well behaved setting. In the untyped case, confluence, progress, and leftmost-outermost normalization are obtained essentially for free. In the typed case, subject reduction up to distributivity holds, as well as strong normalization. The proof of strong normalization, in particular, is a smooth adaptation of Tait's standard reducibility proof for the λ-calculus with pairs.

Acknowledgements. This work has been partially funded by the ANR JCJC grant COCA HOLA (ANR-16-CE40-004-01), the ECOS-Sud grant QuCa (A17C03), and the French-Argentinian International Research Project SINFIN.

A   Proofs Appendix

Lemma 2.3 (Substitutivity of $\to_{\mathsf{dist}}$).

1. Left substitutivity: if $t \to_{\mathsf{dist}} t'$ then $t\{x\leftarrow s\} \to_{\mathsf{dist}} t'\{x\leftarrow s\}$.
2. Right substitutivity: if $s \to_{\mathsf{dist}} s'$ then $t\{x\leftarrow s\} \to_{\mathsf{dist}}^* t\{x\leftarrow s'\}$.

Proof.

1. By induction on the relation $\to_{\mathsf{dist}}$. Base cases:
   - Let $t = (\lambda y.u)r \mapsto_\beta u\{y\leftarrow r\} = t'$. Then,

$$t\{x\leftarrow s\} = ((\lambda y.u)r)\{x\leftarrow s\} = (\lambda y.u\{x\leftarrow s\})r\{x\leftarrow s\}$$
$$\mapsto_\beta (u\{x\leftarrow s\})\{y\leftarrow r\{x\leftarrow s\}\} = (u\{y\leftarrow r\})\{x\leftarrow s\} = t'\{x\leftarrow s\}$$

   - Let $t = \pi_i\langle u_1, u_2\rangle \mapsto_{\pi_i} u_i = t'$. Then,

$$t\{x\leftarrow s\} = (\pi_i\langle u_1, u_2\rangle)\{x\leftarrow s\} = \pi_i\langle u_1\{x\leftarrow s\}, u_2\{x\leftarrow s\}\rangle$$
$$\mapsto_{\pi_i} u_i\{x\leftarrow s\} = t'\{x\leftarrow s\}$$

   - Let $t = \langle u, r\rangle p \mapsto_{@_\times} \langle up, rp\rangle = t'$. Then,

$$t\{x\leftarrow s\} = (\langle u, r\rangle p)\{x\leftarrow s\} = \langle u\{x\leftarrow s\}, r\{x\leftarrow s\}\rangle(p\{x\leftarrow s\})$$
$$\mapsto_{@_\times} \langle u\{x\leftarrow s\}p\{x\leftarrow s\}, r\{x\leftarrow s\}p\{x\leftarrow s\}\rangle = \langle up, rp\rangle\{x\leftarrow s\} = t'\{x\leftarrow s\}$$

   - Let $t = \pi_i(\lambda y.u) \mapsto_{\pi_\lambda} \lambda y.\pi_i u = t'$, Then,

$$t\{x\leftarrow s\} = \pi(\lambda y.u)\{x\leftarrow s\} = \pi(\lambda y.u\{x\leftarrow s\})$$
$$\mapsto_{\pi_\lambda} \lambda y.\pi_i(u\{x\leftarrow s\}) = (\lambda y.\pi_i u)\{x\leftarrow s\} = t'\{x\leftarrow s\}$$

   We treat the inductive cases compactly via contexts. First note that a straightforward induction on C shows that $C\langle t\rangle\{x\leftarrow s\} = C\{x\leftarrow s\}\langle t\{x\leftarrow s\}\rangle$, where the substitution $C\{x\leftarrow s\}$ on contexts is defined as expected. Now, consider $t = C\langle u\rangle \to_a C\langle r\rangle = t'$ with $u \mapsto_a r$, for some $a \in \{\beta, @_\times, \pi_1, \pi_2, \pi_\lambda\}$. By *i.h.*, $u\{x\leftarrow s\} \mapsto_a r\{x\leftarrow s\}$. Hence,

$$t\{x\leftarrow s\} = C\langle u\rangle\{x\leftarrow s\} = C\{x\leftarrow s\}\langle u\{x\leftarrow s\}\rangle$$
$$\to_a C\{x\leftarrow s\}\langle r\{x\leftarrow s\}\rangle = C\langle r\rangle\{x\leftarrow s\} = t'\{x\leftarrow s\}$$

2. By induction on t.
   - Let $t = x$. Then,

$$t\{x\leftarrow s\} = s \to_{\mathsf{dist}} s' = t\{x\leftarrow s'\}$$

   - Let $t = y$. Then,

$$t\{x\leftarrow s\} = y \to_{\mathsf{dist}}^* y = t\{x\leftarrow s'\}$$

- Let $t = \lambda y.u$. By *i.h.*, $u\{x\leftarrow s\} \rightarrow^*_{\text{dist}} u\{x\leftarrow s'\}$. Then,

$$t\{x\leftarrow s\} = \lambda y.u\{x\leftarrow s\} \rightarrow^*_{\text{dist}} \lambda y.u\{x\leftarrow s'\} = t\{x\leftarrow s'\}$$

- Let $t = ur$. By *i.h.*, $u\{x\leftarrow s\} \rightarrow^*_{\text{dist}} u\{x\leftarrow s'\}$ and $r\{x\leftarrow s\} \rightarrow^*_{\text{dist}} r\{x\leftarrow s'\}$. Then,

$$t\{x\leftarrow s\} = (u\{x\leftarrow s\})(r\{x\leftarrow s\}) \rightarrow^*_{\text{dist}} (u\{x\leftarrow s'\})(r\{x\leftarrow s'\}) = t\{x\leftarrow s'\}$$

- Let $t = \langle u_1, u_2 \rangle$. By *i.h.*, for $i = 1,2$, $u_i\{x\leftarrow s\} \rightarrow^*_{\text{dist}} u_i\{x\leftarrow s'\}$. Then,

$$t\{x\leftarrow s\} = \langle u_1\{x\leftarrow s\}, u_2\{x\leftarrow s\}\rangle \rightarrow^*_{\text{dist}} \langle u_1\{x\leftarrow s'\}, u_2\{x\leftarrow s'\}\rangle = t\{x\leftarrow s'\}$$

- Let $t = \pi_i u$. By *i.h.* $u\{x\leftarrow s\} \rightarrow^*_{\text{dist}} u\{x\leftarrow s'\}$. Then,

$$t\{x\leftarrow s\} = \pi_i(u\{x\leftarrow s\}) \rightarrow^*_{\text{dist}} \pi_i(u\{x\leftarrow s'\}) = t\{x\leftarrow s'\}$$

$\square$

Lemma 3.2 (Substitution). *If $\Gamma, x : A \vdash t : B$ and $\Gamma \vdash s : A$, then $\Gamma \vdash t\{x\leftarrow s\} : B$.*

Proof. By induction on the derivation of $\Gamma, x : A \vdash t : B$.

- Let $\Gamma, x : A \vdash x : A$ as a consequence of rule (ax). Then, $x\{x\leftarrow s\} = s$, and we have $\Gamma \vdash s : A$.
- Let $\Gamma, y : B, x : A \vdash y : B$ as a consequence of rule (ax). Then, $y\{x\leftarrow s\} = y$, and by rule (ax), $\Gamma, y : B \vdash y : B$.
- Let $\Gamma, x : A \vdash t : B$ as a consequence of $\Gamma, x : A \vdash t : C$, $C \equiv B$ and rule $(\equiv)$. Then, by *i.h.*, $\Gamma \vdash t\{x\leftarrow s\} : C$, so, by rule $(\equiv)$, $\Gamma \vdash t\{x\leftarrow s\} : B$.
- Let $\Gamma, x : A \vdash \lambda y.t : B \Rightarrow C$ as a consequence of $\Gamma, x : A, y : B \vdash t : C$ and rule $(\Rightarrow_i)$. Then, by *i.h.*, $\Gamma, y : B \vdash t\{x\leftarrow s\} : C$, so, by rule $(\Rightarrow_i)$, $\Gamma \vdash \lambda y.t\{x\leftarrow s\} : B \Rightarrow C$. Notice that $\lambda y.t\{x\leftarrow s\} = (\lambda y.t)\{x\leftarrow s\}$.
- Let $\Gamma, x : A \vdash tr : B$ as a consequence of $\Gamma, x : A \vdash t : C \Rightarrow B, \Gamma, x : A \vdash r : C$, and rule $(\Rightarrow_e)$. Then, by *i.h.*, $\Gamma \vdash t\{x\leftarrow s\} : C \Rightarrow B$ and $\Gamma \vdash r\{x\leftarrow s\} : C$, so, by rule $(\Rightarrow_e)$, $\Gamma \vdash t\{x\leftarrow s\}r\{x\leftarrow s\} : B$. Notice that $t\{x\leftarrow s\}r\{x\leftarrow s\} = (tr)\{x\leftarrow s\}$.
- Let $\Gamma, x : A \vdash \langle t_1, t_2 \rangle : B_1 \wedge B_2$ as a consequence of $\Gamma, x : A \vdash t_i : B_i$, $i = 1,2$, and rule $(\wedge_i)$. Then, by *i.h.*, $\Gamma \vdash t_i\{x\leftarrow s\} : B_i$, so, by rule $(\wedge_i)$, $\Gamma \vdash \langle t_1\{x\leftarrow s\}, t_2\{x\leftarrow s\}\rangle : B_1 \wedge B_2$. Notice that $\langle t_1\{x\leftarrow s\}, t_2\{x\leftarrow s\}\rangle = \langle t_1, t_2\rangle\{x\leftarrow s\}$.
- Let $\Gamma, x : A \vdash \pi_1 t : B$ as a consequence of $\Gamma, x : A \vdash t : B \wedge C$ and rule $(\wedge_{e_1})$. Then, by *i.h.*, $\Gamma \vdash t\{x\leftarrow s\} : B \wedge C$, so, by rule $(\wedge_{e_1})$, $\Gamma \vdash \pi_1(t\{x\leftarrow s\}) : B$. Notice that $\pi_1(t\{x\leftarrow s\}) = \pi_1 t\{x\leftarrow s\}$.
- Let $\Gamma, x : A \vdash \pi_2 t : B$ as a consequence of $\Gamma, x : A \vdash t : B \wedge B$ and rule $(\wedge_{e_1})$. Analogous to previous case. $\square$

References

1. Aczel, P.: A general Church-Rosser theorem. University of Manchester, Technical report (1978)
2. Aït-Kaci, H., Garrigue, J.: Label-selective λ-calculus syntax and confluence. Theor. Comput. Sci. **151**(2), 353–383 (1995)
3. Arbiser, A., Miquel, A., Ríos, A.: The lambda-calculus with constructors: syntax, confluence and separation. J. Funct. Program. **19**(5), 581–631 (2009)
4. Bruce, K.B., Di Cosmo, R., Longo, G.: Provable isomorphisms of types. Math. Struct. Comput. Sci. **2**(2), 231–247 (1992)
5. Di Cosmo, R.: Isomorphisms of types: from λ-calculus to information retrieval and language design. Progress in Theoretical Computer Science, Birkhauser (1995)
6. Di Cosmo, R.: A short survey of isomorphisms of types. Math. Struct. Comput. Sci. **15**(5), 825–838 (2005)
7. Díaz-Caro, A., Dowek, G.: The probability of non-confluent systems. In: Ayala-Rincón, M., Bonelli, E., Mackie, I. (eds.) Proceedings of the 9th International Workshop on Developments in Computational Models. Electronic Proceedings in Theoretical Computer Science, vol. 144, pp. 1–15. Open Publishing Association (2014)
8. Díaz-Caro, A., Dowek, G.: Proof normalisation in a logic identifying isomorphic propositions. In: Geuvers, H. (ed.) 4th International Conference on Formal Structures for Computation and Deduction (FSCD 2019). Leibniz International Proceedings in Informatics (LIPIcs), vol. 131, pp. 14:1–14:23. Schloss Dagstuhl-Leibniz-Zentrum fuer Informatik (2019)
9. Klop, J.W.: Combinatory reduction systems. Ph.D. thesis, Utrecht University (1980)
10. Nipkow, T.: Higher-order critical pairs. In: Proceedings of the Sixth Annual Symposium on Logic in Computer Science (LICS 1991), Amsterdam, The Netherlands, 15–18 July 1991, pp. 342–349 (1991)
11. Petit, B.: Semantics of typed lambda-calculus with constructors. Log. Methods Comput. Sci. **7**(1), 1–24 (2011)
12. Raamsdonk, F.: Outermost-fair rewriting. In: de Groote, P., Roger Hindley, J. (eds.) TLCA 1997. LNCS, vol. 1210, pp. 284–299. Springer, Heidelberg (1997). https://doi.org/10.1007/3-540-62688-3_42
13. Støvring, K.: Extending the extensional lambda calculus with surjective pairing is conservative. Log. Methods Comput. Sci. **2**(2:1), 1–14 (2006)

Polynomial Time over the Reals
with Parsimony

Emmanuel Hainry[1], Damiano Mazza[2], and Romain Péchoux[1(✉)]

[1] Project Mocqua, LORIA, CNRS, Inria, Université de Lorraine, Nancy, France
{hainry,pechoux}@loria.fr
[2] CNRS, UMR 7030, LIPN, Université Paris 13, Villetaneuse, France
damiano.mazza@lipn.univ-paris13.fr

Abstract. We provide a characterization of Ko's class of polynomial time computable functions over real numbers. This characterization holds for a stream based language using a parsimonious type discipline, a variant of propositional linear logic. We obtain a first characterization of polynomial time computations over the reals on a higher-order functional language using a linear/affine type system.

1 Introduction

Motivations. The notion of polynomial time computations over the reals has been deeply studied in the last decades, e.g. [1–4]. Several programming languages studying mathematical properties of real functions such as computable functions [5,6], Lipschitz-functions [7], or analytical functions [8] have been introduced and studied but no programming language characterizing polynomial time over the reals has emerged. A programming language based characterization of polynomial time over the reals would be highly valuable as it would provide a programmer the opportunity to write libraries of efficient programs where any computation can be approximated in feasible time in the output precision.

This contrasts with studies on discrete domains which have led to the development by the *Implicit Computational Complexity* community of several programming languages capturing various time and space complexity classes using, among other techniques, a linear type discipline, for example see [9–12].

Characterizing complexity classes over the reals requires both convergence within a given time or space bound on inductive data (a finite approximation of the real number) and divergence on coinductive data (the infinite real number representation). If this latter requirement is not fulfilled then the calculus cannot be complete with respect to computability over the reals. Due to the divergence requirement, a characterization of polynomial time over the reals cannot be obtained as a straightforward extension of the results on discrete domains that enforce convergence.

E. Hainry, D. Mazza and R. Péchoux—This work was supported by ANR-14-CE25-0005 Elica: Expanding Logical Ideas for Complexity Analysis.

© Springer Nature Switzerland AG 2020
K. Nakano and K. Sagonas (Eds.): FLOPS 2020, LNCS 12073, pp. 50–65, 2020.
https://doi.org/10.1007/978-3-030-59025-3_4

Results. This paper presents a first characterization of polynomial time over the reals based on a functional higher order language. For that purpose, we consider the non-uniform parsimonious lambda-calculus that was shown to characterize the complexity classes P/poly and L/poly in [13]. Parsimony can be viewed as a logical system, a variant of multiplicative affine logic endowed with an exponential modality !(−). Contrarily to any known variants of linear and affine logics, the exponential modality satisfies *Milner's law* $!A \cong A \otimes !A$. Hence it allows the programmer to encode streams (infinite lists). Non-uniformity means that we do not restrict to ultimately constant streams but allow any stream on a finite alphabet, i.e., generated by arbitrary functions with finite codomain, seen as oracles. The parsimonious calculus also enjoys the necessary property of normalizing in polynomial time on non-stream data (Theorem 1).

We characterize the class of polynomial time computable functions over the real interval $[-1,1]$: the n-th digit of the output can be computed in time polynomial in n (Theorem 2). Real numbers are encoded using non-uniform streams of signed binary digits $(-1, 0, 1)$ and functions are encoded as uniform contexts that can be fed with a non-uniform real encoding (the input) under parsimony requirements.

To our knowledge, this characterization is the first linear logic based characterization of polynomial time computations over the real line. It is obtained in a very natural way by extending the indexed uniform parsimonious calculus of [14] to a non-uniform setting with streams of Church numerals as basic construct. Moreover, the semantics of the language has been improved by adopting a convention similar to [15] that uses explicit substitutions.

Related Work. The parsimonious calculus can be viewed as an finite-depth/infinite-width alternative to the infinitary λ-calculus [28] where terms have finite width and infinite depth.

Studies on complexity properties of stream-based first order programming languages have already been developed using interpretation methods [16]. These only focus on soundness though. The paper [17] provides a characterization of polynomial time over the reals on first order programs using type-2 polynomial interpretations, which are however known to be untractable both at the level of inference and checking. In [18], it is shown that algebras and coalgebras may be encoded in the light affine lambda calculus while preserving polynomial time normalization properties. The paper [19] explores applications of light logics to infinitary calculi, showing a polynomially-bounded productivity result, with no connection however to real number computation.

On function algebras, [20] and [21] provide a characterization of elementary and polynomial time computable real functions, respectively. The function coalgebra defined in [22] characterizes the complexity class of stream functions whose n-th output bit is computable in L.

Another interesting and orthogonal line of work is the one of [23,24] extracting certified programs for exact real number computations from constructive proofs where time complexity is not considered.

2   Preliminaries: Complexity over the Reals

We consider the signed binary representation of real numbers that consists in (infinite) sequences of digits in $\{1, 0, -1\}$. This representation allows numbers to be approximated from below but also from above. It is well known [3] that from a computability point of view, dyadic (i.e. infinite sequences of numbers of the shape $\frac{p}{2^n}; p \in \mathbb{Z}, n \in \mathbb{N}$), Cauchy and signed binary representations are equivalent. Note however that using dyadic numbers instead of a dyadic sequence gives a different (bad) notion of computability. Indeed some basic functions such as multiplication by 3 or addition are not computable if reals are restricted to dyadic numbers.

As we are mostly interested in ensuring complexity properties on the fractional part of a real number, we will restrict our analysis to real numbers in $[-1, 1]$. This restriction is standard in the exact real number computation literature [6, 24]. Our analysis can be generalized to the whole real line by just considering a pair consisting in an integer and a fractional part.

Definition 1. *Any real number* $r \in [-1, 1]$ *can be represented by an infinite sequence of digits in* $\{-1, 0, 1\}$.

Formally, r *is represented by* $\{r\} \in \{-1, 0, 1\}^{\mathbb{N}}$, *noted* $r \lhd \{r\}$, *if*

$$r = \sum_{i=1}^{\infty} \{r\}_i 2^{-i}.$$

Computing a function consists in mapping a representation of a real to a representation of its image. Based on Definition 1, a Turing machine computing a function under a signed binary encoding will work with an infinite sequence of digits, written on a read-only input tape. The result will be written on a write-only output tape. Since the output too is infinite, the use of machines that do not halt is needed. Moreover, if we have two different representations of the same real r, then the computed outputs must represent the same real $f(r)$.

By convention, in this paper "Turing machine" will always mean a machine as just described. They are sometimes called oracle Turing Machines in the literature to exhibit the fact that the input is not a finite object but can be given by an oracle. For such a machine M and a given infinite sequence of signed digits $\{r\} \in \{-1, 0, 1\}^{\mathbb{N}}$, let $M(\{r\}) \in \{-1, 0, 1\}^{\mathbb{N}}$ be the infinite sequence of digits written (and obtained as a limit) on the output tape of the machine.

Definition 2. *A function* $f : [-1, 1] \to [-1, 1]$ *is computable if and only if there exists a Turing machine* M *such that* $\forall r \in [-1, 1]$, *the following diagram commutes:*

$$
\begin{array}{ccc}
r & \lhd & \{r\} \\
\downarrow f & & \downarrow M \\
f(r) & \lhd & M(\{r\}).
\end{array}
$$

The above definition implies that if a real function is computable then it must be continuous. See [3] which calls this property the *fundamental property of computable functions*.

Due to the infinite nature of computations, the complexity of real functions cannot be defined in a standard way. Ko's definition of complexity [2] associates with n the time needed to obtain precision 2^{-n}.

Definition 3. $f : \mathbb{N} \to \mathbb{N}$ *is a complexity measure for a Turing machine M if and only if $\forall n \in \mathbb{N}, \forall \{r\} \in \{-1, 0, 1\}^{\mathbb{N}}$, the n-th digit of $M(\{r\})$, noted $M(\{r\})_n$, is output in time less than or equal to $f(n)$.*

Definition 4. *A Turing machine M has* polynomial time complexity *if there is a polynomial $P \in \mathbb{N}[X]$ that is a complexity measure for M.*

The class of functions in $[-1, 1] \to [-1, 1]$ computed by machines that have polynomial time complexity is denoted $\mathrm{P}([-1, 1])$.

Although the representations we mentioned (dyadic, Cauchy, signed) are equivalent from a computability point of view, they are not strictly equivalent in terms of complexity. However, the complexity class $\mathrm{P}([-1, 1])$ introduced above is equal to Ko's class of polynomial time computable functions on the dyadic representation. Indeed, from the proof of computability equivalence in [3], the translations from one representation to the other may be computed in polynomial time.

Functions computable in polynomial time can be characterized using the notion of modulus of continuity.

Definition 5 (Modulus of continuity). *Given $f : [-1, 1] \to [-1, 1]$, we say that $m : \mathbb{N} \to \mathbb{N}$ is a modulus of continuity for f if and only if*

$$\forall n \in \mathbb{N}, \forall r, s \in [-1, 1], |r - s| < 2^{-m(n)} \implies |f(r) - f(s)| < 2^{-n}.$$

Proposition 1. $f \in \mathrm{P}([-1, 1])$ *iff there exist two computable functions $m : \mathbb{N} \to \mathbb{N}$ and $\psi : [-1, 1] \times \mathbb{N} \to [-1, 1]$ such that*

1. *m is a polynomial modulus of continuity for f,*
2. *ψ is a polynomial time computable approximation function for f (i.e. $\forall d \in [-1, 1], \forall n \in \mathbb{N}, |\psi(d, n) - f(d)| \le 2^{-n}$).*

The above proposition is known since [2] and has been explicitly stated and formalized in [21].

Summing up, functions in $\mathrm{P}([-1, 1])$ enjoy the property of being computable in polynomial time in every (dyadic) point and of having a polynomial modulus of continuity. We hence seek a stream-based programming language with a polynomially-bounded access to streams, with the aim of reproducing this property.

3 Parsimonious Stream Programming Language

Syntax. The language under consideration will be a non-uniform version of the infinitary parsimonious lambda-calculus of [14]. Terms are defined by the following grammar:

(Patterns) $\ni p ::= a \otimes b \mid !x$

(Terms) $\ni t, u ::= a \mid x_i \mid \lambda a.t \mid t\,u \mid t \otimes u \mid t[p := u] \mid !_f \overline{u} \mid t :: u \mid \mathsf{nstrm}_i$

where: $f \in \mathbb{N} \to \mathbb{N}_k$, with $\mathbb{N}_k = \{0, \ldots, k-1\}$; $\overline{u}$ denotes a sequence of k terms $u_0, \ldots, u_{k-1}$; $a, b, c, \ldots$ range over a countable set of *affine variables*; and $x, y, z, \ldots$ range over a countable set of *exponential variables*. Exponential variables correspond to streams and are indexed by an integer $i \in \mathbb{N}$. Intuitively, x_i is the $i+1$-th element of the stream x. We always consider terms up to renaming of bound variables.

For a given function $f : \mathbb{N} \to \mathbb{N}_k$, the term $!_f \overline{u}$, called *box*, is a stream generator: $!_f(u_0, u_1, \ldots, u_{k-1})$ intuitively represents the stream $u_{f(0)} :: u_{f(1)} :: u_{f(2)} :: \cdots$. The precise semantics of $!_f$ will be explained later. We use $\mathbf{u}, \mathbf{v}, \ldots$ to range over boxes. Since any f is allowed, the syntax is infinitary, except when $k = 1$, in which case f can only be the constant zero function and we simply write $!u_0$. These are called *uniform boxes*, and a term (or context) containing only uniform boxes is called *uniform*.

The explicit substitution notation $t[p := u]$ is inspired by [15] and is syntactically equivalent to the let $p := u$ in t construct of [13,14]. It correspond to either a pair destructor $t[a \otimes b := u]$ or to a stream destructor $t[!x := u]$.

The *depth* $d(t)$ of a term t is the maximum number of nested boxes.

The language also includes a stream constructor $::$ as well as a pair constructor $\otimes$ and a family of constants nstrm_i, with $i \in \mathbb{N}$, representing streams of Church numerals (see Example 1 below) in increasing order, starting from $\underline{i}$. Let the size $|t|$ of a term t be the number of symbols in t.

Let $\diamond_1, \ldots, \diamond_n$ be special symbols called *holes*. A context, written $C\langle \diamond_1, \ldots, \diamond_n \rangle$ is a particular term with at most one occurence of each hole $\diamond_i$. We denote by $C\langle t_1, \ldots, t_n \rangle$ the result of substituting the term t_i to the hole $\diamond_i$ in C, an operation which may capture variables. A one-hole context, written $C\langle \diamond \rangle$ is a particular case of context with a single hole.

Example 1. Given $n \in \mathbb{N}$, the n-th *Church numeral* can be encoded as

$$\underline{n} = \lambda f.\lambda a.x_0(x_1(\ldots x_{n-1}\, a \ldots))[!x := f],$$

i.e. applications of the n first elements $x_0, \ldots, x_{n-1}$ of the stream f.

Example 2. The head function is encoded by the term

$$head = \lambda a.x_0[!x := a]$$

returning the element of index 0 in a stream a.

The tail function is encoded by the term

$$tail = \lambda a.!x_1[!x := a]$$

returning the stream of elements of the stream a starting from index 1 (i.e. $!x_1$).

Parsimony. Among terms of the language, we distinguish a family of terms called parsimonious preventing duplication of stream data and exponentiation of standard data. As we shall see later, parsimony will be entailed by the typing discipline (Lemma 1) and will ensure polynomial time normalization on non stream data (Theorem 1).

For that purpose, we first need to define a notion of slice.

Definition 6. *A* slice *of a term is obtained by removing all components but one from each box. Let $S(t)$ be the set of slices of term t:*

$$S(\alpha) := \{\alpha\} \quad if \, \alpha \in \{a, x_i\}$$
$$S(!_f(u_0, \ldots, u_{k-1})) := \bigcup_{i=0}^{k-1}\{!_f\nu_i \mid \nu_i \in S(u_i)\}$$
$$S(t_1 \otimes t_2) := \{\tau_1 \otimes \tau_2 \mid \tau_1 \in S(t_1), \tau_2 \in S(t_2)\}$$
$$S(t_1 \, t_2) := \{\tau_1 \, \tau_2 \mid \tau_1 \in S(t_1), \tau_2 \in S(t_2)\}$$
$$S(t_1 :: t_2) := \{\tau_1 :: \tau_2 \mid \tau_1 \in S(t_1), \tau_2 \in S(t_2)\}$$
$$S(t_1[p := t_2]) := \{\tau_1[p := \tau_2] \mid \tau_1 \in S(t_1), \tau_2 \in S(t_2)\}$$
$$S(\lambda a.t) := \{\lambda a.\tau_1 \mid \tau_1 \in S(t)\}$$

Example 3. In general, a slice does not belong to the set of (syntactically correct) terms:

$$S(tail \, !_f(0,1)) = \{(\lambda a.!x_1[!x := a]) \, !_f(0), (\lambda a.!x_1[!x := a]) \, !_f(1)\}.$$

Definition 7. *A term t is* parsimonious *if:*

1. *affine variables appear at most once in t,*
2. *For all $s \in S(t)$, two occurrences of an exponential variable in s have distinct indices,*
3. *box subterms do not contain free affine variables,*
4. *if an exponential variable appears free in t, then*
   (a) *it appears in at most one box,*
   (b) *in each slice of this box, it appears at most once,*
   (c) *if it appears in a box and outside a box, the occurrences outside a box have an index strictly smaller than those inside.*

Example 4. To illustrate Definition 7, let us see some (counter)-examples. The standard encoding of Church numerals $\lambda f.\lambda x.f \, (\ldots (f \, x) \ldots)$ breaks point 1. This is the reason why the encoding of Example 1 is used. $!_f(x_1)\otimes!_g(x_2)$ is forbidden because of point 4a. $!_f(x_0 \otimes x_1, y_0 \otimes x_1)$ is forbidden as point 4b is violated (but it respects point 2). $x_0\otimes!_f(x_2, x_1)$ is allowed: it respects points 4b and 4b. These counter-examples are rejected as they entail either a stream duplication or a stream data duplication, whose iteration would make it possible to compute a function with an exponential modulus of continuity.

Semantics. For $k \in \mathbb{N}$, we write t^{+n} for the term obtained by replacing all free occurrences of exponential variables x_i with x_{i+n}. We write t^{++} for t^{+1} and t^{x++} to denote the same operation applied *only* to the free occurrences of the variable x. The $++$ operator is extended to sequences by $(u_0, \ldots, u_{k-1})^{++} = (u_0^{++}, \ldots, u_{k-1}^{++})$. Also, in case all free occurrences of x have strictly positive index, we write t^{x--} for the operation which decreases indices by 1. Given a function $f : \mathbb{N} \to \mathbb{N}_k$, let f^{+i}, $i \in \mathbb{N}$, be the function in $\mathbb{N} \to \mathbb{N}_k$ defined by $\forall n \in \mathbb{N}$, $f^{+i}(n) = f(n + i)$. We define *structural congruence*, denoted by $\approx$, as the smallest congruence on terms such that

$$!_f \overline{u} \approx u_{f(0)} :: !_{f+1} \overline{u}^{++},$$

$$\mathsf{nstrm}_i \approx \underline{i} :: \mathsf{nstrm}_{i+1}$$

where $\underline{i}$ denotes the Church numeral encoding i described in Example 1. In particular, $\forall i > 1, !_f \overline{u} \approx u_{f(0)} :: u_{f(1)}^{++} :: \ldots :: u_{f(i-1)}^{+(i-1)} :: !_{f+i} \overline{u}$ holds.

A one-hole context is *shallow* if the hole does not occur inside a box. A subclass of shallow contexts is that of *substitution* contexts, defined by:

$$[-] ::= \diamond \mid [-][p := t].$$

We write $t[-]$ instead of $[-]\langle t \rangle$. The base reduction rules of our language are:

$$
\begin{aligned}
(\lambda a.t)[-] \, u &\to_\beta t\{u/a\}[-] \\
t[a \otimes b := (u \otimes w)[-]] &\to_\otimes t\{u/a, w/b\}[-] \\
S\langle x_0 \rangle[!x := (t :: u)[-]] &\to_{\mathsf{pop}} S^{x--}\langle t \rangle[!x := u][-]
\end{aligned}
$$

where S is a shallow context or a term (i.e., the occurrence x_0 may actually not appear) and $t\{u/a\}$ is the standard capture-free substitution.

The operational semantics, denoted by $\to$, is defined by closing the above rules under shallow contexts and the rule stating that $t \to t'$ and $u \approx t$ implies $u \to t'$.

Example 5. Consider the term *tail* of Example 2 and let $!_f(\underline{0}, \underline{1})$ be a stream of Boolean numbers with $f : \mathbb{N} \to \{0, 1\}$ such that $f(2k) = 0$ and $f(2k + 1) = 1$, for each $k \in \mathbb{N}$, i.e. $!_f(\underline{0}, \underline{1}) \approx \underline{0} :: \underline{1} :: \underline{0} :: \underline{1} :: \ldots$ As *tail* $= \lambda s.!x_1[!x := s]$, we have the following reduction:

$tail \, !_f(\underline{0}, \underline{1})$

$\to_\beta !x_1[!x := !_f(\underline{0}, \underline{1})]$ $\qquad\qquad \approx (x_1 :: !x_2)[!x := \underline{0} :: !_{f+1}(\underline{0}, \underline{1})]$

$\to_{\mathsf{pop}} (x_0 :: !x_1)[!x := !_{f+1}(\underline{0}, \underline{1})]$ $\qquad \approx (x_0 :: !x_1)[!x := \underline{1} :: !_{f+2}(\underline{0}, \underline{1})]$

$\to_{\mathsf{pop}} (\underline{1} :: !x_0)[!x := !_{f+2}(\underline{0}, \underline{1})]$ $\qquad \approx (\underline{1} :: x_0 :: !x_1)[!x := \underline{0} :: !_{f+3}(\underline{0}, \underline{1})]$

$\to_{\mathsf{pop}} \cdots$

Type System. Types are defined inductively by:

$$A, B ::= \alpha \mid A \multimap B \mid A \otimes B \mid !A \mid \forall \alpha.A.$$

α being a type variable. The type system, **nuPL$_\forall$**, is adapted from the uniform type system of [14] and non-uniform type system of [13] and is defined in Fig. 1. The notations Γ and Δ will be used for environments attributing types to variables. Judgments are of the shape $\Gamma; \Delta \vdash t : A$, Γ and Δ being two disjoint environments; meaning that term t has type A under the affine environment Δ and the exponential environment Γ. As usual, let Γ, Γ' represent the disjoint union of Γ and Γ'. Given a sequence of terms $\bar{t} = (t_1, \ldots, t_n)$ and a sequence of types $\bar{A} = (A_1, \ldots, A_n)$, let $\bar{t} : \bar{A}$ be a shorthand notation for $\forall i, t_i : A_i$. Given a sequence of exponential variables $\bar{x}$, let $\bar{x}_0$ denote the sequence obtained by indexing every variable of $\bar{x}$ by 0. The type Nat is a notation for the type $\forall \alpha.!(\alpha \multimap \alpha) \multimap \alpha \multimap \alpha$.

As usual a term t is *closed* if $; \vdash t : A$ can be derived, for some type A. A type A is !-free if it does not contain any occurrence of the modality !. A closed term t is of !-free type if there exists a !-free type A such that $; \vdash t : A$ can be derived.

In what follows, if A is a type with free occurrences of the type variable α and B is a type, we denote by $A[B/\alpha]$ the type obtained by replacing every occurrence of α in A with B. Let $A[]$ be a notation for $A[B/\alpha]$, for some arbitrary type B. By abuse of notation, $\text{Nat}[]$ will denote the type $!(A \multimap A) \multimap A \multimap A$, for some arbitrary type A.

Definition 8 (Rank). *The rank $r(A)$ of a type A is defined by:*

$$r(\alpha) = 0 \qquad\qquad r(A \multimap B) = r(A \otimes B) = max(r(A), r(B))$$
$$r(\forall \alpha.A) = r(A) \qquad\qquad\qquad r(!A) = r(A) + 1$$

The rank $r(t)$ of a closed term t is the maximum rank of types occurring in the typing derivation for t.

The rank of a term is always well-defined as polymorphism is restricted to !-free types in rule $\forall E$, hence $r(\forall \alpha.A) = r(A[B/\alpha])$.

Example 6. The numerals of Example 1 can be given the type Nat. We may encode unary successor and predecessor by:

$$succ = \lambda n.\lambda f.\lambda a.z_0(n \ (!z_1) \ a)[!z := f] : \text{Nat} \multimap \text{Nat}$$
$$pred = \lambda n.\lambda f.\lambda a.n \ ((\lambda b.b) :: (!z_0)) \ a[!z := f] : \text{Nat} \multimap \text{Nat}$$

Properties of **nuPL$_\forall$**. The type system enjoys some interesting properties. First, typable terms with no free exponential variables are parsimonious.

Lemma 1 (Parsimony). *If $; \Delta \vdash t : A$ then t is parsimonious.*

Second, the system enjoys subject reduction on terms with no free exponential variables:

Lemma 2 (Subject reduction). *If $; \Delta \vdash t : A$ and $t \to t'$ then $; \Delta \vdash t' : A$.*

$$\frac{}{\Gamma; \Delta, a : A \vdash a : A} \text{ (Var)} \qquad \frac{}{; \vdash \text{nstrm}_i : !\text{Nat}} \text{ (Nat)}$$

$$\frac{\Gamma; \Delta, a : A \vdash t : B}{\Gamma; \Delta \vdash \lambda a.t : A \multimap B} \text{ (}\multimap\text{I)} \qquad \frac{\Gamma; \Delta \vdash t : A \multimap B \quad \Gamma'; \Delta' \vdash u : A}{\Gamma, \Gamma'; \Delta, \Delta' \vdash t\, u : B} \text{ (}\multimap\text{E)}$$

$$\frac{\Gamma; \Delta \vdash t : A \quad \Gamma'; \Delta' \vdash u : B}{\Gamma, \Gamma'; \Delta, \Delta' \vdash t \otimes u : A \otimes B} \text{ (}\otimes\text{I)} \qquad \frac{\Gamma; \Delta \vdash u : A \otimes B \quad \Gamma'; \Delta', a : A, b : B \vdash t : C}{\Gamma, \Gamma'; \Delta, \Delta' \vdash t[a \otimes b := u] : C} \text{ (}\otimes\text{E)}$$

$$\frac{\Gamma, x : A; \Delta, a : A \vdash t : B}{\Gamma, x : A; \Delta \vdash t^{x^{++}}\{x_0/a\} : B} \text{ (abs)} \qquad \frac{\Gamma; \Delta \vdash t : A \quad \Gamma'; \Delta' \vdash u : !A}{\Gamma, \Gamma'; \Delta, \Delta' \vdash t :: u : !A} \text{ (coabs)}$$

$$\frac{; \overline{a} : \overline{A} \vdash \overline{u}_0 : A \quad \dots \quad ; \overline{a} : \overline{A} \vdash \overline{u}_{k-1} : A}{\Gamma, \overline{x} : \overline{A}; \vdash !_f \overline{u}\{\overline{x}_0/\overline{a}\} : !A} \text{ (!I)} \qquad \frac{\Gamma; \Delta \vdash u : !A \quad \Gamma', x : A; \Delta' \vdash t : B}{\Gamma, \Gamma'; \Delta, \Delta' \vdash t[!x := u] : B} \text{ (!E)}$$

$$\frac{\Gamma; \Delta \vdash t : A \quad \alpha \notin FV(\Gamma \cup \Delta)}{\Gamma; \Delta \vdash t : \forall \alpha.A} \text{ (}\forall\text{I)} \qquad \frac{\Gamma; \Delta \vdash t : \forall \alpha.A \quad B \text{ is !-free}}{\Gamma; \Delta \vdash t : A[B/\alpha]} \text{ (}\forall\text{E)}$$

Fig. 1. Non-uniform parsimonious logic type system

The proof of subject reduction is standard after observing that $\approx$ preserves typability, i.e. if $; \Delta \vdash t : A$ and $t \approx t'$ then $; \Delta \vdash t' : A$.

Last, we can show a polynomial time normalization result on closed terms of !-free type. Let $\Lambda_{d,r}$ be the set of closed terms of !-free type of depth smaller than d and rank smaller than r.

Theorem 1. *For every $d, r \in \mathbb{N}$, there is a polynomial $P_{d,r}$ such that every term $t \in \Lambda_{d,r}$ normalizes in $P_{d,r}(|t|)$ steps.*

Proof. The proof is a rather straightforward adaptation of the proof of [13] to the considered calculus.

4 A Characterization of Polynomial Time over the Reals

Before proving the main result (Theorem 2), we introduce some preliminary notions and encodings. A function f is closed under the relation $\mathcal{R}$ if $\forall x, \forall y, x \mathcal{R} y \Rightarrow f(x) = f(y)$.

Signed Bits. Consider the type $\mathsf{SB} = o \multimap o \multimap o \multimap o$ for encoding the signed binary digits $\{-1, 0, 1\}$, for some propositional variable o. Constants $\mathsf{b} \in \{-1, 0, 1\}$ can be represented by the terms $\lambda a.\lambda b.\lambda c.t$ with t equal to a, b or c depending on whether b is equal to 1, 0 or -1, respectively. By abuse of notation, we will use b to denote both the term and the constant it represents.

Real Numbers. Let *toReal* be a function from $!SB \to [-1,1]$ closed under congruence $\approx$ and reduction $\to$ such that $toReal(b :: t) = \frac{b}{2} + \frac{1}{2}toReal(t)$.

Any real number $r \in [-1,1]$ can be represented by a box $\mathbf{r} = !_f(-1,0,1)$ of type $!SB$ as, by definition of *toReal*, we have

$$toReal(\mathbf{r}) = \sum_{i=0}^{\infty} r_{f(i)} 2^{-(i+1)}.$$

Function. A function $f : [-1,1] \to [-1,1]$ is *parsimoniously computable* if there is a uniform context $t_f \langle \diamond_1, \ldots, \diamond_n \rangle$ such that for each closed term t of type $!SB$ we have:

$$; \vdash t_f \langle t, \ldots, t \rangle : !SB \text{ and } toReal(t_f \langle t, \ldots, t \rangle) = f(toReal(t)).$$

This definition can be generalized to n-ary functions over $[-1,1]$ by considering contexts of the shape $t_f \langle \overline{t_1}, \ldots, \overline{t_n} \rangle$ as we will see in the example computing the average of two real numbers described in Sect. 5.

In the above definition, the context is required to be uniform to ensure that the only real numbers we deal with are part of the input, thus preventing a non-computable oracle such as Chaitin's Ω [25] to be used.

Theorem 2. *The set of parsimoniously computable functions is exactly* $P([-1,1])$.

Proof. The proof is in 2 directions: *Soundness* and *Completeness*.

- For Soundness, we demonstrate that any parsimoniously computable function f computed by a context $t_f \langle \diamond \rangle$ is in $P([-1,1])$. For that purpose, consider the family of prefix functions computed by the terms $get_n : !SB \multimap SB^{\otimes n}$:

$$get_n = \lambda a.x_0 \otimes (\ldots \otimes x_{n-1})[!x := a],$$

where $SB^{\otimes 1} = SB$ and $SB^{\otimes n+1} = SB \otimes SB^{\otimes n}$, outputting the n-th element of a stream s given as input, $n > 0$. Then, the term:

$$t_f^n \langle t \rangle = get_n \ t_f \langle t \rangle$$

can be typed by $SB^{\otimes n}$.

For each n, let $toReal_n : SB^{\otimes n} \to [-1,1]$ be the function closed under reduction $\to$ and such that:

$$toReal_{n+1}(b \otimes t) = \frac{b}{2} + \frac{1}{2}toReal_n(t)$$

$$toReal_1(b) = \frac{b}{2}$$

For any $n \geq 1$ and any representation t of a real number r (i.e. $r = toReal(t)$), we have that:

$$|toReal(t_f \langle t \rangle) - toReal_n(t_f^n \langle t \rangle)| \leq 2^{-n}.$$

This is straightforward as $t_f^n \langle t \rangle$ outputs a truncation of the n first signed digits of $t_f \langle t \rangle$. Moreover $t_f^n \langle t \rangle$ is a closed term of !-free type ($SB^{\otimes n}$). Consequently, it belongs to $\Lambda_{d,r}$, for some depth d and some rank r, and we can apply Theorem 1: it normalizes in $P_{d,r}(|t_f^n \langle t \rangle|)$ steps, that is in $Q(n)$ steps for some polynomial Q.

- For Completeness, we show that any function in $P([-1,1])$, computed by a Turing Machine M, is parsimoniously computable by exhibiting a uniform context with the good properties simulating M.

  For that purpose, we first show how to encode iteration, duplication, and any polynomial in order to compute the polynomial time bound of the machine M.

  Then, we show how to encode signed binary strings representing real numbers, how to encode operations on these strings: case, push, and pop. These operations correspond to basic tape manipulations in the Turing machine.

  We also show how to encode the modulus of continuity and, finally, we encode the semantics of the Turing machine: configurations, transition function, and machinery, reusing previously introduced term for iteration.

Iteration. An iteration scheme $It(n, step, base):=n \ !(step) \ base$ corresponding to the following typing derivation, can be defined on $\mathtt{Nat}$:

$$\frac{\begin{array}{cc} \vdots & \vdots \\ ; \Delta \vdash step : A \multimap A \quad \Gamma; \Sigma \vdash base : A \end{array}}{\dfrac{\vdots}{\Gamma, \Delta'; \Sigma \vdash It(n, step', base) : A}}$$

where Δ' and $step'$ are obtained from Δ and $step$, respectively, by replacing each affine variable by an exponential variable.

Duplication. We also manage to encode and type duplication on $\mathtt{Nat}$ as follows:

$$\lambda n.It(n, \lambda a.(succ \ m) \otimes (succ \ l)[m \otimes l = a], \underline{0} \otimes \underline{0}) : \mathtt{Nat}[] \multimap \mathtt{Nat} \otimes \mathtt{Nat}$$

Polynomials. Successor of Example 6 can be iterated to obtain addition of type $\mathtt{Nat}[] \multimap \mathtt{Nat} \multimap \mathtt{Nat}$. A further iteration on addition (applied to a unary integer of type $\mathtt{Nat}[]$) leads to multiplication, of type $\mathtt{Nat}[] \multimap \mathtt{Nat}[] \multimap \mathtt{Nat}$. Using addition, multiplication and duplication we may represent any polynomial with integer coefficients as a closed term of type $\mathtt{Nat}[] \multimap \mathtt{Nat}$.

The usual encodings for duplication, addition, multiplication on Church numerals are not handled as they are in need of variable duplication that is not allowed in our formalism (see Example 4).

Signed Binary Strings. Define the strings of signed binary numbers by $\mathsf{SB}^* = \, !(o \multimap o) \multimap \, !(o \multimap o) \multimap \, !(o \multimap o) \multimap o \multimap o$. The signed binary string $w = b_{n-1} \ldots b_0 \in \{-1,0,1\}^n$ can be represented by the term

$$t_w = \lambda a.\lambda b.\lambda c.\lambda d.g_{n-1}(\ldots g_0(d)\ldots)[!z := c][!y := b][!x := a]$$

of type SB^*, where $g_i = x_i, y_i$ or z_i depending on whether $b_i = -1, 0$ or 1. In what follows, let ϵ denote the empty string of SB^*.

Case, Push and Pop. We define a case construct case a of $b \to t_b$, $b \in \{-1,0,1\}$, as syntactic sugar for $\lambda a. t_1 \, t_0 \, t_{-1}$. Let the substitution context $[-]$ be equal to $\diamond[!x := b][!y := c][!z := d]$. We encode the adjunction of one signed bit to a binary string by the term *push* of type $\mathsf{SB} \multimap \mathsf{SB}^* \multimap \mathsf{SB}^*$:

$$push = \text{case } a \text{ of } b \to \lambda b.\lambda c.\lambda d.\lambda e.g_b(a \, (!x_1) \, (!y_1) \, (!z_1) \, e)[-]$$

where $g_b = x_0, y_0$ or z_0 depending on whether $b = 1, 0$ or -1, respectively. In the same way we can encode the term *pop* : $\mathsf{SB}^* \multimap \mathsf{SB}^*$ that removes the first symbol of a String as follows:

$$\lambda a.\lambda b.\lambda c.\lambda d.\lambda e.(a \, ((\lambda f.f) :: (!x_0)) \, ((\lambda f.f) :: (!y_0))((\lambda f.f) :: (!z_0)) \, e)[-].$$

Modulus. We now can encode a term *modulus* of type $\mathsf{Nat}[] \multimap (\mathsf{Nat}[] \multimap \mathsf{Nat}) \multimap \, !\mathsf{SB} \multimap \mathsf{SB}^*$ taking the encodings of a natural number n, a modulus of continuity m, and a stream of signed digits $\{r\}$ (representing the real number r) as inputs and outputting a signed binary string corresponding to the $m(n)$ first bits of $\{r\}$, as *modulus* $= \lambda n.\lambda m.\lambda c.It(m \, n, \lambda a.(push \, x_0 \, a), \epsilon)[!x = c]$.

Configuration and Transitions. A configuration of a Turing Machine can be encoded by $\mathsf{Conf} = \mathsf{State} \otimes (\mathsf{SB}^* \otimes \mathsf{SB}^*)^k \otimes (\mathsf{SB}^* \otimes \mathsf{SB}^*)$, where:

- State is a type allowing to encode the finite set of states of a machine,
- each (internal) tape is encoded by a pair of signed binary string $s \otimes t$: $\mathsf{SB}^* \otimes \mathsf{SB}^*$. s represents the left-hand part of the tape in reverse order and t represents the right-hand part of the tape. The head points on the first digit of t.
- the last tape of type $\mathsf{SB}^* \otimes \mathsf{SB}^*$ is used to store the $m(n)$ first digits of the real number on the input tape.

The initial configuration of a machine computing a function over input t : $!\mathsf{SB}$ with modulus of continuity m can be encoded by:

$$c_0\langle t \rangle = init \otimes (\epsilon \otimes \epsilon)^k \otimes ((modulus \, n \, m \, t) \otimes \epsilon)$$

where *init* is a term encoding the initial state.

Machine. We can encode easily the transition function of the machine by a term *trans* : $\mathtt{Conf} \multimap \mathtt{Conf}$ using a combination of *case* constructs, and *pop* and *push* instructions on the tape. Writing a new symbol just consists in executing sequentially a pop and a push on the right part of a tape. Moving the head just consists in popping a symbol on some part of the tape and pushing on the opposite part. In the same way, we can encode a term *extract* : $\mathtt{Conf} \multimap$ SB computing, from a final configuration, the n-th signed bit computed by the machine. This term can also be encoded using a combination of case constructs as it suffices to read the state and the symbols to whom heads are pointing in order to compute the output.

Now consider the term $sim\langle t\rangle : \mathtt{Nat}[] \to \mathtt{SB}$ defined by:

$$sim\langle t\rangle = \lambda n.extract\ It(P\ n, trans, c_0\langle t\rangle)$$

where P encodes the polynomial time bound of the machine. By construction, $sim\langle t\rangle\ \underline{n}$ computes the term $M(\{r\})_n$, provided that $r \lhd \{r\}$ and $convert(t) = r$ both hold.

Output Stream. We have demonstrated that we can compute each single signed bit of the output. It just remains to show that the output stream can be rebuilt. Consider the term $map : !(\alpha \multimap \beta) \multimap !\alpha \multimap !\beta$:

$$map := \lambda f.\lambda a.!(y_0\ x_0)[!x = a][!y = f]$$

$map\ !sim\langle t\rangle\ \mathtt{nstrm}_0$ computes the infinite stream $M(\{r\})$. Moreover the term $map\ !sim\langle\diamond\rangle\ \mathtt{nstrm}_0$ is uniform and of type $!\mathtt{SB}$. $\qquad\qquad\square$

5   Example: Average of Two Real Numbers

Let us now encode the average of two real numbers in $[-1, 1]$ which is equivalent to addition modulo shift but has the advantage of staying in $[-1, 1]$. Note that the difficulty is that we need to work from left to right in the stream, that is starting from the most significant bit. This uses one digit of each stream and needs a remainder between -2 and 2 coded with 2 signed digits (the remainder will be the sum of those 2 digits), see for example [24] for an Haskell implementation.

The computation of average needs three copies of the streams and is defined as $average\langle a, b\rangle := aux\langle a, b, a, b, a, b\rangle$, with $aux\langle\diamond_1, \ldots, \diamond_6\rangle :=$

$$(map\ (!\lambda n.\pi_5\ It(n, bitr\langle\diamond_5, \diamond_6\rangle), \diamond_3 \otimes \diamond_4 \otimes x_0 \otimes y_0 \otimes 0))\ \mathtt{nstrm}_0)[-],$$

$[-] := \diamond[!x := \diamond_1][!y := \diamond_2]$, and $\pi_5 := \lambda g.e[a \otimes b \otimes c \otimes d \otimes e := g]$ and using the terms It and map defined in Sect. 4.

The main ingredient is the term $bitr\langle a, b\rangle$ that consumes the first signed digit of each stream as well as the previous remainder and computes one digit, the next remainder and the tail of each stream. This term of type $!\mathtt{SB}^{\otimes 2} \otimes \mathtt{SB}^{\otimes 3} \multimap$

$!SB^{\otimes 2} \otimes SB^{\otimes 3}$ will simply be iterated to go through the inputs and is defined by $bitr\langle \diamond_5, \diamond_6 \rangle :=$

$$\lambda g.\text{tail } \diamond_5 \otimes \text{tail } \diamond_6 \otimes (com \; x_0 \; y_0 \; c \; d)[!x := a][!y := b][a \otimes b \otimes c \otimes d \otimes e := g]$$

The two first arguments are encodings of the real numbers in the input. The next two arguments represent the remainder and the last one is the computed digit. The term com is defined by a case analysis on digits (the case term is generalized to any number of arguments).

$$
\begin{aligned}
com = \text{case } x_0, y_0, c, d \text{ of } 1,1,1,1 &\to 1 \otimes 1 \otimes 1 \\
1,1,0,1 &\to 0 \otimes 0 \otimes 1 \\
1,1,0,0 &\to 1 \otimes 1 \otimes 0 \\
1,1,0,-1 &\to 0 \otimes 0 \otimes 0 \\
1,1,-1,-1 &\to -1 \otimes -1 \otimes 0 \\
1,0,1,1 &\to 1 \otimes 0 \otimes 1 \\
\ldots &\to \ldots
\end{aligned}
$$

Indeed, the term com is a long sequence of all the 3^4 cases that happen for the 4 signed digits x_0, y_0, c and d (where $c+d$ represents the remainder). Instead of defining each of these cases one by one, we will give an algorithm to compute those cases:

$$com = \text{case } x_0, y_0, c, d \text{ of } b_1, b_2, b_3, b_4 \to b'_1 \otimes b'_2 \otimes b'_3$$

b'_3 is the result digit, computed by:

$$
\begin{aligned}
b'_3 := &\text{ if } b_1 + b_2 + 2b_3 + 2b_4 > 2 \text{ then } 1 \\
&\text{elseif } b_1 + b_2 + 2b_3 + 2b_4 < -2 \text{ then } -1 \\
&\text{else } 0
\end{aligned}
$$

b'_1 and b'_2 are the remainder bits. As we use the sum of those two digits, we only give how this sum is computed, not the combination of digits that will be chosen to satisfy this constraint.

$$b'_1 + b'_2 = b_1 + b_2 + 2b_3 + 2b_4 - 4b'_3$$

6 Remarks and Future Works

We have provided a first linear logic based characterization of polynomial time over the reals avoiding the use of untractable tools such as type-2 polynomials as in [17].

We now discuss some of the restrictions of our work that can be improved as future work.

- Parsimony forbids duplicating a stream, which is why we had to resort to contexts (rather than plain terms) to achieve completeness. For practical purposes, it would be preferable to add to the language an explicit controlled operator for stream duplication. Here we chose to stick to the "bare" parsimonious calculus and favor theoretical simplicity over practical usability.
- The non-polymorphic part of the type system of Fig. 1 is essentially syntax-directed: rule abs is the exception but it may be repeatedly applied until there are no non-linear variables at depth 0, and then one may proceed with the only applicable rule. We therefore conjecture that, with the due restrictions concerning the presence of polymorphism, type inference is efficiently decidable as in [26,27].
- In the parsimonious calculus, it is impossible to access/manipulate the index i in x_i. The stream $nstrm_i$ is introduced for circumventing this difficulty, which is tied to the nature of the parsimonious calculus: the syntactic tree of a term has finite depth but possibly infinite width (given by boxes). A cleaner solution, currently under investigation, would be to introduce parsimony in a calculus allowing also infinite depth, like the infinitary λ-calculus of [28], in the spirit of [19].

References

1. Müller, N.T.: Subpolynomial complexity classes of real functions and real numbers. In: Kott, L. (ed.) ICALP 1986. LNCS, vol. 226, pp. 284–293. Springer, Heidelberg (1986). https://doi.org/10.1007/3-540-16761-7_78
2. Ko, K.I.: Complexity Theory of Real Functions. Birkhäuser, Basel (1991). https://doi.org/10.1007/978-1-4684-6802-1
3. Weihrauch, K.: Computable Analysis: An Introduction. Springer, Heidelberg (2000). https://doi.org/10.1007/978-3-642-56999-9
4. Kawamura, A., Cook, S.A.: Complexity theory for operators in analysis. TOCT 4(2), 5:1–5:24 (2012). https://doi.org/10.1145/2189778.2189780
5. Brattka, V., Hertling, P.: Feasible real random access machines. J. Comp. 14(4), 490–526 (1998). https://doi.org/10.1006/jcom.1998.0488
6. Ciaffaglione, A., Di Gianantonio, P.: A certified, corecursive implementation of exact real numbers. TCS 351, 39–51 (2006). https://doi.org/10.1016/j.tcs.2005.09.061
7. Di Gianantonio, P., Edalat, A.: A language for differentiable functions. In: Pfenning, F. (ed.) FoSSaCS 2013. LNCS, vol. 7794, pp. 337–352. Springer, Heidelberg (2013). https://doi.org/10.1007/978-3-642-37075-5_22
8. Ehrhard, T., Regnier, L.: The differential lambda-calculus. TCS 309(1–3), 1–41 (2003). https://doi.org/10.1016/S0304-3975(03)00392-X
9. Girard, J.: Light linear logic. Inf. Comput. 143(2), 175–204 (1998). https://doi.org/10.1006/inco.1998.2700
10. Hofmann, M.: Linear types and non-size-increasing polynomial time computation. Inf. Comput. 183(1), 57–85 (2003). https://doi.org/10.1016/S0890-5401(03)00009-9
11. Gaboardi, M., Rocca, S.R.D.: A soft type assignment system for lambda -calculus. In: CSL, pp. 253–267 (2007). https://doi.org/10.1007/978-3-540-74915-8_21
12. Baillot, P., Terui, K.: Light types for polynomial time computation in λ-calculus. Inf. Comput. 207(1), 41–62 (2009). https://doi.org/10.1016/j.ic.2008.08.005

13. Mazza, D., Terui, K.: Parsimonious types and non-uniform computation. In: Halldórsson, M.M., Iwama, K., Kobayashi, N., Speckmann, B. (eds.) ICALP 2015. LNCS, vol. 9135, pp. 350–361. Springer, Heidelberg (2015). https://doi.org/10. 1007/978-3-662-47666-6_28

14. Mazza, D.: Simple parsimonious types and logarithmic space. In: CSL 2015, pp. 24–40 (2015). https://doi.org/10.4230/LIPIcs.CSL.2015.24

15. Accattoli, B., Dal Lago, U.: Beta reduction is invariant, indeed. In: CSL-LICS 2014, pp. 8:1–8:10 (2014). https://doi.org/10.1145/2603088.2603105

16. Gaboardi, M., Péchoux, R.: On bounding space usage of streams using interpretation analysis. Sci. Comput. Program. 111, 395–425 (2015). https://doi.org/10. 1016/j.scico.2015.05.004

17. Férée, H., Hainry, E., Hoyrup, M., Péchoux, R.: Characterizing polynomial time complexity of stream programs using interpretations. TCS 585, 41–54 (2015). https://doi.org/10.1016/j.tcs.2015.03.008

18. Gaboardi, M., Péchoux, R.: Algebras and coalgebras in the light affine lambda calculus. In: ICFP, pp. 114–126 (2015). https://doi.org/10.1145/2858949.2784759

19. Dal Lago, U.: Infinitary lambda calculi from a linear perspective. In: LICS, pp. 447–456 (2016). https://doi.org/10.1145/2933575.2934505

20. Campagnolo, M.L.: The complexity of real recursive functions. In: Calude, C.S., Dinneen, M.J., Peper, F. (eds.) UMC 2002. LNCS, vol. 2509, pp. 1–14. Springer, Heidelberg (2002). https://doi.org/10.1007/3-540-45833-6_1

21. Bournez, O., Gomaa, W., Hainry, E.: Algebraic characterizations of complexity-theoretic classes of real functions. Int. J. Unconv. Comput. 7(5), 331–351 (2011)

22. Leivant, D., Ramyaa, R.: The computational contents of ramified corecurrence. In: Pitts, A. (ed.) FoSSaCS 2015. LNCS, vol. 9034, pp. 422–435. Springer, Heidelberg (2015). https://doi.org/10.1007/978-3-662-46678-0_27

23. Berger, U.: From coinductive proofs to exact real arithmetic: theory and applications. Log. Methods Comput. Sci. 7(1) (2011). https://doi.org/10.2168/LMCS-7(1:8)2011

24. Berger, U., Seisenberger, M.: Proofs, programs, processes. Theory Comput. Syst. 51(3), 313–329 (2012). https://doi.org/10.1007/s00224-011-9325-8

25. Chaitin, G.J.: A theory of program size formally identical to information theory. J. ACM 22(3), 329–340 (1975). https://doi.org/10.1145/321892.321894

26. Baillot, P.: Type inference for light affine logic via constraints on words. Theoret. Comput. Sci. 328(3), 289–323 (2004). https://doi.org/10.1016/j.tcs.2004.08.014

27. Atassi, V., Baillot, P., Terui, K.: Verification of ptime reducibility for system F terms: type inference in dual light affine logic. Log. Methods Comput. Sci. 3(4) (2007). https://doi.org/10.2168/LMCS-3(4:10)2007

28. Kennaway, J., Klop, J.W., Sleep, M.R., de Vries, F.J.: Infinitary lambda calculus. TCS 175(1), 93–125 (1997). https://doi.org/10.1016/S0304-3975(96)00171-5

Session Types Without Sophistry

System Description

Oleg Kiselyov[1]([⊠]) [iD] and Keigo Imai[2]([⊠]) [iD]

[1] Tohoku University, Sendai, Japan
oleg@okmij.org
[2] Gifu University, Gifu, Japan
keigoi@gifu-u.ac.jp

Abstract. Whereas ordinary types approximate the results, session types approximate communication among computations. As a form of typestate, they describe not only what is communicated now but also what is to be communicated next. Writing session-typed programs in an ordinary programming language such an OCaml requires inordinary cleverness to simulate type-level computations and linear typing – meaning the implementation and the error messages are very hard to understand. One is constantly reminded of template metaprogramming in C++.

We present a system exploring a very different approach to session typing: lowering type-level sophistry to ordinary programming, while maintaining the static assurances. Error messages are detailed and customizable, and one can use an ordinary debugger to investigate session-type problems. Our system is a binary-session–typed DSL for service-oriented programming in OCaml, supporting multiple communication channels, internal and external choices, recursion, and also channel delegation.

The key idea is staging: ordinary run-time checks in the generator play the role of "type-checks" from the point of view of the generated program. What is a fancy type to the latter is ordinary data to the generator.

1 Introduction

Whereas ordinary types approximate the results, session types approximate communication among computations. Session types [14,47] are appealing because they can be inferred and statically checked, and because well–session-typed programs "do not go wrong": no two parties attempt to both read from or both write to their communication channel; no computation sends the data its party is not prepared to handle; no program tries to use closed or delegated away channels.[1] Therefore, there have been developed many session-typed communication libraries [21–23,32,35,37,39,41–43]. They are, in essence, DSLs for process orchestration embedded in an extant mature programming language: data pro-

---

[1] Binary session type systems like [14] and its successors, used in many libraries including ours, do not in general prevent deadlocks (see Sect. 5).

© Springer Nature Switzerland AG 2020
K. Nakano and K. Sagonas (Eds.): FLOPS 2020, LNCS 12073, pp. 66–87, 2020.
https://doi.org/10.1007/978-3-030-59025-3_5

cessing parts are programmed as usual; data communication, written via DSL operations, is guaranteed to obey the protocol.

On the other hand, session type systems needed for realistic service-oriented programs are substructural and rather complicated [1,2,6,51], with type-level computations to express duality, with resource-sensitivity, with extensible (type-level) record types and (equi-)recursive types. They are a poor match for the type system of the typical host language such as OCaml, Scala or Haskell, and hence have to be emulated, often with extraordinary sophistication, exploiting the (mis)features of the host type system to the full (see examples in Sect. 5). Although the emulation is possible – after all, the host type systems are Turing-complete – it often feels like programming an actual Turing Machine. Abstraction, error reporting and debugging are lacking. Linear types are a particular challenge [21,39,43]. The emulation invariably also affects end users: as complicated inferred types that quickly become unreadable [39]; as referring to channels by De Bruijn indices rather than by names [21,24,41,42]; and especially as bewildering error messages should something go wrong [22,41].

Having developed session-type libraries ourselves and become familiar with intricacies and frustrations of type-level programming, we cannot help but envy the ordinary term-level programming, which is actually designed for programming. We would like to:

– add a session-typed communication layer to an existing programming language, reusing all its libraries, tools and support;
– take a non-toy, off-the-shelf session-type system such as [51] essentially as it is;
– use the host language itself (rather than its type system) to implement the session-type checking and inference;
– statically guarantee that a well-sessioned program "does not go wrong";
– make error messages customizable and use the host language debugging facilities to debug session types problems.

We have built an embedded DSL satisfying all these desiderata, relying on staging, a form of metaprogramming. The key idea is type checking as a staged computation. Our contributions are as follows:

1. The DSL, called <session>, for service-oriented programming embedded in OCaml. It supports bidirectional communication on arbitrary many channels, internal and external choices, channel delegation, and recursion – over named FIFO pipes. Other back-ends such as UDP or HTTP can be easily added.
2. The showcase of using staging for embedding DSLs with sophisticated type systems, maintaining the static guarantees.
3. The showcase of implementing extensible DSLs. In fact, <session> is built by progressively extending the base DSL with choices and then delegation and recursion. Type-checking operations, in particular, unification, are likewise extensible. Extensible records with record subtyping is one of the extensions.
4. The example of using canonical structures (first proposed for Coq, see Sect. 4.2), e.g., to support communication for arbitrary many, user-defined types.

The next section presents `<session>` on a progression of examples, at the same time reminding of session type systems. Section 2.3 deals with errors and error messages. More interesting details of `<session>` are shown in Sect. 3. We then expound two implementation techniques characteristic of `<session>`: staging in Sect. 4.1 and canonical structures in Sect. 4.2. (The lack of space precludes the description of extensible mutually recursive functions and unification: we refer to the source code and the comments therein.) Section 5 discusses the related work.

The complete code is available at the following URL:

http://okmij.org/ftp/Computation/types.html#sessions.

2   Session Types by Example

This section recalls the binary session types (specifically, Yoshida and Vasconcelos' liberal system [51, §3]), by example, using `<session>`. The section hence also serves as an introduction to `<session>`. Figure 1 presents the DSL in full (as an OCaml signature), which we will explain step by step.

Ordinary type systems such as the Hindley-Milner system and its variations deal with (potentially open) expressions, such as x+1>y. Assuming the free variables x and y have the type int, the type system judges the expression well-typed and infers its type as bool. The type is an approximation of the expression's result – computed statically, that is, before evaluating it. In fact, we cannot evaluate the sample expression by itself since it is not a complete program: it is open. In a sound type system, the type correctly approximates an expression's result (if it ever comes), from which follows that a well-typed program "does not go wrong". For example, we may use our sample expression in a conditional **if** x+1>y **then** ... **else** ..., without worrying what to do should x+1>y happen to return, say, a string.

2.1   Basic Communication

Session type systems deal not with expressions to evaluate but with communicating processes to run, such as the process

$$y_1?[z_1] \text{ in } y_2?[z_2] \text{ in } y_2![z_1>z_2]; \text{inact} \tag{1}$$

in the conventional process calculus notation, employed in [51]. This process has two communication channels, or, to be precise, *endpoints*,[2] y_1 and y_2, which are represented by free variables. (Our process is hence a mere process fragment; we complete it soon.) It is to receive a value on the endpoint y_1, bind it to the

---

[2] What we call an endpoint, Yoshida and Vasconcelos [51, §3] call a "polarized channel", following Gay and Hole [12].

variable z_1, receive another value on y_2 binding it to z_2, and send on y_2 the result of the comparison of z_1 and z_2. After that, the process is finished.

Our <session> is a (Meta)OCaml library to write processes and orchestrate them. It represents a process – to be precise, a perhaps infinite *sequence* of computations and communications – as an OCaml value of the abstract type th (named for "thread"). An endpoint is represented as a value of the type ep. The sample process (1) is written as[3]

```
let p1 y1 y2 =  recv y1 Int @@ fun z1 →
                recv y2 Int @@ fun z2 →
                send y2 Bool < .~z1 > .~z2 >. @@
                finish
⤳ val p1 : ep → ep → th =  <fun>
```

(the last line shows the type inferred by OCaml for p1). We use OCaml's let-statement to assign the process a name for easy reference, and make explicit its free endpoint variables y1 and y2. Comparing the sample process in the two notations, (1) and ours, shows them quite similar. Our notation however clearly distinguishes the binding occurrences of z1 and z2 (and we write finish instead of "inact" for the ended process). Also explicit in the p1 code are Int and Bool, which may be regarded as type annotations on the communicated values. That these annotations are mandatory is a drawback of the embedding (although not that big), which we discuss in Sect. 4.2.

The p1 code also betrays staging. Staging is what MetaOCaml [25, 26] adds to OCaml: the facility to generate code to compile and execute later. To be precise, MetaOCaml adds the type α code for values representing the generated code, and two facilities to produce such values. One, akin to quote in Lisp, is enclosing an expression in so-called "brackets", for example: <1 > 2>.. The bracketed expression is not evaluated; rather, it becomes (a fragment of) the generated code. The other facility, called "escape", is like Lisp unquote. It can be understood as poking a hole in a bracketed expression, turning it into a code template. In p1 code, < .~z1 > .~z2 >. is such a template, with two holes to be filled by the code values bound to the variables z1 and z2 – producing the code of the comparison expression. Although bracketed expressions are not evaluated, they are type checked. For example, in order for < .~z1 > .~z2 >. to be well-typed, with the type bool code, the variables z1 and z2 should be of the type int code – or a type error is raised. Thus MetaOCaml statically guarantees that the generated code is well-typed – and also free from scoping errors (like unbound or unintentionally bound identifiers): unlike Lisp quotations, MetaOCaml is hygienic. Staging is crucial in our approach to session typing, as detailed in Sect. 4.1. Staging also lets <session> distinguish process computations (which are put in brackets) from process communications (described by the combinators such as recv and send). Thus <session> is a DSL for orchestration.

---

[3] The right-associative infix operator @@ of low precedence is application: f @@ x + 1 is the same as f (x + 1) but avoids the parentheses. The operator is the analogue of $ in Haskell.

(a) Types

type proc	top-level process
type th	communication thread
type ep	session endpoint
type shared	shared name, e.g., host:name

(b) Basics

val proc   : th → proc
val (‖)   : proc → proc → proc

val new_shared : string → shared

val request : shared → (ep → th) → th
val accept : shared → (ep → th) → th
val send   : ep → α trep → α code → th → th
val recv   : ep → α trep → (α code → th) → th

val othr   : unit code → th → th
val let_   : α code → (α code → th) → th
val finish : th

(c) Debugging, logging, etc

val describe_ep : ep → string code
val describe_sh : shared → string code
val debuglog   : string → th → th

(d) Inference, execution, deployment

val infer   : α trep → α → string
val proc_run   : proc → unit
val proc_deploy : proc → unit code list

(e) Internal and external choices

type label = string
val branch : ep → (label * th) list → th
val select : ep → label → th → th
val ifte   : bool code → then_:th → else_:th → th

(f) Delegation

val deleg_to   : ep → ep → th → th
val deleg_from : ep → (ep → th) → th

(g) Iteration

val toploop : (th → th) → th
val loop : ep list → (th → th) → th

Fig. 1. The syntax of <session>, as OCaml module signatures

(a) Environments

type envd   (in text, Δ)   Linear environment: finite map from ep to sess
type envg   (in text, Γ)   Non-linear environment: finite map from shared to sess

(b) Type formulas, as an extensible data type sess

type sess = ..
type sess += Var **of** var **ref** | End

(c) Basic communication extension

type sess += Send : α trep * sess → sess | Recv : α trep * sess → sess

(d) External and internal choices, based on row types [33]

type sess += Bra : rows → sess | Sel : rows → sess
and rows =
| Row : (label * sess) * rows → rows
| RowVar : rowvar **ref** → rows
| RowClosed

(e) Delegation

type sess += DSend : sess * sess → sess | DRecv : sess * sess → sess

(f) Recursion

type sess += Mu : id * sess → sess | RecVar : id * bool*(*dual*)* → sess

Fig. 2. Session types (see the explanations text; trep will be explained in Sect. 4.2)

Type-checking a `<session>` expression in OCaml gives its OCaml type that says nothing about communication (see, for example, the type of p1). Evaluating the expression gives its session type (as well as the code to run, to be discussed in Sect. 2.2); the error case is detailed in Sect. 2.3. The expression p1 however is open (represents an incomplete process fragment) and cannot be evaluated. We can still get its session type, by evaluating infer Fun(EP,Fun(EP,TH)) p1, which supplies the two "assumed" endpoints, obtaining:[4]

$$ep\_hyp\text{--}12/13 \qquad\qquad : \text{Recv}(int,End) \qquad\qquad (2)$$

$$ep\_hyp\text{--}14/15 \qquad\qquad : \text{Recv}(int,Send(bool,End)) \qquad (3)$$

Unlike the ordinary type (which is a single formula), a session type is like an environment: a finite map from names to formulas, see Fig. 2. To be precise, a session type is a pair of environments: the linear Δ (which [51] calls "typing") and the non-linear Γ (called sorting in [51]). They are so named because in the system of [51], endpoints are to be used linearly, but shared points, discussed later, do not have to be. Shown above is the linear environment inferred for p1

---

[4] It should also be possible to supply a session type and check an expression against it, to verify its communication obeys the protocol stated in the type. After all, if we can infer a session type, we can check against it. However, we have not yet offered this facility in the public library interface.

(Γ is empty). The environment specifies the communication pattern for the two endpoints of p1 in order for it to be well-sessioned (the concrete names for those hypothetical endpoints, correspond to the free variables y1 and y2, are made up by infer).

Session types (environments and type formulas) are the ordinary data types in <session>. The type formulas are an extensible data type, because we keep extending the syntax of formulas as we add more features to <session>. The type formulas describe the communication protocol: the approximation, or pattern, of the actual communication over a channel (endpoint). End is the end of interactions; Send(t,s) means sending a value of the type t (represented as "type representation" data type trep, see Sect. 4.2) with further interactions being described by s. Recv(t,s) is the protocol of receiving a value of the type t and then continuing as s. Thus, the process fragment p1, according to its inferred session type, communicates on two endpoints. From one endpoint, (2), it reads an integer and closes it; for the other, (3), it reads an integer, then sends a boolean and closes.

2.2   Sessions

A session, whose type we have just discussed, is a series of interactions between two parties over a channel. (This paper deals only with binary sessions.) A session begins when two parties rendez-vous at a "common point" and establish a fresh channel; it concludes when the communications over the channel end (as we will see, <session> detects the end as part of the session type inference, and automatically arranges for closing the channel and freeing its resources.) The rendez-vous point is called shared in <session>, created on the base of a name, such as a host name, known to all parties. The exact representation of shared depends on the underlying low-level communication library: for a TCP/IP back-end, shared may be a socket_addr; for the FIFO pipe backend, shared is represented by two (unidirectional) pipes, whose names are derived from the supplied known name. There may be many rendez-vous at the same shared – all of which, however, establish channels with the same protocol. This is the basic assumption of structured communication behind session type systems. Therefore, shared itself may be assigned a session type, describing the common protocol of these channels.

A rendez-vous is performed when one process executes accept and the other request, see Fig. 1, on the same shared. (In TCP/IP terms, when one process "connects" and the other "accepts" the connection.) As the result, a fresh private communication channel is created; each of the two processes receive the respective endpoint of it and can start communication.

To complete our running example p1 we create two channels, in two consecutive rendez-vous on two different shared:

```
let a =  new_shared "sha" and b =  new_shared "shb"
let pc =  request b @@ fun y2 → accept a @@ fun y1 → p1 y1 y2
```

Why one shared or one channel would not suffice is discussed in Sect. 2.3; on the other hand, which operation to use, request or accept, is arbitrary at this point of developing the example. The party communicating with pc is the process q:

```
let q =
  accept b  @@ fun x2 →
  request a  @@ fun x1 →
  send x1 Int .<1>. @@
  send x2 Int .<2>. @@
  recv x2 Bool @@ fun z →
  othr .<Printf.printf "got_%b\n" .~z>. @@
  finish
```

Since q is meant to communicate with pc, the choice of accept and request is no longer arbitrary. The operation othr lets us perform computations other than communication, specified as an arbitrary OCaml code enclosed in brackets. In case of q, this computation is printing, of the received value.

Both pc and q have no free endpoints and can be regarded as "top-level processes": cast as proc. Top-level processes can be combined to run in parallel:

```
let r =  proc pc || proc q
```

The inferred session type of proc pc is

$$\text{sh>sha–49} \qquad : \text{Recv(int, End)} \qquad (4)$$

$$\text{sh>shb–50} \qquad : \text{Send(int, Recv(bool, End))} \qquad (5)$$

which is the non-linear environment Γ for proc pc; as top-level processes have no free endpoints, the linear environment Δ is always empty. The environment Γ associates shared with session types. Process proc pc rendez-vous on two shared, which hence show in the printed Γ. Here, sh>sha–49 is the internal identifier for the shared point with the name "sha" created earlier, and similar with for "shb". Comparing (4) with the earlier (2) illustrates what we have explained already: the session type of a shared is the session type of channels created at its rendez-vous. However, (5) and (3) are not the same: they look "symmetric", or dual. Indeed, when two processes communicate over a channel, one sends and the other receives. Thus the session types of two endpoints of the same channel have to be dual. The session type of a channel is taken to be the session type of the ep of the accept-ing process – or the dual to the session type of the ep of the request-or.

The inferred session type, or Γ, for proc q is the same as for proc pc ((4) and (5)), which means the parallel composition r is well-sessioned. When pc is sending an integer, q will be waiting to receive it. Evaluating r does more than just the session type inference and checking. We also get the code for the processes to run in parallel. The top-level r is the parallel composition of two complete th, and hence two pieces of code are produced. Here is the first one, corresponding to proc pc:[5]

---

[5] To improve readability, we adjusted indentation and removed module references, while the rest is left as-is. Variables lv_77 and lv_78 are generated via let-insertion.

```
1   <let lv_78 = {sh_arname = "/tmp/SHshb−50.fifo"; sh_name = "shb−50"} in
2   let lv_77 = {sh_arname = "/tmp/SHsha−49.fifo"; sh_name = "sha−49"} in
3   let rawep_79 = sh_request lv_78 in
4   let rawep_80 = sh_accept lv_77 in
5   let x_81 = int_of_string (ep_read rawep_80) in
6   ep_close rawep_80;
7   (let x_82 = int_of_string (ep_read rawep_79) in
8     ep_write rawep_79 (if x_81 > x_82 then "T" else "F");
9     ep_close rawep_79;
10    ())>.
```

Clearly seen are the calls to the low-level communication library, as well as the serialization/deserialization code such as int_of_string, converting sent and received values to/from strings, that is, the sequence of bytes to exchange over the channel. The serialization/deserialization code is generated by <session>.

Lines 5 through 10 are the code generated for the process fragment p1, with the variable rawep_80 standing for y1 and rawep_79 to y2. Noticeable are the ep_close calls to close and deallocate the endpoints, which were not present in p1. A call to close an endpoint is inserted as part of session type inference, as soon as it is determined that the endpoint's communication is complete. For example, when the inferred session type of p' in recv y1 Int @@ p' does not mention y1, this endpoint can be closed right after recv completes. Just as the automatic memory management, the automatic endpoint management eliminates the class of subtle bugs, as well as relieving the programmer of a chore.

The generated code for the processes can be extracted by proc_deploy (see Fig. 1), stored into a file, compiled and then deployed on communication nodes. Alternatively, <session> provides proc_run to run the generated code as separate (fork-ed) processes, for testing. One may do make tests to test-execute r (and all other examples that come with <session>.)

2.3   What If One Makes a Mistake: OCaml Types V. Session Types

There are many opportunities for mistakes. This section shows what happens if we make some of them. After all, detection and reporting mistakes is the main reason to use a type system in the first place.

Some mistakes are caught already by the OCaml type checker, for example:

```
let p1' y1 y2 = recv y1 T.Int @@ fun z1 → recv y2 T.Int @@ fun z2 →
  send y2 T.Bool <."z1 > ."z2>.
  ^^^^^^^^^^^^^^^^^^^^^^^^^^^
```
Error: This expression has type th → th but an expression was expected of type th

```
let p1'' y1 y2 = recv y1 T.Int @@ fun z1 →recv y2 T.Int @@ fun z2 →
  send y2 T.Bool <."z1 + ."z2>. @@ finish
  ^^^^^^^^^^
```
Error: This expression has type int but an expression was expected of type bool

with the detailed error message. The type errors mean that p1' and p1'' are not well-formed processes.

In Sect. 2.2 we have created two shared for pc, saying that one would not suffice. Let us see what happens if we do use only one shared (e.g., by mistake):

```
let a =  new_shared "sha"
let pc₁ =  request a @@ fun y2 → accept a @@ fun y1 → p1 y1 y2
```

This code type-checks in OCaml, meaning it is a well-formed `<session>` expression. It is legitimate, after a rendez-vous on a shared do another rendez-vous on the same shared, with the same or different process[6] – but not in the case of p1. All channels created on the same shared should be used with the same communication protocol. However, a glance at (2) and (3) tells the two endpoints of p1 are used rather differently. Therefore, pc_1, albeit a well-formed `<session>` expression, is not well-sessioned. Indeed, its evaluation ends in an exception that the types Send(int,Recv(bool,End) and Recv(int,End), inferred separately for shared a, are not unifiable. Session-typing problems are reported as exceptions, carrying the problem descriptor (e.g., unification failure) and the details (the non-unifiable types themselves) – so that one may print a custom error messages upon catching it, along with the backtrace. Standard tools like Emacs or other IDEs understand such backtraces, thus allowing to investigate the problem.

When the session-type inference succeeds, it returns the session type plus the code generated for the process (which can be extracted, for the complete process, with proc_deploy). The evaluation of pc_1 ended in an exception, and hence no code has been generated. Contrapositively, if the code is successfully generated, it represents a well-sessioned process. This is a *static* guarantee, from the process point-of-view – we know the process shall obey the protocol before running its generated code.

When defining the fragment p1 in Sect. 2.1 we meant it to communicate on two endpoints, denoted by the variables y1 and y2. Nothing stops the caller of p1, however, from supplying the same endpoint value for both variables (i.e., make y1 and y2 alias the same endpoint):

```
let pc₂ =  request b @@ fun y2 → p1 y2 y2
```

This time evaluating pc_2 produces no errors: after all, it expresses a legitimate communication behavior – only not the intended one and not corresponding to the process q. Therefore, evaluating proc pc_2 ‖ proc q raises an exception that the two processes make non-unifiable assumptions about the protocol associated with "shb", namely, Send(int,Recv(bool,End)) vs. Recv(bool,End). One can then look closely into the inferred session types for pc_2 and its fragments, possibly using the OCaml debugger, identifying the source of the problem.

The process q defined in Sect. 2.2 accepted on shared point b and requested on a; therefore, its party pc should first request on b and accept on a. It is very easy to confuse the two operations and write

```
let pc₃ =  accept b @@ fun y2 → request a @@ fun y1 → p1 y1 y2
```

---

[6] The code does not say that pc_1 rendez-vous with itself, which is impossible. Communications on a shared are synchronous (i.e. request and response blocks until its counterpart becomes available) while those on session endpoints are asynchronous.

Although this code defines a legitimate process, it cannot be a party to q. There-fore, proc pc₃ ‖ proc q raises an exception that the two processes make different assumptions about the protocol of the shared b, viz., Recv(int,Send(bool,End)) and Send(int,Recv(bool,End)). The two inferred types look dual, which is a hint at a request/accept confusion.

Thus, when a <session> expression passes the OCaml type check, the com-putations within the corresponding process are well-typed and "won't go wrong", and the process itself is well-formed ("syntactically correct"). Further, when the <session> expression successfully evaluates, it produces the code for the process, whose computations and, in addition, communications are statically assured to do no wrong.

```
1   let srv ep =                              14   let cli ep =
2     loop_with_val (.< 0 >., [ep]) @@        15     select ep "add" @@
3       fun continue acc →                    16     send ep T.Int .<1234>. @@
4     branch ep                               17     recv ep T.Int @@ fun acc0 →
5     ["add",                                 18     select ep "add" @@
6       recv ep T.Int @@ fun x →              19     send ep T.Int .<5678>. @@
7       let_ .<.~x + .~acc>. @@ fun acc →     20     recv ep T.Int @@ fun acc1 →
8       send ep T.Int acc @@                  21     select ep "quit" @@
9       continue acc                          22     recv ep T.Int @@ fun ans →
10    "quit",                                 23     othr .<printf "sum:_%d\n" .~ans>. @@
11      send ep T.Int acc @@                  24     finish
12      finish
13    ]

25  let p =  let sh =  new_shared "sh" in proc (accept sh srv) ‖ proc (request sh cli)
```

Fig. 3. Example: an arithmetic server

3   Elaborate Examples: Choice, Recursion and Delegation

Arithmetic Server. Figure 3 shows a more interesting example with external and internal choices and recursions. This is the standard example of the so-called "arithmetic server", which is common in literature. Function srv is a server which takes an endpoint ep and iterates over a loop via construct loop_with_val. The loop construct is supplied a pair of the initial value .< 0 >. of an accumulator and the endpoint [ep] which are used in the following body of iteration. It binds itself to variable continue and the accumulator to acc. Note that the construct itself does *not* iterate but just produce the code for iteration. The loop body offers two labels "add" and "quit" via external choice construct branch. Here, labels represented by two strings then become part of the type for external choice, which is an ordinary runtime value in (Meta)OCaml. In the "add" branch, an integer is received, bound to x and added to the accumulator. The result is rebound to acc and sent back to the client. The server then recurs (with the updated acc) to handle further requests. On "quit", the server reports the accumulator to the client and terminates. Client's function cli should be understood similarly.

Compatibility of srv and cli is checked at Line 25. Thanks to equi-recursive nature of session types, this program actually typechecks. The example exhibits a form of *session subtyping* in `<session>` implemented via *row types*, following the Links language [5]. By evaluating infer Fun(EP,TH) srv, we get the following type which describes the server's protocol:

$$\text{Mu}(18, \text{Bra}(\text{quit:Send}(\text{int},\text{End}) + \text{add:Recv}(\text{int},\text{Send}(\text{int},\text{RecVar18})) + \text{RClosed})) \tag{6}$$

Session $\text{Mu}(id, t)$ denotes a (equi-)recursive type, with $\text{RecVar}id$ bound to the whole $\text{Mu}(id, t)$ expression. $\text{Bra}(l_1{:}t_1 + \ldots + l_n{:}t_n + \text{RClosed})$ shows an external choice among labels $l_1, \ldots, l_n$ where t_i describes communication after l_i is chosen. RClosed in the end says that the choice is *closed*, disallowing other labels. In total, the above session type (correctly) specifies the recursive behavior of the server with two operations quit and add. Similarly, infer Fun(EP,TH) cli yields the client's type which is dual to the type above:

$$\begin{aligned}
&\text{Sel}(\text{add:Send}(\text{int},\text{Recv}(\text{int},\\
&\quad \text{Sel}(\text{add:Send}(\text{int},\text{Recv}(\text{int},\\
&\qquad \text{Sel}(\text{quit:Recv}(\text{int},\text{End}) + \text{RMeta21}))) + \text{RMeta22}))) + \text{RMeta23})
\end{aligned} \tag{7}$$

Note that the type (7) does not show any recursive structure as well. Session $\text{Sel}(l_1{:}t_1 + \ldots + l_n{:}t_n + \text{RMeta}id)$ is an internal choice, where $\text{RMeta}id$ is a *row variable* which can contain more alternatives, enabling session subtyping. The type unification invoked by (||) at Line 25 confirms that the session (6) and (7) are *dual* to each other; thus the programmer can conclude cli and srv have no deadlock, in an *earlier* stage. Moreover, such type features come without annotations like enter in [41] (see Sect. 5), thanks to the flexibility of metaprogramming.

Example with Delegation. Delegation allows one to pass a session-typed channel to another peer, enabling dynamic change of the communication topology in a system[7]. Figure 4 is the Travel Agency example from [21] (originally in [18]). The scenario is played by three participants: customer, agency and service. Process customer knows agency while customer and service initially do not know each other, and agency mediates a deal between customer and service by delegation. We use accumulator-less loop combinator in this example. Upon quote request from customer, agency replies a rate (fixed to 350 for simplicity) and re-starts from the beginning, and if customer agrees on the price (label "accept"), agency delegates the rest of the session to service in Line 12 using deleg_to. Process service accepts the delegation in Line 18 using deleg_from, and consumes the rest of session by receiving the delivery address (of type string) and then sending the delivery date ("2020−04−01"). Note that the original OCaml implementation in

---

[7] Ours deleg_from and deleg_to are called throw and catch in [51] (we changed the names to avoid association with exceptions).

```
1   let agency agc_ch svc_ch =
2     accept agc_ch @@ fun cus_ep →
3     loop [cus_ep] @@ fun continue →
4       branch cus_ep
5       ["quote", begin
6         recv cus_ep String @@ fun dest →
7         send cus_ep Int .< 350 >. @@
8         continue
9       end;
10      "accept", begin
11        request svc_ch @@ fun svc_ep →
12        deleg_to svc_ep cus_ep @@
13        finish
14      end]
15
16  let service svc_ch =
17    accept svc_ch @@ fun svc_ep →
18    deleg_from svc_ep @@ fun cus_ep →
19    recv cus_ep String @@ fun address →
20      send cus_ep
21        String .< "2020−04−01" >. @@
22      finish
23
24  let customer ch =
25    request ch @@ fun ep →
26    loop [ep] @@ fun continue →
27      select ep "quote" @@
28      send ep String
29        .< "Tokyo_to_Akita" >. @@
30      recv ep Int @@ fun cost →
31      ifte .< .~cost < 400 >. ~then_: begin
32        select ep "accept" @@
33        send ep String
34          .< "Tokyo,_JP" >. @@
35        recv ep String @@ fun date →
36        finish
37      end
38      ~else_: continue
```

Fig. 4. Example: travel agency

[21] uses *lenses* to convey delegated (linear) variables in types, while we use an ordinary, term-level variables, resulting in less complication in (OCaml) types.

Note also that there is a subtle difference in *ownership* control of session type systems [14, 51] from usual notion of *linearity*. That is, some primitives assume implicit *presence* of End types in continuation—for example, send ep 350 finish has Send(Int,End) in ep—while the delegation requires *absence* of a session in continuation, as in the end of agency above. To avoid such ambiguity, implementations (e.g. [23, 32, 39]) usually require the channel to be explicitly closed in the end of a session, while <session> does not demand such annotation.

4   Notable Implementation Techniques

4.1   Staging

We now describe and justify staged embedded DSLs as an implementation technique of supporting session- and other advanced type systems in an existing (staged) language.

Session types with no safety or usability compromises call for a language system designed for them, e.g., Links [5], which offers session types natively. Achieving this golden standard, and implementing and supporting a programming language requires time, effort and investment beyond the reach of many. Not only one has to implement a type checker, but also the whole compiler – as well as libraries, tools, build systems. One has to maintain them, write documentation, advertise and build community.

DSLs embedded in a mature, well supported host language are an attractive alternative. The host language provides the compilation, infrastructure, community – letting the DSL author concentrate on expressing domain-specific constructs and types as terms and types of the host language. The first problem comes when the DSL type system significantly differs from that of the host language – which is the case of session types, the form of *type-state* [46]. It requires advanced, modal or substructural type systems [7,19,49], rarely offered by a host language. One has to resort to emulation, whose problems we detailed in the Introduction. The main problem, for the implementor, is that type systems are rarely designed for writing code. Using a host type system as a programming language in which to emulate an advanced DSL type system is excruciating.

Staging helps, by letting the DSL implementor map DSL constructs *and* DSL types to host language terms. Whatever the DSL type checking and inference is needed, can be programmed in the host language itself (rather than in its type system). That seems inadequate as DSL type errors will be reported too late: not when compiling a DSL program but when running it. One has to remember, however, that with staging, there are two (potentially more) run-times: the run-time of the code generator and the run-time of the generated code. It is the latter that corresponds to the traditional run-time, and which "should do no wrong". The run-time of the generator, from the point of view of the generated program, is a sort of "compile-time". Run-time errors in the generator are akin to the traditional type-error and compiler diagnostics: an indication that a compiler gave up on the source program and produced no object code. On the other hand, when the code is generated, one has the confidence it has passed the checks of both the host and the DSL type systems.

We now show a concrete illustration of the approach. Since <session> is rather advanced, we use a similar but simpler example, also featuring type-state: a DSL with operations to open, write to and close an arbitrary number of communication channels – and the type system that prevents using a channel after it has been closed. The manual closing of channels allows for more accurate and timely management of scarce resources than achievable with, say, region discipline. This is the example described in [29, §6]. Although seemingly simple, embedding this DSL in Haskell required heavy and unwieldy type-level programming, with the predictable result of large inferred types, fragile inference and confusing error messages [29, §6.2].

Let us see if we can do better with staging. Figure 5 presents the interface, sample code, and most of the implementation (see the accompanying source code for full details and more examples.)[8] Most operations should be self-explanatory. The left-associative // is the "semicolon", to compose DSL expressions. The main assumption is the factoring of the DSL into communication (channel operations) and computations. The latter are represented as string code whereas the former are as values of the type comm. Such a factoring is common: monadic IO in Haskell, Lwt and Async libraries in OCaml are just a few other examples.

---

[8] The language is quite like the STATE language in [27, §7]: the imperative part of Reynolds' Idealized Algol, as pointed out by Bob Atkey. Instead of var we write ch.

Interface	Sample code

type comm   **type** ch

```
let p =
  open_ "/tmp/a1" @@ fun ch1 →
  open_ "/tmp/a2" @@ fun ch2 →
  write ch1 <"s1">. //
  close ch1 //
  write ch2 <string_of_int 5>. //
  close ch2
```

val (//) : comm → comm → comm
val skip : comm

val close : ch → comm
val write : ch → string code → comm
val open_ :
    string → (ch → comm) → comm
val if_ : bool code → then_:comm → else_:comm → comm

Implementation: types	"Type" errors

```
type ch_id = string
type ch_status = Closed | Active
type ch =
  {chch: out_channel code; chid: ch_id}
module M =
  Map.Make(struct type t = ch_id let compare = compare end)
type styp = ch_status M.t
type comm = {c_code: unit code; c_chan: styp}
```

```
exception NotClosed of ch_id
exception UsedAfterClosed of ch_id
exception ClosedOnlyInOneBranch of
    bool * ch_id
```

```
let skip =
  {c_code = <()>.;
   c_chan = M.empty}

let close = fun {chch;chid} →
  {c_code = <close_out ~chch>.;
   c_chan = M.singleton chid Closed}

let write = fun {chch;chid} str →
  {c_code = <output_string ~chch ~str>.;
   c_chan = M.singleton chid Active}
```

```
let (//) = fun c1 c2 →
  let c_code =
    < ~(c1.c_code); ~(c2.c_code) >. in
  let merger chid c1t c2t =
    match (c1t,c2t) with
    | (None,ct) | (ct,None) → ct
    | (Some Active, ct)      → ct
    | (Some Closed, Some _) →
        raise (UsedAfterClosed chid) in
  let c_chan =
    M.merge merger c1.c_chan c2.c_chan
  in {c_code;c_chan}
```

Fig. 5. The writeDSL: interface, sample code, implementation

The sample DSL expression p, when evaluated, produces the expected code of opening, writing to, and closing output channels. If instead of ch1 we close ch2, the evaluation of p ends with a UsedAfterClose exception mentioning the offending channel – and produces no code.

The key is the realization of comm as an "annotated code": a record carrying the code generated for the DSL expression. The field c_chan of the record is the annotation: the DSL type associated with the code. As in <session>, it is a finite map (implemented with OCaml's Stdlib.Map) of channel ids ch_id and their statuses Closed or Active. The close operation generates code to close the channel – and the annotation that the channel, which should be active before, becomes Closed. Likewise, the write operation annotates the channel writing code with the fact that the channel was and to remain Active. The composition c1 // c2 merges not only the code but also the annotations, thus inferring the DSL type (channel statuses) for the composed expression. The merging is done by Stdlib.Map.merge operation, with merger determining which associations from the input maps get to the output map, and how to deal with merge conflicts. If a channel remains active after c1, its status in c1 // c2 is determined by its status in c2. On the other hand, if the channel is Closed in c1 and yet appears in c2's annotation, it is the "use after close" error, and reported by throwing an exception.

4.2   Canonical Structures

To put it simply, Canonical Structures is a facility to obtain a value of a given type – for example, a value of the type int→string, that is, the function to "show" an integer. Since there are many such functions, the user has to register the "canonical" value of this type. In the simplest case, searching for a canonical instance is a mere look up in the database of registered values. Instead of a canonical value itself, however, the database may provide a rule how to make it, from some other registered values (e.g., how to "show" a pair if we can show its components). Querying this database of facts and rules is quite like the evaluation of a Prolog/Datalog query.

From the point of view of the Curry-Howard correspondence, finding a term of a given type is finding a proof of a proposition. This is how this facility was developed in Coq, as a programmable unification technique for proof search, as expounded in [34].[9] Our implementation, inspired by that remarkable paper, is an attempt to explain it in plain OCaml, experiment with and use beyond Coq.

The rudiment of canonical structures is already present in OCaml, in the form of the registry of printers for user-defined types. It is available only at the top-level, however, and deeply intertwined with it. We have implemented this facility for all programs, as a plain, small, self-contained library, with no compiler or other magic. It can be used independently from <session>. Unlike the OCaml top-level–printer or Haskell type-class resolution, searching for a canonical instance is fully user-programmable. One may allow "overlapping instances", or prohibit them, insisting on uniqueness. One may allow for backtracking, fully or in part.

In <session> the canonical structures are used to look up the code for serializers and deserializers, to print types, and to implement infer to infer session types of process fragments with an arbitrary number of free endpoint variables.

Our implementation of Canonical Structures is user-level. Therefore, the look up of canonical values happens at run-time – rather than at compile time, as in type-class resolution. The look-up failures are also reported at run-time. It should be stressed, however, that in <session>, Canonical Structures are used only during code generation. The run-time errors at that point are run-time

---

[9] That tutorial paper also compares canonical structures to related approaches, in particular, implicits and type classes.

errors in the generator. From the point of view of the generated code, these are "compile-time" errors. Therefore, Canonical Structures in metaprograms roughly correspond to type classes in ordinary programs.

Since our Canonical Structures are implemented completely outside the compiler, the types of values to look up have to be explicitly specified as values of the α trep data type, which represents types at the value level. For example, a value Fun(Int,Bool) represents the type int→bool (and itself has the type (int→bool) trep). The data type can be easily extended with representations of user-defined data types (the <session> code shows a few examples). The trep values may be regarded as type annotations; in particular, as with other type annotations, if the user sets them wrong, the type error is imminent. Therefore, they are not an additional source of mistakes, but still cumbersome. If a compiler could somehow "reflect" an inferred type of an expression and synthesize a trep value, these annotations could be eliminated. We are contemplating how such reflection facility could be supported by OCaml, taking inspiration from the run-time-type proposal [13] and type-level implicits proposals [10,50].

5   Related Work

The session type system employed in <session> is essentially the same as the liberal system [51, §3]. However, we distinguish threads th and endpoint-closed top-level processes. Only the latter may be parallel-composed. The reason is not of principle but practicality: web application and other such services do not spawn processes at will but rely on a worker pool, for better control of resources.

Links [5,33] has session types on top of linear types and row polymorphism. Its core calculus GV [31,48] has stronger properties like global progress, determinism, and termination, while [51] can lead to a deadlock with two or more sessions. We chose [51] as it has more liberal form of parallel composition. Adopting our approach to GV (and extending to exception handling [9]) is future work.

Several implementations have been done in Haskell [22,32,35,37,41,42] and compared in [38] in detail. They are also established in Rust [23] (using its substructural types) and Scala [43] (based on dynamic linearity checking).

Implementation of session types in OCaml, firstly done by Padovani [39] and then Imai et al. [20,21], seems a touchstone to spread into wider range of programming languages since it does not have substructural types nor any *fancy* features like type classes or implicits. The key issues are (1) static checking of *linearity*, (2) inference of *dual* session types and (3) encoding of *branching labels*. For (1), static checking of linearity in [39] is based on a parameterised monad of [41]. Imai et al. [21] provides a handy way to operate on multiple sessions using type-level indexes encoded by polymorphic *lenses* [8,40], based on the idea by Garrigue [11,20]. However, it requires much elaboration on types; for example, the type signature of the send primitive involves *six* type variables because of index-based manipulation for linearity and partially due to polarity encoding, which we will explain in the following (2).

For duality (2), there is a subtle tension between type inference, readability of types, and type compatibility. Pucella and Tov [41] showed a manual construction of duality witness in various languages including OCaml, while it can be automatically generated by type classes (and type functions [28]) in Haskell. On the other hand, Padovani adopts an encoding into i/o types by Dardha et al. [6], achieving duality inference by OCaml's typechecker, which is also applied by Scalas et al. in Scala [43]. Dardha et al's encoding, however, is quite verbose, to the point that the resulting session types are hard to understand for humans (for details, see [21, § 6.2]). To mitigate it, the implementation of [39] provides the *type decoder*. Imai et al. resolved it by having *polarities* in types, however, it introduces complication on types, as we mentioned above. Furthermore, the polarity-based encoding has a type compatibility issue in delegations [21, in the end of § 3.3]. Summarizing the above, duality encoding in types has problems of (a) manual construction, as in [20,41], (b) type decoder [39] or (c) compatibility problem [21], while our <session> does not have such problems at all.

Furthermore, duality is not just a swapping of output and input when a recursion variable occurs in a carried type, as pointed out independently by Bernardi et al. [2] and Bono et al. [3] which is usually overlooked (see [38, § 10.3.1]). Instead, we use $\overline{\mu\alpha.T} = \mu\alpha.\overline{T}[\overline{\alpha}/\alpha]$ in the Links language [33, § 12.4.1].

Type-level branching labels (3) are another obstacle for having session types in languages like Rust and Scala (e.g. [23,43]) from which our approach does not suffer, as we have labels at the ordinary, term-level.

Hu et al. [18] showed a binary session extension to Java, *SessionJava*, including syntax extensions for protocols and session-based control structures. By contrast, <session> implements binary session types as a library on top of Meta-OCaml, using only standard staging features like brackets and escape. Their work also includes *session delegation protocol* over distributed environment, which is orthogonal to the syntax and can possibly be added to <session>.

Scribble [44] is an implementation of *multiparty* session types [15] in various programming languages via code generation, including Java [16,17], Go [4], and F# [36]. Multiparty session types take a top-down approach to generate session types from a global description of protocol called *global type*. On the other hand, Lange et al. [30] directly verifies session types via model checking. Extending <session> to the multiparty setting is future work.

6   Conclusions

We have presented the session-typed DSL <session> for service-oriented programming embedded in MetaOCaml. It was an experiment to see how the "type checking as staging" idea really works in practice, for a non-trivial, type-state–based type system and a non-trivial DSL. Overall, we are satisfied with our implementation experience: we have provided the same or even stronger guarantees than the other, mainstream implementations; we emit helpful error diagnostics; and we enjoyed programming in a mature implementation language rather than in a bare Post system. There is room for improvement (such as the trep annotations discussed in Sect. 4.2), and we are considering proposals to OCaml developers.

We have not yet implemented session-type annotations – that is, define the protocol as a session type, and then check that a process satisfies it. However, this is easy to add. We also want to extend our approach to group communication and multiparty session types.

The topic of this paper has been implementing session-type DSLs rather than developing session type systems themselves. Nevertheless, `<session>` turns out a good tool to prototype variations and extensions of session types. In the future work we plan to investigate one such extension: cancellation and failure modes.

Acknowledgments. We thank anonymous reviewers for many, helpful comments and suggestions. This work was partially supported by JSPS KAKENHI Grant Number 18H03218 and 17K12662.

References

1. Bernardi, G., Dardha, O., Gay, S.J., Kouzapas, D.: On duality relations for session types. In: Maffei, M., Tuosto, E. (eds.) TGC 2014. LNCS, vol. 8902, pp. 51–66. Springer, Heidelberg (2014). https://doi.org/10.1007/978-3-662-45917-1_4
2. Bernardi, G., Hennessy, M.: Using higher-order contracts to model session types. Logical Methods Comput. Sci. **12**(2) (2016). https://doi.org/10.2168/LMCS-12(2:10)2016
3. Bono, V., Messa, C., Padovani, L.: Typing copyless message passing. In: Barthe, G. (ed.) ESOP 2011. LNCS, vol. 6602, pp. 57–76. Springer, Heidelberg (2011). https://doi.org/10.1007/978-3-642-19718-5_4
4. Castro, D., Hu, R., Jongmans, S.S., Ng, N., Yoshida, N.: Distributed programming using role parametric session types in go. In: 46th ACM SIGPLAN Symposium on Principles of Programming Languages, vol. 3, pp. 29:1–29:30. ACM (2019). https://doi.org/10.1145/3290342
5. Cooper, E., Lindley, S., Wadler, P., Yallop, J.: Links: web programming without tiers. In: de Boer, F.S., Bonsangue, M.M., Graf, S., de Roever, W.-P. (eds.) FMCO 2006. LNCS, vol. 4709, pp. 266–296. Springer, Heidelberg (2007). https://doi.org/10.1007/978-3-540-74792-5_12
6. Dardha, O., Giachino, E., Sangiorgi, D.: Session types revisited. In: PPDP 2012: Proceedings of the 14th Symposium on Principles and Practice of Declarative Programming, pp. 139–150. ACM, New York (2012)
7. Fluet, M., Morrisett, G., Ahmed, A.: Linear regions are all you need. In: Sestoft, P. (ed.) ESOP 2006. LNCS, vol. 3924, pp. 7–21. Springer, Heidelberg (2006). https://doi.org/10.1007/11693024_2
8. Foster, J.N., Greenwald, M.B., Moore, J.T., Pierce, B.C., Schmitt, A.: Combinators for bidirectional tree transformations: a linguistic approach to the view-update problem. ACM Trans. Program. Lang. Syst. **29**(3), 17 (2007). https://doi.org/10.1145/1232420.1232424
9. Fowler, S., Lindley, S., Morris, J.G., Decova, S.: Exceptional asynchronous session types: session types without tiers. PACMPL **3**(POPL), 28:1–28:29 (2019)
10. Furuse, J.: Typeful PPX and value implicits. In: OCaml 2015: The OCaml Users and Developers Workshop (2015). https://bitbucket.org/camlspotter/ppx_implicits

11. Garrigue, J.: Safeio (a mailing-list post) (2006). https://github.com/garrigue/safeio

12. Gay, S., Hole, M.: Subtyping for session types in the Pi-calculus. Acta Informatica **42**(2/3), 191–225 (2005). https://doi.org/10.1007/s00236-005-0177-z

13. Henry, G., Garrigue, J.: Runtime types in OCaml. In: OCaml 2013: The OCaml Users and Developers Workshop (2013). https://ocaml.org/meetings/ocaml/2013/proposals/runtime-types.pdf

14. Honda, K., Vasconcelos, V.T., Kubo, M.: Language primitives and type discipline for structured communication-based programming. In: Hankin, C. (ed.) ESOP 1998. LNCS, vol. 1381, pp. 122–138. Springer, Heidelberg (1998). https://doi.org/10.1007/BFb0053567

15. Honda, K., Yoshida, N., Carbone, M.: Multiparty asynchronous session types. J. ACM **63**(1), 9:1–9:67 (2016). http://doi.acm.org/10.1145/2827695

16. Hu, R., Yoshida, N.: Hybrid session verification through endpoint API generation. In: Stevens, P., Wąsowski, A. (eds.) FASE 2016. LNCS, vol. 9633, pp. 401–418. Springer, Heidelberg (2016). https://doi.org/10.1007/978-3-662-49665-7_24

17. Hu, R., Yoshida, N.: Explicit connection actions in multiparty session types. In: Huisman, M., Rubin, J. (eds.) FASE 2017. LNCS, vol. 10202, pp. 116–133. Springer, Heidelberg (2017). https://doi.org/10.1007/978-3-662-54494-5_7

18. Hu, R., Yoshida, N., Honda, K.: Session-based distributed programming in Java. In: Vitek, J. (ed.) ECOOP 2008. LNCS, vol. 5142, pp. 516–541. Springer, Heidelberg (2008). https://doi.org/10.1007/978-3-540-70592-5_22

19. Igarashi, A., Kobayashi, N.: Resource usage analysis. ACM Trans. Program. Lang. Syst. **27**(2), 264–313 (2005)

20. Imai, K., Garrigue, J.: Lightweight linearly-typed programming with lenses and monads. J. Inf. Process. **27**, 431–444 (2019). https://doi.org/10.2197/ipsjjip.27.431

21. Imai, K., Yoshida, N., Yuen, S.: Session-ocaml: a session-based library with polarities and lenses. In: Jacquet, J.-M., Massink, M. (eds.) COORDINATION 2017. LNCS, vol. 10319, pp. 99–118. Springer, Cham (2017). https://doi.org/10.1007/978-3-319-59746-1_6

22. Imai, K., Yuen, S., Agusa, K.: Session type inference in Haskell. In: Proceedings Third Workshop on Programming Language Approaches to Concurrency and communication-cEntric Software, PLACES 2010, Paphos, Cyprus, 21st March 2010, pp. 74–91 (2010). https://doi.org/10.4204/EPTCS.69.6

23. Jespersen, T.B.L., Munksgaard, P., Larsen, K.F.: Session types for rust. In: WGP 2015: Proceedings of the 11th ACM SIGPLAN Workshop on Generic Programming, pp. 13–22. ACM (2015). https://doi.org/10.1145/2808098.2808100

24. Kiselyov, O.: Typed tagless final interpreters. In: Gibbons, J. (ed.) Generic and Indexed Programming. LNCS, vol. 7470, pp. 130–174. Springer, Heidelberg (2012). https://doi.org/10.1007/978-3-642-32202-0_3

25. Kiselyov, O.: The design and implementation of BER MetaOCaml. In: Codish, M., Sumii, E. (eds.) FLOPS 2014. LNCS, vol. 8475, pp. 86–102. Springer, Cham (2014). https://doi.org/10.1007/978-3-319-07151-0_6

26. Kiselyov, O.: Reconciling Abstraction with High Performance: A MetaOCaml approach. Foundations and Trends in Programming Languages, Now Publishers (2018)

27. Kiselyov, O.: Effects without monads: non-determinism - back to the Meta Language. Electron. Proc. Theor. Comp. Sci. **294**, 15–40 (2019). https://arxiv.org/abs/1905.06544

28. Kiselyov, O., Peyton Jones, S., Shan, C.-c.: Fun with type functions. In: Roscoe, A.W., Jones, C.B., Wood, K.R. (eds.) Reflections on the Work of C.A.R. Hoare, pp. 301–331. Springer, London (2010). https://doi.org/10.1007/978-1-84882-912-1_14

29. Kiselyov, O., Shan, C.-c.: Lightweight monadic regions. In: Gill, A. (ed.) Haskell '08: Proceedings of the First ACM SIGPLAN Symposium on Haskell, pp. 1–12. ACM Press, New York, 25 September 2008

30. Lange, J., Yoshida, N.: Verifying asynchronous interactions via communicating session automata. In: Dillig, I., Tasiran, S. (eds.) CAV 2019. LNCS, vol. 11561, pp. 97–117. Springer, Cham (2019). https://doi.org/10.1007/978-3-030-25540-4_6

31. Lindley, S., Morris, J.G.: A semantics for propositions as sessions. In: Vitek, J. (ed.) ESOP 2015. LNCS, vol. 9032, pp. 560–584. Springer, Heidelberg (2015). https://doi.org/10.1007/978-3-662-46669-8_23

32. Lindley, S., Morris, J.G.: Embedding session types in Haskell. In: Haskell 2016: Proceedings of the 9th International Symposium on Haskell, pp. 133–145. ACM (2016). https://doi.org/10.1145/2976002.2976018

33. Lindley, S., Morris, J.G.: Lightweight Functional Session Types (2017). In [45 §12]

34. Mahboubi, A., Tassi, E.: Canonical structures for the working Coq user. In: Blazy, S., Paulin-Mohring, C., Pichardie, D. (eds.) ITP 2013. LNCS, vol. 7998, pp. 19–34. Springer, Heidelberg (2013). https://doi.org/10.1007/978-3-642-39634-2_5

35. Neubauer, M., Thiemann, P.: An implementation of session types. In: Jayaraman, B. (ed.) PADL 2004. LNCS, vol. 3057, pp. 56–70. Springer, Heidelberg (2004). https://doi.org/10.1007/978-3-540-24836-1_5

36. Neykova, R., Hu, R., Yoshida, N., Abdeljallal, F.: A session type provider: compile-time API generation of distributed protocols with refinements in f#. In: Proceedings of the 27th International Conference on Compiler Construction, CC 2018, February 24–25, 2018, Vienna, Austria, pp. 128–138. ACM (2018). https://doi.org/10.1145/3178372.3179495

37. Orchard, D., Yoshida, N.: Effects as sessions, sessions as effects. In: POPL 2016: 43th Annual ACM SIGPLAN-SIGACT Symposium on Principles of Programming Languages, pp. 568–581. ACM (2016). https://doi.org/10.1145/2837614.2837634

38. Orchard, D., Yoshida, N.: Session Types with Linearity in Haskell (2017). In [45 §10]

39. Padovani, L.: A simple library implementation of binary sessions. J. Func. Program. **27**, e4 (2016)

40. Pickering, M., Gibbons, J., Wu, N.: Profunctor optics: modular data accessors. Art Sci. Eng. Program. **1**(2), Article 7 (2017). https://doi.org/10.22152/programming-journal.org/2017/1/7

41. Pucella, R., Tov, J.A.: Haskell session types with (almost) no class. In: Gill, A. (ed.) Proceedings of the 1st ACM SIGPLAN Symposium on Haskell, pp. 25–36. ACM Press, New York, 25 September 2008

42. Sackman, M., Eisenbach, S.: Session types in Haskell: updating message passing for the 21st century. Technical report, Imperial College London, June 2008. http://pubs.doc.ic.ac.uk/session-types-in-haskell/

43. Scalas, A., Yoshida, N.: Lightweight session programming in scala. In: ECOOP 2016: 30th European Conference on Object-Oriented Programming. LIPIcs, vol. 56, pp. 21:1–21:28. Dagstuhl (2016). https://doi.org/10.4230/LIPIcs.ECOOP.2016.21

44. Scribble: Scribble home page (2019). http://www.scribble.org

45. Simon Gay, A.R. (ed.): Behavioural Types: from Theory to Tools. River Publisher (2017). https://www.riverpublishers.com/research_details.php?book_id=439

46. Strom, R.E., Yellin, D.M.: Extending typestate checking using conditional liveness analysis. IEEE Trans. Softw. Eng. **19**(5), 478–485 (1993)
47. Takeuchi, K., Honda, K., Kubo, M.: An interaction-based language and its typing system. In: Halatsis, C., Maritsas, D., Philokyprou, G., Theodoridis, S. (eds.) PARLE 1994. LNCS, vol. 817, pp. 398–413. Springer, Heidelberg (1994). https://doi.org/10.1007/3-540-58184-7_118
48. Wadler, P.: Propositions as sessions. J. Funct. Program. **24**(2–3), 384–418 (2014)
49. Walker, D., Crary, K., Morrisett, J.G.: Typed memory management via static capabilities. ACM Trans. Program. Lang. Syst. **22**(4), 701–771 (2000)
50. White, L., Bour, F., Yallop, J.: Modular implicits. In: ML 2014: ACM SIGPLAN ML Family Workshop 2014. Electronic Proceedings in Theoretical Computer Science, vol. 198, pp. 22–63 (2015). https://doi.org/10.4204/EPTCS.198.2
51. Yoshida, N., Vasconcelos, V.T.: Language primitives and type discipline for structured communication-based programming revisited: two systems for higher-order session communication. Electr. Notes Theor. Comput. Sci **171**(4), 73–93 (2007)

Restriction on Cut in Cyclic Proof System for Symbolic Heaps

Kenji Saotome[1(✉)], Koji Nakazawa[1], and Daisuke Kimura[2]

[1] Nagoya University, Nagoya, Japan
saotomekenji@sqlab.jp, knak@i.nagoya-u.ac.jp
[2] Toho University, Funabashi, Japan
kmr@is.sci.toho-u.ac.jp

Abstract. It has been shown that some variants of cyclic proof systems for symbolic heap entailments in separation logic do not enjoy the cut elimination property. To construct complete system, we have to consider the cut rule, which requires some heuristics to find cut formulas in bottom-up proof search. Hence, we hope to achieve some restricted variant of cut rule which does not change provability and does not interfere with automatic proof search without heuristics. This paper gives a limit on this challenge. We propose a restricted cut rule, called the presumable cut, in which cut formula is restricted to those which can occur below the cut. This paper shows that there is an entailment which is provable with full cuts in cyclic proof system for symbolic heaps, but not with only presumable cuts.

1 Introduction

Separation logic is an extension of Hoare logic for verifying programs manipulating heap memories. It is successful as theoretical base to achieve (semi-)automatic verification systems for low level languages and low-level programming languages which is often developed with C language.

One of the keys for automation is to solve the entailment checking problem for separation logic formulas with inductive predicates, which represent recursively structured data on heaps. To obtain decidability, some restrictions are required. One of them is to restrict formulas to (extended) symbolic heaps, which are considered sufficient to represent assertions in real verification systems, and for which some decidability results have been obtained [1,2,10–12,14,17]. Some of them [1,2,17] are based on proof theoretic approaches, which have some advantages: it provides evidences of correctness for valid entailments, and it can be easily extended by adding inference rules.

Cyclic proof systems are adopted for the entailment checking for symbolic heaps with general inductive predicates [4,5,17]. Cyclic proofs are proofs with cycles, which correspond to use of induction hypotheses. They are considered suitable for automated inductive reasoning since we need not to decide formulas to be proved by induction a priori. However, there are few results on fundamental properties of cyclic proof systems.

© Springer Nature Switzerland AG 2020
K. Nakano and K. Sagonas (Eds.): FLOPS 2020, LNCS 12073, pp. 88–105, 2020.
https://doi.org/10.1007/978-3-030-59025-3_6

Cut-elimination property is one of such properties of logical systems. It is important not only from theoretical interest, but also from application, since it ensures that provability is not changed by existence of the cut rule, which is not good for bottom-up proof search since we have to find cut formulas. However, it is shown in [13] that we cannot eliminate cuts from the cyclic proof system for symbolic heaps. The existing cyclic proof systems [4,5,17] are cut-free systems, and neither completeness nor decidability has been proved for the systems in [4,5], and the system in [17] requires additional mechanism called the spatial factorization and a relatively strong restriction for inductive predicates to achieve completeness and decidability. Hence we hope that we can restrict the cut rule as not to interfere with automated proof search.

This paper gives a limit on this challenge for a cyclic proof system for symbolic heaps. It shows that it seems hard to restrict the cut rule as not to interfere with automated proof search. In other words, some heuristics seem unavoidable to find cut formulas for full power of provability.

First, we propose a restricted variant of the cut rule, called *presumable cuts*. A formula is called *presumable* from a sequent if it is obtained by bottom-up applications of inference rules except for cut from the sequent, and a cut is called presumable if the cut formula is presumable. Presumable cuts can be applied without heuristics, so it is preferable that any conclusion which is provable with cuts can be proved with only presumable cuts. We call this property *quasi cut-elimination property*.

One counterexample to the cut elimination in [13] is $\mathrm{lsne}(x, y) \vdash \mathrm{slne}(x, y)$, where the predicates are defined as

$$\mathrm{lsne}(x, y) = x \mapsto y \mid \exists z.(x \mapsto z * \mathrm{lsne}(z, y)),$$
$$\mathrm{slne}(x, y) = x \mapsto y \mid \exists z.(\mathrm{slne}(x, z) * z \mapsto y).$$

They showed that the entailment can be proved with cuts, but is not provable without cut. Its cyclic proof with a cut is

$$
\cfrac{
\cfrac{x \mapsto y \vdash x \mapsto y}{x \mapsto y \vdash \mathrm{slne}(x, y)}
\qquad
\cfrac{
\cfrac{\vdots \;(1)}{x \mapsto z * \mathrm{lsne}(z, y) \vdash x \mapsto z * \mathrm{slne}(z, y)} \qquad \cfrac{\vdots \;(2)}{x \mapsto z * \mathrm{slne}(z, y) \vdash \mathrm{slne}(x, y)}
}{x \mapsto z * \mathrm{lsne}(z, y) \vdash \mathrm{slne}(x, y)} \;(\text{Cut})
}{\mathrm{lsne}(x, y) \vdash \mathrm{slne}(x, y)}
\qquad ,
$$

where both (1) and (2) are cut free. The underlined cut formula $x \mapsto z * \mathrm{slne}(z, y)$ is presumable since it is obtained by unfolding $\mathrm{slne}(x, y)$. From this example, we may expect that any entailment provable with cuts can be proved with only presumable cuts, that is, the quasi cut-elimination property holds for the cyclic proof system for symbolic heaps.

The main result of this paper is that the cyclic proof system for symbolic heaps does not satisfy the quasi cut-elimination property. It is proved by a counterexample entailment which is provable with cuts but not provable with only presumable cuts. It means that the proof of this entailment requires some heuristics to find a cut formula.

Related Work. There are some results on cut-elimination property for proof systems with infinite paths and cyclic proof systems. For proof systems with infinite paths, cut elimination holds for several logics such as first-order predicate logic [6] and multiplicative additive liner logic with fixed point operators (μ-MALL) [9]. On the other hand, for cyclic proof systems, it does not hold for several logics such as symbolic heap separation logic [13], μ-MALL [9], and sequent style system for Kleene algebra [8]. These results suggest that there is an essential difference between proof systems with infinite paths and cyclic proof systems, which are obtained by restricting proofs in the former systems to regular trees.

Hence, for automated reasoning, it is important to achieve cyclic proof systems with restricted cut rule which is sufficient for provability, that is, the quasi cut-elimination property holds, and which does not require any heuristics to find cut formulas. However, there are few studies on such restriction to the cut rule in cyclic proof systems. The proof system introduced by Chu [7] is implicitly based on the cyclic proof system with restricted form of the cut rule where one of the assumptions must be a bud in the cyclic proof of which the companion stands below the bud. This restriction is a special case of the presumable cut.

We can also find this kind of restriction in the sequent calculi of some modal logics [16], for which the cut elimination does not hold but the cut rule can be restricted, without changing provability, to that with a cut formula which is a subformula of the bottom sequent of the cut. This restricted cut is also a special case of the presumable cut.

Structure of the Paper. We introduce a cyclic proof system for symbolic heaps in Sect. 2. In Sect. 3, we propose the presumable cuts and the quasi cut-elimination property. In Sect. 4, we show that the cyclic proof system defined in Sect. 2 does not satisfy the quasi cut-elimination property. We give concluding remark in Sect. 5.

2   Cyclic Proof System for Symbolic Heaps

We define the logic SL_1 of symbolic heaps in separation logic, and the cyclic proof system CSL_1ID^ω for symbolic heaps.

2.1   Symbolic Heaps

We define the formulas of the separation logic with the singleton heap $\mapsto$ and the separating conjunction $*$ in a standard way [15].

We use the metavariables $x, y, z,\ldots$ for variables, and $P, Q,\ldots$ for predicate symbols. Each predicate symbol is supposed to have a fixed arity.

Definition 1 (Symbolic heaps). *Let* nil *be a term constant, and* $\top$ *and* emp *be propositional constants. A term, denoted by* $t, u,\ldots$, *is defined as either a variable or* nil. *We use the boldface metavariables* $\boldsymbol{x}$ *and* $\boldsymbol{t}$ *for finite sequences of* *variables and terms, respectively. The* pure formulas Π *and the* spatial formulas Σ *are defined as follows.*

$$\Pi ::= \top \mid t = u \mid t \neq u \mid \Pi \wedge \Pi, \qquad \Sigma ::= \mathrm{emp} \mid P(t) \mid t \mapsto u \mid \Sigma * \Sigma.$$

The formulas of SL_1 are (quantifier-free) symbolic heaps A, which is defined as $\Pi \wedge \Sigma$. We define $FV(A)$ as the set of free variables in A.

We use the following notation. For $I = \{1, \cdots, n\}$, we write $\bigwedge_{i \in I} \Pi_i$ for $\Pi_1 \wedge \cdots \wedge \Pi_n$. Similarly, we write $*_{i \in I} \Sigma_i$ for $\Sigma_1 * \cdots * \Sigma_n$. When A is $\Pi_1 \wedge \Sigma_1$ and B is $\Pi_2 \wedge \Sigma_2$, we write $A * B$ for $\Pi_1 \wedge \Pi_2 \wedge \Sigma_1 * \Sigma_2$. Similarly, we write $A \wedge \Pi$ for $\Pi_1 \wedge \Pi \wedge \Sigma_1$ and $A * \Sigma$ for $\Pi_1 \wedge \Sigma_1 * \Sigma$.

Each predicate P is supposed to be accompanied with its definition clauses as

$$P(\boldsymbol{x}) := \exists \boldsymbol{y}_1.A_1 \mid \exists \boldsymbol{y}_2.A_2 \mid ... \mid \exists \boldsymbol{y}_n.A_n,$$

where each A_i is a quantifier-free symbolic heap whose free variables are in $\boldsymbol{x}$ or $\boldsymbol{y}_i$.

Substitutions of terms are finite mappings from term variables to terms. A substitution θ is called a renaming, if θ is injective and $\theta(x)$ is a variable for any x in its domain.

We identify formulas up to commutativity and associativity for $*$, commutativity, associativity, and idempotence for $\wedge$, and symmetry for $=$ and $\neq$. $\top$ is a unit for $\wedge$. We use $\equiv$ for syntactic identity modulo these identifications.

Definition 2 (Extended subformula). *The* extended subformulas *of a symbolic heap $\bigwedge_{i \in I} \Pi_i \wedge *_{j \in J} \Sigma_j$ are defined as formulas obtained by renaming from the formulas of the form $\bigwedge_{i \in I'} \Pi_i \wedge *_{j \in J'} \Sigma_j$ for $I' \subseteq I$ and $J' \subseteq J$. ExSub(A) is defined as the set of extended subformulas of A.*

2.2   Semantics of Symbolic Heap

In the following, for a mapping f, the domain and the image of f are denoted as $\mathrm{dom}(f)$ and $\mathrm{img}(f)$, respectively.

A store, denoted by s, is a function from variables to natural numbers $\mathbb{N}$. It is extended to a mapping on terms by $s(\mathrm{nil}) = 0$. We write $s[\boldsymbol{x} := \boldsymbol{a}]$ for the store which is the same as s except the values of $\boldsymbol{x}$ are $\boldsymbol{a}$. A heap, denoted by h, is a finite partial function from $\mathbb{N} \setminus \{0\}$ to $\mathbb{N}$. $h = h_1 + h_2$ means $\mathrm{dom}(h_1) \cap \mathrm{dom}(h_2) = \emptyset$, $\mathrm{dom}(h) = \mathrm{dom}(h_1) \cup \mathrm{dom}(h_2)$, and $h(n) = h_i(n)$ for $n \in \mathrm{dom}(h_i)$ ($i \in \{1, 2\}$). A pair (s, h) is called a *heap model*.

Definition 3 (Interpretation of formulas). *The interpretation of a formula* A *in* (s, h), *denoted by* $s, h \models A$, *is inductively defined as follows.*

$$s \models t = u \quad \overset{def}{\Longleftrightarrow} \quad s(t) = s(u),$$

$$s \models t \neq u \quad \overset{def}{\Longleftrightarrow} \quad s(t) \neq s(u),$$

$$s \models \Pi_1 \wedge \Pi_2 \quad \overset{def}{\Longleftrightarrow} \quad s \models \Pi_1 \text{ and } s \models \Pi_2,$$

$$s, h \models t \mapsto u \quad \overset{def}{\Longleftrightarrow} \quad \text{dom}(h) = \{s(t)\} \text{ and } h(s(t)) = s(u),$$

$$s, h \models P^{(0)}(t) \qquad\qquad never\ holds,$$

$$s, h \models P^{(m+1)}(t) \quad \overset{def}{\Longleftrightarrow} \quad s[y := b], h \models A[P_1^{(m)}, ..., P_k^{(m)}/P_1, ..., P_K](t, y),$$
$$\text{for some definition clause } \exists y.A \text{ of } P \text{ containing } P_1, ..., P_K,$$

$$s, h \models P(t) \quad \overset{def}{\Longleftrightarrow} \quad s, h \models P^{(m)}(t) \text{ for some } m,$$

$$s, h \models \Sigma_1 * \Sigma_2 \quad \overset{def}{\Longleftrightarrow} \quad \text{there exist } h_1 \text{ and } h_2 \text{ such that } h = h_1 + h_2,$$
$$s, h_1 \models \Sigma_1, \text{ and } s, h_2 \models \Sigma_2,$$

$$s, h \models \Pi \wedge \Sigma \quad \overset{def}{\Longleftrightarrow} \quad s \models \Pi \text{ and } s, h \models \Sigma,$$

where $P^{(m)}$ *is an auxiliary notation for defining* $s, h \models P(t)$ *and* $A[P_1^{(m)}, ..., P_K^{(m)}/P_1, ..., P_K]$ *is the formula obtained by replacing each* P_i *by* $P_i^{(m)}$.

2.3   Inference Rules of CSL_1ID^ω

The cyclic proof system CSL_1ID^ω consists of standard inference rules [4,14].

Definition 4 (Sequent). *Let* A *and* B *be symbolic heaps.* $A \vdash B$ *is called a sequent.* A *is called the antecedent of* $A \vdash B$, *and* B *is called the succedent of* $A \vdash B$. *We use the metavariable* e *for sequents. A sequent* $A \vdash B$ *is defined to be valid, denoted by* $A \models B$, *if and only if, for any heap model* (s, h) *such that* $s, h \models A$, $s, h \models B$ *holds.*

Definition 5 (Inference rules of CSL_1ID^ω). *The inference rules of* CSL_1ID^ω *are the following.*

$$\frac{}{A \vdash A}\ (Id) \quad \frac{}{A * t \mapsto u_1 * t \mapsto u_2 \vdash B}\ (\mapsto L) \quad \frac{}{t \neq t \wedge A \vdash B}\ (NEQL)$$

$$\frac{A \vdash C \quad C \vdash B}{A \vdash B}\ (cut) \quad \frac{A \vdash B}{\Pi \wedge A \vdash B}\ (Wk) \quad \frac{A \vdash C \quad B \vdash D}{A * B \vdash C * D}\ (*)$$

$$\frac{t \neq u \wedge A \vdash B}{t \neq u \wedge A \vdash t \neq u \wedge B}\ (NEQR)$$

$$\frac{t = u \wedge A[u/x] \vdash B[u/x]}{t = u \wedge A[t/x] \vdash B[t/x]}\ (EQL) \quad \frac{A \vdash B}{A \vdash t = t \wedge B}\ (EQR)$$

$$\frac{A \vdash B}{A * \text{emp} \vdash B}\ (EL1) \quad \frac{A * \text{emp} \vdash B}{A \vdash B}\ (EL2)$$

$$\frac{A \vdash B}{A \vdash B * \mathrm{emp}} \ (ER1) \qquad \frac{A \vdash B * \mathrm{emp}}{A \vdash B} \ (ER2)$$

$$\frac{C_1(\boldsymbol{x}, \boldsymbol{y}_1) * A \vdash B \quad \cdots \quad C_n(\boldsymbol{x}, \boldsymbol{y}_n) * A \vdash B}{P(\boldsymbol{x}) * A \vdash B} \ (Case) \qquad \frac{A \vdash C_i(\boldsymbol{u}, \boldsymbol{t}) * B}{A \vdash P(\boldsymbol{u}) * B} \ (PR)$$

where the definition clauses of the predicate P are the following

$$P(\boldsymbol{x}) := \exists \boldsymbol{y}_1.C_1(\boldsymbol{x}, \boldsymbol{y}_1) \mid \cdots \mid \exists \boldsymbol{y}_n.C_n(\boldsymbol{x}, \boldsymbol{y}_n).$$

In (PR), i satisfies $1 \le i \le n$, and the terms $\boldsymbol{t}$ are arbitrary. In (Case), the variables $\boldsymbol{y}_i$ are fresh. The formula C in (cut) is called the cut formula.

2.4 Cyclic Proof in CSL_1ID^ω

The cyclic proofs in CSL_1ID^ω are defined in a similar way to [4–6].

A derivation tree (denoted by D) in CSL_1ID^ω of a sequent e is defined in a usual way by the inference rules of CSL_1ID^ω.

Definition 6 (Bud, companion, and pre-proof). A bud is a leaf sequent of a CSL_1ID^ω derivation tree that is not an axiom. A companion for a bud e is an occurrence of a sequent of which e is a substitution instance.

A pre-proof P is defined as a pair (D, R) where D is a derivation tree and R is a function such that, for each bud occurrence e, $R(e)$ is a companion for e.

Definition 7 (Path). A proof-graph $G(P)$ of a pre-proof $P = (D, R)$ is a directed graph structure D in the bottom-up manner with additional edges from buds to companions assigned by R. A path in P is a path in $G(P)$.

Definition 8 (Trace). Let $(e_i)_{i \ge 0}$ be a path in $P = (D, R)$. A trace along $(e_i)_{i \ge 0}$ is a sequence of inductive predicates $(C_i)_{i \ge 0}$ such that each C_i occurs in the antecedent of e_i, and satisfies the following conditions:

(a) If e_i is the conclusion of (Case) in D, then either $C_i = C_{i+1}$ or C_i is unfolded in the rule instance and C_{i+1} appears as a subformula of the unfolding result. In the latter case, i is called a progressing point.

(b) If e_i is the conclusion of a rule other than (Case), then C_{i+1} is the subformula occurrence in e_{i+1} corresponding C_i in e_i.

(c) If e_i is a bud, C_{i+1} is the corresponding occurrence of the predicate to C_i in e_i.

If a trace contains infinitely many progressing points, it is called an infinitely progressing trace.

Definition 9 (Cyclic proof). A pre-proof P of CSL_1ID^ω is called a cyclic proof if it satisfies the global trace condition: for any infinite path $(e_i)_{i \ge 0}$ in P, there is a number j and an infinitely progressing trace along the path $(e_i)_{i \ge j}$.

Note that when e_i is the conclusion of (cut) and e_{i+1} is its right assumption, there is no trace along the path containing e_i and e_{i+1} since e_{i+1} contains no formula corresponding C_i in e_i. Hence, if a pre-proof contains an infinite path which passes through right assumptions of cuts infinitely many times, then it is not a cyclic proof since it cannot satisfy the global trace condition.

Example 1. A cyclic proof of $\mathrm{ls}(x,y) * \mathrm{ls}(y,z) \vdash \mathrm{ls}(x,z)$ in CSL_1ID^ω is given as follows, where the predicate ls is defined by

$$\mathrm{ls}(x,y) := x = y \wedge \mathrm{emp} \mid \exists x'.(x \neq y \wedge x \mapsto x' * \mathrm{ls}(x',y)).$$

Intuitively, $\mathrm{ls}(x,y)$ represents linear list segments.

$$
\cfrac{
\cfrac{\mathrm{ls}(y,z) \vdash \mathrm{ls}(y,z)}{
\cfrac{x = y \wedge \mathrm{ls}(y,z) \vdash \mathrm{ls}(y,z)}{
\cfrac{x = y \wedge \mathrm{ls}(y,z) \vdash \mathrm{ls}(x,z)}{
x = y \wedge \mathrm{emp} * \mathrm{ls}(y,z) \vdash \mathrm{ls}(x,z)
}\,(EL)
}\,(EQL)
}\,(Wk)
\qquad
\cfrac{
\cfrac{
\cfrac{
\cfrac{
\cfrac{x \mapsto x' \vdash x \mapsto x' \qquad \underline{\mathrm{ls}(x',y)} * \mathrm{ls}(y,z) \vdash \mathrm{ls}(x',z)\,(\dagger)}{x \mapsto x' * \underline{\mathrm{ls}(x',y)} * \mathrm{ls}(y,z) \vdash x \mapsto x' * \mathrm{ls}(x',z)}\,(*)
}{x \neq y \wedge x \mapsto x' * \underline{\mathrm{ls}(x',y)} * \mathrm{ls}(y,z) \vdash x \mapsto x' * \mathrm{ls}(x',z)}\,(Wk)
}{x \neq y \wedge x \mapsto x' * \underline{\mathrm{ls}(x',y)} * \mathrm{ls}(y,z) \vdash x \neq y \wedge x \mapsto x' * \mathrm{ls}(x',z)}\,(NEQ)
}{x \neq y \wedge x \mapsto x' * \underline{\mathrm{ls}(x',y)} * \mathrm{ls}(y,z) \vdash \mathrm{ls}(x,z)}\,(PR)
}
}{\underline{\mathrm{ls}(x,y)} * \mathrm{ls}(y,z) \vdash \mathrm{ls}(x,z)\,(\dagger)}\,(Case)
$$

The sequents marked (†) are corresponding bud and companion. This pre-proof contains only one infinite path, which contains the trace, indicated by underlines, progressing at (Case) infinitely many times. Hence, it satisfies the global trace condition.

Example 2. A cyclic proof of $\mathrm{ls}^3(x_1,y_1,x_1) \vdash \mathrm{ls}^3(y_1,x_1,y_1)$ is given as follows, where ls^3 is a ternary variant of list-segment predicate defined by

$$\mathrm{ls}^3(x,y,z) := x = y \wedge y = z \wedge \mathrm{emp}$$
$$\mid \exists x'.(x = y \wedge y \neq z \wedge x \mapsto x' * \mathrm{ls}^3(x',x',z))$$
$$\mid \exists x'.(x \neq y \wedge x \mapsto x' * \mathrm{ls}^3(x',y,z)).$$

Intuitively, $\mathrm{ls}^3(x,y,z)$ represents a list segment from x to z through y, and has the same meaning as $\mathrm{ls}(x,y) * \mathrm{ls}(y,z)$.

$$
\cfrac{
\overset{(1)}{\mathrm{ls}^3(x_1,y_1,x_1) \vdash \mathrm{ls}(x_1,y_1) * \mathrm{ls}(y_1,x_1)} \qquad \overset{(2)}{\mathrm{ls}(x_1,y_1) * \mathrm{ls}(y_1,x_1) \vdash \mathrm{ls}^3(y_1,x_1,y_1)}
}{\mathrm{ls}^3(x_1,y_1,x_1) \vdash \mathrm{ls}^3(y_1,x_1,y_1)}\,(cut)
,
$$

where the subproofs (1) and (2) are in Fig. 1.

The sequents marked (α), (β), and (γ) are each corresponding bud and companion, which make three infinite paths separately. Since each infinite path contains infinitely progressing trace, this satisfies the global trace condition.

This cyclic proof of $\mathrm{ls}^3(x_1,y_1,x_1) \vdash \mathrm{ls}^3(y_1,x_1,y_1)$ contains the (cut) with the cut formula $\mathrm{ls}(x_1,y_1) * \mathrm{ls}(y_1,x_1)$, which contains the predicate ls which does not occur in the conclusion. However, we can also construct another proof with the cut formula $\mathrm{ls}^3(x_1,y_1,y_1) * \mathrm{ls}^3(y_1,x_1,x_1)$ since $\mathrm{ls}^3(x,y,y)$ has the same meaning as $\mathrm{ls}(x,y)$.

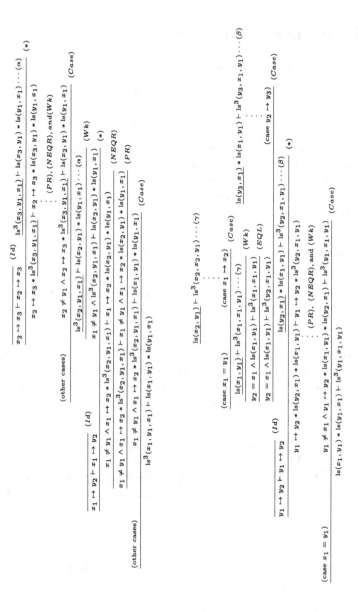

Fig. 1. Subproofs for $\mathrm{ls}^3(x_1, y_1, x_1) \vdash \mathrm{ls}^3(y_1, x_1, y_1)$

Theorem 1 (Soundness of CSL_1ID^ω). *If (D, R) is a cyclic proof in CSL_1ID^ω, then every sequent in D is valid.*

The proof of this theorem is similar to [4,6].

3   Quasi Cut-Elimination Property

3.1   Failure of Cut Elimination in CSL_1ID^ω

As [13] shows, we cannot eliminate cut for CSL_1ID^ω.

Theorem 2 ([13]). *CSL_1ID^ω does not satisfy cut-elimination property.*

For the predicates lsne and slne defined in Sect. 1, the sequent $\mathrm{lsne}(x, y) \vdash \mathrm{slne}(x, y)$ is provable, but it cannot be proved in CSL_1ID^ω without cut.

The cut rule cannot be completely removed from CSL_1ID^ω, so, as a workaround, it is expected to achieve some restriction on the cut rule which does not interfere with automatic proof search.

3.2   Presumable Cut and Quasi Cut-Elimination Property

In this section, we propose a restriction on the cut rule. We can consider this restriction not only for CSL_1ID^ω, but also for usual sequent-calculus-style proof system S and some suitable notion of subformulas $\mathrm{ExSub}(A)$. We call inference rules except for cut *non-cut rules*.

Definition 10 (Presumable formula). *Let $A \vdash B$ be a sequent in S. We inductively define the set $\mathcal{R}_S(A \vdash B)$ of reachable sequents from $A \vdash B$ in S, and the set $\mathcal{P}_S(A \vdash B)$ of presumable formulas from $A \vdash B$ simultaneously as the smallest set which satisfies the following property:*

(a) $A \vdash B \in \mathcal{R}_S(A \vdash B)$.
(b) If $A' \vdash B' \in \mathcal{R}_S(A \vdash B)$ and we have a rule instance
$$\frac{A_1'' \vdash B_1'' \quad \cdots \quad A_n'' \vdash B_n''}{A' \vdash B'} \ (r)$$
where (r) is either a non-cut rule in S or the cut rule of which cut formula is in $\mathcal{P}_S(A \vdash B)$, then $A_i'' \vdash B_i'' \in \mathcal{R}_S(A \vdash B)$ for $1 \leq i \leq n$.
(c) If $A' \vdash B' \in \mathcal{R}_S(A \vdash B)$ and $C \in \mathrm{ExSub}(A') \cup \mathrm{ExSub}(B')$, then $C \in \mathcal{P}_S(A \vdash B)$.

A presumable cut (pcut) *in a proof of $A \vdash B$ is a cut of which the cut formula is presumable from $A \vdash B$.*

Definition 11 (Quasi cut-elimination property). *If every $A \vdash B$ which is provable in S with cuts can be proved only with presumable cuts, we say that S satisfies the quasi cut-elimination property.*

Remark 1. The counterexample $\mathrm{lsne}(x,y) \vdash \mathrm{slne}(x,y)$ to the cut elimination of CSL_1ID^ω can be proved only with presumable cuts as follows.

$$
\cfrac{
\cfrac{
\cfrac{x \mapsto y \vdash x \mapsto y}{x \mapsto y \vdash \mathrm{slne}(x,y)}\ (PR)
\quad
\cfrac{
\cfrac{x \mapsto x' \vdash x \mapsto x' \quad \mathrm{lsne}(x',y) \vdash \mathrm{slne}(x',y)\ (\dagger)}{x \mapsto x' * \mathrm{lsne}(x',y) \vdash x \mapsto x' * \mathrm{slne}(x',y)}\ (*)
\quad
\cfrac{x \mapsto x' * \mathrm{slne}(x',y) \vdash x \mapsto x' * \mathrm{slne}(x',y)}{x \mapsto x' * \mathrm{slne}(x',y) \vdash \mathrm{slne}(x,y)}\ (PR)
}{x \mapsto x' * \mathrm{lsne}(x',y) \vdash \mathrm{slne}(x,y)}\ (pcut)
}{\mathrm{lsne}(x,y) \vdash \mathrm{slne}(x,y)\ (\dagger)}\ (Case)
$$

We use $x \mapsto x' * \mathrm{slne}(x',y)$ as the cut formula in this proof. By applying (PR) to $\mathrm{lsne}(x,y) \vdash \mathrm{slne}(x,y)$, we have $\mathrm{lsne}(x,y) \vdash x \mapsto x' * \mathrm{slne}(x',y)$ as its assumption. Hence $x \mapsto x' * \mathrm{slne}(x',y)$ is a presumable from $\mathrm{lsne}(x,y) \vdash \mathrm{slne}(x,y)$.

3.3   Restricting Cuts in Sequent Calculi

In the bottom-up proof search, it is hard to apply the cut rule since we have to find a cut formula. If candidates of the cut formula are not limited, we have to find a suitable cut formula by heuristics. The notion of the presumable cuts is intended to limit the range of the cut formulas to the formulas which can occur in a sequent under the cut.

Such restriction is not very new, and we can find a similar restriction in the proof system for symbolic heaps in [7]. They did not explicitly describe, but their system can be seen as a cyclic proof system with a restricted cut rule, where one of assumptions is a bud whose companion is located below the cut. We call this restricted cut the *normal bud cut*. The cut formula must occur below the cut, and hence the normal bud cut can be seen as a stricter restriction than the presumable cut. They showed that $\mathrm{lsne}(x,y) \vdash \mathrm{slne}(x,y)$ is provable with normal bud cuts.

One may wonder what happens if we remove the condition "normal" from the normal bud cut, that is, if we consider only cuts where one of assumptions is a bud whose companion is located anywhere in the proof. In fact such restriction does not restrict anything on cut formulas, since any cut in a cyclic proof can be transformed to a "bud cuts" in a cyclic proof forest with the same cut formula as in Fig. 2, where both of two cuts in the right proof forest are cuts where one of assumptions is a bud.

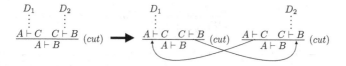

Fig. 2. Cut to bud cuts

We can also find another similar restriction on cuts for sequent calculus of propositional modal logics [16]. For modal logics S5, K4B, and so on, the sequent calculi do not satisfy the cut elimination property. Takano [16] proposed the restriction on cuts where the cut formula must be a subformula of the bottom sequent, and the restricted cuts and full cuts have the same provability power. In those systems (and usual sequent calculi for propositional logics), every non-cut rule satisfies the subformula property in a local sense, that is, every formula in the assumptions occurs in the conclusion as its subformula, so such restriction on cut formulas is stricter than the presumable cuts. Hence, Takano's results shows that these systems are examples of sequent calculi satisfying the quasi cut-elimination whereas not satisfying the full cut-elimination.

4   Failure of Quasi Cut Elimination in CSL_1ID^ω

In this section, we show that $\mathrm{ls}^3(x_1, y_1, x_1) \vdash \mathrm{ls}^3(y_1, x_1, y_1)$ is a counterexample to the quasi cut-elimination property for CSL_1ID^ω, where ls^3 is defined in Example 2.

Before the proof, we explain why $\mathrm{ls}^3(x_1, y_1, x_1) \vdash \mathrm{ls}^3(y_1, x_1, y_1)$ is a counterexample. Similarly to the counterexample $\mathrm{lsne}(x, y) \vdash \mathrm{slne}(x, y)$ to the cut-elimination property, $\mathrm{ls}^3(x_1, y_1, x_1)$ and $\mathrm{ls}^3(y_1, x_1, y_1)$ have the same meaning but are syntactically different. We can unfold the former only at x_1 and the latter at y_1, and hence, when we prove $\mathrm{ls}^3(x_1, y_1, x_1) \vdash \mathrm{ls}^3(y_1, x_1, y_1)$ its proof has the following form with the cut formula such as $\mathrm{ls}^3(x_1, y_1, y_1) * \mathrm{ls}^3(y_1, x_1, x_1)$, which can be unfolded at both x_1 and y_1:

$$
\dfrac{
\begin{array}{c} D_1 \\ \vdots \\ \mathrm{ls}^3(x_1, y_1, x_1) \vdash \mathrm{ls}^3(x_1, y_1, y_1) * \mathrm{ls}^3(y_1, x_1, x_1) \end{array}
\quad
\begin{array}{c} D_2 \\ \vdots \\ \mathrm{ls}^3(x_1, y_1, y_1) * \mathrm{ls}^3(y_1, x_1, x_1) \vdash \mathrm{ls}^3(y_1, x_1, y_1) \end{array}
}{
\mathrm{ls}^3(x_1, y_1, x_1) \vdash \mathrm{ls}^3(y_1, x_1, y_1)
} \; (cut)
,
$$

where we can construct a cycle within D_1 by unfolding at x_1, and another cycle within D_2 by unfolding at y_1. However, such a formula $\mathrm{ls}^3(x_1, y_1, y_1) * \mathrm{ls}^3(y_1, x_1, x_1)$ is not presumable from $\mathrm{ls}^3(x_1, y_1, x_1) \vdash \mathrm{ls}^3(y_1, x_1, y_1)$. Hence, we cannot construct the proof of this form with only presumable cuts.

In the following, we prove that $\mathrm{ls}^3(x_1, y_1, x_1) \vdash \mathrm{ls}^3(y_1, x_1, y_1)$ is a counterexample to the quasi cut-elimination property. We have already shown in Example 2 that it is provable with cuts, so we will prove that $\mathrm{ls}^3(x_1, y_1, x_1) \vdash \mathrm{ls}^3(y_1, x_1, y_1)$ is not provable with only presumable cuts.

The rules (Case) and (PR) for ls^3 are the following:

$$
\dfrac{e_a \quad e_b \quad e_c}{A * \mathrm{ls}^3(x, y, z) \vdash B} \; (Case)
,
$$

where e_a is $x = y \wedge y = z \wedge A * \mathrm{emp} \vdash B$, e_b is $x = y \wedge y \neq z \wedge A * x \mapsto x' * \mathrm{ls}^3(x', x', z) \vdash B$, and e_c is $x \neq y \wedge A * x \mapsto x' * \mathrm{ls}^3(x', y, z) \vdash B$ for fresh x'.

$$
\dfrac{A \vdash x = y \wedge y = z \wedge \mathrm{emp}}{A \vdash B * \mathrm{ls}^3(x, y, z)} \; (PR1)
,
$$

$$
\dfrac{A \vdash x = y \wedge y \neq z \wedge x \mapsto t * \mathrm{ls}^3(t, t, z)}{A \vdash B * \mathrm{ls}^3(x, y, z)} \; (PR2)
,
$$

$$\frac{A \vdash B * x \neq y \wedge x \mapsto t * \mathrm{ls}^3(t, y, z)}{A \vdash B * \mathrm{ls}^3(x, y, z)} \ (PR3)$$
,

where t is an arbitrary term.

We suppose for a contradiction that there is a cyclic proof (D, R) of $\mathrm{ls}^3(x_1, y_1, x_1) \vdash \mathrm{ls}^3(y_1, x_1, y_1)$ in $CSL_1 ID^\omega$ with only presumable cuts. In the following Lemma 1, we prove that the presumable formulas for $\mathrm{ls}^3(x_1, y_1, x_1) \vdash \mathrm{ls}^3(y_1, x_1, y_1)$ is limited to the form defined in Definition 12. In Lemma 6, we will see that (D, R) has an infinite path $(e_i)_{i \geq 0}$, which passes through right branches of (pcut) infinitely many times, which contradicts the global trace condition. Therefore, $CSL_1 ID^\omega$ does not satisfy the quasi cut-elimination property.

We call a spatial formula *predicate-free* if it contains no predicate symbol except $\mapsto$.

Definition 12. *We define the set S of symbolic heaps as $S = \{\Pi \wedge \Sigma_{pf} * \mathrm{ls}^3(t_1, t_2, t_3) \mid \Sigma_{pf}$ is predicate free, and t_1, t_2, t_3 are terms$\} \cup \{\Pi \wedge \Sigma_{pf} \mid \Sigma_{pf}$ is predicate free$\}$.*

Lemma 1 (Presumable formulas). *We have $\mathcal{P}_{CSL_1 ID^\omega}(\mathrm{ls}^3(x_1, y_1, x_1) \vdash \mathrm{ls}^3(y_1, x_1, y_1)) \subseteq S$.*

Proof. Let e_0 be $\mathrm{ls}^3(x_1, y_1, x_1) \vdash \mathrm{ls}^3(y_1, x_1, y_1)$ and $S_\vdash$ be $\{A' \vdash B' \mid A', B' \in S\}$. We can prove $\mathcal{P}_{CSL_1 ID^\omega}(e_0) \subseteq S$ and $\mathcal{R}_{CSL_1 ID^\omega}(e_0) \subseteq S_\vdash$ by induction on $\mathcal{P}_{CSL_1 ID^\omega}(e_0)$ and $\mathcal{R}_{CSL_1 ID^\omega}(e_0)$. $\square$

Then, we define the path $(e_i)_{i \geq 0}$ in (D, R).

Definition 13. *The path $(e_i)_{i \geq 0}$ in the cyclic proof (D, R) of $\mathrm{ls}^3(x_1, y_1, x_1) \vdash \mathrm{ls}^3(y_1, x_1, y_1)$ is defined as follows:*

(a) e_0 is defined as $\mathrm{ls}^3(x_1, y_1, x_1) \vdash \mathrm{ls}^3(y_1, x_1, y_1)$.

(b) When e_i is a conclusion $A * \mathrm{ls}^3(x, y, z) \vdash B$ of (Case), one of the assumptions is of the form $A * x \neq y \wedge x \mapsto x' * \mathrm{ls}^3(x', y, z) \vdash B$. Define e_{i+1} as this assumption.

(c) When e_i is a conclusion of (*), the rule application is of the form

$$\frac{A \vdash C \quad B \vdash D}{A * B \vdash C * D} \ (*).$$

If the spatial part of B or D is emp, define e_{i+1} as $A \vdash C$. Otherwise, define e_{i+1} as $B \vdash D$.

(d) When e_i is a conclusion of (pcut), the rule application is of the form

$$\frac{A \vdash C \quad C \vdash B}{A \vdash B} \ (pcut).$$

If the spatial formula of C is the same as B, define e_{i+1} as $A \vdash C$. Otherwise, define e_{i+1} as $C \vdash B$.

(e) When e_i is a bud, define e_{i+1} as the companion of e_i.
(f) For the other rules, there is exactly one assumption, and define e_{i+1} as it.

Lemma 2. *Let (s,h) be a heap model.*

1. *If Σ_{pf} is predicate-free, x occurs in Σ_{pf}, and $s, h \models \Sigma_{pf}$, we have $s(x) \in \text{dom}(h) \cup \text{img}(h)$.*
2. *If $s, h \models \text{ls}^3(t_1, t_2, t_3)$, we have either $s(t_i) \in \text{dom}(h) \cup \text{img}(h)$ or $s(t_1) = s(t_2) = s(t_3)$.*

Definition 14. *A pure formula Π is called* injective *if $t = u \notin \Pi$ for any $t \not\equiv u$.*

Let $x_1, x_2, \ldots$ be fixed variables. We introduce the following abbreviations: For $m \geq 1$, $x_1 \mapsto^* x_m * \text{ls}^3(x_m, t, t')$ denotes either $\text{ls}^3(x_1, t, t')$ or $x_1 \mapsto x_2 * x_2 \mapsto x_3 * \cdots * x_{m-1} \mapsto x_m * \text{ls}^3(x_m, t, t')$ (for $m \geq 2$). **emp** denotes $\text{emp} * \text{emp} * \cdots * \text{emp}$.

Definition 15. *For natural numbers $m < n \leq k$, we define the set $\mathcal{H}_{m,n,k}$ of heap models as follows:*

$$\mathcal{H}_{m,n,k} = \{(s, h) \mid s \text{ is injective}, s(x_i) = i (1 \leq i \leq m), s(y_1) = n$$
$$\text{dom}(h) = [1, k], h(i) = i + 1 (1 \leq i \leq k - 1), \text{and } h(k) = 1\},$$

where $[n, m]$ denotes the interval $\{i \mid n \leq i \leq m\}$ for natural numbers n and m.

Note that for any $m < n \leq k$, $\mathcal{H}_{n,m,k}$ is trivially non-empty, and the size of $\text{dom}(h)$ is k for any $(s, h) \in \mathcal{H}_{n,m,k}$.

Lemma 3. *Suppose that Π is injective, $m < n \leq k$, and $(s, h) \in \mathcal{H}_{m,n,k}$. We have $s, h \models \Pi \wedge x_1 \mapsto^* x_m * \text{ls}^3(x_m, y_1, x_1)$.*

Lemma 4. *Suppose that $m < n \leq k$, $(s, h) \in \mathcal{H}_{m,n,k}$, $h = h_1 + h_2$, and $s(t_i) \in [1, k]$ for $1 \leq i \leq 3$. $s, h_1 \models \text{ls}^3(t_1, t_2, t_3)$ holds if and only if (s, h_1) satisfies one of the following conditions:*

(1) $s(t_1) = s(t_2) = s(t_3)$ and $\text{dom}(h_1) = \emptyset$,
(2) $s(t_3) = 1$, not $s(t_1) = s(t_2) = s(t_3)$, $\text{dom}(h_1) = [s(t_1), k]$, and $s(t_2) \in \text{dom}(h_1)$,
(3) $1 < s(t_3) \leq s(t_1)$, not $s(t_1) = s(t_2) = s(t_3)$, $\text{dom}(h_1) = [1, s(t_3) - 1] \cup [s(t_1), k]$, and $s(t_2) \in \text{dom}(h_1)$,
(4) $s(t_1) < s(t_3)$, $\text{dom}(h_1) = [s(t_1), s(t_3) - 1]$, and $s(t_2) \in \text{dom}(h_1)$.

Lemma 5. *Let C be a formula of the form $\Pi \wedge \Sigma_{pf} * \text{ls}^3(t_1, t_2, t_3)$, where Σ_{pf} is predicate-free. If Π_1 and Π_2 are injective, and*

$$\Pi_1 \wedge x_1 \mapsto^* x_m * \text{ls}^3(x_m, y_1, x_1) * \text{emp} \vdash C \text{ and}$$

$$C \vdash \Pi_2 \wedge \text{ls}^3(y_1, x_1, y_1) * \text{emp}$$

are valid, then C is satisfiable and of the form either

$$\Pi \wedge x_1 \mapsto^* x_n * \text{ls}^3(x_n, y_1, x_1) * \text{emp} \text{ for some } n \leq m, \text{ or}$$

$$\Pi \wedge \text{ls}^3(y_1, x_1, y_1) * \text{emp},$$

and Π is injective.

Proof. Let A be $\Pi_1 \wedge x_1 \mapsto^* x_m * \mathrm{ls}^3(x_m, y_1, x_1) * \mathbf{emp}$, B be $\Pi_2 \wedge \mathrm{ls}^3(y_1, x_1, y_1) * \mathbf{emp}$, and V be $\{x_1, \ldots, x_m, y_1\}$, which is the set of variables contained in the spatial part of A.

By Lemma 3, every $(s, h) \in \mathcal{H}_{m,n,k}$ $(m < n \leq k)$ is a model of A, and $A \vdash C$ is valid, and hence (s, h) is also a model of C. It implies that C is satisfiable.

(i) We show that Π is injective. Assume that there are t and u such that $t = u \in \Pi$ and $t \not\equiv u$. For $(s, h) \in \mathcal{H}_{m,m+1,m+1}$, we have $s \models \Pi$, and hence $s(t) = s(u)$, which contradicts that s is injective.

(ii) We show that either $t_1 \not\equiv t_2$ or $t_2 \not\equiv t_3$ holds. Otherwise, we have $t_1 \equiv t_2 \equiv t_3$. For any $(s, h) \in \mathcal{H}_{m,m+1,k}$, we have $s, h \models \Sigma_{pf} * \mathrm{ls}^3(t_1, t_1, t_1)$. By the definition of ls^3, we have $s, h \models \Sigma_{pf}$. In particular, there are heap models $(s, h_1) \in \mathcal{H}_{m,m+1,m+1}$ and $(s, h_2) \in \mathcal{H}_{m,m+1,m+2}$ such that $s, h_1 \models \Sigma_{pf}$ and $s, h_2 \models \Sigma_{pf}$. However, the sizes of $\mathrm{dom}(h_1)$ and $\mathrm{dom}(h_2)$ are $m + 1$ and $m + 2$, respectively, which contradicts that Σ_{pf} is predicate-free.

(iii) We show that any variable in $\Sigma_{pf} * \mathrm{ls}^3(t_1, t_2, t_3)$, which is the spatial part of C, are in V. Assume that z is a variable in $\Sigma_{pf} * \mathrm{ls}^3(t_1, t_2, t_3)$ but not in V. For any $(s, h) \in \mathcal{H}_{m,m+1,m+1}$ we have $s, h \models C$. Since $z \notin V$, for any $i \notin \mathrm{dom}(h) \cup \mathrm{img}(h) \cup \mathrm{img}(s)$, $s' = s[z \mapsto i]$ is injective, and $s', h \in \mathcal{H}_{m,m+1,m+1}$, and hence $s', h \models C$. Since $s'(z) = i \notin \mathrm{dom}(h) \cup \mathrm{img}(h)$, by Lemma 2.1, z is not contained in Σ_{pf}. Therefore, z is either t_1, t_2, or t_3. By Lemma 2.2, $t_1 \equiv t_2 \equiv t_3$ holds, which contradicts (ii).

(iv) We show that both x_1 and y_1 occur in $\Sigma_{pf} * \mathrm{ls}^3(t_1, t_2, t_3)$. Assume that x_1 does not occur in $\Sigma_{pf} * \mathrm{ls}^3(t_1, t_2, t_3)$. For any $(s, h) \in \mathcal{H}_{m,m+1,m+1}$, we have $s, h \models C$. For any $i \notin \mathrm{dom}(h) \cup \mathrm{img}(h) \cup \mathrm{img}(s)$, $s' = s[x_1 \mapsto i]$ is injective, and we have $s', h \models C$. Since $C \models B$ is valid, $s', h \models B$ holds, and hence $s', h \models \mathrm{ls}^3(y_1, x_1, y_1)$. Since s' is injective, we have $s'(y_1) \neq s'(x_1)$. By Lemma 2, $s'(x_1) \in \mathrm{dom}(h) \cup \mathrm{img}(h)$, which contradicts $s'(x_1) = i \notin \mathrm{dom}(h) \cup \mathrm{img}(h)$. For y_1, it is similarly proved.

(v) We show that $y_1 \mapsto t$ does not occur in C. For any $(s, h) \in \mathcal{H}_{m,m+1,m+2}$, we have $s, h \models C$. If $y_1 \mapsto t$ occurs in C, we have $h(s(y_1)) = s(t)$. By definition of $\mathcal{H}_{m,m+1,m+2}$, we have $s(t) = m + 2$. By (iii), we have $t \in V$, and hence $s(t) \in [1, m] \cup \{m + 1\}$, which contradicts $s(t) = m + 2$.

(vi) We show that $t \mapsto y_1$ does not occur in C. For any $(s, h) \in \mathcal{H}_{m,m+2,m+2}$, we have $s, h \models C$. If $t \mapsto y_1$ occurs in C, we have $h(s(t)) = s(y_1)$. By definition of $\mathcal{H}_{m,m+1,m+2}$, we have $s(t) = m + 1$. By (iii), we have $t \in V$, and hence $s(t) \in [1, m] \cup \{m + 2\}$, which contradicts $s(t) = m + 1$.

(vii) We show that, if $x_i \mapsto x_j$ occurs in C, we have $1 \leq i \leq m - 1$ and $j = i + 1$. For any $(s, h) \in \mathcal{H}_{m,m+1,m+1}$, we have $s, h \models C$. If $x_i \mapsto x_j$ occurs in C, we have $h(s(x_i)) = s(x_j)$. By definition of $\mathcal{H}_{m,m+1,m+1}$, we have $i + 1 = j$ and $1 \leq i \leq m - 1$.

By (i)–(vii), we prove the lemma. For $(s, h) \in \mathcal{H}_{m,m+2,m+2}$, since we have $s, h \models C$, we can divide h to h_1 and h_2 such that $h = h_1 + h_2$, $s, h_1 \models \mathrm{ls}^3(t_1, t_2, t_3)$, and $s, h_2 \models \Sigma_{pf}$. Then, (s, h_1) satisfies one of four conditions of Lemma 4. Since Π is injective, $s(t_1) = s(t_2) = s(t_3)$ does not hold by (ii), so (1) of Lemma 4 is not the case. If $m + 2 \in \text{dom}(h_2)$, Σ_{pf} contains $z \mapsto t$ for some $z \in V$ by (iii) such that $s(z) = m + 2$. Then, z must be y_1, which contradicts (v). Hence $m + 2 \in \text{dom}(h_1)$ holds, so (4) of Lemma 4 is not the case since $s(t_3) - 1 < m + 2$. Therefore, we have either

(a) $\text{dom}(h_1) = [1, s(t_3) - 1] \cup [s(t_1), m + 2]$ and $1 \neq s(t_3) \leq s(t_1)$, or

(b) $\text{dom}(h_1) = [s(t_1), m + 2]$ and $s(t_3) = 1$.

Case (a). Since $s(x_1) = 1 \notin \text{dom}(h_2) \cup \text{img}(h_2)$ holds by the definition of $\mathcal{H}_{m,m+2,m+2}$, x_1 does not occur in Σ_{pf} by Lemma 2.1, and hence either t_1 or t_2 is x_1 by (iv). Since we have $1 \leq s(t_3) - 1 < s(t_1)$ in this case, we have $t_2 \equiv x_1$. By (iv), (v), (vi), either t_1 or t_3 is y_1. If $t_3 \equiv y_1$ holds, we have $t_1 \equiv y_1$ since $s(t_3) \leq s(t_1)$ holds. If $t_1 \equiv y_1$ and $t_3 \not\equiv y_1$ hold, we have $m + 1 \in \text{dom}(h_2)$. However, there is no $z \in V$ such that $s(z) = m + 1$. Therefore, we have $t_1 \equiv t_3 \equiv y_1$. In this case, $\text{dom}(h_1) = [1, m + 2]$ and $\text{dom}(h_2) = \emptyset$ hold, and hence C is of the form $\Pi \wedge \text{ls}^3(y_1, x_1, y_1) * \textbf{emp}$.

Case (b). We have $t_3 \equiv x_1$ since $s(t_3) = 1$. If t_1 is y_1, then $m + 1 \in \text{dom}(h_2)$ holds, and then Σ_{pf} must contain $z \mapsto t$ for some $z \in V$ by (iii) such that $s(z) = m + 1$, but there is no such z. Hence we have $t_1 \not\equiv y_1$, and then we have $t_2 \equiv y_1$ by (iv), (v), (vi). Since $t_1 \in V - \{y_1\}$ holds, we have $t_1 \equiv x_n$ for some $n \leq m$. Then, we have $\text{dom}(h_1) = [n, m + 2]$ and $\text{dom}(h_2) = [1, n - 1]$. By (iii) and (vii), the form of C is $\Pi \wedge x_1 \mapsto^* x_n * \text{ls}^3(x_n, y_1, x_1) * \textbf{emp}$.

From the above, the form of C is either

$$\Pi \wedge x_1 \mapsto^* x_n * \text{ls}^3(x_n, y_1, x_1) * \textbf{emp} \text{ for some } n, \text{ or}$$

$$\Pi \wedge \text{ls}^3(y_1, x_1, y_1) * \textbf{emp}$$

and Π is injective by (i).   □

Lemma 6. *Every sequent e_i in the path $(e_i)_{i \geq 0}$ is of the following form:*

$$\Pi_1 \wedge x_1 \mapsto^* x_m * \text{ls}^3(x_m, y_1, x_1) * \textbf{emp} \vdash \Pi_2 \wedge \text{ls}^3(y_1, x_1, y_1) * \textbf{emp}, \qquad (\dagger)$$

where Π_1 and Π_2 are injective and the antecedent of e_i is satisfiable. Hence, e_i is not an axiom and the path $(e_i)_{i \geq 0}$ is an infinite path.

Proof. First, the antecedent of $(\dagger)$ is satisfiable by Lemma 3.

Secondly, we show that e_i is of the form $(\dagger)$ by induction on i. For $e_0 \equiv \text{ls}^3(x_1, y_1, x_1) \vdash \text{ls}^3(y_1, x_1, y_1)$, it is trivial. Under the assumption that e_n is of the form of $(\dagger)$, we prove that for e_{n+1}. We will give only nontrivial cases.

Case (PR). Any assumption of (PR) whose conclusion is e_n must be invalid, so it is not the case.

Case (pcut). By Lemma 1, the cut formula is of the form either $\Pi \wedge \Sigma_{pf} * \textbf{emp}$ or $\Pi \wedge \Sigma_{pf} * \text{ls}^3(t_1, t_2, t_3) * \textbf{emp}$, where Σ_{pf} is predicate-free. For the former case, we can see that one of the assumptions is invalid, so it is not the case. For the latter case, e_{n+1} is of the form $(\dagger)$ by Lemma 5.   □

Lemma 7. *The path $(e_i)_{i \geq 0}$ passes through right branches of (pcut) infinitely many times.*

Proof. By Lemma 6, $(e_i)_{i \geq 0}$ is an infinite path, hence (Case) must be applied to $(e_i)_{i \geq 0}$ infinitely many times by the global trace condition. When (Case) is applied, the number of $\mapsto$ increases. Any proof trees of cyclic proofs are finite, hence the number of $\mapsto$ in $(e_i)_{i \geq 0}$ must decrease infinitely many times.

By Lemma 6, any sequents on the path $(e_i)_{i \geq 0}$ is form (†) and the number of $\mapsto$ in $(e_i)_{i \geq 0}$ decreases only when it passes through the right branch of (pcut). Hence the path $(e_i)_{i \geq 0}$ must pass through right branches of (pcut) infinitely many times. □

Theorem 3 (Failure of quasi cut elimination for CSL_1ID^ω). CSL_1ID^ω *does not satisfy the quasi cut-elimination property.*

Proof. $\mathrm{ls}^3(x_1, y_1, x_1) \vdash \mathrm{ls}^3(y_1, x_1, y_1)$ is a counterexample. First, $\mathrm{ls}^3(x_1, y_1, x_1) \vdash \mathrm{ls}^3(y_1, x_1, y_1)$ can be proved in CSL_1ID^ω as in Example 2. Secondly, we show $\mathrm{ls}^3(x_1, y_1, x_1) \vdash \mathrm{ls}^3(y_1, x_1, y_1)$ can not be proved in CSL_1ID^ω with only (pcut). Suppose that there is a cyclic proof (D, R) of $\mathrm{ls}^3(x_1, y_1, x_1) \vdash \mathrm{ls}^3(y_1, x_1, y_1)$ with only (pcut). By Lemma 7, (D, R) has a path which passes through right branches of (pcut) infinitely many times. However, at each right branch of (pcut), no trace is connected, and hence (D, R) cannot satisfy the global trace condition, which contradicts that (D, R) is a cyclic proof. □

Even if we change the definition of the extended subformula from renaming variables to replacing variables by arbitrary terms, the above proof shows that CSL_1ID^ω does not satisfy the quasi cut-elimination property, since all of the presumable formulas from $\mathrm{ls}^3(x_1, y_1, x_1) \vdash \mathrm{ls}^3(y_1, x_1, y_1)$ still remain in S after the change of the definition. Hence, the restriction of [7] properly changes the provability from the system with full cuts.

Corollary 1. *In CSL_1ID^ω, if we impose the condition that one of assumption of a cut is a bud whose companion is located below the cut, the provability properly weakens.*

5   Concluding Remark

This paper has proposed a restriction for the cut rule, called presumable cut, in sequent-calculus-style proof systems, and a relaxed variant of the cut-elimination, the quasi cut-elimination property. In general, the cut rule requires some heuristics to find the cut formula in the bottom-up proof search, whereas the presumable cut limits the cut formula to those which can occur below the cut.

It has been shown in [13] that the cyclic proof systems for symbolic heaps in separation logic do not enjoy the cut-elimination property, and we hope that those enjoy the quasi cut-elimination property. However, this paper showed that a cyclic proof system CSL_1ID^ω does not enjoy the quasi cut-elimination by giving a counterexample $ls^3(x_1, y_1, x_1) \vdash ls^3(y_1, x_1, y_1)$. It shows a limit on automatic proof search in cyclic proof systems.

As future work, we will study on the quasi cut-elimination property for other cyclic proof systems such as the logic of bunched implications [3] and the first-order predicate logic. Another direction is relaxing the condition of presumable cuts. For the example $ls^3(x_1, y_1, x_1) \vdash ls^3(y_1, x_1, y_1)$, we can prove it in $CSL_1 ID^\omega$ with the cut formula $ls^3(x_1, y_1, y_1) * ls^3(y_1, x_1, x_1)$, which is a separating conjunction of two presumable formulas. It is an interesting question whether we can restrict the cut formulas to separating conjunctions of some bounded number of presumable formulas.

References

1. Berdine, J., Calcagno, C., O'Hearn, P.W.: A decidable fragment of separation logic. In: Lodaya, K., Mahajan, M. (eds.) FSTTCS 2004. LNCS, vol. 3328, pp. 97–109. Springer, Heidelberg (2004). https://doi.org/10.1007/978-3-540-30538-5_9

2. Berdine, J., Calcagno, C., O'Hearn, P.W.: Symbolic execution with separation logic. In: Yi, K. (ed.) APLAS 2005. LNCS, vol. 3780, pp. 52–68. Springer, Heidelberg (2005). https://doi.org/10.1007/11575467_5

3. Brotherston, J.: Formalised inductive reasoning in the logic of bunched implications. In: Nielson, H.R., Filé, G. (eds.) SAS 2007. LNCS, vol. 4634, pp. 87–103. Springer, Heidelberg (2007). https://doi.org/10.1007/978-3-540-74061-2_6

4. Brotherston, J., Distefano, D., Petersen, R.L.: Automated cyclic entailment proofs in separation logic. In: Bjørner, N., Sofronie-Stokkermans, V. (eds.) CADE 2011. LNCS (LNAI), vol. 6803, pp. 131–146. Springer, Heidelberg (2011). https://doi.org/10.1007/978-3-642-22438-6_12

5. Brotherston, J., Gorogiannis, N., Petersen, R.L.: A generic cyclic theorem prover. In: Jhala, R., Igarashi, A. (eds.) APLAS 2012. LNCS, vol. 7705, pp. 350–367. Springer, Heidelberg (2012). https://doi.org/10.1007/978-3-642-35182-2_25

6. Brotherston, J., Simpson, A.: Sequent calculi for induction and infinite descent. J. Logic Comput. **21**(6), 1177–1216 (2011)

7. Chu, D., Jaffar, J., Trinh, M.: Automatic induction proofs of data-structures in imperative programs. In: Proceedings of PLDI, vol. 2015, pp. 457–466 (2015)

8. Das, A., Pous, D.: Non-wellfounded proof theory for (kleene+action) (algebras+lattices). In: Proceedings of CSL 2018 LIPIcs, vol. 119, pp. 19:01–19:18 (2018)

9. Doumane, A.: On the infinitary proof theory of logics with fixed points. Ph.D. thesis, Paris 7 (2017)

10. Iosif, R., Rogalewicz, A., Simacek, J.: The tree width of separation logic with recursive definitions. In: Bonacina, M.P. (ed.) CADE 2013. LNCS (LNAI), vol. 7898, pp. 21–38. Springer, Heidelberg (2013). https://doi.org/10.1007/978-3-642-38574-2_2

11. Iosif, R., Rogalewicz, A., Vojnar, T.: Deciding entailments in inductive separation logic with tree automata. In: Cassez, F., Raskin, J.-F. (eds.) ATVA 2014. LNCS, vol. 8837, pp. 201–218. Springer, Cham (2014). https://doi.org/10.1007/978-3-319-11936-6_15

12. Katelaan, J., Matheja, C., Zuleger, F.: Effective entailment checking for separation logic with inductive definitions. In: Vojnar, T., Zhang, L. (eds.) TACAS 2019. LNCS, vol. 11428, pp. 319–336. Springer, Cham (2019). https://doi.org/10.1007/978-3-030-17465-1_18
13. Kimura, D., Nakazawa, K., Terauchi, T., Unno, H.: Failure of cut-elimination in cyclic proofs of separation logic. Comupt. Softw. **37**(1), 39–52 (2020)
14. Kimura, D., Tatsuta, M.: Decidability for entailments of symbolic heaps with arrays. https://arxiv.org/abs/1802.05935 (2018)
15. Reynolds, J.C.: Separation logic: a logic for shared mutable data structures. In: Proceedings of LICS, vol. 2002, pp. 55–74 (2002)
16. Takano, M.: Subformula property as a substitute for cut-elimination in modal propositional logics. Math. Japonica **37**, 1129–1145 (1992)
17. Tatsuta, M., Nakazawa, K., Kimura, D.: Completeness of cyclic proofs for symbolic heaps with inductive definitions. In: Lin, A.W. (ed.) APLAS 2019. LNCS, vol. 11893, pp. 367–387. Springer, Cham (2019). https://doi.org/10.1007/978-3-030-34175-6_19

On the Effectiveness of Higher-Order Logic Programming in Language-Oriented Programming

Matteo Cimini[✉]

University of Massachusetts Lowell, Lowell, MA 01854, USA
matteo_cimini@uml.edu

Abstract. In previous work we have presented LANG-N-PLAY, a functional language-oriented programming language with languages as first-class-citizens. Language definitions can be bound to variables, passed to and returned by functions, and can be modified at run-time before being used. LANG-N-PLAY programs are compiled and executed in the higher-order logic programming language λProlog. In this paper, we describe our compilation methods, which highlight how the distinctive features of higher-order logic programming are a great fit in implementing a language-oriented programming language.

Keywords: Higher-order logic programming · Language-oriented programming · Functional programming

1 Introduction

Language-oriented programming [8, 14, 31] is a paradigm that has received a lot of attention in recent years. Behind this paradigm is the idea that different parts of a programming solution should be expressed with different problem-specific languages. For example, programmers can write JavaScript code for their web application and enjoy using JQuery to access DOM objects in some parts of their code, and WebPPL to do probabilistic programming in other parts [16]. To realize this vision, *language workbenches* have emerged as sophisticated tools to assist programmers with the creation, reuse and composition of languages.

Languages as first-class citizens [7] is an approach to language-oriented programming that advocates that language definitions should have the same status as any other expression in the context of a general-purpose programming language. In this approach language definitions are *run-time values*, just like integers, for example, and they can be the result of computations, bound to variables, passed to and returned by functions, and inserted into lists, to name a few possibilities.

LANG-N-PLAY [6, 7] is a functional language-oriented programming language with languages as first-class citizens. LANG-N-PLAY is implemented in a combination of OCaml and the higher-order logic programming language λProlog [24].

© Springer Nature Switzerland AG 2020
K. Nakano and K. Sagonas (Eds.): FLOPS 2020, LNCS 12073, pp. 106–123, 2020.
https://doi.org/10.1007/978-3-030-59025-3_7

The core of the language implementation is, however, an interpreter written in λProlog. Specifically, LANG-N-PLAY programs are compiled into λProlog terms and executed with such interpreter.

To implement language-oriented programming operations, the features of higher-order logic programming have proved to be exceptionally fitting. In particular, formulae as first-class citizens make it easy to have a run-time data type for languages and implement operations that manipulate languages at run-time, including switching evaluation strategies on demand (call-by-value vs call-by-name). Furthermore, hypothetical reasoning [15] (i.e. deriving implicative goals)[1] makes it easy to execute programs with arbitrary languages defined by programmers, as well as switch from a language to another during computation.

Goal of the Paper. Our goal is to demonstrate that higher-order logic programming can be a great fit for implementing language-oriented systems. To this aim, we describe our compilation methods and highlight how the distinctive features of higher-order logic programming have been a natural fit in this context.

Ultimately, LANG-N-PLAY allows for non-trivial language-oriented programming scenarios, and yet its interpreter is 73 lines of λProlog code. This is remarkable in the context of language-oriented systems.

Roadmap of the Paper. Section 2 reviews higher-order logic programming as adopted in λProlog. Section 3 gives a general overview of the implementation of LANG-N-PLAY before diving into specific aspects. Section 4 discusses our implementation of (programmer-defined) language definitions. Section 5 covers our implementation of the LANG-N-PLAY operations that manipulate languages. Section 6 provides details on our implementation w.r.t. using languages to execute programs. Section 7 covers the scenario of switching strategies at run-time. Section 8 discusses related work, and Sect. 9 concludes the paper.

2   Higher-Order Logic Programming

λProlog is a flagship representative of higher-order logic programming languages [24]. This section reviews its features. We do not give a complete account of λProlog. Instead, we discuss the features that play a role in the next sections. λProlog extends Prolog with the following elements: types, formulae as first-class citizens, higher-order abstract syntax, and hypothetical reasoning.

Typed Logic Programming. λProlog programs are equipped with a signature that defines the entities that are involved in the program. Programs must follow the typing discipline that is declared in this signature or they would be rejected. For example, if we were to implement a simple language with numbers and additions, we would have the following declarations.

---

[1] To remain in line with λProlog terminology we use the terms *hypothetical reasoning* throughout this paper, see [24].

```
kind typ type.
kind expression type.

type int typ.
type zero -> expression.
type succ expression -> expression.
type plus expression -> expression -> expression.
```

The keyword **kind** declares the entities in the program. The keyword **type** is used to specify how to create terms of such entities.

As in Prolog, the computation takes place through the means of logic programming rules. Logic programming rules can derive formulae, which are built with predicates. Predicates, as well, must be declared with a type in λProlog. For example, a type checking relation and a reduction relation can be declared as follows.

```
type typeOf expression -> typ -> prop.
type step expression -> expression -> prop.

typeOf zero int.
typeOf (succ E) int :-  typeOf E int.

    ... reduction rules, here omitted ...
```

The keyword **prop** denotes that **typeOf** and **step** build a formula when applied to the correct type of arguments.

Formulae as First-Class Citizens. λProlog extends Prolog also in that formulae can be used in any well-typed context. For example, below we intentionally split our type checker in an unusual way.

```
type getFormula expression -> prop -> prop.
type check expression -> prop.

getFormula zero true.
getFormula (succ E) (typeOf E int).

check E :- getFormula E F, F.
```

The predicate **getFormula** takes two arguments. The first is an expression and is an input, and the second is a proposition and is an output. The predicate **getFormula** returns the formula we should check to establish that the term is well-typed (the output type is ignored for the sake of this example). This example shows that formulae can be arguments. Furthermore, after **check** calls **getFormula** to retrieve the formula F, this formula can be used as a premise in the rule, as shown in the last line.

Higher-Order Abstract Syntax (HOAS). HOAS is an approach to syntax in which the underlying logic can appeal to a native λ-calculus for modeling aspects related to binding [25]. Suppose that we were to add the operators of the λ-calculus, we would define the following.

```
type abs (expression -> expression) -> expression.
type app expression -> expression -> expression.

step (app (abs R) V) (R V) :- value V.
```

The argument of abs is an abstraction from an expression to an expression. To model the identity function we write (abs x\ x), where the highlighted part of this term points out the syntax used by λProlog for writing HOAS abstractions. In the beta-reduction rule above we have that R is an abstraction and therefore we can use it with a HOAS application (R V) to produce a term. λProlog takes care of performing the substitution for us.

Hypothetical Reasoning. λProlog also extends Prolog with hypothetical reasoning [24] (i.e. deriving implicative goals [15]). To appreciate this feature consider the following logic program.

```
flyTo london nyc.
flyTo chicago portland.
connected X X.
connected X Z :- flyTo X Y, connected Y Z.
```

The city london and portland are not connected. However, in λProlog we can write the formula:

```
connected nyc chicago => connected london portland
```

This formula asks: "Were nyc connected to chicago, would london be connected to portland?". At run-time the query connected london portland is interrogated in the logic program in which the fact connected nyc chicago is added.

3   Basic Overview of Lang-n-Play

LANG-N-PLAY is a functional language-oriented programming language [7]. Programmers can define their own languages and use them to execute programs. LANG-N-PLAY is implemented partly in OCaml and partly in λProlog. Precisely, the following is the architecture of LANG-N-PLAY.

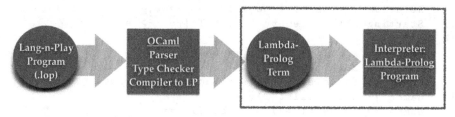

Programs are parsed and type checked in OCaml. These two aspects are not discussed in the paper because they do not play a role in our message about the effectiveness of higher-order logic programming.

Next, LANG-N-PLAY programs are compiled into λProlog. The interpreter of LANG-N-PLAY programs is a λProlog logic program. Our OCaml compilation produces the λProlog term that represents the LANG-N-PLAY program, and gives it to this interpreter. Programmers do not launch the interpreter manually. Our OCaml code is interfaced to the ELPI interpreter of λProlog through the ELPI OCaml package [9], and loads an external file that contains the interpreter written in λProlog.

In this paper we discuss the part that is enclosed in the red rectangle, as it is the core of the implementation of LANG-N-PLAY, and highlights how higher-order logic programming can accommodate the features of LANG-N-PLAY.

Our interpreter defines a kind for LANG-N-PLAY expressions called expLO, and defines two relations for reduction steps and detecting values.

```
type stepLO expLO -> expLO -> prop.
type valueLO expLO -> prop.
```

The suffix LO in the names of operators and relations are meant to recall that we are in a language-oriented language. We introduce the elements of expLO as we encounter them in the next sections. There are a number of aspects of LANG-N-PLAY that we do not discuss in this paper. For example, although LANG-N-PLAY includes common features of functional programming such as booleans, if-then-else, lists, letrec, and import, we omit discussing them because they are not relevant to this paper.

4   Defining Languages

LANG-N-PLAY provides syntax for defining languages. Below is the example of a definition of a language with lists and an operator elementAt which accesses an element of a list based on its position (position 0 is the first element).

```
1    {!
2    Type T ::= int | (list T),
3    Expression e ::= zero | (succ e) | nil | (cons e e)
4                          | (elementAt e e),
5    Value v ::= zero | (succ v) | nil | (cons v v),
6    Context C ::= (succ E) | (cons C e) | (cons v C)
7                     | (elementAt C e) | (elementAt v C),
8    Environment Gamma ::= [x : T],
9    Relation ::= Gamma |- e : T | e --> e,
10   StartingCall ::= empty |- e : T | e --> e.
11
12   Gamma |- x : T <== x : T in Gamma,
13   Gamma |- zero : int,
14   Gamma |- (succ e) : int <== Gamma |- e : int,
15   Gamma |- nil : (list T),
16   Gamma |- (cons e1 e2) : (list T) <==
17           Gamma |- e1 : T /\ Gamma |- e2 : (list T),
18   Gamma |- (elementAt e1 e2) : T <==
19           Gamma |- e1 : int /\ Gamma |- e2 : (list T),
20   (elementAt zero (cons V1 V2)) --> V1,
21   (elementAt (succ V) (cons V1 V2)) --> (elementAt V V2)
22   !}
```

Languages are defined within {! ... !}, as in lines 1–22. LANG-N-PLAY makes use of a domain-specific language that closely resembles the way researchers define and share languages in operational semantics. (The Ott language achieved the same effect over ten years ago [28], and we adopt a similar syntax).

As typical, languages define a grammar (lines 2–10) and an inference system (lines 12–21). An inference system may define a type system and a reduction semantics.

The syntax for defining grammars is quite standard. As in many language workbenches [8,14,31], language definitions can use lists with [...]. For example, Environment Gamma ::= [x : T] means Gamma is a list of formulae of that shape. LANG-N-PLAY provides the operation in for testing membership on lists, as in line 12. Furthermore, there are two special grammar categories, Relation and Starting Call. The former simply declares relations, and the latter informs LANG-N-PLAY on how to call the type checker and the evaluator.

The syntax for defining inference systems is also rather familiar to operational semantics practitioners. Perhaps, the biggest departure is that the horizontal line of an inference rule is replaced with an inverse implication <== that can be read "*provided that*", and we use an explicit syntactic and-operator when we have multiple premises.

The language definition above serves as our running example throughout the paper. We refer to the lines 2–21 as *listLines* in what follows.

4.1 λProlog Implementation of Language Definitions

It is rather natural to compile language definitions such as the one above into λProlog because operational semantics is based on inference systems. These, in turn, map naturally to logic programming rules. For example, the language above compiles to the following (we show only an excerpt).

```
typeOf nil (list T).
typeOf (cons E1 E2) (list T) :- typeOf E1 T,
                                typeOf E2 (list T).
typeOf (elementAt E1 E2) T :- typeOf E1 int,
                              typeOf E2 (list T).
step (elementAt zero (cons V1 V2)) V1 :- value V1,
                                         value V2.
step (elementAt (succ V) (cons V1 V2)) (elementAt V V2)
                               :- value V1, value V2.
```

The fact that language definitions map well to higher-order logic programs has been previously demonstrated with the work of Twelf [26], and λProlog [24].

Since LANG-N-PLAY handles programmer-defined languages that may be manipulated at run-time, we accommodate languages with an internal representation. In particular, the language above is represented with a list of formulae with the following operator:

```
type language (list prop) -> expLO.
```

Therefore, the language *listLines* is compiled as follows.

```
 1  language
 2  [
 3  typeOf nil (list T) ;
 4  typeOf (cons E1 E2) (list T) :- typeOf E1 T,
 5                                   typeOf E2 (list T) ;
 6  typeOf (elementAt E1 E2) T :- typeOf E1 int,
 7                                typeOf E2 (list T) ;
 8  step (elementAt zero (cons V1 V2)) V1 :- value V1,
 9                                           value V2 ;
10  step (elementAt (succ V) (cons V1 V2)) (elementAt V V2)
11                                :- value V1, value V2 ;
12  value nil ;
13  value (cons V1 V2) :- value V1, value V2 ;
14  step (elementAt E1 E2) (elementAt E1' E2) :- step E1 E1';
15  step (elementAt V1 E2) (elementAt V1 E2') :- step E2 E2';
16  ... the rest of contextual reduction rules ...
17  ]
```

This is our run-time representation for languages. Notice that since we need only the reduction rules to execute programs we compile inference rules only (not grammar), with the exception of values and evaluation contexts, which are turned into rules.

We shall refer to the list of elements at lines 3–16 as *listsInLP*.

5   Operations on Languages

LANG-N-PLAY provides a handful of operations on language definitions. Below we discuss the following operations: let-binding, union of languages, functions on languages, and removal of rules.

Let-Binding. LANG-N-PLAY can bind a language definition to a variable in typical ML-style, as in

```
let lists = {!
  ... listLines ...
!} in lists
```

Therefore, our interpreter includes a let-operation and its reduction semantics.

```
type letLO expLO -> (expLO -> expLO ) -> expLO.
stepLO (letLO V R) (R V) :- valueLO V.
```

The code above is then compiled to

```
letLO (language [ listsInLP ]) (lists\ lists)
```

which reduces to (language [*listsInLP*]) in one step. (This example also shows that languages can be the result of computations.)

Language Union. Another operation of LANG-N-PLAY is language union, performed with the binary operator U. For example, notice that the language for lists is unsafe: if we called `elementAt` asking for the 4-th element of a list that contains only 2 elements we would get stuck, because there is no specified behavior for that case. We can add reduction rules that cover those cases as follows. (We refer to the language created by the union operation below as `safeLists`).

```
lists U {!
    Expression e ::= myError,
    Error er ::= myError,
    (elementAt zero nil) --> myError,
    (elementAt (succ V) nil) --> myError,
!}
```

This code adds the error to the language and adds appropriate reduction rules. Our interpreter includes the language union operation and its reduction semantics.

```
type unionLO expLO -> expLO -> expLO.
stepLO
        (unionLO (language Rules1) (language Rules2))
        (language Result)
        :- append Rules1 Rules2 Result.
```

where **append** is a polymorphic list append defined in the interpreter (straightforward and here omitted). The union operation above is compiled as

```
1  unionLO
2      (language [ listsInLP ])
3      (language [ step (elementAt zero nil) myError ;
4                  step (elementAt (succ V) nil) myError])
```

which reduces to (language [*listsInLP + rules in lines 3-4*]) in one step.

Removal of Rules. LANG-N-PLAY includes an operation for removing rules from a language. For example, the union above adds two extra rules but the sole rule `step (elementAt V nil) myError :- value V` would be sufficient.

To modify `safeLists` and create the more compact language that has only one rule we can execute the following LANG-N-PLAY program.

```
1  (remove
2      (elementAt zero nil) --> myError)
3      from (remove (elementAt (succ V) nil) --> myError
4              from safeLists)
5  ) U {! (elementAt V nil) --> myError !}
```

The operation **remove** takes in input a rule and a language, and returns a language. This code removes one of the rules from `safeLists` at lines 3 and 4. The language so produced is then used in the removal of the other rule at lines 1–3. Line 5 adds the safe reduction rule for `elementAt` with a union operation.

Our interpreter includes the rule removal operation and its reduction semantics.

```
type removeLO prop -> expLO -> expLO.
stepLO (removeLO Formula (language Rules))
        (language Result)
      :- listRemove Formula Rules Result.
```

where listRemove is a polymorphic predicate that matches elements of a list with a given element and removes the element if the match succeeds. This predicate is also defined in the interpreter (straightforward and here omitted).

The remove operations above, excluding the union at line 5, are compiled as

```
1  removeLO
2      (step (elementAt zero nil) myError)
3      (removeLO
4          step (elementAt (succ V) nil) myError :- value V
5          (language [ listsInLP +
6              step (elementAt zero nil) myError ;
7              step (elementAt (succ V) nil) myError :- value V
8              ]
9          )
10     )
```

which reduces to (language [*listsInLP*]) in two steps.

λProlog grants us a powerful equality on formulae and the removal operation is far from performing a textual match on the rule to remove. For example, the following two rules are equal in λProlog.

$$(*) \quad \texttt{step (elementAt (succ MyVar) nil) myError :- value MyVar}$$
$$=$$
$$\texttt{step (elementAt (succ V) nil) myError :- value V}$$

Therefore, we obtain the same results if we used the formula (*) at line 4. Thanks to λProlog, formulae are up-to renaming of variables and alpha-equivalence of HOAS abstractions.

Functions on Languages. As typical in programming languages, we often would like to pack instructions in functions for the sake of abstraction. LANG-N-PLAY provides functions on languages. For example, instead of performing language union inline we can create a function that adds the desired safety checks, as in

```
let addSafeAccess mylan =
mylan U {! Expression e ::= myError ,
           Error er ::= myError ,
           (elementAt V nil) --> myError ,
        !}
in (addSafeAccess lists)
```

Our interpreter includes abstractions and applications, as well as their reduction semantics.

```
type absLO (expLO -> expLO ) -> expLO.
type appLO expLO -> expLO -> expLO.
stepLO (appLO (absLO R) V) (R V) :- valueLO V.
```

LANG-N-PLAY compiles the let-binding above in the following way.

```
letLO
  (addSafeAccess\
    (appLO addSafeAccess (language [... listsInLP ...])))
  (absLO mylan\
    (unionLO
      mylan
      (language [
          step (elementAt (succ V) nil) myError :- value V
                ])
    )
  )
```

This program reduces the letLO operation in one step and we obtain

```
(appLO
  (absLO mylan\ unionLO mylan
      (language [
          step (elementAt (succ V) nil) myError :- value V
                ])
    (language [... listsInLP ...])))
```

In turn, this program reduces in one step to

```
unionLO
  (language [... listsInLP ...])))
  (language [
          step (elementAt (succ V) nil) myError :- value V
                ])
```

which produces the expected language in one step.

6   Executing Programs and Language Switch

Of course, languages can be used to execute programs. The code below shows the LANG-N-PLAY expression to do so. (For readability, we use standard notation for numbers and lists rather than sequences of succ and cons).

```
{! ... listsLines ... !}> elementAt 1 [1,2,3]
```

We call this type of expression *program execution* and is of the form *language > program*. The program above returns a value together with the language with which it has been computed:

```
        Value = 2 in {! listsLines !}.
```

Our interpreter includes the operation for executing programs and its reduction semantics.

```
type execLO expLO -> program -> expLO.

stepLO (execLO (language Language) Prg)
       (execLO (language Language) Prg')
       :- (Language => (step Prg Prg')).
```

In the declaration at the top, program is the kind for programs. Intuitively, elements of program are S-expressions, i.e. a top-level operator followed by a series of arguments, which, too, can be programs. Notice that the language argument of execLO (first argument) is an expression. Although above we have explicitly written the language to be used, that component can be an expression that evaluates to a language, for example as in

```
lists> elementAt 1 [1,2,3], or
(addSafeAccess lists)> elementAt 1 [1,2,3]
```

The reduction rule for execLO deserves some words. The key idea is that we use hypothetical reasoning. In Sect. 2 we have seen that we can use this feature to temporarily add facts and run an augmented logic program. Above, instead, we do not add a fact but a list of formulae Language. Moreover, this list of formulae is not a list of facts but a list of rules (rules such as step (elementAt zero (cons V1 V2)) V1 :- value V1, value V2.). This has the effect of augmenting the logic program that we are currently running (which is our LANG-N-PLAY interpreter!) with new rules. In particular, these rules define the operational semantics of the language that we need to execute. The interpreter then interrogates (step Prg Prg') to compute the step from these new rules[2].

For example, the code above compiles to

```
execLO (language [... listsInLP ...]) (elementAt 1 [1,2,3])
```

The current logic program (that is, our LANG-N-PLAY interpreter) is augmented with the rules *listsInLP* and we execute the query
(step (elementAt 1 [1, 2, 3]) Prg').
This produces $Prg' = $ (element 0 [2,3]). (Notice that the query asks for one step). LANG-N-PLAY keeps executing until a value is produced. Therefore at the second step we run the query (step (elementAt 0 [2,3]) Prg'). This query returns the result $Prg' = 2$, which our interpreter detects as a value. The execution of programmer-defined languages and the execution of LANG-N-PLAY operations are never confused because the former makes use of the predicate step and the latter makes use of the predicate stepLO.

The way our interpreter recognizes that we have obtained a value is through the predicate valueLO, which our interpreter defines with

```
valueLO (execLO (language Language) Prg)
        :- (Language => (value Prg)).
```

---

[2] We are guaranteed that the rules use the predicate step for reductions because the OCaml part of LANG-N-PLAY (see the figure on Sect. 3, page 4) specifically generates the λProlog term to use step. Similarly for value.

Let us recall that once *listsInLP* is loaded in the current logic program it also contains the rules that define the values of the loaded language, defined with the predicate `value`. These rules are, for example, `value zero.` and `value succ V : − value V.`, and so on. Then we run the query (`value Prg`) to detect if `Prg` is a term that the loaded language defines as a value.

Language Switch. LANG-N-PLAY also allows for switching languages at run-time. Consider the following program.

```
let pairs = {!
  Type T ::= (times T T),
  Expression e ::= pair e e | fst e | snd e,
  Value v ::= (pair v v),
  Context C ::= (pair C e) | (pair v C)
             | (fst C) | (snd C),
  Gamma |- (pair e1 e2) : (times T1 T2) <==
              Gamma |- e1 : T1 /\ Gamma |- e2 : T2,
  Gamma |- (fst e) : T1 <==
              Gamma |- e : (times T1 T2),
  Gamma |- (snd e) : T2 <==
              Gamma |- e : (times T1 T2),
  (fst (pair V1 V2)) --> V1,
  (snd (pair V1 V2)) --> V2
!} in
lists> elementAt (pairs> fst (pair 1 0)) [1,2,3]
```

This code defines a language with pairs. Afterwards, it makes use of the list language to perform a list access. However, the first argument of `elementAt` (the position) is computed by executing another program in another language. In particular, the position is computed by executing `fst (pair 1 0)` in the language `pairs`.

This program returns the following value (recall that position 1 asks for the second element of the list).

Value = 2 in {! listsLines !}.

Implementing this language switch is easy with higher-order logic programming. When we execute

```
execLO (language [... listsInLP ...])
       (elementAt
          (execLO (language [ rules of pairs ])
                  (fst (pair 1 0)))
          [1,2,3])
```

The interpreter adds the rules *listsInLP* and evaluates the program that starts with `elementAt`. When the interpreter encounters another `execLO` it applies the same reduction rule of `execLO` that we have seen. This has the effect of adding the language with pairs on top of the language with lists. This augmented language is then used to evaluate `fst (pair 1 0)` with the query (`step (fst (pair 1 0)) Prg'`). The nested `execLO` detects when `fst (pair 1 0)` evaluates to a value in the way described above, that is, the query (`value 1`) succeeds. At this point, `execLO` simply leaves the value it has just computed in the context in which it has been executed. Therefore, `elementAt` simply continues with the value 1 as first argument, oblivious as to how this value has been computed.

Remark on the Semantics of Language Switch. The semantics of language switch is such that the current language is *extended* with new rules. Therefore, the switch does not replace a language with a completely different language. The semantics we adopt is in 1-1 correspondence with the semantics of hypothetical reasoning. We believe that this facilitates writing correct programs because the child language must at least share some values with the parent language, as the nested computation leaves a value in the context of the parent. Therefore, this value must be understood by the parent language.

Notice that the overall result is 2 in the language {! *listsLines* !} that does not contain pairs. Indeed, pairs has been added and then removed by λProlog after the nested execLO has finished.

7   Valuehood Abstractions

Strategies play a central role in computing. Examples of notable strategies are call-by-value and call-by-name in the λ-calculus. In LANG-N-PLAY we can define the λ-calculus in a way that allows the strategy to be chosen at run-time. We do so with valuehood abstractions:

```
let lambda vh : strategy =
    {! Expression e ::= (abs @x e) | (app e e),
       Value v ::= (abs @x e),
       Context C ::= (app C e),
       Environment Gamma ::= [x : T],
       (app (abs @x e) vh ) --> e[ vh /x],
    !}
```

Here, lambda is not a language definition. It is, instead, a valuehood abstraction. This is a function that takes in input a kind of expression called strategy. The variable vh is bound in the body of lambda and can appear as a variable in inference rules, as highlighted. The meaning is that it will be discovered later whether the inference rule fires when the variable is a value or an ordinary expression. The two strategies are represented with the constants EE and VV, respectively. The application (lambda EE) returns the language with the reduction rule (app (abs @x e) e2) --> e[e2/x], which fires irrespective of whether e2 is a value or not, in call-by-name style. The application (lambda VV), instead, return the language with rule (app (abs @x e) v) --> e[v/x], which fires when the argument is a value, in call-by-value style.

To realize this, we take advantage of formulae as first-class citizens. The compilation of lambda is:

```
absLO vh\
language [step (app (abs R) ARG) (R ARG) :- (vh ARG)]
```

The variable vh is a HOAS abstraction from terms to formulae. Intuitively, when we pass EE we want to say that the premise (vh ARG) should not add any additional conditions. We do so by compiling EE to the function (x\ true). The application (lambda EE) is then compiled into an ordinary application appLO.

For (lambda EE), after the parameter passing we end up with
    language [step (app (abs R) ARG) (R ARG) :- ((x\ true) ARG)]
which λProlog converts to
    language [step (app (abs R) ARG) (R ARG) :- true]
When we pass VV, instead, we want to say that the premise (vh ARG) should be
satisfied only so long that ARG is a value. To do so, we compile the constant VV
to (x\ value x). When we execute (lambda VV) we end up with
    language [step (app (abs R) ARG) (R ARG) :- ((x\ value x) ARG)]
which λProlog converts to
    language [step (app (abs R) ARG) (R ARG) :- value ARG].
Therefore, we place a new premise to check that ARG is a value.

8   Related Work

The main related work is the vision paper [7]. We have used a variant of the
example in [7] to demonstrate our compilation methods. We have also addressed
remove with a different example, and the example on language switch is new.

There are two main differences between [7] and this paper.

– [7] proposes the approach of languages as first-class citizens and exemplifies
  it with an example in LANG-N-PLAY. [7] does not discuss any implementation
  details of LANG-N-PLAY. On the contrary, this paper's focus is entirely on the
  implementation mechanisms that we have adopted and, most importantly,
  this paper demonstrates that the distinctive features of higher-order logic
  programming are a great fit for language-oriented systems.
– This paper extends the work in [7] by adding language switches.

The K framework is a rewrite-based executable framework for the specification
of programming languages [27]. Differently from LANG-N-PLAY, the K framework
does not offer language-oriented programming features such as language switch
and the updating of languages at run-time. On the other hand, K has been
used to define real-world programming languages such as C [10] and Java [2],
to name a few, while LANG-N-PLAY has not. The style of language definitions
in LANG-N-PLAY is that of plain operational semantics. Therefore, defining real-
world programming languages can become a cumbersome task, and we have not
ventured into that task yet. An interesting feature of the K framework is that it
automatically derives analyzers and verifiers from language specifications [29].
This work inspires us towards adding similar features to LANG-N-PLAY.

A number of systems have been created to support language-oriented programming [3,17,18,21,30]. Features such as language switch and the updating
of languages at run-time are rather sophisticated in this research area, and not
many systems offer these features [4,12,19,20]. However, some language workbenches do provide these functionalities, such as Racket [13], Neverlang [30]
and Spoofax [18]. Racket provides special syntax for defining languages and its
implementation is based on macros. Language definitions are macro-expanded

into Racket's core functional language. Spoofax and Neverlang have an internal ad hoc representation of languages. Languages can be accessed and updated at run-time in Neverlang, for example, making use of the run-time loading features of the JVM to add parts to languages represented as objects. To our knowledge, LANG-N-PLAY is the only language-oriented system that is implemented in *higher-order* logic programming.

LANG-N-PLAY is *not* more expressive than other systems. The goal of this paper is not to provide a system that surpasses the state of the art. LANG-N-PLAY is also a young tool (2018) compared to the mentioned systems, some of which boast decades of active development. The goal of our paper is, instead, about the effectiveness of higher-order logic programming in language-oriented programming. It is hard to compare our implementation to others at a quantitative level (lines of code) because systems such as Racket, Neverlang and Spoofax are very large and mature systems that offer all sorts of language services. We were not able to single out an isolated meaningful part of these systems to compare with our interpreter. Nonetheless, we believe that it is generally remarkable that we could implement the interpreter of a full language-oriented programming language with sophisticated features in 73 lines of code.

9 Conclusion

This paper describes the compilation methods that we have adopted in the implementation of LANG-N-PLAY, and provides evidence that high-order logic programming can be a great fit for implementing language-oriented systems.

The following aspects of higher-order logic programming have been particularly fitting:
(We add numbers, as some features have been helpful in more than one way).

- *Formulae as first-class citizens #1:* List of formulae naturally models language definitions in operational semantics, providing a readily available run-time data type. This makes it easy to implement operations that manipulate languages (such as union and rule removal) during execution.
- *Formulae as first-class citizens #2:* It models naturally the switch of evaluation strategy at run-time. This is thanks to the fact that we can pass premises to rules. These premises may or may not add new conditions under which existing rules can fire.
- *Hypothetical reasoning #1:* It naturally models the execution of a program with a given operational semantics, possibly created at run-time.
- *Hypothetical reasoning #2:* It naturally models the switch from executing a program using a language to executing another program using an extension of that language.

In the future, we would like to strengthen our message by implementing further operations on languages using high-order logic programming. We would like to implement operations such as language unification and restriction [11], grammar inheritance, language embedding, and aggregation from the Manticore system [21], and renaming and remapping from Neverlang [30]. There is notable work in [5, 22, 23] on inferring the dependencies of languages, which we also plan to implement.

Some systems compile languages and programs into proof assistants. For example, Ott compiles into Coq, HOL and Isabelle [28], so that users can carry out proofs in these systems. Currently, LANG-N-PLAY compiles into λProlog solely to execute programs. However, a subset of λProlog is also the specification language of the proof assistant Abella [1]. In the future, we would like to explore the verification of LANG-N-PLAY programs after compilation to λProlog/Abella code.

We point out that language workbenches offer a variety of editor services among syntax colouring, highlighting, outlining, and reference resolution, to name a few. Currently, LANG-N-PLAY is not equipped with a comfortable IDE. Inspired by the work on language workbenches, we would like to improve the usability of our system.

References

1. Baelde, D., et al.: Abella: a system for reasoning about relational specifications. Journal of Formalized Reasoning 7(2) (2014). https://doi.org/10.6092/issn.1972-5787/4650. http://jfr.unibo.it/article/download/4650/4137
2. Bogdanas, D., Rosu, G.: K-Java: a complete semantics of Java. In: Proceedings of the 42nd Symposium on Principles of Programming Languages, pp. 445–456. ACM (2015). https://doi.org/10.1145/2676726.2676982
3. Bousse, E., Degueule, T., Vojtisek, D., Mayerhofer, T., Deantoni, J., Combemale, B.: Execution framework of the gemoc studio (tool demo). In: Proceedings of the 2016 ACM SIGPLAN International Conference on Software Language Engineering SLE 2016, pp. 84–89. ACM, New York (2016)
4. van den Brand, M.G.J., et al.: The ASF+SDF meta-environment: a component-based language dvelopment environment. In: Wilhelm, R. (ed.) CC 2001. LNCS, vol. 2027, pp. 365–370. Springer, Heidelberg (2001). https://doi.org/10.1007/3-540-45306-7_26
5. Butting, A., Eikermann, R., Kautz, O., Rumpe, B., Wortmann, A.: Modeling language variability with reusable language components. In: Proceedings of the 22nd International Systems and Software Product Line Conference SPLC 2018. ACM, New York (2018)
6. Cimini, M.: Lang-n-play: a functional programming language with languages as first-class citizens (2018). https://github.com/mcimini/lang-n-play
7. Cimini, M.: Languages as first-class citizens (vision paper). In: Proceedings of the 11th ACM SIGPLAN International Conference on Software Language Engineering SLE 2018, pp. 65–69. ACM, New York (2018). https://doi.org/10.1145/3276604.3276983
8. Dmitriev, S.: Language oriented programming: the next programming paradigm (2004). http://www.onboard.jetbrains.com/is1/articles/04/10/lop/mps.pdf
9. Dunchev, C., Guidi, F., Coen, C.S., Tassi, E.: ELPI: fast, embeddable, \lambda prolog interpreter. In: Proceedings of the Logic for Programming, Artificial Intelligence, and Reasoning - 20th International Conference, LPAR-20 2015, Suva, Fiji, 24–28 November 2015, pp. 460–468 (2015). https://doi.org/10.1007/978-3-662-48899-7_32

10. Ellison, C., Rosu, G.: An executable formal semantics of C with applications. In: Field, J., Hicks, M. (eds.) Proceedings of the 39th Symposium on Principles of Programming Languages, pp. 533–544. ACM (2012). https://doi.org/10.1145/2103656.2103719

11. Erdweg, S., Giarrusso, P.G., Rendel, T.: Language composition untangled. In: LDTA 2012, pp. 7:1–7:8. ACM, New York (2012)

12. Erdweg, S., Rendel, T., Kästner, C., Ostermann, K.: SugarJ: library-based syntactic language extensibility. SIGPLAN Not. 46(10), 391–406 (2011). https://doi.org/10.1145/2076021.2048099. http://doi.acm.org/10.1145/2076021.2048099

13. Flatt, M., PLT: reference: racket. Technical report PLT-TR-2010-1. PLT Design Inc. (2010). https://racket-lang.org/tr1/

14. Fowler, M.: Language workbenches: the killer-app for domain specific languages? (2005). http://www.martinfowler.com/articles/languageWorkbench.html

15. Gabbay, D., Reyle, U.: N-prolog: an extension of prolog with hypothetical implications I. J. Logic Program. 1(4), 319–355 (1984). http://www.sciencedirect.com/science/article/pii/0743106684900293

16. Goodman, N.D., Stuhlmüller, A.: The design and implementation of probabilistic programming languages (2014). http://dippl.org. Accessed 10 Feb 2020

17. JetBrains: JetBrains MPS - Meta Programming System. http://www.jetbrains.com/mps/

18. Kats, L.C.L., Visser, E.: The spoofax language workbench: rules for declarative specification of languages and ides. In: OOPSLA, vol. 45, pp. 444–463. ACM, New York, October 2010. http://doi.acm.org/10.1145/1932682.1869497

19. Kelly, S., Lyytinen, K., Rossi, M.: MetaEdit+ a fully configurable multi-user and multi-tool CASE and CAME environment. In: Constantopoulos, P., Mylopoulos, J., Vassiliou, Y. (eds.) CAiSE 1996. LNCS, vol. 1080, pp. 1–21. Springer, Heidelberg (1996). https://doi.org/10.1007/3-540-61292-0_1

20. Kienzle, J., et al.: Concern-oriented language development (COLD): fostering reuse in language engineering. Comput. Lang. Syst. Struct. 54, 139–155 (2018)

21. Krahn, H., Rumpe, B., Völkel, S.: MontiCore: a framework for compositional development of domain specific languages. Int. J. Softw. Tools Technol. Transf. 12(5), 353–372 (2010). https://doi.org/10.1007/s10009-010-0142-1

22. Kühn, T., Cazzola, W., Olivares, D.M.: Choosy and picky: configuration of language product lines. In: Proceedings of the 19th International Conference on Software Product Line SPLC 2015, pp. 71–80. ACM, New York (2015). https://doi.org/10.1145/2791060.2791092. http://doi.acm.org/10.1145/2791060.2791092

23. Méndez-Acuña, D., Galindo, J.A., Degueule, T., Combemale, B., Baudry, B.: Leveraging software product lines engineering in the development of external DSLs: a systematic literature review. Comput. Lang. Syst. Struct. 46, 206–235 (2016). https://doi.org/10.1016/j.cl.2016.09.004

24. Miller, D., Nadathur, G.: Programming with Higher-Order Logic, 1st edn. Cambridge University Press, New York (2012)

25. Pfenning, F., Elliott, C.: Higher-order abstract syntax. SIGPLAN Not. 23(7), 199–208 (1988). https://doi.org/10.1145/960116.54010

26. Pfenning, F., Schürmann, C.: System description: twelf—a meta-logical framework for deductive systems. CADE 1999. LNCS (LNAI), vol. 1632, pp. 202–206. Springer, Heidelberg (1999). https://doi.org/10.1007/3-540-48660-7_14

27. Rosu, G., Şerbănuţă, T.F.: An overview of the K semantic framework. J. Logic Algebraic Program. 79(6), 397–434 (2010)

28. Sewell, P., et al.: Ott: effective tool support for the working semanticist. In: Proceedings of the 12th ACM SIGPLAN International Conference on Functional Programming ICFP 2007, pp. 1–12. ACM, New York (2007)
29. Stefanescu, A., Park, D., Yuwen, S., Li, Y., Rosu, G.: Semantics-based program verifiers for all languages. In: Proceedings of the 2016 ACM SIGPLAN International Conference on Object-Oriented Programming, Systems, Languages, and Applications, OOPSLA 2016, part of SPLASH 2016, Amsterdam, The Netherlands, 30 October–4 November 2016, pp. 74–91 (2016). https://doi.org/10.1145/2983990.2984027
30. Vacchi, E., Cazzola, W.: Neverlang: a framework for feature-oriented language development. Comput. Lang. Syst. Struct. **43**, 1–40 (2015)
31. Ward, M.P.: Language oriented programming. Softw.-Concepts Tools **15**, 147–161 (1995)

Declarative Pearl: Deriving Monadic Quicksort

Shin-Cheng Mu[1]([⊠]) and Tsung-Ju Chiang[2]

[1] Academia Sinica, Taipei, Taiwan
scm@iis.sinica.edu.tw
[2] National Taiwan University, Taipei, Taiwan

Abstract. To demonstrate derivation of monadic programs, we present a specification of sorting using the non-determinism monad, and derive pure quicksort on lists and state-monadic quicksort on arrays. In the derivation one may switch between point-free and pointwise styles, and deploy techniques familiar to functional programmers such as pattern matching and induction on structures or on sizes. Derivation of stateful programs resembles reasoning backwards from the postcondition.

Keywords: Monads · Program derivation · Equational reasoning · Nondeterminism · State · Quicksort

1 Introduction

This pearl presents two derivations of quicksort. The purpose is to demonstrate reasoning and derivation of monadic programs. In the first derivation we present a specification of sorting using the non-determinism monad, from which we derive a pure function that sorts a list. In the second derivation we derive an imperative algorithm, expressed in terms of the state monad, that sorts an array.

Before we dive into the derivations, we shall explain our motivation. Program derivation is the technique of formally constructing a program from a problem specification. In functional derivation, the specification is a function that obviously matches the problem description, albeit inefficiently. It is then stepwise transformed to a program that is efficient enough, where every step is justified by mathematical properties guaranteeing that the program *equals* the specification, that is, for all inputs they compute exactly the same output.

It often happens, for certain problem, that several answers are equally preferred. In sorting, for example, the array to be sorted might contain items with identical keys. It would be inflexible, if not impossible, to decide in the specification how to resolve the tie: it is hard to predict how quicksort arranges items with identical keys before actually deriving quicksort.[1] Such problems are better modelled as non-deterministic mappings from the input to all valid outputs. The derived program no longer equals but *refines* the specification.[2]

---

[1] Unless we confine ourselves to stable sorting.

[2] This is standard in imperative program derivation—Dijkstra [6] argued that we should take non-determinism as default and determinism as a special case.

© Springer Nature Switzerland AG 2020
K. Nakano and K. Sagonas (Eds.): FLOPS 2020, LNCS 12073, pp. 124–138, 2020.
https://doi.org/10.1007/978-3-030-59025-3_8

To cope with non-determinism, there was a trend in the 90's generalising from functions to relations [1,4]. Although these relational calculi are, for advocates including the authors of this paper, concise and elegant, for those who were not following this line of development, these calculi are hard to comprehend and use. People, in their first and often only exposure to the calculi, often complained that the notations are too bizarre, and reasoning with inequality (refinement) too complex. One source of difficulties is that notations of relational calculus are usually *point-free*—that is, about composing relations instead of applying relations to arguments. There have been attempts (e.g. [5,13]) designing *pointwise* notations, which functional programmers are more familiar with. Proposals along this line tend to exhibit confusion when functions are applied to non-deterministic values—β-reduction and η-conversion do not hold. One example [13] is that $(\lambda x \to x - x)\,(0\ []\ 1)$, where $([])$ denotes non-deterministic choice, always yields 0, while $(0\ []\ 1) - (0\ []\ 1)$ could be 0, 1, or -1.

Preceding the development of relations for program derivation, another way to model non-determinism has gained popularity. Monads [12] were introduced into functional programming as a way to rigorously talk about side effects including IO, state, exception, and non-determinism. Although they are considered one of the main obstacles in learning functional programming (in particular Haskell), monads have gained wide acceptance. In this pearl we propose a calculus of program derivation based on monads—essentially moving to a Kleisli category. Problem specifications are given as Kleisli arrows for non-deterministic monads, to be refined to deterministic functional programs through calculation. One of the benefits is that functional programmers may deploy techniques they are familiar with when reasoning about and deriving programs. These include both point-free and pointwise reasoning, and induction on structures or sizes of data types. An additional benefit of using monads is that we may talk about effects other than non-determinism. We demonstrate how to, from a specification of quicksort on lists, construct the imperative quicksort for arrays. All the derivations and theorems in this pearl are verified in the dependently typed programming language Agda.[3]

2   Monads

A monad consists of a type constructor $m :: * \to *$ paired with two operators, can be modelled in Haskell as a type class:

```
class Monad m where
    {·}  :: a → m a
    (≫=) :: m a → (a → m b) → m b.
```

The operator $\{\cdot\}$ is usually called *return* or *unit*. Since it is used pervasively in this pearl, we use a shorter notation for brevity. One can either think of it

---

[3] https://scm.iis.sinica.edu.tw/home/2020/deriving-monadic-quicksort/.

as mimicking the notation for a singleton set, or C-style syntax for a block of effectful program. They should satisfy the following *monad laws*:

$$m \ggeq \{\cdot\} = m,$$
$$\{x\} \ggeq f = f\ x,$$
$$(m \ggeq f) \ggeq g = m \ggeq (\lambda x \to f\ x \ggeq g).$$

A standard operator $(\gg) :: \mathsf{Monad}\ m \Rightarrow m\ a \to m\ b \to m\ b$, defined by $m_1 \gg m_2 = m_1 \ggeq \lambda\_ \to m_2$, is handy when we do not need the result of m_1. Monadic functions can be combined by Kleisli composition $(\gggeq)$, defined by $f \gggeq g = \lambda x \to f\ x \ggeq g$.

Monads usually come with additional operators corresponding to the effects they provide. Regarding non-determinism, we assume two operators $\emptyset$ and $(\talloblong)$, respectively denoting failure and non-deterministic choice:

class $\mathsf{Monad}\ m \Rightarrow \mathsf{MonadPlus}\ m$ **where**
  $\emptyset\ :: m\ a$
  $(\talloblong) :: m\ a \to m\ a \to m\ a.$

It might be a good time to note that this pearl uses type classes for two purposes: firstly, to be explicit about the effects a program uses. Secondly, the notation implies that it does not matter which actual implementation we use for m, as long as it satisfies all the properties we demand—as Gibbons and Hinze [7] proposed, we use the properties, not the implementations, when reasoning about programs. The style of reasoning in this pearl is not tied to type classes or Haskell, and we do not strictly follow the particularities of type classes in the current Haskell standard.[4]

It is usually assumed that $(\talloblong)$ is associative with $\emptyset$ as its identity:

$$\emptyset \talloblong m = m = m \talloblong \emptyset, \qquad (m_1 \talloblong m_2) \talloblong m_3 = m_1 \talloblong (m_2 \talloblong m_3).$$

For the purpose of this pearl, we also demand that $(\talloblong)$ be idempotent and commutative. That is, $m \talloblong m = m$ and $m \talloblong n = n \talloblong m$. Efficient implementations of such monads have been proposed (e.g. [10]). However, we use non-determinism monad only in specification. The derived programs are always deterministic.

The laws below concern interaction between non-determinism and $(\ggeq)$:

$$\emptyset \ggeq f = \emptyset, \tag{1}$$
$$m \gg \emptyset = \emptyset, \tag{2}$$
$$(m_1 \talloblong m_2) \ggeq f = (m_1 \ggeq f) \talloblong (m_2 \ggeq f), \tag{3}$$
$$m \ggeq (\lambda x \to f_1\ x \talloblong f_2\ x) = (m \ggeq f_1) \talloblong (m \ggeq f_2). \tag{4}$$

Left-zero (1) and left-distributivity (3) are standard—the latter says that $(\talloblong)$ is algebraic. When mixed with state, right-zero (2) and right-distributivity (4) imply that each non-deterministic branch has its own copy of the state [14].

---

[4] For example, we overlook that a Monad must also be $\mathsf{Applicative}$, $\mathsf{MonadPlus}$ be $\mathsf{Alternative}$, and that functional dependency is needed in a number of places.

3 Specification

We are now ready to present a monadic specification of sorting. Bird [3] demonstrated how to derive various sorting algorithms from relational specifications. In Sects. 4 and 5 we show how quicksort can be derived in our monadic calculus.

We assume a type Elm (for "elements") associated with a total preorder ($\leqslant$). To sort a list xs :: List Elm is to choose, among all permutation of xs, those that are sorted:

$$slowsort :: \text{MonadPlus } m \Rightarrow \text{List Elm} \rightarrow m \text{ (List Elm)}$$
$$slowsort = perm \ggg filt \ sorted,$$

where $perm$ :: MonadPlus $m \Rightarrow$ List $a \rightarrow m$ (List a) non-deterministically computes a permutation of its input, $sorted$ :: List Elm $\rightarrow$ Bool checks whether a list is sorted, and $filt \ p \ x$ returns x if $p \ x$ holds, and fails otherwise:

$$filt :: \text{MonadPlus } m \Rightarrow (a \rightarrow \text{Bool}) \rightarrow a \rightarrow m \ a$$
$$filt \ p \ x = guard \ (p \ x) \ggg \{x\}.$$

The function $guard \ b = \textbf{if} \ b \ \textbf{then} \ \{\} \ \textbf{else} \ \emptyset$ is standard. The predicate $sorted$ :: List Elm $\rightarrow$ Bool can be defined by:

$$sorted \ [\,] \qquad = \text{True}$$
$$sorted \ (x : xs) = all \ (x \leqslant) \ xs \wedge sorted \ xs.$$

The following property can be proved by a routine induction on ys:

$$sorted \ (ys \mathbin{+\!\!+} [x] \mathbin{+\!\!+} zs) \ \equiv \tag{5}$$
$$sorted \ ys \wedge sorted \ zs \wedge all \ (\leqslant x) \ ys \wedge all \ (x \leqslant) \ zs.$$

Now we consider the permutation phase. As shown by Bird [3], what sorting algorithm we end up deriving is often driven by how the permutation phase is performed. The following definition of $perm$, for example:

$$perm \ [\,] \qquad = \{[\,]\}$$
$$perm \ (x : xs) = perm \ xs \ggg insert \ x,$$

where $insert \ x \ xs$ non-deterministically inserts x into xs, would lead us to insertion sort. To derive quicksort, we use an alternative definition of $perm$:

$$perm :: \text{MonadPlus } m \Rightarrow \text{List } a \rightarrow m \text{ (List } a)$$
$$perm \ [\,] \qquad = \{[\,]\}$$
$$perm \ (x : xs) = split \ xs \ggg \lambda(ys, zs) \rightarrow liftM2 \ (\mathbin{+\!\!+}[x]\mathbin{+\!\!+}) \ (perm \ ys) \ (perm \ zs).$$

where $liftM2 \ (\oplus) \ m_1 \ m_2 = m_1 \ggg \lambda x_1 \rightarrow m_2 \ggg \lambda x_2 \rightarrow \{x_1 \oplus x_2\}$, and $split$ non-deterministically splits a list. When the input has more than one element, we split the tail into two, permute them separately, and insert the head in the middle. The monadic function $split$ is given by:

$split :: \mathsf{MonadPlus}\ m \Rightarrow \mathsf{List}\ a \to m\ (\mathsf{List}\ a \times \mathsf{List}\ a)$
$split\ [] \qquad = \{([],[])\}$
$split\ (x : xs) = split\ xs \ggg \lambda(ys, zs) \to \{(x : ys, zs)\} [\!] \{(ys, x : zs)\}.$

This completes the specification. One may argue that the second definition of
perm is not one that, as stated in Sect. 1, "obviously" implied by the problem
description. Bird [3] derived the second one from the first in a relational setting,
and we can also show that the two definitions are equivalent.

4   Quicksort on Lists

In this section we derive a divide-and-conquer property of *slowsort*. It allows us
to refine *slowsort* to the well-known recursive definition of quicksort on lists, and
is also used in the next section to construct quicksort on arrays.

Refinement. We will need to first define our concept of program refinement.
We abuse notations from set theory and define:

$$m_1 \subseteq m_2 \equiv m_1 [\!] m_2 = m_2.$$

The righthand side $m_1 [\!] m_2 = m_2$ says that every result of m_1 is a possible
result of m_2. When $m_1 \subseteq m_2$, we say that m_1 *refines* m_1, m_2 can be *refined to*
m_1, or that m_2 *subsumes* m_1. Note that this definition applies not only to the
non-determinism monad, but to monads having other effects as well. We denote
$(\subseteq)$ lifted to functions by $(\dot\subseteq)$:

$$f \dot\subseteq g \ = \ (\forall x : f\ x \subseteq g\ x).$$

That is, f refines g if $f\ x$ refines $g\ x$ for all x. When we use this notation, f and
g are always functions returning monads, which is sufficient for this pearl.
   One can show that the definition of $(\subseteq)$ is equivalent to $m_1 \subseteq m_2 \equiv (\exists\ n :
m_1 [\!] n = m_2)$, and that $(\subseteq)$ and $(\dot\subseteq)$ are both reflexive, transitive, and anti-
symmetric $(m \subseteq n \wedge n \subseteq m \equiv n = m)$. Furthermore, $(\ggg)$ respects refinement:

Lemma 1. *Bind* $(\ggg)$ *is monotonic with respect to* $(\subseteq)$. *That is,* $m_1 \subseteq m_2 \Rightarrow$
$m_1 \ggg f \subseteq m_2 \ggg f$, *and* $f_1 \dot\subseteq f_2 \Rightarrow m \ggg f_1 \subseteq m \ggg f_2$.

Having Lemma 1 allows us to refine programs in a compositional manner. The
proof of Lemma 1 makes use of (3) and (4).

Commutativity and *Guard*. We say that m and n commute if

$$m \ggg \lambda x \to n \ggg \lambda y \to f\ x\ y \ = \ n \ggg \lambda y \to m \ggg \lambda x \to f\ x\ y.$$

It can be proved that *guard* p commutes with all m if non-determinism is the
only effect in m—a property we will need many times. Furthermore, having
right-zero (2) and right-distributivity (4), in addition to other laws, one can

prove that non-determinism commutes with other effects. In particular, non-determinism commutes with state.

We mention two more properties about *guard*: *guard* $(p \wedge q)$ can be split into two, and *guards* with complementary predicates can be refined to **if**:

$$guard\ (p \wedge q)\ =\ guard\ p \gg guard\ q, \tag{6}$$

$$(guard\ p \gg m_1)\ [\!]\ (guard\ (\neg \cdot p) \gg m_2)\ \sqsupseteq\ \textbf{if}\ p\ \textbf{then}\ m_1\ \textbf{else}\ m_2. \tag{7}$$

Divide-and-Conquer. Back to *slowsort*. We proceed with usual routine in functional programming: case-analysis on the input. For the base case, *slowsort* $[\,] = \{[\,]\}$. For the inductive case, the crucial step is the commutativity of *guard*:

$$
\begin{aligned}
&slowsort\ (p : xs) \\
={}&\ \{\ \text{expanding definitions, monad laws}\ \} \\
&split\ xs \gg \lambda(ys, zs) \rightarrow \\
&perm\ ys \gg \lambda ys' \rightarrow perm\ zs \gg \lambda zs' \rightarrow \\
&filt\ sorted\ (ys' \mathbin{+\!\!+} [p] \mathbin{+\!\!+} zs') \\
={}&\ \{\ \text{by (5)}\ \} \\
&split\ xs \gg \lambda(ys, zs) \rightarrow \\
&perm\ ys \gg \lambda ys' \rightarrow perm\ zs \gg \lambda zs' \rightarrow \\
&guard\ (sorted\ ys' \wedge sorted\ zs' \wedge all\ (\leqslant p)\ ys' \wedge all\ (p \leqslant)\ zs') \gg \\
&\{ys' \mathbin{+\!\!+} [p] \mathbin{+\!\!+} zs'\} \\
={}&\ \{\ \text{(6) and that } guard \text{ commutes with non-determinism}\ \} \\
&split\ xs \gg \lambda(ys, zs) \rightarrow guard\ (all\ (\leqslant p)\ ys \wedge all\ (p \leqslant)\ zs') \gg \\
&(perm\ ys \gg filt\ sorted) \gg \lambda ys' \rightarrow \\
&(perm\ zs \gg filt\ sorted) \gg \lambda zs' \rightarrow \\
&\{ys' \mathbin{+\!\!+} [p] \mathbin{+\!\!+} zs'\}.
\end{aligned}
$$

Provided that we can construct a function *partition* such that

$$\{partition\ p\ xs\}\ \subseteq\ split\ xs \gg filt\ (\lambda(ys, zs) \rightarrow all\ (\leqslant p)\ ys \wedge all\ (p \leqslant)\ zs),$$

we have established the following divide-and-conquer property:

$$
\begin{aligned}
slowsort\ (p : xs)\ \sqsupseteq\ \ &\{partition\ p\ xs\} \gg \lambda(ys, zs) \rightarrow \\
&slowsort\ ys \gg \lambda ys' \rightarrow slowsort\ zs \gg \lambda zs' \rightarrow \\
&\{ys' \mathbin{+\!\!+} [p] \mathbin{+\!\!+} zs'\}.
\end{aligned} \tag{8}
$$

The derivation of *partition* proceeds by induction on the input. In the case for $xs := x : xs$ we need to refine two guarded choices, $(guard\ (x \leqslant p) \gg \{x : ys, zs\})\ [\!]\ (guard\ (p \leqslant x) \gg \{ys, x : zs\})$, to an **if** branching. When x and p equal, the specification allows us to place x in either partition. For no particular reason, we choose the left partition. That gives us:

$$
\begin{aligned}
&partition\ p\ [\,] &&= ([\,], [\,]) \\
&partition\ p\ (x : xs) &&= \textbf{let}\ (ys, zs) = partition\ p\ xs \\
& &&\ \textbf{in if}\ x \leqslant p\ \textbf{then}\ (x : ys, zs)\ \textbf{else}\ (ys, x : zs).
\end{aligned}
$$

Having *partition* derived, it takes only a routine induction on the length of input lists to show that $\{\cdot\} \cdot qsort \subseteq slowsort$, where *qsort* is given by:

$$
\begin{aligned}
qsort\ [] \quad &= [] \\
qsort\ (p : xs) &= \textbf{let}\ (ys, zs) = partition\ p\ xs \\
&\quad\ \textbf{in}\ qsort\ ys \mathbin{+\!\!+} [p] \mathbin{+\!\!+} qsort\ zs.
\end{aligned}
$$

As is typical in program derivation, the termination of derived program is shown separately afterwards. In this case, *qsort* terminates because the input list decreases in size in every recursive call—for that we need to show that, in the call to *partition*, the sum of lengths of *ys* and *zs* equals that of *xs*.

5   Quicksort on Arrays

One of the advantages of using a monadic calculus is that we can integrate effects other than non-determinism into the program we derive. In this section we derive an imperative quicksort on arrays, based on previously established properties.

5.1   Operations on Arrays

We assume that our state is an Int-indexed, unbounded array containing elements of type e, with two operations that, given an index, respectively read from and write to the array:

class Monad $m \Rightarrow$ MonadArr e m **where**
   read :: Int $\rightarrow$ m e
   write :: Int $\rightarrow$ e $\rightarrow$ m ().

They are assumed to satisfy the following laws:

read-write:	$read\ i \ggg write\ i\ =\ \{()\},$
write-read:	$write\ i\ x \ggg read\ i\ =\ write\ i\ x \ggg \{x\},$
write-write:	$write\ i\ x \ggg write\ i\ x'\ =\ write\ i\ x',$
read-read:	$read\ i \ggg \lambda x \rightarrow read\ i \ggg \lambda x' \rightarrow f\ x\ x' =$
	$read\ i \ggg \lambda x \rightarrow f\ x\ x\ .$

Furthermore, we assume that (1) *read i* and *read j* commute; (2) *write i x* and *write j y* commute if $i \neq j$; (3) *write i x* and *read j* commute if $i \neq j$.

More operations defined in terms of *read* and *write* are shown in Fig. 1, where #*xs* abbreviates *length xs*. The function *readList i n*, where n is a natural number, returns a list containing the n elements in the array starting from index i. Conversely, *writeList i xs* writes the list *xs* to the array with the first element being at index i. In imperative programming we often store sequences of data into an array and return the length of the data. Thus, functions *writeL*, *write2L* and *write3L* store lists into the array before returning their lengths. These *read*

$readList$ :: MonadArr e m ⇒ Int → Nat → m (List e)
$readList$ i 0 $= \{[\,]\}$
$readList$ i $(1 + k) = liftM2\ (:)\ (read\ i)\ (readList\ (i+1)\ k)$,

$writeList$ :: MonadArr e m ⇒ Int → List e → m ()
$writeList$ i $[\,]$ $= \{()\}$
$writeList$ i $(x : xs) = write\ i\ x \gg writeList\ (i+1)\ xs$,

$writeL$ i xs $= writeList\ i\ xs \gg \{\#xs\}$,
$write2L$ i (xs, ys) $= writeList\ i\ (xs + ys) \gg \{(\#xs, \#ys)\}$,
$write3L$ i $(xs, ys, zs) = writeList\ i\ (xs + ys + zs) \gg \{(\#xs, \#ys, \#zs)\}$.

$swap\ i\ j = read\ i \ggeq \lambda x \to read\ j \ggeq \lambda y \to write\ i\ y \gg write\ j\ x$.

Fig. 1. Operations for reading and writing chunks of data.

and $write$ family of functions are used only in the specification; the algorithm we construct should only mutate the array by $swap$ing elements.

Among the many properties of $readList$ and $writeList$ that can be induced from their definitions, the following will be used in a number of crucial steps:

$$writeList\ i\ (xs + ys) \ =\ writeList\ i\ xs \gg writeList\ (i + \#xs)\ ys. \qquad (9)$$

A function f :: List a → m (List a) is said to be *length preserving* if f $xs \ggeq$ $\lambda ys \to \{(ys, \#ys)\} = f\ xs \ggeq \lambda ys \to \{(ys, \#xs)\}$. It can be proved that $perm$, and thus $slowsort$, are length preserving.

On "composing monads" In the sections to follow, some readers may have concern seeing $perm$, having class constraint MonadPlus m, and some other code having constraint MonadArr e m in the same expression. This is totally fine: mixing two such subterms simply results in an expression having constraint (MonadPlus m, MonadArr e m). No *lift*ing is necessary.

We use type classes to make it clear that we do not specify what exact monad $perm$ is implemented with. It could be one monolithic monad, a monad built from monad transformers [8], or a free monad interpreted by effect handlers [11]. All theorems and derivations about $perm$ hold regardless of the actual monad, as long as the monad satisfies all properties we demand.

5.2 Partitioning an Array

While the list-based *partition* is relatively intuitive, partitioning an array *in-place* (that is, using at most $O(1)$ additional space) is known to be a tricky phase of array-based quicksort. Therefore we commence our discussion from deriving in-place array partitioning from the list version. The partition algorithm we end up deriving is known as the *Lomuto scheme* [2], as opposed to Hoare's [9].

Specification. There are two issues to deal with before we present a specification for an imperative, array-based partitioning, based on list-based *partition*. Firstly, *partition* is not tail-recursive, while many linear-time array algorithms are implemented as a tail-recursive for-loop. Thus we apply the standard trick constructing a tail-recursive algorithm by introducing accumulating parameters. Define (we write the input/outputs of *partition* in bold font for clarity):

$$partl :: \mathsf{Elm} \to (\mathsf{List\ Elm} \times \mathsf{List\ Elm} \times \mathsf{List\ Elm}) \to (\mathsf{List\ Elm} \times \mathsf{List\ Elm})$$
$$partl\ p\ (ys, zs, \boldsymbol{xs}) = \mathbf{let}\ (\boldsymbol{us}, \boldsymbol{vs}) = partition\ p\ \boldsymbol{xs}$$
$$\mathbf{in}\ (ys +\!\!+ \boldsymbol{us}, zs +\!\!+ \boldsymbol{vs}).$$

In words, *partl* p $(ys, zs, \boldsymbol{xs})$ partitions $\boldsymbol{xs}$ into $(\boldsymbol{us}, \boldsymbol{vs})$ with respect to pivot p, but appends ys and zs respectively to $\boldsymbol{us}$ and $\boldsymbol{vs}$. It is a generalisation of *partition* because *partition* p xs = *partl* p $([],[], xs)$. By routine calculation exploiting associativity of $(+\!\!+)$, we can derive a tail-recursive definition of *partl*:

$$partl\ p\ (ys, zs, [\,]) \quad = (ys, zs)$$
$$partl\ p\ (ys, zs, \boldsymbol{x} : \boldsymbol{xs}) = \mathbf{if}\ \boldsymbol{x} \leqslant p\ \mathbf{then}\ partl\ p\ (ys +\!\!+ [\boldsymbol{x}], zs, \boldsymbol{xs})$$
$$\mathbf{else}\quad partl\ p\ (ys, zs +\!\!+ [\boldsymbol{x}], \boldsymbol{xs}).$$

It might aid our understanding if we note that, if we start *partl* with initial value $([],[], xs)$ we have the invariant that ys contains elements that are at most p, and elements in zs are larger than p. The calculations below, however, do not rely on this observation.[5]

Our wish is to construct a variant of *partl* that works on arrays. That is, when the array contains $ys +\!\!+ zs +\!\!+ \boldsymbol{xs}$, the three inputs to *partl* in a consecutive segment, when the derived program finishes its work we wish to have $ys +\!\!+ \boldsymbol{us} +\!\!+ zs +\!\!+ \boldsymbol{vs}$, the output of *partl*, stored consecutively in the array.

This brings us to the second issue: *partition*, and therefore *partl*, are stable (that is, elements in each partition retain their original order), which is a strong requirement for array-based partitioning. It is costly to mutate $ys +\!\!+ zs +\!\!+ \boldsymbol{xs}$ into $ys +\!\!+ \boldsymbol{us} +\!\!+ zs +\!\!+ \boldsymbol{vs}$, since it demands that we retain the order of elements in zs while inserting elements of $\boldsymbol{us}$. For sorting we do not need such a strong postcondition. It is sufficient, and can be done more efficiently, to mutate $ys +\!\!+ zs +\!\!+ \boldsymbol{xs}$ into $ys +\!\!+ \boldsymbol{us} +\!\!+ ws$, where ws is some permutation of $zs +\!\!+ \boldsymbol{vs}$. It is handy allowing non-determinism: we introduce a *perm* in our specification, indicating that we do not care about the order of elements in ws.

Define *second* :: Monad $m \Rightarrow (b \to m\ c) \to (a, b) \to m\ (a, c)$, which applies a monadic function to the second component of a tuple:

$$second\ f\ (x, y) = f\ y \ggg \lambda y' \to \{(x, y')\}.$$

Our new wish is to construct an array counterpart of *second perm · partl* p. Let the function be

---

[5] It might be worth noting that *partl* causes a space leak in Haskell, since the accumulators become thunks that increase in size as the input list is traversed. It does not matter here since *partl* merely serves as a specification of *ipartl*.

$$ipartl :: (\mathsf{MonadPlus}\ m, \mathsf{MonadArr}\ \mathsf{Elm}\ m) \Rightarrow$$
$$\mathsf{Elm} \to \mathsf{Int} \to (\mathsf{Nat} \times \mathsf{Nat} \times \mathsf{Nat}) \to m\ (\mathsf{Nat} \times \mathsf{Nat}).$$

The intention is that in a call $ipartl\ p\ i\ (ny, nz, nx)$, p is the pivot, i the index where $ys \mathbin{+\!\!+} zs \mathbin{+\!\!+} \boldsymbol{xs}$ is stored in the array, and ny, nz, nx respectively the lengths of ys, zs, and xs. A specification of $ipartl$ is:

$$writeList\ i\ (ys \mathbin{+\!\!+} zs \mathbin{+\!\!+} \boldsymbol{xs}) \gg ipartl\ p\ i\ (\#ys, \#zs, \#\boldsymbol{xs}) \subseteq$$
$$second\ perm\ (partl\ p\ (ys, zs, \boldsymbol{xs})) \ggg write2L\ i.$$

That is, under assumption that $ys \mathbin{+\!\!+} zs \mathbin{+\!\!+} \boldsymbol{xs}$ is stored in the array starting from index i (initialised by $writeList$), $ipartl$ computes $partl\ p\ (ys, zs, \boldsymbol{xs})$, possibly permuting the second partition. The resulting two partitions are still stored in the array starting from i, and their lengths are returned.

Derivation. We start with fusing $second\ perm$ into $partl$, that is, to construct $partl'\ p \mathrel{\dot\subseteq} second\ perm \cdot partl\ p$.[6] If we discover an inductive definition of $partl'$, it can then be used to construct an inductive definition of $ipartl$. With some routine calculation we get:

$$partl' :: \mathsf{MonadPlus}\ m \Rightarrow \mathsf{Elm} \to (\mathsf{List}\ \mathsf{Elm})^3 \to m\ (\mathsf{List}\ \mathsf{Elm} \times \mathsf{List}\ \mathsf{Elm})$$
$$partl'\ p\ (ys, zs, []) \quad = \{(ys, zs)\}$$
$$partl'\ p\ (ys, zs, \boldsymbol{x} : \boldsymbol{xs}) =$$
$$\textbf{if}\ \boldsymbol{x} \leqslant p\ \textbf{then}\ perm\ zs \ggg \lambda zs' \to partl'\ p\ (ys \mathbin{+\!\!+} [\boldsymbol{x}], zs', \boldsymbol{xs})$$
$$\textbf{else}\quad perm\ (zs \mathbin{+\!\!+} [\boldsymbol{x}]) \ggg \lambda zs' \to partl'\ p\ (ys, zs', \boldsymbol{xs}).$$

For an intuitive explanation, rather than permuting the second list zs after computing $partl$, we can also permute zs in $partl'$ before every recursive call.

The specification of $ipartl$ now becomes

$$writeList\ i\ (ys \mathbin{+\!\!+} zs \mathbin{+\!\!+} \boldsymbol{xs}) \gg ipartl\ p\ i\ (\#ys, \#zs, \#\boldsymbol{xs}) \subseteq \tag{10}$$
$$partl'\ p\ (ys, zs, \boldsymbol{xs}) \ggg write2L\ i.$$

To calculate $ipartl$, we start with the right-hand side of ($\subseteq$), since it contains more information to work with. We try to push $write2L$ leftwards until the expression has the form $writeList\ i\ (ys \mathbin{+\!\!+} zs \mathbin{+\!\!+} xs) \gg ...$, thereby constructing $ipartl$. This is similar to that, in imperative program calculation, we *work backwards from the postcondition* to construct a program that works under the given precondition [6].

We intend to construct $ipartl$ by induction on xs. For $xs := []$, we get $ipartl\ p\ i$ $(ny, nz, 0) = \{(ny, nz)\}$. For the case $x : xs$, assume that the specification is met for xs. Just for making the calculation shorter, we refactor $partl'$, lifting the recursive calls and turning the main body into an auxiliary function:

---

[6] We will discover a stronger specification $partl'\ p \mathrel{\dot\subseteq} snd3\ perm \setminus (second\ perm \cdot partl\ p)$, where $snd3\ f\ (x, y, z) = f\ y \ggg \lambda y' \to \{(x, y', z)\}$. We omit the details.

$partl'\ p\ (ys, zs, x : \boldsymbol{xs}) = dispatch\ \boldsymbol{x}\ p\ (ys, zs, \boldsymbol{xs}) \ggeq partl'\ p,$
  where $dispatch\ \boldsymbol{x}\ p\ (ys, zs, \boldsymbol{xs}) =$
    if $\boldsymbol{x} \leqslant p$ **then** $perm\ zs \ggeq \lambda zs' \rightarrow \{(ys \mathbin{+\!\!+} [\boldsymbol{x}], zs', \boldsymbol{xs})\}$
          else $perm\ (zs \mathbin{+\!\!+} [\boldsymbol{x}]) \ggeq \lambda zs' \rightarrow \{(ys, zs', \boldsymbol{xs})\}.$

We calculate:

$\quad partl'\ p\ (ys, zs, x : \boldsymbol{xs}) \ggeq write2L\ i$
$=\quad$ { definition of $partl'$ }
$\quad (dispatch\ \boldsymbol{x}\ p\ (ys, zs, \boldsymbol{xs}) \ggeq partl'\ p) \ggeq write2L\ i$
$\sqsupseteq\quad$ { monad laws, inductive assumption }
$\quad (dispatch\ \boldsymbol{x}\ p\ (ys, zs, \boldsymbol{xs}) \ggeq write3L\ i) \ggeq ipartl\ p\ i$
$=\quad$ { by (9), monad laws }
$\quad dispatch\ \boldsymbol{x}\ p\ (ys, zs, \boldsymbol{xs}) \ggeq \lambda(ys', zs', \boldsymbol{xs}) \rightarrow$
$\quad writeList\ i\ (ys' \mathbin{+\!\!+} zs') \gg writeList\ (i + \#(ys' \mathbin{+\!\!+} zs'))\ \boldsymbol{xs} \gg$
$\quad ipartl\ p\ i\ (\#ys', \#zs', \#\boldsymbol{xs})$
$=\quad$ { $perm$ preserves length, commutativity }
$\quad writeList\ (i + \#ys + \#zs + 1)\ \boldsymbol{xs} \gg$
$\quad dispatch\ \boldsymbol{x}\ p\ (ys, zs, \boldsymbol{xs}) \ggeq \lambda(ys', zs', \boldsymbol{xs}) \rightarrow$
$\quad writeList\ i\ (ys' \mathbin{+\!\!+} zs') \gg$
$\quad ipartl\ p\ i\ (\#ys', \#zs', \#\boldsymbol{xs})$
$=\quad$ { definition of $dispatch$, function calls distribute into **if** }
$\quad writeList\ (i + \#ys + \#zs + 1)\ \boldsymbol{xs} \gg$
$\quad$ **if** $\boldsymbol{x} \leqslant p$ **then** $perm\ zs \ggeq \lambda zs' \rightarrow writeList\ i\ (ys \mathbin{+\!\!+} [\boldsymbol{x}] \mathbin{+\!\!+} zs') \gg$
$\qquad\qquad\qquad\qquad ipartl\ p\ i\ (\#ys + 1, \#zs', \#\boldsymbol{xs})$
$\qquad\quad$ **else** $perm\ (zs \mathbin{+\!\!+} [\boldsymbol{x}]) \ggeq \lambda zs' \rightarrow writeList\ i\ (ys \mathbin{+\!\!+} zs') \gg$
$\qquad\qquad\qquad\qquad ipartl\ p\ i\ (\#ys, \#zs', \#\boldsymbol{xs}).$

We pause here to see what has happened: we have constructed a precondition $writeList\ (i + \#ys + \#zs + 1)\ \boldsymbol{xs}$, which is part of the desired precondition: $writeList\ i\ (ys \mathbin{+\!\!+} zs \mathbin{+\!\!+} (\boldsymbol{x} : \boldsymbol{xs}))$. To recover the latter precondition, we will try to turn both branches of **if** into the form $writeList\ i\ (ys \mathbin{+\!\!+} zs \mathbin{+\!\!+} [\boldsymbol{x}]) \ggeq ....$ That is, we try to construct, in both branches, some code that executes under the precondition $writeList\ i\ (ys \mathbin{+\!\!+} zs \mathbin{+\!\!+} [\boldsymbol{x}])$—that the code generates the correct result is guaranteed by the refinement relation.

It is easier for the second branch, where we can simply refine $perm$ to $\{\cdot\}$:

$\quad perm\ (zs \mathbin{+\!\!+} [\boldsymbol{x}]) \ggeq \lambda zs' \rightarrow writeList\ i\ (ys \mathbin{+\!\!+} zs') \gg$
$\quad ipartl\ p\ i\ (\#ys, \#zs', \#\boldsymbol{xs})$
$\sqsupseteq\quad$ { since $\{xs\} \subseteq perm\ xs$ }
$\quad writeList\ i\ (ys \mathbin{+\!\!+} zs \mathbin{+\!\!+} [\boldsymbol{x}]) \gg ipartl\ p\ i\ (\#ys, \#zs + 1, \#\boldsymbol{xs}).$

For the first branch, we focus on its first line:

$\quad perm\ zs \ggeq \lambda zs' \rightarrow writeList\ i\ (ys \mathbin{+\!\!+} [\boldsymbol{x}] \mathbin{+\!\!+} zs')$
$=\quad$ { by (9), commutativity }

$writeList\ i\ ys \gg perm\ zs \ggg \lambda zs' \rightarrow writeList\ (i + \#ys)\ ([x] + zs')$
$\supseteq$ { introduce $swap$, see below }
  $writeList\ i\ ys \gg writeList\ (i + \#ys)\ (zs + [x]) \gg$
  $swap\ (i + \#ys)\ (i + \#ys + \#zs)$
$=$ { by (9) }
  $writeList\ i\ (ys + zs + [x]) \gg swap\ (i + \#ys)\ (i + \#ys + \#zs).$

Here we explain the last two steps. Operationally speaking, given an array containing $ys + zs + [x]$ (the precondition we wanted, initialized by the $writeList$ in the last line), how do we mutate it to $ys + [x] + zs'$ (postcondition specified by the $writeList$ in the first line), where zs' is a permutation of zs? We may do so by swapping x with the leftmost element of zs, which is what we did in the second step. Formally, we used the property:

$$perm\ zs \ggg \lambda zs' \rightarrow writeList\ i\ ([x] + zs') \supseteq$$
$$writeList\ i\ (zs + [x]) \gg swap\ i\ (i + \#zs). \tag{11}$$

Now that both branches are refined to code with precondition $writeList$ $i\ (ys + zs + [x])$, we go back to the main derivation:

$writeList\ (i + \#ys + \#zs + 1)\ xs \gg$
if $x \leqslant p$ **then** $writeList\ i\ (ys + zs + [x]) \gg$
                 $swap\ (i + \#ys)\ (i + \#ys + \#zs) \gg$
                 $ipartl\ p\ i\ (\#ys + 1, \#zs, \#xs)$
            else $writeList\ i\ (ys + zs + [x]) \gg$
                 $ipartl\ p\ i\ (\#ys, \#zs + 1, \#xs)$
$=$ { distributivity of **if**, (9) }
  $writeList\ i\ (ys + zs + (x : xs)) \gg$
  if $x \leqslant p$ **then** $swap\ (i + \#ys)\ (i + \#ys + \#zs) \gg$
                  $ipartl\ p\ i\ (\#ys + 1, \#zs, \#xs)$
             else $ipartl\ p\ i\ (\#ys, \#zs + 1, \#xs)$
$=$ { **write-read** and definition of $writeList$ }
  $writeList\ i\ (ys + zs + (x : xs)) \gg$
  $read\ (i + \#ys + \#zs) \ggg \lambda x \rightarrow$
  if $x \leqslant p$ **then** $swap\ (i + \#ys)\ (i + \#ys + \#zs) \gg$
                  $ipartl\ p\ i\ (\#ys + 1, \#zs, \#xs)$
             else $ipartl\ p\ i\ (\#ys, \#zs + 1, \#xs).$

We have thus established the precondition $writeList\ i\ (ys + zs + (x : xs))$. In summary, we have derived:

$ipartl :: MonadArr\ Elm\ m \Rightarrow Elm \rightarrow Int \rightarrow (Int \times Int \times Int) \rightarrow m\ (Int \times Int)$
$ipartl\ p\ i\ (ny, nz, 0)\quad = \{(ny, nz)\}$
$ipartl\ p\ i\ (ny, nz, 1 + k) =$
  $read\ (i + ny + nz) \ggg \lambda x \rightarrow$
  if $x \leqslant p$ **then** $swap\ (i + ny)\ (i + ny + nz) \gg ipartl\ p\ i\ (ny + 1, nz, k)$
             else $ipartl\ p\ i\ (ny, nz + 1, k).$

5.3   Sorting an Array

Now that we have *ipartl* derived, the rest of the work is to install it into quicksort. We intend to derive $iqsort :: \mathsf{MonadArr\ Elm}\ m \Rightarrow \mathsf{Int} \to \mathsf{Nat} \to m\ ()$ such that *isort i n* sorts the *n* elements in the array starting from index *i*. We can give it a formal specification:

$$writeList\ i\ xs \gg iqsort\ i\ (\#xs) \subseteq slowsort\ xs \ggeq writeList\ i. \tag{12}$$

That is, when *iqsort i* is run from a state initialised by *writeList i xs*, it should behave the same as *slowsort xs* $\ggeq$ *writeList i*.

The function *iqsort* can be constructed by induction on the length of the input list. For the case $xs := p : xs$, we start from the left-hand side *slowsort* $(p : xs) \ggeq$ *writeList i* and attempt to transform it to *writeList i* $(p : xs) \gg ...$, thereby construct *iqsort*. We present only the hightlights of the derivation. Firstly, *slowsort* $(p : xs) \ggeq writeList\ i$ can be transformed to:

$$partl'\ p\ ([], [], xs) \ggeq \lambda(ys, zs) \to$$
$$perm\ ys \ggeq \lambda ys' \to writeList\ i\ (ys' + [p] + zs) \gg$$
$$iqsort\ i\ (\#ys) \gg iqsort\ (i + \#ys + 1)\ (\#zs).$$

For that to work, we introduced two *perm* to permute both partitions generated by *partition*. We can do so because *perm* $\ggg$ *perm* = *perm* and thus *perm* $\ggg$ *slowsort* = *slowsort*. The term *perm zs* was combined with *partition p*, yielding *partl' p*, while *perm ys* will be needed later. We also needed (9) to split *writeList i* $(ys' + [x] + zs')$ into two parts. Assuming that (12) has been met for lists shorter than *xs*, two subexpressions are folded back to *iqsort*.

Now that we have introduced *partl'*, the next goal is to embed *ipartl*. The status of the array before the two calls to *iqsort* is given by *writeList i* $(ys' + [p] + zs)$. That is, $ys' + [p] + zs$ is stored in the array from index *i*, where *ys'* is a permutation of *ys*. The postcondition of *ipartl*, according to the specification (10), ends up with *ys* and *zs* stored consecutively. To connect the two conditions, we use a lemma that is dual to (11):

$$perm\ ys \ggeq \lambda ys' \to writeList\ i\ (ys' + [p]) \supseteq$$
$$writeList\ i\ ([p] + ys) \gg swap\ i\ (i + \#ys). \tag{13}$$

This is what the typical quicksort algorithm does: swapping the pivot with the last element of *ys*, and (13) says that it is valid because that is one of the many permutations of *ys*. With (13) and (10), the specification can be refined to:

$$writeList\ i\ (p : xs) \gg$$
$$ipartl\ p\ (i + 1)\ (0, 0, \#xs) \ggeq \lambda(ny, nz) \to swap\ i\ (i + ny) \gg$$
$$iqsort\ i\ (\#ys) \gg iqsort\ (i + \#ys + 1)\ (\#zs).$$

In summary, we have derived:

$iqsort :: \mathsf{MonadArr\ Elm}\ m \Rightarrow \mathsf{Int} \to \mathsf{Nat} \to m\ ()$

$iqsort\ i\ 0 = \{()\}$

$iqsort\ i\ n = read\ i \ggg \lambda p \to$
$\qquad ipartl\ p\ (i+1)\ (0,0,n-1) \ggg \lambda(ny, nz) \to$
$\qquad swap\ i\ (i+ny) \gg$
$\qquad iqsort\ i\ ny \gg iqsort\ (i+ny+1)\ nz.$

6   Conclusions

From a specification of sorting using the non-determinism monad, we have derived a pure quicksort for lists and a state-monadic quicksort for arrays. We hope to demonstrate that the monadic style is a good choice as a calculus for program derivation that involves non-determinism. One may perform the derivation in pointwise style, and deploy techniques that functional programmers have familiarised themselves with, such as pattern matching and induction on structures or on sizes. When preferred, one can also work in point-free style with ($\ggg$). Programs having other effects can be naturally incorporated into this framework. The way we derive stateful programs echos how we, in Dijkstra's style, reason backwards from the postcondition.

A final note: ($\ggg$) and ($\dot{\subseteq}$) naturally induce the notion of (left) factor, ($\backslash$) :: $(a \to m\ b) \to (a \to m\ c) \to b \to m\ c$, defined by the Galois connection:

$$f \ggg g \ \dot{\subseteq}\ h \ \equiv\ g \ \dot{\subseteq}\ f \backslash h.$$

Let $h :: a \to m\ c$ be a monadic specification, and $f :: a \to m\ b$ performs the computation half way, then $f \backslash h$ is the most non-deterministic (least constrained) monadic program that, when ran after the postcondition set up by f, still meets the result specified by h. With ($\backslash$), $ipartl$ and $iqsort$ can be specified by:

$ipartl\ p\ i \ \dot{\subseteq}\ write3L\ i \backslash ((second\ perm \cdot partl\ p) \ggg write2L\ i),$
$iqsort\ i \ \ \dot{\subseteq}\ writeL\ i \backslash (slowsort \ggg writeList\ i).$

In relational calculus, the *factor* is an important operator that is often associated with weakest precondition. We unfortunately cannot cover it due to space constraints.

Acknowledgements. The authors would like to thank Jeremy Gibbons for the valuable discussions during development of this work.

References

1. Backhouse, R.C., de Bruin, P.J., Malcolm, G., Voermans, E., van der Woude, J.: Relational catamorphisms. In: Möller, B. (ed.) Proceedings of the IFIP TC2/WG2.1 Working Conference on Constructing Programs, pp. 287–318. Elsevier Science Publishers (1991)

2. Bentley, J.L.: Programming Pearls, 2nd edn. Addison-Wesley, Boston (2000)
3. Bird, R.S.: Functional algorithm design. Sci. Comput. Program. **26**, 15–31 (1996)
4. Bird, R.S., de Moor, O.: Algebra of programming. In: International Series in Computer Science. Prentice Hall (1997)
5. Bird, R., Rabe, F.: How to calculate with nondeterministic functions. In: Hutton, G. (ed.) MPC 2019. LNCS, vol. 11825, pp. 138–154. Springer, Cham (2019). https://doi.org/10.1007/978-3-030-33636-3_6
6. Dijkstra, E.W.: A Discipline of Programming. Prentice Hall, Upper Saddle River (1976)
7. Gibbons, J., Hinze, R.: Just do it: simple monadic equational reasoning. In: Danvy, O. (ed.) International Conference on Functional Programming, pp. 2–14. ACM Press (2011)
8. Gill, A., Kmett, E.: The monad transformer library (2014). https://hackage.haskell.org/package/mtl
9. Hoare, C.A.R.: Algorithm 63: partition. Commun. ACM **4**(7), 321 (1961)
10. Kiselyov, O.: How to restrict a monad without breaking it: the winding road to the Set monad, July 2013. http://okmij.org/ftp/Haskell/set-monad.html
11. Kiselyov, O., Ishii, H.: Freer monads, more extensible effects. In: Reppy, J.H. (ed.) Symposium on Haskell, pp. 94–105. ACM Press (2015)
12. Moggi, E.: Computational lambda-calculus and monads. In: Parikh, R. (ed.) Logic in Computer Science, pp. 14–23. IEEE Computer Society Press (1989)
13. de Moor, O., Gibbons, J.: Pointwise relational programming. In: Rus, T. (ed.) AMAST 2000. LNCS, vol. 1816, pp. 371–390. Springer, Heidelberg (2000). https://doi.org/10.1007/3-540-45499-3_27
14. Pauwels, K., Schrijvers, T., Mu, S.-C.: Handling local state with global state. In: Hutton, G. (ed.) MPC 2019. LNCS, vol. 11825, pp. 18–44. Springer, Cham (2019). https://doi.org/10.1007/978-3-030-33636-3_2

Language-Integrated Query with Nested Data Structures and Grouping

Rui Okura[✉] and Yukiyoshi Kameyama

University of Tsukuba, Tsukuba, Japan
`rui@logic.cs.tsukuba.ac.jp, kameyama@acm.org`

Abstract. Language-integrated query adds to database query the power of high-level programming languages such as abstraction, compositionality, and nested data structures. Cheney et al. designed a two-level typed language for it and showed that any closed term of suitable type can be normalized to a single SQL query which does not have nested data structures nor nested SELECT clauses.

This paper extends their language to cover the GROUP BY clause in SQL to express grouping and aggregate functions. Although the GROUP BY clause is frequently used, it is not covered by existing studies on efficient implementation of language-integrated queries. In fact, it seems impossible to express composition of two aggregate functions by a single aggregate function, therefore, there exists a query with nested GROUP BY clauses which has no equivalent query without nested one. However, since several database engines such as PostgreSQL allow nested queries, we can still ask if it is possible to convert an arbitrary query with grouping and aggregation to a single query in SQL which allows nested queries, but disallows nested data structures such as a table of tables.

This paper solves the latter question affirmatively. Our key observation is that the GROUP BY clause in SQL does two different kinds of things: manipulating input/output data and grouping with aggregation, the former can be transformed, but may have complex types, while the latter cannot be transformed, but has simple types. Hence, we decouple the GROUP BY clause and introduce primitives into our language-integrated query to obtain a calculus which can express GROUP BY. We then show our language has the normalization property that every query is converted to a single query which does not have nested data structures. We conduct simple benchmarks which show that queries in our language can be transformed to efficient SQL queries.

Keywords: Database · Language-integrated query · Grouping · Aggregation · Normalization · Type safety

1 Introduction

Language-integrated query is gaining increasingly bigger attention by integrating a database query language such as SQL with a high-level programming language. Microsoft's LINQ[1] [1] is a typical example used by various applications. Existing languages for language-integrated query allow one to interact with a database management

---

[1] https://docs.microsoft.com/en-us/dotnet/csharp/linq/.

© Springer Nature Switzerland AG 2020
K. Nakano and K. Sagonas (Eds.): FLOPS 2020, LNCS 12073, pp. 139–158, 2020.
https://doi.org/10.1007/978-3-030-59025-3_9

system, construct abstraction mechanisms and complex data structures, and compute over them.

A classic problem in language-integrated queries is the query-avalanche problem; composing two queries and executing the result of the composition may sometimes need a huge number of transactions with a database [2]. Another classic problem is that nested data structures such as a list of lists are allowed in language-integrated queries, while they are not allowed in SQL, hence they are not directly implementable. Cooper [3] proposed normalization on queries to solve these problems. He showed that a closed query of non-nested type[2] can be always transformed ('normalized') to a form which does not use abstractions, nested data structures, or nested comprehensions, hence can be translated to SQL. Moreover, the result of normalization is a single SQL query, solving the query avalanche problem. Cheney et al. [4] formalized his idea in a two-level typed language with quotation and anti-quotation to give theoretical foundation for it, and Suzuki et al. [5] implemented it via tagless-final encoding [6] as an extensible type-safe framework. However, none of the studies mentioned above targeted the features of grouping and aggregate functions, which are indispensable in many realistic queries.

This paper addresses the problem of introducing grouping and aggregate functions into language-integrated queries while keeping efficient implementation. Grouping (the GROUP BY clause in SQL) classifies data records based on the given *keys*, and computes aggregated values for each group of records. Aggregation is a reduction operation, which computes a single value from a list of values in each group.

An example in SQL is given as follows:

```
SELECT p.orderId AS oid, SUM(p.quantity) AS sales
FROM products AS p
GROUP BY p.orderId
```

This query gets data records from the products table, classifies them into groups based on the orderId key, and returns, for each group, a record which consists of an orderId and the summation of the quantity. SUM is called an *aggregate* function, which computes the sum of all records for each group, and the GROUP BY clause specifies the key for this grouping. Following Cheney et al., we write $\mathbf{for}(x \leftarrow L)\ M$ for the following SQL query:

```
SELECT M
FROM L AS x
```

and we temporally introduce a new construct $\mathbf{gfor}(x \leftarrow L;\ K)\ M$ for the SQL query with grouping:

```
SELECT M
FROM L AS x
GROUP BY K
```

---

[2] We say that a table type (a bag type of a record type) is not nested, if each component type of the record is a basic type such as string, integer, or floating-point number.

While the GROUP BY clause is simple to handle in SQL, it is problematic as a construct in language-integrated query, which will be explained as follows.

First, there seems no normalization rules for the combination of **gfor** and another control structure such as **for** or **gfor** itself. A normalization rule is a rule to transform a query to a normal form which directly corresponds to an SQL query, and Cheney et al. showed a number of normalization rules such as $\mathbf{for}(x \leftarrow \mathbf{for}(y \leftarrow L) M) N \rightsquigarrow \mathbf{for}(y \leftarrow L) \mathbf{for}(x \leftarrow M) N$ which are sufficient to flatten nested control structures[3]. On the other hand, **gfor** does not seem to have such normalization rules which work in general. For instance, $\mathbf{gfor}(x \leftarrow \mathbf{for}(y \leftarrow L) M; K) N$ cannot be normalized to a natural candidate $\mathbf{for}(y \leftarrow L) (\mathbf{gfor}(x \leftarrow M; K) N)$, which is semantically different. There are other combinations of constructors such as **gfor-gfor** which also suffer from the same problem. Informally it is explained by an example: suppose we are given a table for GPAs for all students in a university, which has several schools and each school has departments. We want to determine, for each school, the department whose students' average GPA is the best among the departments in the school. Clearly, we need to compute average per department, and then take the maximum value per school, each of which corresponds to grouping and aggregate functions AVG and MAX. Therefore, we need to have nested **gfor** constructs to obtain the correct result.

It follows that our target language for SQL need to have *subqueries*, which means an input (or an output) of a query is the result of another query. Several SQL dialects including PostgreSQL[4] indeed allow subqueries, hence we also assume that our SQL backend allows (an arbitrary nesting of) subqueries.

Although allowing subqueries in SQL solves the problem of nested control structures, we still have a problem of nested data structures. To see this, let Q_1 be $\mathbf{gfor}(x \leftarrow L; K) M$ where M has a nested data structure such that each component type of the record is a bag of a basic type. Let Q_2 be a query $\mathbf{for}(y \leftarrow Q_1) N$ whose type is not nested. We expect that Q_2 is normalized to a query which is translated to a single SQL, in particular, the resulting query has no nested data structures. Unfortunately, normalization does not work for this query, since it contains **gfor** which is a barrier for any normalization to occur. One may think that the **for** construct in Q_1 (at the outermost position of Q_2) can be moved inward, and we can rewrite Q_2 into $\mathbf{gfor}(x \leftarrow L; K) \mathbf{for}(y \leftarrow M) N$, which can be further transformed. However, this rewriting has another problem; if N has an aggregate function which operates on grouping outside of Q_2, the aggregate function goes under this **gfor**, rather than grouping outside of Q_2, leading to an incorrect result. Namely, this rewriting may not be semantics-preserving.

In summary, having **gfor** in language-integrated query causes a big problem and most desirable properties which Cheney et al. proved for the language without **gfor** will be lost. Hence, it has been an open problem to have grouping and aggregate functions in language-integrated query, while keeping the desirable properties such as normalization to non-nested data structures.

---

[3] Queries that has a **for** construct inside another **for** construct are called queries with nested control structures.

[4] http://postgresql.org.

This paper solves the problem above under the assumption that the normal form may contain nested control structures. We start by observing that the **gfor** construct in language-integrated queries does too many things; it performs not only grouping, but also aggregation and construction of (possibly complicated) output. In the context of this study, these processes have quite different nature, and should be treated separately.

- Grouping and Aggregation; examples are taking an average score among a department, and getting the maximum average score among a school. These operations, if combined with other control structures, cannot be transformed, while their input and output types are restricted to basic types. (Note that aggregate functions are provided in the target SQL, and they work on a collection of basic values and return a reduced value of the same type as input.)
- Output Construction; an example is constructing a nested list whose element is a student-score pair whose score is above the average in her department. This operation may have complicated types (arbitrarily nested types), however, they are standard operations made from **for**, hence, they can be transformed by Cheney et al.'s normalization rules.

Since **gfor** is a combination of them, we cannot normalize it, nor its data type may be nested, and we got stuck. A lesson learned from here is that we should *decouple* the two, then we can normalize output construction to normal form, while grouping/aggregation have non-nested types, hence there are no obstacles to obtain a normal form without nested data structures. This is a rather simple idea but as far as we know, there is no similar research in this direction, and the present paper is a straightforward realization of this simple idea.

We design our source language based on Cooper's work and Cheney et al.'s work, and add the functionality of grouping and aggregate functions by a new construct instead of the **gfor** construct. The new construct captures only the first process of the above two, namely, grouping and aggregation, while the second process is represented by the existing constructs provided by Cheney et al. We argue that most functionality of GROUP BY in SQL can be recovered by combining the new constructs and existing ones by some sort of rewriting. We introduce a type system and then give a set of transformation rules which transform all the typable queries of an appropriate type[5] to a single SQL query, thus avoiding the Query Avalanche problem completely.

The rest of this paper is organized as follows. Section 2 informally discusses how to resolve nested clauses with grouping. Section 3 introduces our languages and transformation rules, and Sect. 4 introduces adding grouping to the language. The performance measurements for our language and implementation are explained in Sect. 5. Finally, we state concluding remarks in Sect. 6.

2   Examples of Grouping and Aggregation

In this section, we consider several examples for language-integrated query, and informally discuss our new primitives for aggregation and grouping. Formal development will be presented in the next section.

---

[5] An SQL-convertible query must compute a bag of records whose fields are of base types. Hence, we normalize queries of such types only.

A database used in our example has two tables in Fig. 1.

	products			orders	
pid	name	price	oid	pid	qty
110	shirt	100	1	110	2
111	T-shirt	200	1	111	3
210	pants	500	2	110	5
310	suit	1000	2	210	10
			2	310	15
			3	310	20

Fig. 1. Sample database tables

The products table (left) has the columns of product ID (pid), name (name), and price (price), while the orders table (right) has the columns of order ID (oid), product ID (pid), and quantity (qty). Let us first introduce a query without grouping and aggregation as follows:

$$Q = \textbf{for}(p \leftarrow \textbf{table}(\text{``products''}))$$
$$\textbf{for}(o \leftarrow \textbf{table}(\text{``orders''}))$$
$$\textbf{where}\ (p.\text{pid} = o.\text{pid})$$
$$\textbf{yield}\ \{\text{oid} = o.\text{oid}, \text{sales} = p.\text{price} * o.\text{qty}\}$$

which corresponds to the following SQL query:

```
SELECT o.oid AS oid, p.price * o.qty AS sales
FROM products AS p, orders AS o
WHERE p.pid = o.pid
```

The collection is a multiset, or a *bag*. The above query scans tables, and returns a bag of records consisting of two fields oid and sales, whose values are order ID and qty multiplied by the price. In this paper, we do not consider the value NULL, and assume all fields have some values of appropriate type.

The next query uses an aggregate function without grouping, shown below:

$$Q_0 = \textbf{yield}\ \mathcal{A}_\alpha(\textbf{for}(p \leftarrow \textbf{table}(\text{``products''}))$$
$$\textbf{for}(o \leftarrow \textbf{table}(\text{``orders''}))$$
$$\textbf{where}\ (p.\text{pid} = o.\text{pid})$$
$$\textbf{yield}\ \{\text{sales} = p.\text{price} * o.\text{qty}\})$$
$$\text{Where}\ \alpha = \{(\text{sales}, \text{SUM}, \text{sales\_sum})\}$$

which corresponds to the following SQL query:

```
SELECT SUM(p.price * o.qty) AS sales_sum
FROM products AS p, orders AS o
WHERE p.pid = o.pid
```

where SUM is an *aggregate* function, which computes the sum of $p.$price $*$ $o.$qty for *all* collections in the constructed table, and $\mathcal{A}_\alpha$ is the new operator in our language, standing for aggregation.

The role of the new operator $\mathcal{A}_\alpha$ is to apply aggregate functions to the components specified in α. The component values are taken from its argument. In the above example $\alpha = \{(\text{sales}, \text{SUM}, \text{sales\_sum})\}$ specifies that $\mathcal{A}_\alpha$ should retrieve values from the sales field of the argument, applies SUM to the values, and returns the value with the field name sales_sum. Thus, the above query in our language does exactly the same thing as the query in SQL.

Clearly the notation in our language is heavier than the corresponding expression in SQL, but it is justified by the following argument. The essential difference between the two is the position the function SUM appears at: in SQL (the lower query), SUM appears at deep inside of the query, while in our language (the upper query), it appears at the outermost position. Since SUM in our language appears remotely from its real argument, we need to specify which field name it will pick up, and the heavier notation above is necessary. But our notation has a merit that the target table of aggregate functions is clearer. In the above example, the target table of SUM is the argument computed by the **for** expression, while the target of SUM in SQL is determined by its external context which is not always clear. In this example, there are no GROUP BY clauses in the query so the target table is the whole expression, but in general, there may be several GROUP BY clauses around SUM, and they form a sort of binder-bindee correspondence. But, since they are not really binders (no variables are used to make the correspondence explicit), the correspondence is fragile under rewriting, or normalization. When designing normalization rules, we always need to consider if the binder-bindee correspondence is kept correctly, which is quite cumbersome, and sometimes impossible (note that our language has the standard lambda binding and function application, hence substitution for variables may occur at any time of computation).

We then add the functionality of grouping to the $\mathcal{A}_\alpha$ operator. The extended operator is denoted by $\mathcal{G}_{(\kappa,\alpha)}$ where α is the specification for aggregate functions as in $\mathcal{A}_\alpha$. The extra parameter κ is a list of field names and considered as grouping keys on which grouping takes place. To show an example, we perform grouping with the example above.

$$Q_1 = \mathcal{G}_{(\text{oid},\alpha)}(\mathbf{for}(p \leftarrow \mathbf{table}(\text{``products''}))$$
$$\mathbf{for}(o \leftarrow \mathbf{table}(\text{``orders''}))$$
$$\mathbf{where}\ (p.\text{pid} = o.\text{pid})$$
$$\mathbf{yield}\ \{\text{oid} = o.\text{oid}, \text{sales} = p.\text{price} * o.\text{qty}\})$$
$$\text{Where}\ \alpha = \{(\text{sales}, \text{SUM}, \text{sales\_sum})\}$$

which corresponds to the following SQL query:

```
SELECT o.oid AS oid, SUM(p.price * o.qty) AS sales_sum
FROM products AS p, orders AS o
WHERE p.pid = o.pid
GROUP BY o.oid
```

In the lower query, we have added the order ID field to the record created dynamically, which will be the grouping key as specified by the GROUP BY clause on the last line. In the upper query, we also do the same thing, and in addition to it, the grouping operator specifies not only α, but also the order ID field as the grouping key. When we execute the upper query, it groups the table created by the **for** clause based on the order ID field, computes the sum of qty multiplied by price for each group, and then returns a record consisting of the order ID field, and the summation.

The merit and demerit of expressing grouping and aggregate functions in terms of the $\mathcal{G}_{(\kappa,\alpha)}$ operator inherit those for the $\mathcal{A}_\alpha$ operator. In addition, one query in SQL may have more than one GROUP BY clause, and then the correspondence between the GROUP BY clause and aggregate functions are even more complicated, and will be error prone. On the contrary, our grouping and aggregate functions are expressed by a single operator, hence we seldom make any 'scope'-related issues. Note that $\mathcal{G}_{(\kappa,\alpha)}$ is a natural extension of $\mathcal{A}_\alpha$, but for a technical reason, $\mathcal{G}_{(\cdot,\alpha)}$ (no grouping keys) is equivalent to **yield** $\mathcal{A}_\alpha$, which returns a singleton consisting of $\mathcal{A}_\alpha$. Modulo this small twist, the former extends the latter, and $\mathcal{A}_\alpha$ exists only for the purpose of explanation.

In SQL, we can group records, aggregate values, and construct complicated data from them all in one query. As we discussed in the previous section, it is problematic to do all three things in a single primitive, therefore, our language does not have such a super operator. Instead, our operator $\mathcal{G}_{(\kappa,\alpha)}$ can do grouping and aggregation only. The resulting value of applying this operator to an expression is a bag of records consisting of the results of aggregate functions, whose types are not nested. Any operation after applying aggregate functions are disallowed by this primitive. For instance, the following query has no direct counterpart in our language:

```
SELECT o.oid AS oid,
       SUM(p.price * o.qty)/SUM(o.qty) AS average
FROM products AS p, orders AS o
WHERE p.pid = o.pid
GROUP BY o.oid
```

where we divide one aggregated value by another. It is still no problem to pre-compute values before aggregation such as SUM(p.price * o.qty).

We can recover the lost expressiveness by simple rewriting. A query which is equivalent to the above one may be written in our language as follows:

$$Q_2 = \textbf{for}(q \leftarrow \mathcal{G}_{(\text{oid},\alpha)}(\textbf{for}(p \leftarrow \textbf{table}(\text{``products''}))$$
$$\textbf{for}(o \leftarrow \textbf{table}(\text{``orders''}))$$
$$\textbf{where } (p.\text{pid} = o.\text{pid})$$
$$\textbf{yield } \{\text{oid} = o.\text{oid}, \text{sales} = p.\text{price} * o.\text{qty},$$
$$\text{qty} = o.\text{qty}\}))$$
$$\textbf{yield } \{\text{oid} = q.\text{oid}, \text{average} = q.\text{sales\_sum}/q.\text{qty\_sum}\}$$
$$\text{Where } \alpha = \{(\text{sales}, \text{SUM}, \text{sales\_sum}), (\text{qty}, \text{SUM}, \text{qty\_sum})\}$$

Thus we divide one big process performed by the GROUP BY clause into a combination of triply nested control structures **for**-$\mathcal{G}_{(\kappa,\alpha)}$-**for**. It is arguable that this decomposition (or 'decoupling') is beneficial for performance, but we believe that, as long as the nested data structures are concerned, our decomposition is the only way to normalize *all* queries systematically into a single SQL query which has subqueries but does not have nested data structures.

The above query in our language corresponds to the following query in SQL:

```
SELECT q.oid AS oid, q.sales_sum / q.qty_sum AS average
FROM (SELECT o.oid AS oid,
             SUM(p.price * o.qty) AS sales_sum,
             SUM(o.qty) AS qty_sum
      FROM products AS p, orders AS o
      WHERE p.pid = o.pid
      GROUP BY o.oid) AS q
```

which uses a subquery and performs badly if we compare it with the above single SQL query. In this paper, we do not talk about optimization of queries which will be reported in a separate paper.

3   The Language with Aggregate Functions

This section explains the base language for language-integrated query in the existing studies, and introduces our language with aggregate functions. Grouping will be added to the language in the next section.

3.1   Base Language

The base language Quel is essentially the same as Cooper's source language [3] without effects (which is 'nearly the same' as Nested Relational Calculus [7]), and Cheney et al.'s T-LINQ [4] without quotation and code generation. Figure 2 gives the syntax of types and terms in Quel where t denotes a name of a database table, and l denotes a field name of a record.

Base types	$O ::= \text{Int} \mid \text{Bool} \mid \text{String}$
Types	$A, B ::= O \mid A \rightarrow B \mid \text{Bag } A \mid \{\overline{l : A}\}$
Type environment	$\Gamma ::= \phi \mid \Gamma, x : A$
Terms	$L, M, N ::= \lambda x.\, M \mid M\, N \mid \oplus (\overline{M}) \mid M \uplus N \mid x \mid c$
	$\mid \textbf{for}(x \leftarrow M)\, N \mid \textbf{where } L\, M \mid \textbf{yield } M \mid []$
	$\mid \textbf{exists } M \mid \textbf{table}(t) \mid \{\overline{l = M}\} \mid L.l$

Fig. 2. Types and terms of Quel

Types are either a basic type (integers, booleans, and strings), a function type $A \rightarrow B$, a bag type $\text{Bag } A$, or a record type $\{\overline{l : A}\}$ where $\overline{l : A}$ is abbreviation of a sequence $l_1 : A_1, \cdots, l_k : A_k$ for some $k \geq 0$. The bag type is the type for multisets in which the order of elements is irrelevant and the number of elements matters. A record type $\{\overline{l : O}\}$ where O is a basic type is called a *flat* type. The bag type of a flat record type is also called a flat type. Flat types are important in the study of language-integrated query, since SQL allows only values of flat types.

Terms are either lambda terms augmented with a primitive operator $\oplus$, a variable x, a constant c, $\{\overline{l = M}\}$ (record), $L.l$ (selection), or constructed by database primitives such as $M \uplus N$ (multiset union), $\textbf{for}(x \leftarrow M)\, N$ (bag comprehension) $\textbf{where } L\, M$ (conditional), $\textbf{yield } M$ (singleton), $\textbf{exists } M$ (emptiness test), and $\textbf{table}(t)$ (database table with name t). The term $\textbf{for}(x \leftarrow M)\, N$ corresponds to the SELECT statement in SQL, which computes N for each element in (the value of) M, and returns their multiset union. The term $\textbf{where } L\, M$ returns the value of M if L returns true, and returns the empty bag $[]$ otherwise. The term $\textbf{yield } M$ creates a singleton multiset consisting of the value of M. The term $\textbf{exists } M$ is the emptiness test for a multiset M and returns a boolean value. The variable x in $\lambda x.\, M$ and $\textbf{for}(x \leftarrow L)\, M$ are bound in M. As usual, we identify two terms which are α-equivalent.

3.2 The Language Quela

We add aggregate functions to Quel, and call the extended language Quela. Figure 3 defines new syntax in Quela where a sequence of dots means the corresponding syntax in Quel.

$$\text{Terms } L, M, N ::= \ldots \mid \mathcal{A}_\alpha(L)$$

$$\text{A-Spec} \quad \alpha ::= \{(l, \odot, l')\}$$

Fig. 3. Terms of Quela

The term $\mathcal{A}_\alpha(L)$ applies aggregate functions to L as specified by α. Here, α is a finite collection of triples of a field name in the input, an aggregate function $\odot$ such as MAX, MIN, AVG, COUNT, and SUM[6] and a field name in the output. An example of α is $\{(l_1, \text{MAX}, l_1'), (l_2, \text{SUM}, l_2')\}$, which means that we apply MAX to the values of the l_1 field and SUM to the values of the l_2 field, and returns a record consisting of these data with new field names l_1' and l_2'.

Quela has the standard call-by-value, left-to-right semantics. Let us explain how the term $\mathcal{A}_\alpha(L)$ is evaluated where $\alpha = \{(l_1, \odot_1, l_1'), \cdots, (l_k, \odot_k, l_k')\}$. L is an expression of record type whose fields contain $l_1, \cdots, l_k$. For each $i \leq k$, we apply the aggregate function $\odot_i$ to the l_i-component of the value of L to get an aggregated value which we call v_i. Then we return a record $\{l_1' = v_1, \cdots, l_k' = v_k\}$ as the result. For instance, suppose L is a bag with two elements $[\{l_1 = 10, l_2 = 20\}, \{l_1 = 30, l_2 = 10\}]$. Then the term $\mathcal{A}_{\{(l_1, \text{SUM}, l_1'), (l_2, \text{MAX}, l_2')\}}(L)$ is evaluated to $\{l_1' = 40, \ l_2' = 20\}$.

Quela is a statically typed language, and Fig. 4 lists a few interesting typing rules.

$$\text{FOR} \quad \frac{\Gamma \vdash M : \mathsf{Bag}\ A \quad \Gamma, x : A \vdash N : \mathsf{Bag}\ B}{\Gamma \vdash \mathbf{for}(x \leftarrow M)\ N : \mathsf{Bag}\ B}$$

$$\text{EXISTS} \quad \frac{\Gamma \vdash M : \mathsf{Bag}\ \{\overline{l_i : O_i}\}}{\Gamma \vdash \mathbf{exists}\ M : Bool}$$

$$\text{AGGREGATION}$$
$$\frac{\Gamma \vdash L : \mathsf{Bag}\ \{\overline{k_j : O_j}\} \quad \alpha = \{\overline{(l_i, \odot_i, l_i')}\} \quad \overline{l_i} \subseteq \overline{k_j} \quad \odot_i : \mathsf{Bag}\ O_j \to O_j \ (\text{for all } l_i \ s.t.\ l_i = k_j)}{\Gamma \vdash \mathcal{A}_\alpha(L) : \{\overline{l_i' : O_j}\} \ (\text{for all } l_i \ s.t.\ l_i = k_j)}$$

Fig. 4. Type system of Quela

The first typing rule represents the one for the **for**-construct, or bag comprehension. The term $\mathbf{for}(x \leftarrow M)\ N$ computes a bag N for each element x in M, and takes the multi-set union for all the results. Hence, M and N must have bag types, and x is bound in N. The second one is for the **exists**-construct. Here we need to constrain that the argument M must have a flat bag type (notice that the type of each field is a basic type O_i). Otherwise, we cannot normalize such a term to an SQL query where nested data structures are not allowed. The third typing rule is for aggregate application $\mathcal{A}_\alpha(L)$. The A-Spec α specifies which aggregate function should be used for each field of the given record. We require that, for each l_i, there exists k_j such that $k_j = l_i$. Then the aggregate function $\odot_i$ must have the type $\mathsf{Bag}\ O_j \to O_j$. It is important to restrict all the type of fields O_j must be basic types. This is again for the sake of guaranteeing the non-nested property of normal forms in Quela. This restriction does not affect the expressiveness of Quela, since we can always insert a **for**-expression between $\mathcal{A}_\alpha$ and L to throw away unused fields of non-basic types.

Other typing rules are standard in simply typed lambda calculus, and omitted here.

---

[6] In this study the set of aggregate functions is left unspecified, but we assume that they must operate on simple types. See the type system.

3.3 Normalization of Quela

Cooper has shown that any query of an appropriate type in his language can be normalized to a simple form which directly corresponds to a single SQL query, thus solving the query avalanche problem.

We have the same property for Quela. More precisely, given a closed term in Quela which has a flat bag type (a bag-of-record type whose fields are of basic types) can be transformed to normal form, which is directly convertible to an SQL query. In the rest of this section, we explain how we can show this property. Note that we assume that the target SQL to allow subqueries (or nested queries), so nested control structures are not problematic. However, the normal form must not create or manipulate nested data structures (such as a record of records, or a table of tables), our goal is to eliminate the latter.

Figure 11 in the appendix shows normalization rules essentially proposed by Cheney et al., after slight adjustment for Quela. For the newly added primitive $\mathcal{A}_\alpha(L)$ we do not have normalization rules[7] as explained in earlier sections. ($\mathcal{A}_\alpha(L)$ is a 'barrier' for normalization.) Hence, we need to add the term $\mathcal{A}_\alpha(L)$ to the normal form of appropriate type. Figure 5 defines the normal form for Quela.

Query	$U ::= U_1 \uplus U_2 \mid [\,] \mid F$
Comprehension	$F ::= \mathbf{for}(x \leftarrow H)\, F \mid H \mid Z$
Table	$H ::= \mathbf{table}(t)$
Body	$Z ::= \mathbf{where}\, B\, Z \mid \mathbf{yield}\, R$
Record	$R ::= \{\overline{l = B}\} \mid x \mid \mathcal{A}_\alpha(U)$
Primitive	$B ::= \mathbf{exists}\, U \mid \oplus(\overline{B}) \mid x.l \mid c$
A-Spec	$\alpha ::= \{\overline{(l, \odot, l')}\}$

Fig. 5. Normal form of Quela

For the term $\mathcal{A}_\alpha(U)$, U must be of flat bag type, and so is the whole term, hence no nested data structures are used in this term, which is the key of our proof of the non-nested property.

We will formally state the desirable properties on 'non-nestedness' of the result of our translation. Here, we take the minimalist approach, and we define flat types, instead of defining nested data types and non-nested data types in general. We call a record type whose components are basic types as flat record types. A flat bag type is the type Bag F where F is a flat record type. Flat types are either basic types, flat record types, or flat bag types.

Theorem 1. *1. Normalization rules for Quela preserve typing, namely, $\Gamma \vdash L : A$ and $L \rightsquigarrow M$, then $\Gamma \vdash M : A$.*

---

[7] When L is an empty bag, we can transform the whole expression, but it is a special case which does not contribute general patterns.

2. *For any typable term, normalization weakly terminates, namely, If $\Gamma \vdash L : A$, then there is a normal form N such that $L \rightsquigarrow N$.*
3. *Suppose N is normal form, and $\vdash N : F$ is derivable where F is a flat type. Then its type derivation contains only flat types.*

The item 3 is crucial in our work, as it implies that all closed normal form of flat type does not use any nested data structures as intermediate data, which is necessary for it to be translated to an SQL query.

Let us briefly mention the proof of the theorem.

Item 1 can be proved by straightforward induction.

Item 2 is proved by making an analogy; Quela's aggregation is a 'barrier' for normalization since it has no transformation (normalization) rules. In Cheney et al.'s work, the **exists** primitive is similar, as it has no transformation rules other than the rare cases when its argument happens to be a value. Hence, as far as we are concerned with weak normalization property, we can treat our aggregation primitive just like the **exists** primitive, and the proof of Cheney et al.'s weak normalization theorem can be re-used without essential modification.

Item 3 is proved by induction on type derivation for a slightly stronger lemma: if $\Gamma \vdash N : \mathsf{Bag}\ \{\overline{l_i : O_i}\}$ is derivable for some $\Gamma = x_1 : F_1, \cdots, x_n : F_n$ where F_i are flat types, and N is normal form, then the typing derivation does not contain non-flat types. For this inductive proof, it is essential that our aggregation operator works over terms of flat types only. The rest of the proof is easy and omitted.

Note that, for this property to hold, we need to restrict the argument of $\mathcal{A}_\alpha$ be flat types; otherwise the item 3 does not hold in general.

The normal form is actually easy to translate to an SQL query. Figure 6 gives the translation for only one important case.

$$\llbracket \mathbf{yield}\ \mathcal{A}_\alpha(U) \rrbracket = \textbf{SELECT}\ \overline{\odot(e)\ \textbf{AS}\ l'}$$
$$\textbf{FROM}\ \overline{t\ \textbf{AS}\ y}\ \textbf{WHERE}\ B$$
$$where\ \llbracket U \rrbracket = \textbf{SELECT}\ \overline{e\ \textbf{AS}\ l}\ \textbf{FROM}\ \overline{t\ \textbf{AS}\ y}\ \textbf{WHERE}\ B$$
$$and\ \alpha = \{(\overline{l, \odot, l'})\}$$

Fig. 6. Translation to SQL

For a normal form N, we write $\llbracket N \rrbracket$ for its translation to SQL. For $\mathcal{A}_\alpha(U)$, we first convert U to an SQL query, and then apply aggregate functions $\odot_i$ for each e_i designated by the field l_i. We finally collect all fields and return the answer.

3.4 Comparison with Classic Results

The statement of Theorem 1 in the previous subsection resembles the 'conservativity' property studied in classical database theory. Among all, Libkin and Wong [8] formulated a simple calculus with aggregation, and proved that, for any query whose type has height n, there exists an equivalent query which has height n or lower. Here the height is the depth of nested data structures, and by taking n as 0, we have a statement which is very similar to the item 3 of Theorem 1.

However, there are several differences between Libkin and Wong's work and ours, and their result does not subsume ours (and vice versa).

The first difference is that the primitive data structure in their language is sets, whereas ours is bags (multi-sets). This difference is minor, as we can adjust their theory to the one based on multi-sets.

The second, more essential difference is that they have more normalization rules than we have; one of their rules (in our syntax) is:

$$\mathcal{A}_{(1,\mathrm{SUM},\mathrm{l}')}(L_1 \cup L_2) = \mathcal{A}_{(1,\mathrm{SUM},\mathrm{l}')}(L_1) + \mathcal{A}_{(1,\mathrm{SUM},\mathrm{l}')}(L_2)$$

They regard this equation as a left-to-right rewrite rule. This rewriting often makes a query rather inefficient; it replaces an aggregation to normal addition, and if $L_1 \cup L_2$ in the above equation is replaced by a union of 100 bags, then the right-hand side will be the sum of 100 elements, which is clearly slower to execute than an aggregate function.

The third difference is that their language does not have grouping, whereas ours has, as we will see in the next section. Adding grouping to the language would make the above efficiency problem even more serious; there is no simple way to express grouping and aggregation for $L_1 \cup L_2$ in terms of those for L_1 and those for L_2.

One may wonder why we successfully get the same (or very similar) theorem while our set of normalization rules is strictly smaller than theirs. The trick is that, our primitives for aggregation (and grouping) are finer than those primitives in existing studies.[8] The aggregation primitive in Libkin and Wong's study is:

$$\Sigma\{\{e_1 \mid x \in e_2\}\}$$

where e_1 and e_2 are expressions for queries and x is bound in e_1. The above primitive sums up the result of $e_1[a_i/x]$ for all $a_i \in e_2$. As the syntax reveals, their primitive can manipulate input of Σ by the expression e_1, whereas our primitive $\mathcal{A}_\alpha$ cannot. In our language, constructing e_1 from $x \in e_2$ should be expressed by another expression (it can be written as $\mathbf{for}(x \leftarrow e_2)\ [e_1]$ if we ignore labels and the difference of set and multi-set), and we can recover their aggregation primitive by combining these two. The bonus of this decomposition is Theorem 1.

In summary, while we obtained nothing new in theory (a very similar theorem is already known in old days, which can be adjusted to our setting), we claim that we have made solid progress towards a practical theory as advocated by Cheney et al., since much more efficient queries can be generated by our method. In the subsequent sections we will back up our claim by adding groping and showing performance.

---

[8] In the introduction of the present paper, we already explained it against SQL's GROUP BY.

4   Adding Grouping to the Language

The language Quela in the previous section does not have grouping, and this section extends it to the language Quelg, which has grouping.

One might think that this extension is a big step, however, surprisingly, the difference is quite small, since grouping with aggregation behaves quite similar to aggregation. As before, the grouping operator cannot be normalized but works on terms of flat types, so it does not affect the important property that the normal form does not have nested data structures.

We briefly explain in this section the extended language and its properties.

The extended syntax is defined in Fig. 7. We introduce a new operator $\mathcal{G}_{(\kappa,\alpha)}(L)$ for grouping and aggregation, where κ is a list of field names, and represents the keys of this grouping, and α is the same as α in $\mathcal{A}_\alpha(L)$.

$$\text{Terms } L, M, N ::= \dots \mid \ \mathcal{G}_{(\kappa,\alpha)}(L)$$

Fig. 7. Syntax of Quelg

Intuitively, $\mathcal{G}_{(\kappa,\alpha)}(L)$ gets an input table from (the result of computing) L, performs grouping based on the keys in κ, and then apply aggregate functions listed in α. The result of this computation is a table whose element is a record consisting of the keys and the fields with the results of aggregate functions. As a simple example, the term $\mathcal{G}_{(\mathrm{oid},\{(\mathrm{qty},\mathrm{MAX},\mathrm{qty\_max})\})}(\mathbf{table}(\text{``orders''}))$ evaluates to $[\{\mathrm{oid} = 1, \mathrm{qty\_sum} = 3\}, \{\mathrm{oid} = 2, \mathrm{qty\_sum} = 15\}, \{\mathrm{oid} = 3, \mathrm{qty\_sum} = 20\}]$.

Typing rules for Quelg are those for Quela plus the rule shown in Fig. 8.

GROUPING
$$\frac{\Gamma \vdash L : \mathbf{Bag}\ \{\overline{\kappa_i : O_i}, \overline{l_i : O_i'}\} \quad \kappa = \{\overline{l_i}\} \quad \alpha = \{(\overline{l_i, \odot_i, l_i'})\} \quad \odot_i : \mathbf{Bag}\ O_i' \to O_i'}{\Gamma \vdash \mathcal{G}_{(\kappa,\alpha)}(L) : \mathbf{Bag}\ \{\overline{\kappa_i : O_i}, \overline{l_i' : O_i'}\}}$$

Fig. 8. Type system of Quelg

The new typing rule is for grouping. To type $\mathcal{G}_{(\kappa,\alpha)}(L)$, we need to have L is a flat bag type $\mathbf{Bag}\ \{\overline{\kappa_i : O_i}, \overline{l_i : O_i'}\}$. The keys for grouping κ must appear in this list, and here we assume that κ_i appears in the first half of this sequence. The aggregate functions specified in α must be of function type from a bag of a basic type to the basic type. Finally, $\mathcal{G}_{(\kappa,\alpha)}(L)$ has the same type as L.

For the language Quelg, the normal form becomes a bit more complicated than those for Quela, because the new primitive for grouping returns a value of bag type, and it is still normal, hence each syntactic category of bag type must have the new primitive as normal form. Figure 9 defines the normal form for Quelg.

$$
\begin{array}{lll}
\text{Query} & U ::= U_1 \uplus U_2 \mid [\,] \mid F \\
\text{Comprehension} & F ::= \textbf{for}(x \leftarrow H)\, F \mid Z \\
& H ::= \textbf{table}(t) \mid \mathcal{G}_{(\kappa,\alpha)}(U) \\
\text{Body} & Z ::= \textbf{where}\, B\, Z \mid \textbf{yield}\, R \mid H \\
\text{Record} & R ::= \{\overline{l = B}\} \mid x \\
\text{Primitive} & B ::= \textbf{exists}\, U \mid \oplus(\overline{B}) \mid x.l \mid c \\
\text{A-Spec} & \alpha ::= \{\overline{(l, \odot, l')}\} \\
& \kappa ::= \overline{l}
\end{array}
$$

Fig. 9. Normal form of Quelg

Finally, we define the translation from a normal form in Quelg to an SQL query. Figure 10 defines the most interesting case.

$$
\begin{aligned}
[\![\mathcal{G}_{(\overline{\kappa},\alpha)}(U)]\!] &= \textbf{SELECT}\ \overline{\odot(x.l)\ \textbf{AS}\ l'} \\
&\quad \textbf{FROM}\ [\![U]\!]\ \textbf{AS}\ x \\
&\quad \textbf{GROUP BY}\ \overline{x.\kappa} \\
&\quad and\ \alpha = \{\overline{(l, \odot, l')}\}
\end{aligned}
$$

Fig. 10. Translation from Quelg to SQL

In the case of Quela, we analyzed the translation for U and added aggregate functions to them and we get a simple query (we do not have nested SELECT statements). On the other hand, in Quelg, U in $\mathcal{G}_{(\overline{\kappa},\alpha)}(U)$ may be translated to an SQL query with grouping, in which case we cannot translate the whole term to a non-nested SQL. Hence, we translate it to nested queries. In the right-hand side of the definition in Fig. 10, $[\![U]\!]$ appears inside the FROM clause, which is a subquery. Note, however, that we can translate all normal form in Quelg to a single SQL query, thanks to the property that no nested data structures are used.

5   Implementation and Examples of Normalization

We have implemented normalization in Quelg, and translation to SQL. For this purpose, we embedded Quelg in the programming language OCaml using the tagless-final embedding [6] following Suzuki et al. [5], and use PostgreSQL as the backend database server. The computing environment is Mac OS 10.13.2 with Intel Core i5-7360 CPU with memory 8GB RAM, and our programs run on OCaml 4.07.1, and generated SQL queries on PostgreSQL 11.5. The results of performance measurements will be shown after we explain example queries.

We prepare several concrete queries in Quelg which use aggregate functions and grouping in different ways. The database used here has two tables, the products table and the orders table in Sect. 2.

The first query Q'_3 accesses the orders table, and produces a bag of all orders whose oid matches the given value. The next query Q''_3 accesses the products table, and gets the $Orders$ record from Q'_3, finds all the products which have the same oid field as oid, and returns a bag of records with the oid and sales fields.

$$Q'_3 = \lambda oid.$$
$$\mathbf{for}(o \leftarrow \mathbf{table}(\text{``orders''}))$$
$$\mathbf{where}\ (o.\text{oid} = oid)$$
$$\mathbf{yield}\ o$$

$$Q''_3 = \lambda o.$$
$$\mathbf{for}(p \leftarrow \mathbf{table}(\text{``products''}))$$
$$\mathbf{where}\ (p.\text{pid} = o.\text{pid})$$
$$\mathbf{yield}\ \{\text{oid} = o.\text{oid},$$
$$\text{sales} = p.\text{price} * o.\text{qty}\}$$

We want to compose these kinds of small queries to obtain a large, complicated query. It is easy to achieve in our language, since we can define a generic combinator for composition as follows:

$$compose = \lambda q.\ \lambda r.\ \lambda x.\ \mathbf{for}(y \leftarrow q\ x)\ r\ y$$

Then we only have to apply it to Q'_3 and Q''_3 in this order to obtain a composed query. Here we also perform grouping and aggregation on the results, and we define a new query Q_3 as follows:

$$Q_3 = \lambda x.\ \mathcal{G}_{(\text{oid},\alpha)}(compose\ Q'_3\ Q''_3\ x)$$
$$= \lambda x.\ \mathcal{G}_{(\text{oid},\alpha)}(\mathbf{for}(y \leftarrow Q'_3\ x)\ Q''_3\ y)$$
$$\text{where } \alpha = \{(\text{sales}, \text{SUM}, \text{sales\_sum})\} \quad \dots\ (1)$$

We normalize Q_3 N (for a concrete value N) to obtain the following normal form:

$$Q_3 = \mathcal{G}_{(\text{oid},\alpha)}(\mathbf{for}(o \leftarrow \mathbf{table}(\text{``orders''}))$$
$$\mathbf{for}(p \leftarrow \mathbf{table}(\text{``products''}))$$
$$\mathbf{where}\ (p.\text{pid} = o.\text{pid} \land o.\text{oid} > \text{N})$$
$$\mathbf{yield}\ \{\text{oid} = o.\text{oid}, \text{sales} = p.\text{price} * o.\text{qty}\})$$
$$\text{Where } \alpha = \{(\text{sales}, \text{SUM}, \text{sales\_sum})\}$$

which is immediately translated to SQL as:

```
SELECT x.oid AS oid, SUM(x.sales) AS sales_sum
FROM (SELECT o.oid AS oid, p.price * o.qty AS sales
      FROM products AS p, orders AS o
      WHERE p.pid = o.pid AND o.oid > N) AS x
GROUP BY x.oid                                    ... (2)
```

One can see that a query in Quelg is translated to a single SQL query using subquery.

After implementing our system, we have conducted performance measurement. We measured the execution time of program transformation and SQL generation in our implementation, and the execution time of generated SQL. We tested varying data sizes for the orders and products tables, ranging up to 10,000 records per table.

Table 1 shows the total execution time of the program transformations and SQL generation (from (1) to (2) for the above query), the execution time of SQL generated in Quelg, and that in LINQ with F#. In addition to Q_1 to Q_3 in the previous chapters, we tested several more queries; Q_4 with lambda abstraction, Q_5 with a predicate, Q_6 to Q_8 with nested control structures, and Q_9 with a nested data structure. All queries of our system used in the experiment is available online at http://logic.cs.tsukuba.ac.jp/~rui/quelg/.

Table 1. Time for code generation and execution of SQL

	Quelg		LINQ(F#)
Example	Code generation time	Execution time of SQL	Execution time of SQL
Q_1	0.03 ms	16.19 ms	14.78 ms
Q_2	0.10 ms	14.07 ms	15.13 ms
Q_3	1.16 ms	4.36 ms	Not available
Q_4	0.07 ms	0.95 ms	1.79 ms
Q_5	0.19 ms	7.41 ms	Not available
Q_6	0.43 ms	14.14 ms	Not available
Q_7	0.04 ms	11.25 ms	Not available
Q_8	5.59 ms	18.04 ms	9.56 ms
Q_9	9.31 ms	3732.62 ms	Avalanche

|products| = 10000, |orders| = 10000

Table 1 shows that Microsoft's LINQ failed to generate 5 queries out of 9, whereas our method succeeded to generate all 9 queries, which clearly shows the usefulness of our proposal.

Table 1 also shows the performance of subqueries (nested queries). For instance, Q_7 is a query which uses only one table, but has almost the same execution time as Q_1, which has two tables and has fewer subqueries than Q_7. It re-confirms the standard knowledge that executing subqueries in SQL takes a long time. The query Q_9, which calculates the average value in a subquery, takes about 3 s, and the execution time for subqueries is quite dependent on queries.

Although analyzing the execution time for different kinds of queries is beyond this work, we claim that our initial aim has been achieved, since all the queries used in this experiment have been converted to single SQL queries, which run on a common database engine (PostgreSQL). It is an interesting future work to investigate how one can optimize the generated SQL queries.

6   Conclusion

In this paper, we have given a tiny core language for language-integrated queries which has grouping and aggregate functions, while retaining the pleasant properties: any closed term of flat type (a bag-of-record type whose component types are basic types) can be normalized to a normal form, which corresponds to a single query in SQL where subqueries are allowed.

The key idea of this study is to decouple a complex job of SQL's GROUP BY clause: One is grouping and aggregation which cannot be normalized but have flat types. The other is output construction which can be normalized but may have complex types. By this decoupling, we have succeeded in getting the properties achieved in the earlier work for the language without grouping and aggregation. Our language is not as expressive as the language with the full GROUP BY clause, but by simply rewriting queries using such clauses, our language can host most such queries. To our knowledge, this work is the first success case of (subset of) language-integrated query which has the above pleasant property.

We have implemented our language by embedding our language Quelg in a host language OCaml. We have shown a concrete example and the result of simplistic performance test.

There are many directions for future work, among which the most important ones are performance evaluation against larger examples, optimization of generated SQL, and thorough comparison with other frameworks and languages. For instance, Peyton Jones and Wadler [9] proposed a language with comprehensions which subsume GROUP BY, and Cheney et al. [10] proposed a translation from nested data structures to flat ones in the absence of GROUP BY. Investigating the relation between our work and these works is an interesting future work.

Extending our language to cover other database primitives is also an interesting next step. For example, Kiselyov and Katsushima studied the ORDER BY clause in SQL [11], and it should be easy to add ORDER BY to our language.

Acknowledgments. We would like to thank Oleg Kiselyov and Kenichi Suzuki for development of Quel and its tagless-final implementation. The second author is supported in part by JSPS Grant-in-Aid for Scientific Research (B) No. 18H03218.

A   Normalization Rules of Quel

Normalization rules of Quel are given as follows:

(Stage 1)

$$(\lambda x.N)\, M \rightsquigarrow N[x := M] \qquad\text{(ABS-}\beta)$$

$$\{\overline{l = M}\}.l_i \rightsquigarrow M_i \qquad\text{(RECORD-}\beta)$$

$$\mathbf{for}(x \leftarrow \mathbf{yield}\, M)\, N \rightsquigarrow N[x := M] \qquad\text{(FORYIELD)}$$

$$\mathbf{for}(x \leftarrow \mathbf{for}(y \leftarrow L)\, M)\, N \rightsquigarrow$$
$$\mathbf{for}(y \leftarrow L)\, \mathbf{for}(x \leftarrow M)\, N \ (\text{if } y \notin FV(N)) \qquad\text{(FORFOR)}$$

$$\mathbf{for}(x \leftarrow \mathbf{where}\, L\, M)\, N \rightsquigarrow \mathbf{where}\, L\, \mathbf{for}(x \leftarrow M)\, N \qquad\text{(FORWHERE}_1)$$

$$\mathbf{for}(x \leftarrow [])\, N \rightsquigarrow [] \qquad\text{(FOREMPTY}_1)$$

$$\mathbf{for}(x \leftarrow M_1 \uplus M_2)\, N \rightsquigarrow$$
$$\mathbf{for}(x \leftarrow M_1)\, N \uplus \mathbf{for}(x \leftarrow M_2)\, N \qquad\text{(FORUNIONALL}_1)$$

$$\mathbf{where\ true}\, M \rightsquigarrow M \qquad\text{(WHERETRUE)}$$

$$\mathbf{where\ false}\, M \rightsquigarrow [] \qquad\text{(WHEREFALSE)}$$

(Stage 2)

$$\mathbf{for}(x \leftarrow M)\, (N_1 \uplus N_2) \hookrightarrow$$
$$\mathbf{for}(x \leftarrow M)\, N_1 \uplus \mathbf{for}(x \leftarrow M)\, N_2 \qquad\text{(FORUNIONALL}_2)$$

$$\mathbf{for}(x \leftarrow M)\, [] \hookrightarrow [] \qquad\text{(FOREMPTY}_2)$$

$$\mathbf{where}\, L\, M \uplus N \hookrightarrow$$
$$(\mathbf{where}\, L\, M) \uplus (\mathbf{where}\, L\, N) \qquad\text{(WHEREUNION)}$$

$$\mathbf{where}\, L\, \mathbf{where}\, M\, N \hookrightarrow \mathbf{where}\, L \wedge M\, N \qquad\text{(WHEREWHERE)}$$

$$\mathbf{where}\, L\, \mathbf{for}(x \leftarrow M)\, N \hookrightarrow$$
$$\mathbf{for}(x \leftarrow M)\, \mathbf{where}\, L\, N \qquad\text{(WHEREFOR)}$$

Fig. 11. Normalization rules of Quela

References

1. Meijer, E., Beckman, B., Bierman, G.M.: LINQ: reconciling object, relations and XML in the .net framework. In: Proceedings of the ACM SIGMOD International Conference on Management of Data, Chicago, Illinois, USA, 27–29 June 2006, p. 706 (2006)
2. Grust, T., Rittinger, J., Schreiber, T.: Avalanche-safe LINQ compilation. PVLDB 3(1), 162–172 (2010)
3. Cooper, E.: The script-writer's dream: how to write great SQL in your own language, and be sure it will succeed. In: Gardner, P., Geerts, F. (eds.) DBPL 2009. LNCS, vol. 5708, pp. 36–51. Springer, Heidelberg (2009). https://doi.org/10.1007/978-3-642-03793-1_3
4. Cheney, J., Lindley, S., Wadler, P.: A practical theory of language-integrated query. In: ACM SIGPLAN International Conference on Functional Programming, ICFP 2013, Boston, MA, USA, 25–27 September 2013, pp. 403–416 (2013)

5. Suzuki, K., Kiselyov, O., Kameyama, Y.: Finally, safely-extensible and efficient language-integrated query. In: Proceedings of the 2016 ACM SIGPLAN Workshop on Partial Evaluation and Program Manipulation, PEPM 2016, St. Petersburg, FL, USA, 20–22 January 2016, pp. 37–48 (2016)
6. Carette, J., Kiselyov, O., Shan, C.: Finally tagless, partially evaluated: tagless staged interpreters for simpler typed languages, vol. 19, pp. 509–543 (2009)
7. Wong, L.: Normal forms and conservative extension properties for query languages over collection types. J. Comput. Syst. Sci. **52**(3), 495–505 (1996)
8. Libkin, L., Wong, L.: Aggregate functions, conservative extension, and linear orders. In: Beeri, C., Ohori, A., Shasha, D.E. (eds.) Database Programming Languages (DBPL-4). Workshops in Computing, pp. 282–294. Springer, London (1994). https://doi.org/10.1007/978-1-4471-3564-7_16
9. Peyton Jones, S.L., Wadler, P.: Comprehensive comprehensions. In: Proceedings of the ACM SIGPLAN Workshop on Haskell, Haskell 2007, Freiburg, Germany, 30 September 2007, pp. 61–72 (2007)
10. Cheney, J., Lindley, S., Wadler, P.: Query shredding: efficient relational evaluation of queries over nested multisets. In: International Conference on Management of Data, SIGMOD 2014, Snowbird, UT, USA, 22–27 June 2014, pp. 1027–1038 (2014)
11. Kiselyov, O., Katsushima, T.: Sound and efficient language-integrated query. In: Chang, B.-Y.E. (ed.) APLAS 2017. LNCS, vol. 10695, pp. 364–383. Springer, Cham (2017). https://doi.org/10.1007/978-3-319-71237-6_18

An Efficient Composition of Bidirectional Programs by Memoization and Lazy Update

Kanae Tsushima[1,2]([✉]), Bach Nguyen Trong[1,2], Robert Glück[3], and Zhenjiang Hu[4]

[1] National Institute of Informatics, Tokyo, Japan
{k_tsushima,bach}@nii.ac.jp
[2] The Graduate University for Advanced Studies, SOKENDAI, Kanagawa, Japan
[3] University of Copenhagen, Copenhagen, Denmark
glueck@acm.org
[4] Peking University, Beijing, China
huzj@pku.edu.cn

Abstract. Bidirectional transformations (BX) are a solution to the view update problem and widely used for synchronizing data. The semantics and correctness of bidirectional programs have been investigated intensively during the past years, but their efficiency and optimization are not yet fully understood. In this paper, as a first step, we study different evaluation methods to optimize their evaluation. We focus on the interpretive evaluation of BX compositions because we found that these compositions are an important cause of redundant computations if the compositions are not right associative. For evaluating BX compositions efficiently, we investigate two memoization methods. The first method, minBiGUL_m, uses memoization, which improves the runtime of many BX programs by keeping intermediate results for later reuse. A disadvantage is the familiar tradeoff for keeping and searching values in a table. When inputs become large, the overhead increases and the effectiveness decreases. To deal with large inputs, we introduce the second method, xpg, that uses tupling, lazy update and lazy evaluation as optimizations. Lazy updates delay updates in closures and enables them to use them later. Both evaluation methods were fully implemented for minBiGUL. The experimental results show that our methods are faster than the original method of BiGUL for the non-right associative compositions.

Keywords: Bidirectional transformation · Implementation technique · Efficiency · Optimization · Tupling

1 Introduction

The synchronization of data is a common problem. In the database community this problem is known as "the view update problem" and has been investigated for a long time [1]. Bidirectional transformation (BX) provides a systematic

© Springer Nature Switzerland AG 2020
K. Nakano and K. Sagonas (Eds.): FLOPS 2020, LNCS 12073, pp. 159–178, 2020.
https://doi.org/10.1007/978-3-030-59025-3_10

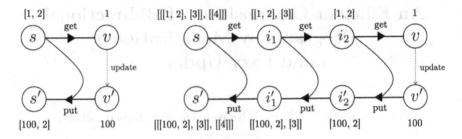

Fig. 1. Evaluating *phead*   **Fig. 2.** Evaluating *phead* õ *phead* õ *phead*

approach to solving this problem. Consider a small BX program of *phead*[1], which consists of two functions: *get* (for getting the head of an input list) and *put* (for reflecting the output to the head of the input). Figure 1 shows an example of the bidirectional behavior of *phead*. Let $[1, 2]$ be the original source s. The function *get* is a projection: *get* of *phead* picks the first element of the given original source $[1, 2]$ and returns 1 as a view v. Supposing that the view is updated to 100, *put* of *phead* will construct a new source s' of $[100, 2]$ from the updated view v' of 100 and the original source s of $[1, 2]$.

The composition of BX programs is a fundamental construct to build more complex BX programs [2,3]. Let bx_1 (defined by get_{bx_1} and put_{bx_1}) and bx_2 (defined by get_{bx_2} and put_{bx_2}) be two bidirectional programs, then their composition $bx_1 \, \tilde{o} \, bx_2$ is defined by

$$get_{bx_1 \tilde{o} bx_2} \ s = get_{bx_2}(get_{bx_1} \ s) \tag{1}$$

$$put_{bx_1 \tilde{o} bx_2} \ s \ v' = put_{bx_1} s \ (put_{bx_2} \ (get_{bx_1} \ s) \ v') \tag{2}$$

Unlike function composition, the composition of bidirectional programs is read left-to-right. We use this order because it is helpful to understand the behavior if we consider data flows from left to right. One feature of this composition is that $put_{bx_1 \tilde{o} bx_2}$ needs to call get_{bx_1} to compute the intermediate result for put_{bx_2} to use, which would introduce an efficiency problem if we compute *put* for composition of many bidirectional programs. Generally, for a composition of $O(n)$ bidirectional programs, we need to call *get* for $O(n^2)$ times. To be concrete, consider the evaluation of the following composition (which will be used as our running example in this paper):

$$lp3 = (phead \ \tilde{o} \ phead) \ \tilde{o} \ phead$$

which is illustrated by Fig. 2 with the original source s being $[[[1, 2], [3]], [[4]]]$ and the updated view 100. To obtain the final updated source s', *put* for *lp3* needs to evaluate *put* of *phead* three times. The first is from i_2 and v' to obtain i'_2, which needs to call *get* twice to compute i_2; the second is from i_1 and i'_2 to

---

[1] The actual program is shown in the next section.

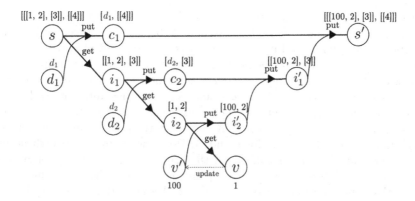

Fig. 3. Evaluating *phead* õ *phead* õ *phead* by keeping complements

obtain i'_1, which needs to call *get* once, and the last is from s and i'_1 to obtain s', which is just a direct *put* computation.

One direct solution to avoid this repeated *get* computation is to compute compositions in a right associative manner. For instance, if we transform *lp3* to *rp3*:

$$rp3 = phead \mathbin{\tilde{\circ}} (phead \mathbin{\tilde{\circ}} phead)$$

then the *put* for *rp3* only needs to compute *get* of *phead* twice, one time less than that for *lp3*. However, this transformation is not always easy to do. For instance, let us consider *breverse*, a bidirectional version of the traditional 'reverse' program for reversing a list. It is defined using *bfoldr*, a bidirectional version of the traditional *foldr*, whose definition is shown in the last part of Sect. 2. Informally, *bfoldr* is a recursive bidirectional program defined in a way like

$$bfoldr\ bx\ \cdots = \cdots (bfoldr\ \cdots) \mathbin{\tilde{\circ}} bx \cdots$$

where the composition is inherently left associative, and the number of composition is dynamically determined by the length of the source list. This makes it hard to do the above transformation statically. The same efficiency problem occurs in all BX languages.

In this paper, we make the first attempt for seriously considering the efficiency of evaluating BX compositions, and solve the problem by introducing two methods based on memoization to gain fast evaluation for (left associative) BX compositions. The first method uses straightforward memoization: "keeping *intermediate states in a table* and using them when needed". This avoids repeated *get* computations and improves the runtime in many cases. However, this simple memoization needs to keep and search values in a table, which may introduce big cost for large inputs. We explain this method in Sect. 3.

To treat large inputs, we propose the second method based on memoization: "keeping *complements in a closure* and using them when needed". Here, complements are information from sources that makes *get* injective, which is in turn needed to evaluate *put*. In the middle *put* and *get* of Fig. 2, we use i_1, $[[1,2],[3]]$ and i_2', $[100,2]$ to obtain the updated source $[[100,2],[3]]$. However, $[1,2]$ is simply replaced by $[100,2]$ and not used to construct the result of *put*. In this case we can use $[...,[3]]$ as a complement. The key idea of the second approach is straightforward: Complements are smaller than intermediate states. For obtaining complements, we tuple *put* and *get*, and produce a new function *pg*. Because *put* produces new complements for *get*, we can shrink the size. Let us reconsider our example *phead* ŏ *phead* ŏ *phead* in Fig. 3, where c_1 and c_2 are complements and d_1 and d_2 are valid views for s and i_1. Here, two points are worth noting. First, after evaluating the leftmost *pg*, the original source s need not be kept because its complete contents are in c_1 and i_1. Second, the complements are smaller than the intermediate states in Fig. 2. Actually, this simple *pg* alone is not yet effective for left associative compositions because it requires two more *puts*, which can be seen on the right side of Fig. 3. To achieve an efficient evaluation, we combine two techniques, lazy update and lazy evaluation. We explain this second method and all optimizations in Sect. 4.

Both methods have been fully implemented for *minBiGUL*, a core bidirectional language, which is a subset of the full bidirectional language *BiGUL*. The experimental results show that our methods are much faster than the original evaluation strategy. We give detailed experimental results in Sect. 5, discuss related work in Sect. 6, and conclude in Sect. 7.

Although we will introduce the basics of bidirectional transformation in the next session, it is not complete due to space limitations. Please refer BiGUL papers [4,5] for the details if needed.

2   Bidirectional Programming Language: minBiGUL

The target language in this paper, minBiGUL, is a very-well behaved subset of BiGUL, which is a simple, yet powerful putback-based bidirectional language.

BiGUL supports two transformations: a forward transformation *get* producing a view from a source and a backward transformation *put* taking a source and a modified view to produce an updated source. Intuitively, if we have a BiGUL program *bx*, these two transformations are the following functions:

$$get \, [\![bx]\!] : s \to v, \quad put \, [\![bx]\!] : s * v \to s$$

BiGUL is well-behaved [6] since two functions *put* $[\![bx]\!]$ and *get* $[\![bx]\!]$ satisfy the round-trip laws as follows:

$$put \, [\![bx]\!] \, s \, (get \, [\![bx]\!] \, s) = s \qquad [\text{GetPut}]$$

$$get \, [\![bx]\!] \, (put \, [\![bx]\!] \, s \, v) = v \qquad [\text{PutGet}]$$

The GetPut law means that if there is no change to the view, there should be no change to the source. The PutGet law means that we can recover the modified view by applying the forward transformation to the updated source.

minBiGUL inherits from BiGUL both transformations, *put* and *get*, which satisfy the two laws above. Because we restrict the 'adaptive case' of BiGUL in minBiGUL, *put* and *get* satisfy one more law, namely the PUTPUT law [7]:

$$put \; [\![bx]\!] \; (put \; [\![bx]\!] \; s \; v') \; v = put \; [\![bx]\!] \; s \; v \qquad [\text{PUTPUT}]$$

The PUTPUT law means that a source update should overwrite the effect of previous source updates. Because minBiGUL satisfies all three laws, GETPUT, PUTGET and PUTPUT, it is very well-behaved [7].

2.1   Syntax

The syntax of minBiGUL is briefly written as follows:

$$bx ::= Skip \; h \mid Replace \mid Prod \; bx_1 \; bx_2 \mid RearrS \; f_1 \; f_2 \; bx \mid RearrV \; g_1 \; g_2 \; bx$$
$$\mid Case \; cond_{sv} \; cond_s \; bx_1 \; bx_2 \mid Compose \; bx_1 \; bx_2$$

A minBiGUL program is either a skip of a function, a replacement, a product of two programs, a source/view rearrangement, a case combinator (without adaptive cases), or a composition of two programs. We use numbers, pairs and lists to construct the program inputs including the source and/or the view.

For source/view rearrangement, BiGUL uses a lambda expression to express how to deconstruct as well as reconstruct data. It is a kind of bijection. However, to be able to implement it in OCaml, the environment used for developing minBiGUL and solutions in the paper, we need to require two functions which one is the inverse of the other. In the above syntax, $f_2 = f_1^{-1}$ and $g_2 = g_1^{-1}$.

To help make demonstration more direct, we provide the following alternatives representation: $Prod \; bx_1 \; bx_2 \equiv bx_1 \times bx_2$, $Compose \; bx_1 \; bx_2 \equiv bx_1 \circ bx_2$. The compose symbol $\tilde{\circ}$ used in the previous section will be replaced with the more common one, $\circ$. In general, $\circ$ has a higher priority than $\times$. Their associativity precedence can be either left or right or mixture, but are not set by default. We need to explicitly write programs that use these operators.

2.2   Semantics

The semantics of *put* and *get* is shown in Definitions 1 and 2, respectively. Instead of using the name v' for the updated view in the *put* direction, like Figs. 1, 2 and 3, we simply use v below. The later definitions also follow this convention.

Definition 1. $put \, [\![bx]\!] \; s \; v$

$put \, [\![Skip \; h]\!] \; s \; v =$
  if $h \; s = v$ then s else $undefined$
$put \, [\![Replace]\!] \; s \; v = v$
$put \, [\![bx_1 \times bx_2]\!] \; (s_1, s_2) \; (v_1, v_2) =$
  $(put \, [\![bx_1]\!] \; s_1 \; v_1, put \, [\![bx_2]\!] \; s_2 \; v_2)$
$put \, [\![RearrS \; f_1 \; f_2 \; bx]\!] \; s \; v =$
  $f_2 \; (put \, [\![bx]\!] \; (f_1 \; s) \; v)$
$put \, [\![RearrV \; g_1 \; g_2 \; bx]\!] \; s \; v =$
  $put \, [\![bx]\!] \; s \; (g_1 \; v)$
$put \, [\![Case \; cond_{sv} \; cond_s \; bx_1 \; bx_2]\!] \; s \; v =$
  if $cond_{sv} \; s \; v$
  then $s' \Leftarrow put \, [\![bx_1]\!] \; s \; v$
  else $s' \Leftarrow put \, [\![bx_2]\!] \; s \; v$
  fi $cond_s \; s'$; return s'
$put \, [\![bx_1 \circ bx_2]\!] \; s \; v =$
  $put \, [\![bx_1]\!] \; s \; (put \, [\![bx_2]\!] \; (get \, [\![bx_1]\!] \; s) \; v)$

Definition 2. $get \, [\![bx]\!] \; s$

$get \, [\![Skip \; h]\!] \; s =$
  $h \; s$
$get \, [\![Replace]\!] \; s = s$
$get \, [\![bx_1 \times bx_2]\!] \; (s_1, s_2) =$
  $(get \, [\![bx_1]\!] \; s_1, get \, [\![bx_2]\!] \; s_2)$
$get \, [\![RearrS \; f_1 \; f_2 \; bx]\!] \; s =$
  $get \, [\![bx]\!] \; (f_1 \; s)$
$get \, [\![RearrV \; g_1 \; g_2 \; bx]\!] \; s =$
  $g_2 \; (get \, [\![bx]\!] \; s)$
$get \, [\![Case \; cond_{sv} \; cond_s \; bx_1 \; bx_2]\!] \; s =$
  if $cond_s \; s$
  then $v' \Leftarrow get \, [\![bx_1]\!] \; s$
  else $v' \Leftarrow get \, [\![bx_2]\!] \; s$
  fi $cond_{sv} \; s \; v'$; return v'
$get \, [\![bx_1 \circ bx_2]\!] \; s =$
  $get \, [\![bx_2]\!] \; (get \, [\![bx_1]\!] \; s)$

The two definitions use if-then-else-fi statements to define the semantics of $put \, [\![Case]\!]$ and $get \, [\![Case]\!]$, where $\Leftarrow$ denotes an assignment. This statement is useful to describe many functions related to $Case$ in this paper. Statement (if E_1 then X_1 else X_2 fi E_2) means "if the test E_1 is true, the statement X_1 is executed and the assertion E_2 must be true, otherwise, if E_1 is false, the statement X_2 is executed and the assertion E_2 must be false." If the values of E_1 and E_2 are distinct, the if-then-else-fi structure is undefined. We can write the equivalent if-then-else statement as follows:

$$\text{if } E_1 \text{ then } X_1 \text{ else } X_2 \text{ fi } E_2; S$$
$$\equiv \text{if } E_1 = true \text{ then } \{X_1; \text{ if } E_2 = true \text{ then } S \text{ else } undefined\}$$
$$\text{else } \{X_2; \text{ if } E_2 = false \text{ then } S \text{ else } undefined\}$$

Also in the semantics of $put \, [\![Case]\!]$ and $get \, [\![Case]\!]$, the return statements are used to express clearly the value of functions. Variables s' and v' wrapped in these returns are necessary for checking the fi conditions.

2.3   Examples

As an example of minBiGUL program, consider the definition of $phead$:

$$phead = RearrS \; f_1 \; f_2 \; bx_s \text{ where: } f_1 = \lambda(s :: ss).(s, ss), \; f_2 = \lambda(s, ss).(s :: ss),$$
$$bx_s = RearrV \; g_1 \; g_2 \; bx_v \text{ where: } g_1 = \lambda v.(v, ()), \; g_2 = \lambda(v, ()).v,$$
$$bx_v = Replace \times (Skip \; (\lambda\_.()))$$

The above program rearranges the source, a non-empty list, to a pair of its head element s and its tail ss, and the view to a pair $(v, ())$, then we can use v to replace s and () to keep ss. Intuitively, $put \, [\![phead]\!] \; s_0 \; v_0$ returns a list whose head is v_0 and tail is the tail of s_0, and $get \llbracket phead \rrbracket\ s_0$ returns the head of the list s_0. For instance, $put \llbracket phead \rrbracket\ [1, 2, 3]\ 100 = [100, 2, 3]$ and $get \llbracket phead \rrbracket\ [1, 2, 3] = 1$. If we want to update the head element of the head element of a list of lists by using the view, we can define a composition like $phead \circ phead$. For example:

$$put \llbracket phead \circ phead \rrbracket\ [[1, 2, 3], [\,], [4, 5]]\ 100 = [[100, 2, 3], [\,], [4, 5]]$$
$$get \llbracket phead \circ phead \rrbracket\ [[1, 2, 3], [\,], [4, 5]] = 1$$

In the same way with $phead$, we can define $ptail$ in minBiGUL. $put \llbracket ptail \rrbracket\ s\ v$ accepts a source list s and a view list v to produce a new list by replacing the tail of s with v. $get \llbracket ptail \rrbracket\ s$ returns the tail of the source list s

Next let us look at another more complex example, $bsnoc$:

$$bsnoc = Case\ cond_{sv}\ cond_s\ bx_1\ bx_2\ where:$$
$$cond_{sv} = \lambda s.\lambda v.(\text{length } v = 1),\quad cond_s = \lambda s.(\text{length } s = 1)$$
$$bx_1 = Replace,\quad bx_2 = RearrS\ f_1\ f_2\ bx_s\ where:$$
$$f_1 = f_2^{-1} = \lambda(x : y : ys).(y, (x : ys)),$$
$$bx_s = RearrV\ g_1\ g_2\ bx_v\ where:$$
$$g_1 = g_2^{-1} = \lambda(v : vs).(v, vs),\quad bx_v = Replace \times bsnoc$$

$put \llbracket bsnoc \rrbracket$ requires the source s and the view v are non-empty lists and the length of v is not larger than the length of s. If $cond_{sv}$ is true, i.e. v is singleton, a replacement will be executed to produce a new list which should be equal to v. Because the length of the new list is 1, the exit condition $cond_s$ comes true, so we obtain the updated source. If v is a list of more than one elements, there will be two rearrangements on the source and the view before conducting a product. The program rearranges the source $x : y : ys$ to a pair of its second element y and a list $x : ys$ created from the remaining elements in the original order, and the view to a pair of its head and tail. Then we can use y to replace the head of the view and pair $(x : ys)$ with the tail of the view to form the input of a recursive call $bsnoc$. The obtained source update in this case should be non-singleton since the value of the exit condition $cond_s$ needs to be false. We omit the behavior description of $get \llbracket bsnoc \rrbracket$ that accepts a source list s, checks $cond_s$ to know how to evaluate the view v, then does one more checking, $cond_{sv}$, before resulting. Intuitively, $put \llbracket bsnoc \rrbracket\ s_0\ v_0$ produces a new list by moving the last element of v_0 to its first position if the length of v_0 is not larger than the length of s_0. $get \llbracket bsnoc \rrbracket\ s_0$ returns another list by moving the first element of the list s_0 to its end position. For instance, $put \llbracket bsnoc \rrbracket\ [1, 2, 3]\ [4, 5, 6] = [6, 4, 5]$ and $get \llbracket bsnoc \rrbracket\ [1, 2, 3] = [2, 3, 1]$.

Now, let us see the minBiGUL definition of $bfoldr$ which is a putback function of an important higher-order function on lists, $foldr$:

$$bfoldr\ bx = Case\ cond_{sv}\ cond_s\ bx_1\ bx_2\ where:$$
$$cond_{sv} = \lambda(s_1, s_2).\lambda v.(s_1 = [\,]),\quad cond_s = \lambda(s_1, s_2).(s_1 = [\,])$$
$$bx_1 = RearrV\ g_1\ g_2\ bx_v\ where:$$
$$g_1 = g_2^{-1} = \lambda[v].(v, [\,]), bx_v = (Skip\ (\lambda\_.())) \times Replace$$

$bx_2 = RearrS \ f_1 \ f_2 \ bx_s$ where:
$f_1 = f_2^{-1} = \lambda((x:xs),e).(x,(xs,e))$, $bx_s = ((Replace \times bfoldr \ bx) \circ bx)$

If we think that a minBiGUL program bx has a type of $MinBiGUL \ s \ v$, the type of $bfoldr$ will be look like $MinBiGUL \ (a,b) \ b \rightarrow MinBiGUL \ ([a],b) \ b$. You can easily find the similarity between the above definition of $bfoldr$ with the following definition of $foldr$:

$$foldr :: (a \rightarrow b \rightarrow b) \rightarrow b \rightarrow [a] \rightarrow b$$
$$foldr \ f \ e \ [\ ] = e$$
$$foldr \ f \ e \ (x:xs) = f \ x \ (foldr \ f \ e \ xs)$$

Each branch in a case of $bfoldr$ corresponds to a pattern of $foldr$. In $bfoldr$, the composition is inherently left associative, and the number of composition is dynamically determined by the length of the source list. Because $\circ$ has a higher priority than $\times$, it is in general not possible to transform $bfoldr$ from the left associative composition style to the right one.

Using $foldr$, we can define other functions like $reverse = foldr \ snoc \ [\ ]$. With $bfoldr$, we can also write the bidirectional version $breverse$ as follows:

$breverse = RearrS \ f_1 \ f_2 \ bx$ where:
$f_1 = f_2^{-1} = \lambda s \rightarrow (s,[\ ])$, $bx = bfoldr \ bsnoc$

3   Adding Memoization: minBiGUL$_m$

When evaluating the composition of several BX programs, the same $gets$ are evaluated repeatedly. This problem was illustrated in Fig. 2. To avoid reevaluating $gets$, and as our first approach to avoid this inefficiency, we introduce memoization in the minBiGUL interpreter. To keep it simple, the intermediate state of a composition is saved in a key-value table where the key is a pair of program bx and source s, and the value is the result of evaluating $get \ [\![bx]\!] \ s$. Later the value in the table is used instead of recomputing it.

The memoizing version, minBiGUL$_m$, needs only two modifications: get_m and put_m (Definitions 3 and 4).

Definition 3. *Memoization version of put*

$put_m \ [\![bx]\!] \ s \ v = $ match bx with
$\quad | \ bx_1 \circ bx_2 \rightarrow put_m \ [\![bx_1]\!] \ s \ (put_m \ [\![bx_2]\!] \ (get_m \ [\![bx_1]\!] \ s) \ v)$
$\quad | \ \_ \rightarrow similar \ to \ put$

Definition 4. *Memoization version of get*

$$get_m \, [\![bx]\!] \, s = \text{match } bx \text{ with}$$
$$| \; bx_1 \circ bx_2 \rightarrow$$
$$\text{try } (Hashtbl.find \; table_g \; (bx, s))$$
$$\text{with } Not\_found \rightarrow$$
$$i \Leftarrow get_m \, [\![bx_1]\!] \, s; \quad Hashtbl.add \; table_g \; (bx_1, s) \, i;$$
$$v \Leftarrow get_m \, [\![bx_2]\!] \, i; \quad Hashtbl.add \; table_g \; (bx_2, i) \, v;$$
$$Hashtbl.add \; table_g \; (bx, s) \, v$$
$$v$$
$$| \; \_ \rightarrow similar \; to \; get$$

The evaluation of $put_m \, [\![bx_1 \circ bx_2]\!] \, s \, v$ includes two recursive calls of put_m and an external call of get_m, which is relatively similar to the evaluation of $put \, [\![bx_1 \circ bx_2]\!] \, s \, v$. Meanwhile, the evaluation of $get_m \, [\![bx_1 \circ bx_2]\!] \, s$ does not merely invoke get_m recursively twice. In case that bx is a composition, the key (bx, s) needs to be looked up in the table and the corresponding value would be used for the next steps in the evaluation. If there is no such key, the value of the intermediate state i and the value of $get \, [\![bx]\!] \, s$ in v will be calculated. These values along with the corresponding keys will also be stored in the table where the interpreter may later leverage instead of reevaluating some states. Note in particular that the interpreter does not save all states when evaluating a program, only the intermediate states of a composition.

4   Tupling and Lazy Updates: xpg

4.1   Tupling: pg

Another solution for saving intermediate states is tupling. If *put* and *get* are evaluated simultaneously, there is potential to reduce the number of recomputed *gets*. The following function, *pg*, accepts the pair of a source and a view as the input to produce a new pair that contains the actual result of the corresponding minBiGUL program.

Definition 5. $pg \, [\![bx]\!](s, v) = (put \, [\![bx]\!] \, s \, v, get \, [\![bx]\!] \, s)$

Now, let us see how we construct *pg* recursively.

$$pg \, [\![Skip \; h]\!](s, v) \overset{1}{=} (\text{if } h \; s = v \text{ then } s \text{ else } undefined, h \; s)$$
$$\overset{2}{=} \text{if } h \; s = v \text{ then } (s, h \; s) \text{ else } undefined$$
$$\overset{3}{=} \text{if } h \; s = v \text{ then } (s, v) \text{ else } undefined$$

The first equality is simply based on the definitions of *pg*, *put* $[\![Skip \; h]\!]$ and *get* $[\![Skip \; h]\!]$. The second one tuples two results of *put* and *get* in the body of the if-expression. This is a trick since in some cases, the result of pg may be undefined although the result is not undefined when evaluating $get\,[\![Skip\ h]\!]$. The last equality is a function application.

$$pg\,[\![Replace]\!](s,v) = (v,s)$$

$$pg\,[\![bx_1 \times bx_2]\!]((s_1,s_2),(v_1,v_2))$$

$$\overset{1}{=} ((put\,[\![bx_1]\!]\ s_1\ v_1, put\,[\![bx_2]\!]\ s_2\ v_2),(get\,[\![bx_1]\!]\ s_1, get\,[\![bx_2]\!]\ s_2))$$

$$\overset{2}{=} (s_1',v_1') \Leftarrow pg\,[\![bx_1]\!](s_1,v_1);$$
$$\quad (s_2',v_2') \Leftarrow pg\,[\![bx_2]\!](s_2,v_2);$$
$$\quad ((s_1',s_2'),(v_1',v_2'))$$

$$pg\,[\![RearrS\ f_1\ f_2\ bx]\!](s,v) \overset{1}{=} (f_2\ (put\,[\![bx]\!]\ (f_1\ s)\ v), get\,[\![bx]\!]\ (f_1\ s))$$

$$\overset{2}{=} (s',v') \Leftarrow pg\,[\![bx]\!](f_1\ s,v);$$
$$\quad (f_2\ s',v')$$

$$pg\,[\![RearrV\ g_1\ g_2\ bx]\!](s,v) \overset{1}{=} (put\,[\![bx]\!]\ s\ (g_1\ v), g_2\ (get\,[\![bx]\!]\ s))$$

$$\overset{2}{=} (s',v') \Leftarrow pg\,[\![bx]\!](s,g_1\ v);$$
$$\quad (s',g_2\ v')$$

Constructions of pg for the replacement, the product and the source/view rearrangements are simple. We just pair put and get, and change them to pg. The values of these pg functions are obtained from the final expression in the corresponding sequences. We only use the return keyword to express explicitly the evaluated value of a function in the situation of $Case$.

$$pg\,[\![Case\ cond_{sv}\ cond_s\ bx_1\ bx_2]\!](s,v)$$

$\overset{1}{=}$ (if $cond_{sv}$ s v if $cond_s$ s
   then $s' \Leftarrow put\,[\![bx_1]\!]$ s v then $v' \Leftarrow get\,[\![bx_1]\!]$ s
   else $s' \Leftarrow put\,[\![bx_2]\!]$ s v else $v' \Leftarrow get\,[\![bx_2]\!]$ s
   fi $cond_s$ s'; return s' ,   fi $cond_{sv}$ s v'; return v')

$\overset{2}{=}$ if $cond_{sv}$ s v && $cond_s$ s then
     $(s',v') \Leftarrow (put\,[\![bx_1]\!]\ s\ v, get\,[\![bx_1]\!]\ s)$;
       if $cond_s$ s' && $cond_{sv}$ s v' then return (s',v') else *undefined*
   else if $cond_{sv}$ s v && not $(cond_s$ $s)$ then
     $(s',v') \Leftarrow (put\,[\![bx_1]\!]\ s\ v, get\,[\![bx_2]\!]\ s)$;
       if $cond_s$ s' && not $(cond_{sv}$ s $v')$ then return (s',v') else *undefined*
   else if not $(cond_{sv}$ s $v)$ && $cond_s$ s then
     $(s',v') \Leftarrow (put\,[\![bx_2]\!]\ s\ v, get\,[\![bx_1]\!]\ s)$;
       if not $(cond_s$ $s')$ && $cond_{sv}$ s v' then return (s',v') else *undefined*
   else if not $(cond_{sv}$ s $v)$ && not $(cond_s$ $s)$ then
     $(s',v') \Leftarrow (put\,[\![bx_2]\!]\ s\ v, get\,[\![bx_2]\!]\ s)$;
       if not $(cond_s$ $s')$ && not $(cond_{sv}$ s $v')$ then return (s',v') else *undefined*

$\overset{3}{=}$ (* with restriction *)
   if $cond_{sv}$ s v && $cond_s$ s

then $(s', v') \Leftarrow pg \, [\![bx_1]\!] (s, v)$

else $(s', v') \Leftarrow pg \, [\![bx_2]\!] (s, v)$

fi $cond_s \, s' \, \&\& \, cond_{sv} \, s \, v'$; return (s', v')

A restriction for $pg \, [\![Case]\!]$ needs to be introduced here. We know that there is one entering condition and one exit condition when evaluating $put \, [\![Case]\!]$ as well as $get \, [\![Case]\!]$. If a tupling occurs, there will be 4 combinations from these conditions. This means two entering conditions of $put \, [\![Case]\!]$ and $get \, [\![Case]\!]$ are not always simultaneously satisfied. The evaluated branches are distinct in the put and get directions for combinations $((cond_{sv} \, s \, v) \, \&\& \, (not(cond_s \, s)))$ and $((not(cond_{sv} \, s \, v)) \, \&\& \, (cond_s \, s))$, which are restricted in this paper. Because they evaluate different bx for put and get, we can not evaluate them efficiently. This does not happen for the others which is used in the construction of $pg \, [\![Case]\!]$.

$pg \, [\![bx_1 \circ bx_2]\!] (s, v)$

$\overset{1}{=} (put \, [\![bx_1]\!] \, s \, (put \, [\![bx_2]\!] \, (get \, [\![bx_1]\!] \, s) \, v), get \, [\![bx_2]\!] \, (get \, [\![bx_1]\!] \, s))$

$\overset{2}{=} v_1 \Leftarrow get \, [\![bx_1]\!] \, s;$ $\qquad\qquad \overset{3}{=} (s_1, v_1) \Leftarrow pg \, [\![bx_1]\!] (s, dummy);$

$\quad (s_2, v_2) \Leftarrow pg \, [\![bx_2]\!] (v_1, v);$ $\qquad\quad (s_2, v_2) \Leftarrow pg \, [\![bx_2]\!] (v_1, v);$

$\quad (s_3, v_3) \Leftarrow pg \, [\![bx_1]\!] (s, s_2);$ $\qquad\quad (s_3, v_3) \Leftarrow pg \, [\![bx_1]\!] (s, s_2);$

$\quad (s_3, v_2)$ $\qquad\qquad\qquad\qquad\qquad\quad (s_3, v_2)$

$\overset{4}{=} (s_1, v_1) \Leftarrow pg \, [\![bx_1]\!] (s, dummy);$

$\quad (s_2, v_2) \Leftarrow pg \, [\![bx_2]\!] (v_1, v);$

$\quad (s_3, v_3') \Leftarrow pg \, [\![bx_1]\!] (s_1, s_2);$

$\quad (s_3, v_2)$

The construction of $pg \, [\![bx_1 \circ bx_2]\!]$ is the most important part in the pg function. The first two equalities comes from mentioned definitions and some basic transformations. The third one rewrites $v_1 \Leftarrow get \, [\![bx_1]\!] \, s$ into $(s_1, v_1) \Leftarrow pg \, [\![bx_1]\!] (s, dummy)$. This is possible when we consider $get \, [\![bx_1]\!] \, s$ as the second element of $pg \, [\![bx_1]\!] (s, dummy)$ where $dummy$ is a special value that makes the $put \, [\![bx_1]\!]$ valid. Since there is no real view, this $dummy$ is necessary to pair with the original source s to form the input of $put \, [\![bx_1]\!]$. In general, $dummy$ depends on the source s, the view v and/or the program bx_1. Programmers can be required to give a way to construct $dummy$, but it may be inessential for ill-typed systems where choosing $dummy$ as v is one of the easiest ways to meet our expectation. That setting is used in our experiments. The last equality changes from $(s_3, v_3) \Leftarrow pg \, [\![bx_1]\!] (s, s_2)$ to $(s_3, v_3') \Leftarrow pg \, [\![bx_1]\!] (s_1, s_2)$, where s and v_3 are replaced with s_1 and v_3' respectively. Because s_1 is a source update of $put \, [\![bx_1]\!] \, s \, dummy$, so under the PutPut law, it is possible to substitute s by s_1. The substitution of v_3 by v_3' is simply replacing the variable name since v_3 and v_3' hold different results of $get \, [\![bx_1]\!] \, s$ and $get \, [\![bx_1]\!] \, s_1$ respectively. Because both variables are no longer used later, this substitution does not affect the outcome of the function.

4.2   Lazy Update: cpg

When evaluating $pg [\![bx_1 \circ bx_2]\!]$, there are three pg calls, of which twice for $pg [\![bx_1]\!]$ and once for $pg [\![bx_2]\!]$. If a given program is a left associative composition, the number of pg calls will be exponential. Therefore, the runtime inefficiency of pg for left associative BX programs is inevitable. To solve that, we introduce a new function, cpg, accumulates updates on the source and the view. $cpg[\![bx]\!](ks, kv, s, v)$ is an extension of $pg [\![bx]\!](s, v)$ where ks and kv are continuations used to hold the modification information, and s and v are used to keep evaluated values same as pg. The output of this function is a 4-tuple (ks, kv, s, v). To be more convenient for presenting the definition of cpg as well as the other functions later, we provide some following utility functions:

$$fst = \lambda(x_1, x_2).x_1, \quad snd = \lambda(x_1, x_2).x_2, \quad con = \lambda ks_1.\lambda ks_2.\lambda x.((ks_1\ x),(ks_2\ x))$$

Definition 6. $cpg[\![bx]\!](ks, kv, s, v)$

> $cpg[\![Skip\ h]\!](ks, kv, s, v) =$ if $h\ s = v$ then (ks, kv, s, v) else *undefined*
>
> $cpg[\![Replace]\!](ks, kv, s, v) = (kv, ks, v, s)$
>
> $cpg[\![bx_1 \times bx_2]\!](ks, kv, s, v) =$
>> $(ks_1, kv_1, s_1, v_1) \Leftarrow cpg[\![bx_1]\!](fst \circ ks, fst \circ kv, fst\ s, fst\ v);$
>>
>> $(ks_2, kv_2, s_2, v_2) \Leftarrow cpg[\![bx_2]\!](snd \circ ks, snd \circ kv, snd\ s, snd\ v);$
>>
>> $(con\ ks_1\ ks_2, con\ kv_1\ kv_2, (s_1, s_2), (v_1, v_2))$
>
> $cpg[\![RearrS\ f_1\ f_2\ bx]\!](ks, kv, s, v) =$
>> $(ks', kv', s', v') \Leftarrow cpg[\![bx]\!](f_1 \circ ks, kv, f_1\ s, v);$
>>
>> $(f_2 \circ ks', kv', s', v')$
>
> $cpg[\![RearrV\ g_1\ g_2\ bx]\!](ks, kv, s, v) =$
>> $(ks', kv', s', v') \Leftarrow cpg[\![bx]\!](ks, g_1 \circ kv, s, g_1\ v);$
>>
>> $(ks', g_2 \circ kv', ks', g_2\ v')$
>
> $cpg[\![Case\ cond_{sv}\ cond_s\ bx_1\ bx_2]\!](ks, kv, s, v) =$
>> if $cond_{sv}\ s\ v$ && $cond_s\ s$
>>
>> then $(ks', kv', s', v') \Leftarrow cpg[\![bx_1]\!](ks, kv, s, v)$
>>
>> else $(ks', kv', s', v') \Leftarrow cpg[\![bx_2]\!](ks, kv, s, v)$
>>
>> fi $cond_s\ s'$ && $cond_{sv}\ s\ v'$; return (ks', kv', s', v')
>
> $cpg[\![bx_1 \circ bx_2]\!](ks, kv, s, v) =$
>> $(ks_1, kv_1, \underline{s_1}, v_1) \Leftarrow cpg[\![bx_1]\!](ks, id, s, dummy);$
>>
>> $(ks_2, kv_2, s_2, v_2) \Leftarrow cpg[\![bx_2]\!](kv_1, kv, v_1, v);$
>>
>> $(ks_1 \circ ks_2, kv_2, ks_1\ s_2, v_2)$

In the places where third and/or fourth argument (s and v) are updated by applications, the computations are also accumulated in ks and/or kv. Thanks to these accumulations, there are only two cpg calls in $cpg [\![bx_1 \circ bx_2]\!]$. The first call $cpg [\![bx_1]\!]$ requires parameter $(ks, id, s, dummy)$ where s and ks are corresponding to the source and the update over source. Since there is no real view here, we need a dummy same as pg. Then the continuation updating on this dummy should be initiated as the identity function. The first cpg call is assigned to a 4-tuple (ks_1, kv_1, s_1, v_1). In the next assignment, a 4-tuple (ks_2, kv_2, s_2, v_2) is assigned by the second cpg call which uses the input as (kv_1, kv, v_1, v) where kv_1 and v_1 are obtained from the result of the first assignment, and kv and v come from the input. It is relatively similar to the second pg call assignment in $pg \llbracket bx_1 \circ bx_2 \rrbracket$. After two cpg calls, a function application, $ks_1\ s_2$, is used to produce the updated source instead of calling recursively one more time like in $pg \llbracket bx_1 \circ bx_2 \rrbracket$.

Suppose that we have a source s_0 and a view v_0. The pair of the updated source and view (s, v) where $s = put \llbracket bx \rrbracket\ s_0\ v_0$ and $v = get \llbracket bx \rrbracket\ s_0$ can be obtained using cpg as follows:

$$(ks, kv, s, v) \Leftarrow cpg\llbracket bx \rrbracket(\lambda\_.s_0, id, s_0, v_0);$$
$$(s, v)$$

In general, the beginning of a continuation should be the identity function. However, to be able to use the function application to get the result of $cpg \llbracket bx_1 \circ bx_2 \rrbracket$, the accumulative function on the source needs to be initiated as the constant function from that source. This constant function helps to retain the discarded things in the source.

The result pair (s, v) obtained from cpg as above should be same with the result of $pg \llbracket bx \rrbracket(s_0, v_0)$. More generally, we have the following relationship:

$$cpg\llbracket bx \rrbracket(ks, kv, s, v) = pg \llbracket bx \rrbracket(ks\ s, kv\ v)$$

Note that, in $cpg \llbracket bx_1 \circ bx_2 \rrbracket$, $\underline{s_1}$ is redundant because this evaluated variable is not used in the later steps. In the next session, we will optimize this redundancy.

4.3 Lazy Computation: kpg

The problem for cpg lies in redundant computations during the evaluation. To prevent such redundant computations from occurring, we introduce an extension named kpg. While cpg evaluates values eagerly, kpg does the opposite. Every value is evaluated lazily in a computation of kpg. The input of $kpg \llbracket bx \rrbracket$ is expanded to a 6-tuple (ks, kv, lks, lkv, s, v) where ks and kv keep the modification information same as cpg, s and v hold evaluated values, and lks and lkv are used for lazy evaluation of actual values. The output of this function is also a 6-tuple (ks, kv, lks, lkv, s, v).

Suppose that we have a source s_0 and a view v_0. The pair of the updated source and view (s, v) where $s = put \llbracket bx \rrbracket\ s_0\ v_0$ and $v = get \llbracket bx \rrbracket\ s_0$ can be obtained using kpg as follows:

$$(ks, kv, lks, lkv, s, v) \Leftarrow kpg\llbracket bx \rrbracket(\lambda\_.s_0, id, id, id, s_0, v_0);$$
$$(lks\ s, lkv\ v)$$

The beginning of accumulative functions lks and lkv are set as the identity function, while ks and kv are initiated as the same with the corresponding ones in cpg. The relationship among kpg, cpg and pg can be shown as follows:

$$kpg\llbracket bx \rrbracket(ks, kv, lks, lkv, s, v) = cpg\llbracket bx \rrbracket(ks \circ lks, kv \circ lkv, s, v)$$
$$= pg \llbracket bx \rrbracket(ks\ (lks\ s), kv\ (lkv\ v))$$

Definition 7. $kpg[\![bx]\!](ks, kv, lks, lkv, s, v)$

$kpg[\![Skip\ h]\!](ks, kv, lks, lkv, s, v) =$
  $es \Leftarrow lks\ s; \quad ev \Leftarrow lkv\ v;$
  if $h\ es = ev$ then (ks, kv, id, id, es, ev) else *undefined*
$kpg[\![Replace]\!](ks, kv, lks, lkv, s, v) = (kv, ks, lkv, lks, v, s)$
$kpg[\![bx_1 \times bx_2]\!](ks, kv, lks, lkv, s, v) =$
  $es \Leftarrow lks\ s; \quad ev \Leftarrow lkv\ v;$
  $(ks_1, kv_1, lks_1, lkv_1, s_1, v_1) \Leftarrow$
      $kpg[\![bx_1]\!](fst \circ ks, fst \circ kv, fst, fst, es, ev);$
  $(ks_2, kv_2, lks_2, lkv_2, s_2, v_2) \Leftarrow$
      $kpg[\![bx_2]\!](snd \circ ks, snd \circ kv, snd, snd, es, ev);$
    $(con\ ks_1\ ks_2,\ con\ kv_1\ kv_2,$
      $con\ (lks_1 \circ fst)\ (lks_2 \circ snd),\ con\ (lkv_1 \circ fst)\ (lkv_2 \circ snd),$
      $(s_1, s_2),\ (v_1, v_2))$
$kpg[\![RearrS\ f_1\ f_2\ bx]\!](ks, kv, lks, lkv, s, v) =$
  $(ks', kv', lks', lkv', s', v') \Leftarrow kpg[\![bx]\!](f_1 \circ ks, kv, f_1 \circ lks, lkv, s, v);$
    $(f_2 \circ ks', kv', f_2 \circ lks', lkv', s', v')$
$kpg[\![RearrV\ g_1\ g_2\ bx]\!](ks, kv, lks, lkv, s, v) =$
  $(ks', kv', lks', lkv', s', v') \Leftarrow kpg[\![bx]\!](ks, g_1 \circ kv, lks, g_1 \circ lkv, s, v);$
    $(ks', g_2 \circ kv', lks', g_2 \circ lkv', s', v')$
$kpg[\![Case\ cond_{sv}\ cond_s\ bx_1\ bx_2]\!](ks, kv, lks, lkv, s, v) =$
  $es \Leftarrow lks\ s; \quad ev \Leftarrow lkv\ v;$
  if $cond_{sv}\ es\ ev\ \&\&\ cond_s\ es$
  then $(ks', kv', lks', lkv', s', v') \Leftarrow kpg[\![bx_1]\!](ks, kv, id, id, es, ev)$
  else $(ks', kv', lks', lkv', s', v') \Leftarrow kpg[\![bx_2]\!](ks, kv, id, id, es, ev)$
  fi $cond_s\ (lks'\ s')\ \&\&\ cond_{sv}\ es\ (lkv'\ v');$ return $(ks', kv', lks', lkv', s', v')$
$kpg[\![bx_1 \circ bx_2]\!](ks, kv, lks, lkv, s, v) =$
  $(ks_1, kv_1, \underline{lks_1}, lkv_1, \underline{s_1}, v_1) \Leftarrow kpg[\![bx_1]\!](ks, id, lks, id, s, dummy);$
  $(ks_2, kv_2, lks_2, lkv_2, s_2, v_2) \Leftarrow kpg[\![bx_2]\!](kv_1, kv, lkv_1, lkv, v_1, v);$
    $(ks_1 \circ ks_2, kv_2, ks_1 \circ lks_2, lkv_2, s_2, v_2)$

In kpg, basically, functions for the updates are kept (but not evaluated) in
lks and lkv. In $kpg\,[\![RearrS]\!]$ and $kpg\,[\![RearrV]\!]$, f_1 and g_1 are accumulated in
lks and lkv. The kept functions are evaluated in $kpg\,[\![Skip]\!]$ and $kpg\,[\![Case]\!]$ by
applications of $lks\ s$ and $lkv\ v$. At the same time, the third and fourth argument of recursive calls are updated with the identity function. This evaluation is
needed because these definitions require the actual values, es and ev. Thanks to
this update, accumulation in kpg, $\underline{lks_1}$ and $\underline{s_1}$ in $kpg\,[\![bx_1 \circ bx_2]\!]$ are not evaluated
as much as possible.

Additionally we did two optimizations in kpg. The first is in $kpg\,[\![bx_1 \times bx_2]\!]$. Because es and ev are not used in this definition, we do not need to evaluate. However, if we accumulate lks and lkv, both might be evaluated independently in two assignments using $kpg\,[\![bx_1]\!]$ and $kpg\,[\![bx_2]\!]$. This includes the same computation. To remove duplicate evaluations, we evaluate actual values es and ev before calling $kpg\,[\![bx_1]\!]$ and $kpg\,[\![bx_2]\!]$. The second is in $kpg\,[\![Case]\!]$ and not shown in the definition. We need to evaluate lks' s' and lkv' v' to check the fi condition before returning the 6-tuple. Such evaluations can be done lazily to make programs run faster. We use the above small optimizations in our implementation.

4.4   Combination of pg and kpg: xpg

The purpose we introduced cpg and kpg is to avoid redundant recursive call and keep the dropped parts from the source in a function. On the other hand, these accumulations in cpg and kpg will be an overhead if they are not necessary. The problem in $pg\,[\![bx_1 \circ bx_2]\!]$ is that there are two recursive calls of $pg\,[\![bx_1]\!]$ and there is no problem in the recursive call of $pg\,[\![bx_2]\!]$. Therefore, we combine pg and kpg to take advantage of both approaches.

Definition 8. $xpg\,[\![bx]\!](s, v)$

$$xpg\,[\![bx]\!](s, v) = \text{match } bx \text{ with}$$
$$\mid bx_1 \circ bx_2 \rightarrow$$
$$(ks_1, kv_1, lks_1, lkv_1, s_1, v_1) \Leftarrow kpg[\![bx_1]\!](\lambda\_.s, id, id, id, s, dummy);$$
$$(s_2, v_2) \Leftarrow xpg\,[\![bx_2]\!](lkv_1\ v_1, v);$$
$$(ks_1\ s_2, v_2)$$
$$\mid \_ \rightarrow similar\ to\ pg$$

Similar to pg, $xpg\,[\![bx]\!]$ accepts a pair of the source and the view (s, v) to produce the new pair. The constructions of $xpg\,[\![bx]\!]$ when bx is not a composition are the same as the ones of $pg\,[\![bx]\!]$. Note that, xpg is called recursively instead of pg. For $xpg\,[\![bx_1 \circ bx_2]\!]$, we use two function calls and a function application to calculate the result. The first call and the function application come from kpg, while the second call is based on pg.

5   Experiments

We have fully implemented and tested all methods [2,3] described in the previous sections. Our target language is untyped. Some dummies used for pg, cpg, kpg and xpg are replaced with the current updated views. This helps a program in the put direction valid.

---

[2] All experiments on macOS 10.14.6, processor Intel Core i7 (2.6 GHz), RAM 16 GB 2400 MHz DDR4, OCaml 4.07.1. The OCaml runtime system options and garbage collection parameters are set as default.

[3] The implementation is available: https://github.com/k-tsushima/pgs.

5.1 Test Cases

We have selected seven test cases (Table 1) to represent non-trivial cases of practical significance. The test cases use left associative compositions because we focus on this kind of inefficiency in this paper. In the last two columns, s and v are the updated source and view, respectively. They are produced by applying put and get to the original source s_0 and view v_0. That is, $s = put\,[\![bx]\!]\,s_0\,v_0$ and $v = get\,[\![bx]\!]\,s_0$, where bx is the program indicated in the second column of the table. Results s and v are independent of the associativity of the composition.

Table 1. Composition test cases (number of compositions $= n$)

No	Name	Type	Input		Output	
			s_0	v_0	s	v
1	lcomp-phead-ldata	Straight line	$[[\ldots[1]\ldots]]$ (n+1 times)	100	$[[\ldots[100]\ldots]]$ (n+1 times)	1
2	lcomp-ptail	Straight line	$[1,\ldots,n{+}1]$	$[1,\ldots,10]$	$s_0\,@\,v_0$	$[\,]$
3	lcomp-ptail-ldata	Straight line	$[L,\ldots,L]$ (n+1 times)	$[L,\ldots,L]$ (10 times)	$[L,\ldots,L]$ (n+11 times)	$[\,]$
4	lcomp-bsnoc	Straight line	$[1,\ldots,n{-}1]$	$[1,\ldots,n{-}1]$	$[1,\ldots,n{-}1]$	$[1,\ldots,n{-}1]$
5	lcomp-bsnoc-ldata	Straight line	$[L,\ldots,L]$ (n-1 times)	$[L,\ldots,L]$ (n-1 times)	$[L,\ldots,L]$ (n-1 times)	$[L,\ldots,L]]$ (n-1 times)
6	breverse	Recursion	$[1,\ldots,n]$	$[1,\ldots,n]$	$[n,\ldots,1]$	$[n,\ldots,1]$
7	breverse-ldata	Recursion	$[L,\ldots,L]$ (n times)	$[L,\ldots,L]$ (n times)	$[L,\ldots,L]$ (n times)	$[L,\ldots,L]$ (n times)

The first five test cases (1–5) are n straight-line (non-recursive) compositions of the same $n+1$ programs. The prefix *lcomp* in the name of a test case indicates that the textual compositions are left associative. The suffix *ldata* indicates that the input size is considered large. The symbol L in the input column stands for a list $L = [T,\ldots,T]$ with $T = [A,\ldots,A]$ of length 10 and $A = [1,\ldots,5]$. They are only intended to generate test data that is large enough for measuring results.

We introduced the composition *phead* ∘ *phead* earlier in Sect. 1. The composition of many *phead*s works similarly. The head of a head element inside a deeply nested list, which is the source, is updated by the changed view. Because of the type of the source, this program is categorized as a *ldata* case.

Next, we briefly explain the behavior of the remaining compositions in Table 1.

The composition of many *ptail*s, in the *put* direction, replaces a part of the tail of the source list by the view list and, in the *get* direction, returns such a tail from the source.

The composition of many *bsnoc*s, in the *put* direction, creates a permutation of the view list if its length is not larger than the length of the source list and, in the *get* direction, produces a permutation of the source list.

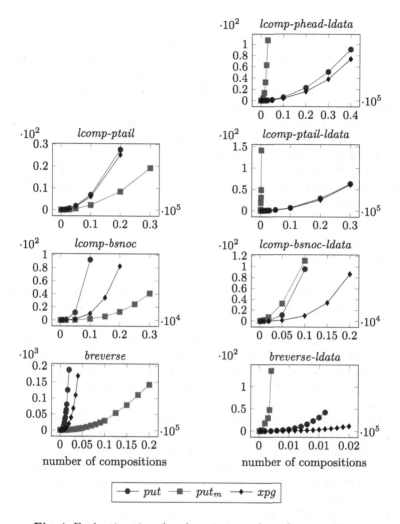

Fig. 4. Evaluation time (secs) against number of compositions

breverse is defined in terms of *bfoldr*, that appeared in Sect. 2. In the *put* direction, it produces a reverse of the view list if its length is not larger than the length of the source list and, in the *get* direction, produces a reverse of the source list. Note that compositions are by the recursions of *breverse* and the number of compositions are dynamically determined by the length of the source list.

5.2 Results

Figure 4 shows the evaluation times for each of the seven test cases using the three methods: *put* in minBiGUL, put_m in minBiGUL$_m$ and *xpg*. We also did similar experiments with *pg*, *cpg* and *kpg*, but their results are slower than the corresponding ones of *xpg*. The slowness was caused by the exponential number of *pg* calls in the case of *pg*, redundant evaluations (*cpg*), and redundant overhead for constructing closures (*kpg*). Therefore we simply omit these results in Fig. 4. As we all know, *put* works poorly for left associative compositions because of the number of reevaluated *gets*. The left part of the figure contains tests using not-large inputs, and we see that put_m is the fastest method for them. However if the input size is large enough, in the cases of the right part of the figure, put_m will be slower quickly due to time for manipulating data in the table. At that time, *xpg* is the most effective method.

Note that this result concerns BX programs that use many compositions. If the number of compositions is small, the original *put* without memoization will be fastest because of the overhead for memoization (put_m) and the overhead for keeping complements in closures (*xpg*).

6   Related Work

Since the pioneering work of lens [7], many BX languages have been proposed [2–4,8–12]. Although much progress has been made on the semantics and correctness of BX programs for the past years, as far as we are aware, little work has been done on optimization of BX programs [13]. Anjorin et al. introduces the first benchmark[4] for BX languages and compared them [14], but a systematic improvement for practical implementation of BX languages is still missing. This paper shows the first attempt of improving efficiency of BX composition evaluation.

The baseline of this work is the BX language BiGUL [4,5], and we compare BiGUL's method (in Sect. 2) with our methods (in Sects. 3 and 4). From experimental results of left associative BX composition programs, we can see that our memoization methods are faster than the original BiGUL's evaluation method. While we focus on BiGUL, our methods are general and should be applicable to other BX languages.

Our work is related to many known optimization methods for unidirectional programs. Memoization [15,16] is a technique to avoid repeated redundant computation. In our case, we show that two specific memoization methods can be used for bidirectional programs. To deal with inefficiency due to compositions, many fusion methods have been studied [17] to merge a composition of two (recursive) programs into one. However, under the context of bidirectional programs, we need to consider not only compositions of recursive programs but also compositions inside a recursive program (as we have seen in *bfoldr*). This paper focuses on the composition inside a recursion, where compositions are produced dynamically at runtime. We tackled the problem by using tupling [18], lazy update and lazy computation [19,20].

---

[4] The BX programs in their benchmark are basically BX programs without composition. Because we focus on the BX programs that include many compositions, their benchmark is not applicable for our evaluation.

7   Conclusion and Future Work

In this paper, we focus on efficiency of composition of BX programs. To achieve fast evaluation, we introduce two different methods using memoization. From the experimental results of left associative BX composition programs, we know that xpg is fastest method if input size is large and put_m is fastest for other left associative programs. This shows that if programmers choose one method based on their BX programs and inputs, they can use an efficient evaluation method.

We will continue our work on the following four points. First is overcoming our limitation in xpg. In xpg, there are two limitations: only for very-well-behaved programs and restriction for $pg [\![Case]\!]$ in Sect. 4.1. To be a practical evaluation method, an extension of the target language is needed. After extension of the language, we can evaluate more various programs for experimental results. Second is introducing an automatic analysis about BX programs and inputs to choose the best evaluation method. Currently, programmers have to choose the evaluation method by themselves based on their BX programs and inputs. If this analysis is achieved, we can reduce programmers' burden. Third is introducing a type system to our target language, especially the datatype of sources and view. If we introduce this, we can avoid runtime errors like statically-typed functional languages. For this, we need to investigate more about how to construct dummy values because the current definition used in our experiments will cause type errors. Fourth is using a lazy language. Although we used a strict language OCaml in this paper, if we use a lazy language, we might get laziness for free.

Acknowledgment. We thank the anonymous reviewers for valuable comments and suggestions. This work has been partially supported by JSPS KAKENHI Grant Number JP17H06099 and ROIS NII Open Collaborative Research 2018.

References

1. Bancilhon, F., Spyratos, N.: Update semantics of relational views. ACM Trans. Database Syst. **6**, 557–575 (1981). ISSN 0362–5915
2. Bohannon, A., Pierce, B.C., Vaughan, J.A.: Relational lenses: a language for updatable views in principles of database systems, pp. 42–67 (2006)
3. Bohannon, A., Foster, J.N., Pierce, B.C., Pilkiewicz, A., Schmitt, A.: Boomerang: resourceful lenses for string data. In: Proceedings of the 35th Annual ACM SIGPLAN-SIGACT Symposium on Principles of Programming Languages, San Francisco, California, USA. ACM, pp. 407–419 (2008). ISBN 978-1-59593-689-9
4. Ko, H.-S., Zan, T., Hu, Z. BiGUL: a formally verified core language for Putback-based bidirectional programming. In: Proceedings of the 2016 ACM SIGPLAN Workshop on Partial Evaluation and Program Manipulation. ACM, St. Petersburg, pp. 61–72 (2016). ISBN 978-1-4503-4097- 7
5. Ko, H.-S., Hu, Z.: An axiomatic basis for bidirectional programming. Proc. ACM Program. Lang. **2**, 41:1–41:29 (2017). ISSN 2475–1421

6. Pacheco, H., Hu, Z., Fischer, S.: Monadic combinators for "Putback" style bidirectional programming. In: Proceedings of the ACM SIGPLAN 2014 Workshop on Partial Evaluation and Program Manipulation, San Diego, California, USA, pp. 39–50. ACM (2014). ISBN 978-1-4503-2619-3
7. Foster, J.N., Greenwald, M.B., Moore, J.T., Pierce, B.C., Schmitt, A.: Combinators for bidirectional tree transformations: a linguistic approach to the view-update problem. ACM Trans. Program. Lang. Syst. **29** (2007). ISSN 0164–0925
8. Buchmann, T.: BXtend - a framework for (bidirectional) incremental model transformations. In: Proceedings of the 6th International Conference on Model-Driven Engineering and Software Development (SCITEPRESS - Science and Technology Publications, Lda, Funchal, Madeira, Portugal, pp. 336–345 (2018). ISBN 978-989-758-283-7
9. Leblebici, E., Anjorin, A., Schürr, A.: Developing eMoflon with eMoflon. In: Di Ruscio, D., Varró, D. (eds.) ICMT 2014. LNCS, vol. 8568, pp. 138–145. Springer, Cham (2014). https://doi.org/10.1007/978-3-319-08789-4_10
10. Samimi-Dehkordi, L., Zamani, B., Rahimi, S.K.: EVL+Strace: a novel bidirectional model transformation approach. Inf. Softw. Technol. **100**, 47–72 (2018). ISSN 0950–5849
11. Cicchetti, A., Di Ruscio, D., Eramo, R., Pierantonio, A.: JTL: a bidirectional and change propagating transformation language. In: Malloy, B., Staab, S., van den Brand, M. (eds.) SLE 2010. LNCS, vol. 6563, pp. 183–202. Springer, Heidelberg (2011). https://doi.org/10.1007/978-3-642-19440-5_11. ISSN 978-3-642-19440-5
12. Hinkel, G., Burger, E.: Change propagation and bidirectionality in internal transformation DSLs. Softw. Syst. Model. **18**, 249–278. ISSN 1619–1366 (2019)
13. Horn, R., Perera, R., Cheney, J.: Incremental relational lenses. Proc. ACM Program. Lang. **2**, 74:1–74:30 (2018). ISSN 2475–1421
14. Anjorin, A., et al.: Benchmarking bidirectional transformations: theory, implementation, application, and assessment. Softw. Syst. Model. **19**(3), 647–691 (2019). https://doi.org/10.1007/s10270-019-00752-x
15. Bellman, R.E.: Dynamic Programming. Dover Publications Inc., New York (2003). ISBN 0486428095
16. Michie, D.: "Memo" functions and machine learning. Nature **218**, 19–22 (1968)
17. Wadler, P.: Deforestation: transforming programs to eliminate trees. Theor. Comput. Sci. **73**, 231–248 (1988). ISSN 0304–3975
18. Fokkinga, M.M.: Tupling and mutumorphisms appeared. In: The Squigollist, vol. 1, no. 4, pp. 81–82, June 1990
19. Henderson, P., Morris Jr., J.H.: A lazy evaluator. In: Proceedings of the 3rd ACM SIGACT-SIGPLAN Symposium on Principles on Programming Languages, Atlanta, Georgia, pp. 95–103. ACM (1976)
20. Hudak, P., Hughes, J., Peyton Jones, S., Wadler, P.: A history of Haskell: being lazy with class. In: Proceedings of the Third ACM SIGPLAN Conference on History of Programming Languages, San Diego, California, pp. 12-1–12-55. ACM (2007). ISBN 978-1-59593-766-7

Implementing, and Keeping in Check, a DSL Used in E-Learning

Oliver Westphal$^{(\boxtimes)}$ and Janis Voigtländer

University of Duisburg-Essen, Duisburg, Germany
{oliver.westphal,janis.voigtlaender}@uni-due.de

Abstract. We discuss a DSL intended for use in an education setting when teaching the writing of interactive Haskell programs to students. The DSL was previously presented as a small formal language of specifications capturing the behavior of simple console I/O programs, along with a trace-based semantics. A prototypical implementation also exists. When going for productive application in an actual course setting, some robustness and usability questions arise. For example, if programs written by students are mechanically checked and graded by the implementation, what guarantees are there for the educator that the assessment is correct? Does the implementation really agree with the on-paper semantics? What else can inform the educator's writing of a DSL expression when developing a new exercise task? Which activities beyond testing of student submissions can be mechanized based on the specification language? Can we, for example, generate additional material to hand to students in support of task understanding, before, and feedback or trusted sample solutions, after their own solution attempts? Also, how to keep the framework maintainable, preserving its guarantees when the expressiveness of the underlying DSL is to be extended? Our aim here is to address these and related questions, by reporting on connections we have made and concrete steps we have taken, as well as the bigger picture.

1 Introduction

We previously presented a small formal specification language for describing interactive behavior of console I/O programs [12]. Given such specifications, we can check whether some candidate program has the specified behavior by repeatedly running the program and matching its traces against the specification, thus either finding a counterexample or gaining sufficient confidence that the program behaves as desired. We plan to use this approach of specification and testing to automatically grade student submissions on the subject of writing interactive programs [8] in our Haskell programming course, and therefore we are developing an implementation. The goal of the implementation is to not only get a working version of the on-paper definitions but a DSL-based framework that makes it easy to design and adapt exercise tasks for use in an e-learning system [9,11].

© Springer Nature Switzerland AG 2020
K. Nakano and K. Sagonas (Eds.): FLOPS 2020, LNCS 12073, pp. 179–197, 2020.
https://doi.org/10.1007/978-3-030-59025-3_11

Central to this goal is a guarantee that if something different is happening than an educator is expecting, then that is not the fault of the DSL implementation itself and instead is therefore fixable by said educator. Moreover, the educator should not be left alone with their mismatch in expectations. The framework's implementation should provide some means for them to investigate what is actually going on and where they are possibly missing a connection. This article is about how we can provide such means.

2   Specification Language Overview

Our specification and testing framework consists of four major components: a way to express specifications that describe read/write behavior of programs, a notion of traces for capturing program runs, a function to determine whether a trace represents program behavior that is valid regarding a specification, and a testing procedure to summarily check programs against specifications.

As an example, take the following program that reads in a natural number and then that many additional numbers and finally prints their sum:

$$main :: \text{IO } ()$$
$$main = \textbf{do } n \leftarrow readLn$$
$$\quad\quad \textbf{let } loop\ xs = \textbf{if } length\ xs == n \textbf{ then } print\ (sum\ xs)$$
$$\quad\quad\quad\quad\quad\quad\quad\quad\quad \textbf{else do } x \leftarrow readLn$$
$$\quad\quad\quad\quad\quad\quad\quad\quad\quad\quad\quad loop\ (x : xs)$$
$$\quad\quad loop\ []$$

A specification for the behavior of this program looks as follows:

$$[\triangleright n]^{\mathbb{N}} \cdot ([\triangleright x]^{\mathbb{Z}} \angle len(x_A) = n_C \searrow \mathbf{E})^{\rightarrow^{\mathbf{E}}} \cdot [\{sum(x_A)\} \triangleright]$$

Testing against the specification is done by randomly generating suitable input sequences (note that for this specification the first input to a program should always be non-negative) and then comparing each trace resulting from running the program on such input with the expectation encoded in the specification. The trace of a program is the sequence of read and written values. For example, given the inputs $2, 7, 13$, the trace of the above program would be ?2 ?7 ?13 !20 stop. We now give a brief overview of specifications, traces, and what/how we test.

2.1   Specifications

There are three atomic forms of specifications: $\mathbf{0}$ is the empty specification, $[\triangleright x]^{\tau}$ is for reading a value typed by $\tau \subseteq \mathbb{Z}$ into a variable x, and $[\Theta \triangleright]$ is for outputting the result of evaluating any term $t \in \Theta$, where Θ represents a set of possible outputs. Variables are always associated with the lists of all values previously read into them. Accessing variables, in terms, can then be done in two different ways: either as x_A, giving precisely the list of all read values for x, or as x_C, giving only the last, most current value.

Two specifications s_1 and s_2 can be composed sequentially, denoted by $s_1 \cdot s_2$. Sequential composition is defined to be associative and to have $\mathbf{0}$ as the neutral element. It will often be performed silently by writing just $s_1 s_2$ instead of $s_1 \cdot s_2$. By $s_1 \angle c \backslash s_2$ we denote the specification that either requires s_1 or requires s_2 to be adhered to, depending on which Boolean value the term c evaluates to under the current variable assignment, where True chooses the branch on the right. Lastly, $s^{\rightarrow \mathbf{E}}$ stands for the repetition of specification s until, inside s, the iteration exit-marker $\mathbf{E}$ is encountered, which behaves similarly to the break command found in many imperative languages (under various names).

2.2 Traces

Traces are sequences $m_0 v_0\, m_1 v_1 \ldots m_n v_n\, \mathsf{stop}$, where $n \in \mathbb{N}$, $m_i \in \{?, !\}$, and $v_i \in \mathbb{Z}$. Here $?v$ denotes the reading of the value v and $!v$ denotes the writing of the value v. Besides these ordinary traces there is also a notion of generalized traces that capture the complete behavior mandated by a specification for a single concrete input sequence. Basically, generalized traces are traces in which each output place is a *set* of all possible outputs a program can make at that point, potentially including the empty output ε to indicate optionality.[1] A covering relation $\prec$ relates ordinary traces and generalized ones. If an ordinary trace t is covered by a generalized trace t_g, denoted by $t \prec t_g$, it means that one can replace each set of outputs in t_g by an element from that set and end up with t. For example, it holds that $?2\,!3\,!8\,\mathsf{stop} \prec ?2\,!\{3,6\}\,!\{\varepsilon,7\}\,!\{8\}\,\mathsf{stop}$.

2.3 Acceptance Criterion

The conditions under which a program run, encoded by a trace, is considered to represent valid behavior regarding a specification are defined by the *accept*-function in Fig. 1 (coming straight from [12]): exactly if $accept(s, k_I)(t, \Delta_I)$ evaluates to True does the ordinary trace t represent behavior valid for specification s. Here Δ_I is the variable assignment mapping each variable occurring in s to the empty list and a continuation argument k is used to keep track of the current iteration context. When entering an iteration, we build a new continuation that either repeats the loop body or restores the previous iteration context, depending on whether it is called with End or Exit. Calls with Exit or End, respectively, happen if we encounter an exit-marker $\mathbf{E}$ or hit the end of a specification, i.e., in the case $accept(\mathbf{0}, k)(t, \Delta)$. The initial continuation k_I takes care of the handling at the top-level of the specification. Hence, k_I is only intended to be called with End at the very end of traversing the specification overall. It then tests whether the remaining trace equals stop, which indicates acceptance of the initially given trace; or else the result of *accept* is False.

---

[1] In the full formulation from [12], consecutive outputs in generalized traces are additionally normalized into a single output action that chooses from a set of value *sequences*. We ignore this detail here in favor of a more straightforward presentation.

2.4   Testing

For the testing of programs against specifications, the *accept*-function is not used directly but is instead modified into a function *traceSet* that takes a specification and describes the set of all generalized traces valid for that specification. Intuitively, *traceSet* is obtained from "solving" $accept(s, k_I)(t, \Delta_I)$ for t.

In almost all cases the set of valid generalized traces for a given specification is infinite. There are two different ways the set of traces can become infinite, one harmless but the other one not so much. The first way is that we can arbitrarily choose a value from a potentially infinite set at every input step. This form of infinity is not really problematic, though, since we can work around it by sampling traces at random instead of computing all possibilities. The second way in which a *traceSet*-result can grow infinitely large is when we consider a specification that exhibits potentially non-terminating behavior. In this case sampling does not help us, since we can get stuck in an endless loop. But as long as we do not choose input values such that the behavior described by a specification becomes non-terminating, we can compute results of *traceSet*.[2] We will treat the *traceSet*-function as a black box here, since its technical details are not important here. Its correctness in the implementation, of course, is! (See Sect. 4.)

The actual testing, for some program p and specification s, is done by repeatedly applying the following steps, resulting in either a counterexample or increased confidence in the appropriateness of p.

1. Use the *traceSet*-function to (randomly) sample a generalized trace for s.
2. From this trace, extract the sequence of inputs.
3. Determine whether the ordinary trace resulting from running p on these inputs is covered by said generalized trace.

3   Comparing Theory and Implementation/Use

Our overall framework is hosted at https://github.com/fmidue/IOTasks. Besides the source code of the implementation, that repository also contains various usage examples. Here, let us consider an example task and compare its formulations in the on-paper version and in the implemented DSL. We take the same example as earlier: reading in a natural number and then as many further integers as that first number says, and finally printing those integers' sum. Recall that the specification $[\triangleright n]^{\mathbb{N}}([\triangleright x]^{\mathbb{Z}} \angle len(x_A) = n_C \diagdown \mathbf{E})^{\rightarrow^{\mathbf{E}}}[\{sum(x_A)\} \triangleright]$ encodes this behavior. Transliterating it into our DSL (which is an EDSL using deep embedding [3]), we get the following Haskell expression:

---

[2] That is easier said than done. We do at the moment not have a general solution to reliably generate "suitable" inputs only, beyond simple typing as expressed by the τ in $[\triangleright x]^{\tau}$, and therefore currently rely on using only specifications that do not involve non-terminating behavior for any well-typed inputs at all.

$$accept([\triangleright x]^\tau \cdot s', k)(t, \Delta) = \begin{cases} accept(s', k)(t', store(x, v, \Delta)), \text{ if } t =?v\,t' \wedge v \in \tau \\ \mathsf{False} \hspace{5.5cm}, \text{ otherwise} \end{cases}$$

$$accept([\Theta \triangleright] \cdot s', k)(t, \Delta) = \begin{cases} accept([(\Theta \setminus \{\varepsilon\}) \triangleright] \cdot s', k)(t, \Delta), \text{ if } \varepsilon \in \Theta \\ \hspace{1.2cm} \vee\; accept(s', k)(t, \Delta) \\ accept(s', k)(t', \Delta) \hspace{1.6cm}, \text{ if } \varepsilon \notin \Theta \wedge t =!v\,t' \\ \hspace{4.4cm} \wedge v \in eval(\Theta, \Delta) \\ \mathsf{False} \hspace{3.7cm}, \text{ otherwise} \end{cases}$$

$$accept((s_1 \angle c \searrow s_2) \cdot s', k)(t, \Delta) = \begin{cases} accept(s_2 \cdot s', k)(t, \Delta), \text{ if } eval(c, \Delta) = \mathsf{True} \\ accept(s_1 \cdot s', k)(t, \Delta), \text{ otherwise} \end{cases}$$

$$accept(s^{\rightarrow \mathbf{E}} \cdot s', k)(t, \Delta) = accept(s, k')(t, \Delta)$$
$$\text{with } k'(cont) = \begin{cases} accept(s, k'), \text{ if } cont = \mathsf{End} \\ accept(s', k), \text{ if } cont = \mathsf{Exit} \end{cases}$$
$$accept(\mathbf{E} \cdot s', k)(t, \Delta) = k(\mathsf{Exit})(t, \Delta)$$
$$accept(\mathbf{0}, k)(t, \Delta) = k(\mathsf{End})(t, \Delta)$$

$$k_I(cont)(t, \Delta) = \begin{cases} \mathsf{True} \hspace{0.6cm}, \text{ if } cont = \mathsf{End} \wedge t = \mathsf{stop} \\ \mathsf{False} \hspace{0.5cm}, \text{ if } cont = \mathsf{End} \wedge t \neq \mathsf{stop} \\ \mathsf{error} \hspace{0.5cm}, \text{ if } cont = \mathsf{Exit} \end{cases}$$

Fig. 1. Trace acceptance.

readInput "n" *nats* <>
tillExit (*branch* (*length* (*getAll* "x") == *getCurrent* "n")
            (*readInput* "x" *ints*)
            exit) <>
writeOutput [*sum* (*getAll* "x")]

Here *sum* :: Num $a \Rightarrow$ Term $[a] \rightarrow$ Term a and *length* :: Term $[a] \rightarrow$ Term Int are redefinitions of the respective standard functions in the context of a Term type constructor. Similarly, *getAll* and *getCurrent* have types String $\rightarrow$ Term $[a]$ and String $\rightarrow$ Term a, respectively.[3]

Values of a Term type can be evaluated under an appropriate variable environment via the function *evalTerm* :: Term $a \rightarrow$ Environment $\rightarrow a$. Our encoding of terms here differs from the original presentation [12], where we used an applicative-style [7] representation for terms that enabled the usage of normal Haskell functions in specifications. The new encoding is useful in case we need access to the syntactic structure of terms (see Sect. 6), as we can preserve this information in the redefinitions. However, if we do not need such inspection of terms, redefining standard functions in the new context most likely does not add

---

[3] There are no guarantees that we can actually use a term constructed with *getAll* or *getCurrent* at any particular instantiation for type a. Checks happen at runtime.

any benefit. For this reason, our implementation is suitably polymorphic over the type constructor for terms used in specifications.

To facilitate checking programs (such as student submissions) against a specification such as the one seen above, we use an approach presented by Swierstra and Altenkirch [10] to acquire an inspectable representation of I/O behavior, plus random testing via QuickCheck [1] to generate test cases and test the candidate program according to the procedure described in Sect. 2.4.

So far, this is essentially the approach described in our previous work [12] (apart from the different term representation).[4] But how do we guarantee that the implementation behaves according to the formal on-paper definitions? That is, if the system tells a student that their submitted solution is correct, is that really the case? And conversely, does the system only reject wrong submissions and does it provide valid explanations in each case? In the next section we will look at exactly these questions. But there are also other important properties an educator might expect from the framework besides technical correctness. Generally, when posing tasks using the implemented system, there are various artifacts in play (some explicit and technical, some more virtual), such as:

- The idea/intention the educator has about what should be done in the task. In the case of the above example, the idea could be something like "I want them to realize a simple I/O loop, so they should write a program that reads a number and then as many further numbers and finally prints a sum."
- The DSL expression (and possibly additional data) capturing, hopefully, the desired behavior.
- The verbal task description handed to students ("Write a program which ...").
- A sample solution; for sanity checking and possibly for later also being handed to students.
- Any supporting material the students get as part of the task description. For example, a run of the sample solution on some specific input sequence.

All of these and potentially further artifacts must be kept in sync with each other in order to arrive at a consistent and usable exercise task. Therefore, we want to provide support for making sure that they indeed are in sync. One potential way to achieve this consistency is to generate some artifacts from others, along with correctness guarantees/arguments for those generators. Another way is to establish processes the educator follows in creating some artifacts either in isolation or together. For example, we can check different hand-written artifacts against each other inside the system itself. A simple example would be to check if a sample solution is accepted by the task specification in DSL form.

We will come back to such issues later. After establishing confidence in the technical core of the implementation, we will show that there are indeed certain provisions an educator can employ to support and verify their usage of

---

[4] A live online demonstration of the prototype implementation for that previous article is available at https://autotool.fmi.iw.uni-due.de/tfpie19, showcasing the approach. (Note that this demo still uses applicative-style terms.)

the framework. For now, Fig. 2 shows our current "bigger picture". The dashed arrows represent activities (creation of artifacts etc.) by the educator, while most of the solid arrows represent technical flow, i.e., where the implementation/system is active. As can already be seen, there are various connections between some source and some target that can be realized via different routes, indicating opportunities for automatic support of educator activities. We will come back to specific ingredients later on.

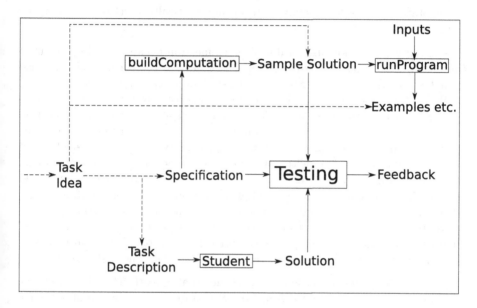

Fig. 2. Artifacts and flow.

4   Validating the Implementation

The guarantees we are going to provide to users of our implementation rely on the correctness of the technical core of the system, i.e., of the components involved in testing solution candidates against specifications. As described earlier (Sect. 2.4), testing is done by repeatedly sampling from the set of generalized traces for a specification and checking if the program under testing produces a matching trace for the same input sequence. The actual semantics of when a specification and a trace match is given by the Boolean-valued *accept*-function defined on specification-trace-pairs (see Fig. 1). The relationship between that semantics and the testing approach is stated as follows [12]:

Let s $\in$ *Spec* and t $\in$ *Tr*, then $accept(s, k_I)(t, \Delta_I) =$ True if and only if there exists a $t_g \in traceSet(s, k_I^T)(\Delta_I)$ such that $t \prec t_g$.

The implementation thus does not need to rely on the *accept*-function to do the testing. However, implementing *accept* anyway gives us a way to check, even programmatically to some extent (i.e., mechanically testing the test framework), whether the implementation behaves according to the on-paper definitions:

- The *accept*-function can be translated almost verbatim to a Haskell program.
- It is clear, from code inspection/review of this program, that both the Haskell and the on-paper version of *accept* compute the same function.
- Therefore, any implementation of the testing approach, no matter how technically involved, can be validated using the *accept*-semantics and turning the statement displayed above into an automatically checkable property or properties.

This reasoning does not just establish the connection between the implemented *traceSet*-function and the on-paper semantics but "in the other direction" also validates that the test framework assesses student submissions correctly.

While the reasoning above is, of course, no substitute for a formal correctness proof, it can still provide us with some confidence that an implementation of *traceSet* behaves correctly. For example, we test properties derived via this approach in our continuous integration setup. Due to that, we can refactor and extend our implementation with confidence and do not need to worry about its correctness after each change. Since at the moment we are mainly interested in exploring different features and implementation details for our framework, validating correctness through automatic tests is sufficient for us so far.

To automatically test that an implementation of *traceSet* behaves as stated above, we need to check two properties corresponding to the two directions of the bi-implication in the statement relating it to *accept*. The first one is:

1. If we have a specification s and a trace t such that $accept(s)(t)$ holds[5], then *the* generalized trace t_g sampled from $traceSet(s)$ for the specific input sequence found in t has to cover t.

To check this property, we need access to a source of pairs of specifications and traces for which $accept(s)(t) = \mathsf{True}$. Systematically building such pairs is not exactly easy. Therefore, our testing of this property currently relies on checking it for hand-written examples, i.e., on unit tests. Instead of writing down specific traces that match a given specification, one can also use full, known to be correct, programs and check that the testing procedure, usually employed for student submissions, never finds any counterexample. This way, one can view each of these unit tests as a very specific property test encoding a weakened version of the above property; the testing procedure itself will still use random inputs.

Fortunately, the property corresponding to the converse direction is far easier to check on a wide range of test cases. That property can be stated as follows:

2. For a specification s, sample a generalized trace using *traceSet*. From this generalized trace t_g, build an ordinary trace t by randomly replacing each output set in t_g by an element of that set (potentially dropping the output there altogether if ε is chosen). Since, by construction, those are exactly the t that are covered by t_g, now $accept(s)(t)$ has to evaluate to True.

---

[5] For notational simplicity, we leave out the continuation and environment here.

Since the only input to this property is a specification s without any further requirements, we are not limited to carefully hand-crafted test cases here but can instead use randomly generated specifications.

Randomly generated specifications have further uses as well. For example, they can be used for certain regression tests, for sanity checking of structural properties of the DSL that we do expect to hold, but which are not explicit from, say, the definition of the *accept*-semantics, such as that specifications form a monoid via sequential composition and neutral element **0**, and even for checking more involved properties of the operations of the specification language, such as the not immediately obvious (but semantically important) equivalence between $s^{\rightarrow \mathbf{E}}$ and $(s \cdot s^{\rightarrow \mathbf{E}} \cdot \mathbf{E})^{\rightarrow \mathbf{E}}$. They also help tie together further components of the overall framework/system under development; see Sect. 5. We even envision to use randomly generated specifications for creating random exercise tasks, in particular in connection with other ideas from Sect. 6 and beyond. So let us make explicit our current strategy for randomly generating specifications here.

4.1   Randomly Generating Specifications

While the basic structure of specifications is fairly simple and does generally not need to fulfill any invariants, there are two non-trivial aspects to randomly generating specifications: terms in general and loops and their termination in particular. First of all, one needs to decide on a set of available functions that can appear in terms. Then, terms can be generated according to this grammar:[6]

$$\langle term \rangle \quad ::= \langle function \rangle \, \langle terms \rangle \qquad\qquad \langle terms \rangle ::= \langle term \rangle \, \langle terms \rangle$$
$$\mid \; \langle var \rangle \qquad\qquad\qquad\qquad\qquad\qquad \mid \; \langle term \rangle$$
$$\mid \; \langle literal \rangle \qquad\qquad\qquad \langle var \rangle \quad ::= getAll \, \langle id \rangle$$
$$\mid \; getCurrent \, \langle id \rangle$$

For loops, we can use the same grammar to generate a condition, but it might be necessary to restrict the set of available functions even further. Otherwise, the generated loop might not be guaranteed to make progress toward termination, therefore leaving us with a specification describing non-terminating behavior. Given the right constraints on the available functions, we can build a terminating loop from three random specifications s_1, s_2, s_3. Our loop skeleton has the form $(s_1 \cdot (s_2 \angle?\diagdown s_3))^{\rightarrow \mathbf{E}}$, i.e., s_1 is a common prefix for every iteration round. Note that we do not have a suffix sequentially after the branching. Since we will insert an exit-marker into one of the branches, a suffix would only ever be used after the branch without that marker. Therefore, it can always be suffixed to that branch. Now we generate a condition c and a specification s^* that guarantees progress toward evaluating c to True. Then our terminating loop is $(s_1 \cdot (s_2^* \angle c \diagdown (s_3 \cdot \mathbf{E})))^{\rightarrow \mathbf{E}}$, where s_2^* is the result of inserting s^* into s_2 at a random position.[7] Alternatively, we can also negate the condition and use the

---

[6] Of course, one has to take scoping and types into account as well.

[7] More precisely, we choose a random and unconditionally reached position.

loop $(s_1 \cdot ((s_2 \cdot \mathbf{E}) \angle not(c) \diagdown s_3^*))^{\to^{\mathbf{E}}}$. A simple way to generate the condition and the progressing specification is to manually define a set of condition and progression pairs and then choose elements of this set at random. For example, we could have a pair with condition $len(x_A) > n$, for some $n > 0$ and variable x, and specification $[\triangleright x]^{\mathbb{Z}}$. Reading into x guarantees that $len(x_A)$ is increasing, eventually exceeding n. Choosing this condition-progression-pair and assuming $s_1 = [\triangleright y]^{\mathbb{N}}$, $s_2 = [\{\varepsilon, 2 \cdot y_C\} \triangleright][\{sum(y_A)\} \triangleright]$, and $s_3 = \mathbf{0}$, we could insert the progressing $[\triangleright x]^{\mathbb{Z}}$ between the two outputs of s_2 and get:

$$([\triangleright y]^{\mathbb{N}} \cdot (([\{\varepsilon, 2 \cdot y_C\} \triangleright][\triangleright x]^{\mathbb{Z}}[\{sum(y_A)\} \triangleright]) \angle len(x_A) > n \diagdown \mathbf{0} \cdot \mathbf{E}))^{\to^{\mathbf{E}}}$$

This method of generating termination conditions relies heavily on the set of hand-written conditions and their respective progressing specifications. In general, the ability to catch implementation errors through testing with randomly generated specifications depends on the possible terms we generate. Consider, for instance, these five specifications generated by our implementation as described:

$$([\{len(y_A)\} \triangleright][\triangleright z]^{\mathbb{Z}}(\mathbf{E} \angle not(len(x_A) > 1) \diagdown [\triangleright x]^{\mathbb{Z}}))^{\to^{\mathbf{E}}}$$

$$[\triangleright n]^{\mathbb{Z}}[\{n_C\} \triangleright][\{n_C - n_C, n_C\} \triangleright](\mathbf{0} \angle null(x_A) \diagdown [\triangleright m]^{\mathbb{Z}})$$

$$[\triangleright m]^{\mathbb{Z}}([\triangleright n]^{\mathbb{Z}} \angle len(n_A) > 0 \diagdown \mathbf{E})^{\to^{\mathbf{E}}}[\{\varepsilon, sum(m_A), m_C\} \triangleright]$$

$$[\{sum(m_A)\} \triangleright](([\triangleright m]^{\mathbb{Z}} \angle null(m_A) \diagdown \mathbf{0}) \angle len(x_A) = len(n_A) \diagdown [\triangleright m]^{\mathbb{Z}})$$

$$[\{\varepsilon, sum(z_A)\} \triangleright][\triangleright n]^{\mathbb{Z}}(\mathbf{0} \angle len(x_A) < n_C * n_C \diagdown ([\triangleright y]^{\mathbb{Z}} \angle n_C = n_C * n_C \diagdown \mathbf{0}))$$

Clearly, most of the generated specifications do not resemble anything a user of the language would write. But for testing an implementation such specifications are precisely what we want, as they potentially trigger edge cases outside the implementer's imagination. We could, of course, attach additional constraints to the generation of specifications. However, too much restricting might lead to some errors never being triggered. On the other hand, restrictions can lead to more useful specifications that resemble actual use cases. For example, it might be a good idea to not allow terms like $x_C = x_C$ in a branching condition when generating specifications for usage in exercise tasks (see Sect. 6), but during validation of an implementation one might explicitly want such edge cases.

5   Empowering the Educator: An Interpreter Semantics

A central problem an educator might have when writing specifications in the DSL so far is the fact that there is no direct way to inspect what behavior a specification represents. When writing normal programs, we are used to a fundamentally different situation: during development we can execute a candidate (the current program version) and play around with different inputs to confirm that we are actually on the right track.

In order to get the same possibility when developing specifications, we wanted an interpreter that given a specification behaves exactly like a program matching that specification would. Essentially, the desire is for a function of the following type: $\llbracket \cdot \rrbracket$ :: Specification $\rightarrow$ IO (). Since specifications conceptually use a global variable environment, our interpreter has to be stateful as well, even beyond the "I/O state". Also, in order to correctly terminate loops, some way to abort a running program part and to recover from such an abort would be handy, to emulate behavior similar to a **break** command. Thus motivated, and in order to keep the interpreter's structure itself simple, we do not target IO () directly but instead the interpreter produces a value of type Semantics (), which is declared as follows:

newtype Semantics a = Semantics { $runSemantics$
$\qquad\qquad\qquad\qquad$ :: Environment $\rightarrow$ IO (Either Exit a, Environment) }
data Exit = Exit
type Environment = [(String, [Int])]

The Semantics type constructor is a monad, in fact, an inlined version of the following monad transformer stack [6]: ExceptT Exit (StateT Environment IO). Thus, it provides us with at least the operations $readLn$, $print$, $gets$, $modify$, $throwError$, and $catchError$. These operations give us everything we need to manage a global state and to abort loops in a convenient way. Additionally using the function $evalTerm$ discussed in Sect. 3, as well as

$$store :: \text{String} \rightarrow \text{Int} \rightarrow \text{Environment} \rightarrow \text{Environment}$$

for the actual updating of environments, the interpreter is then defined thus:

$\llbracket \cdot \rrbracket$ :: Specification $\rightarrow$ Semantics ()
$\llbracket \mathbf{0} \rrbracket \qquad\qquad = return\ ()$
$\llbracket s_1 \cdot \ldots \cdot s_n \rrbracket = \mathbf{do}\ \llbracket s_1 \rrbracket$
$\qquad\qquad\qquad\qquad \vdots$
$\qquad\qquad\qquad \llbracket s_n \rrbracket$
$\llbracket [\,\triangleright x\,]^\tau \rrbracket \qquad = modify \circ store\ x \lll readLn$
$\llbracket [\,\{\varepsilon, \ldots\} \triangleright] \rrbracket = return\ ()$
$\llbracket [\,\{t, \ldots\} \triangleright] \rrbracket = print \lll gets\ (evalTerm\ t)$
$\llbracket s^{\rightarrow \mathbf{E}} \rrbracket \qquad = \mathbf{let}\ loop = \mathbf{do}\ \llbracket s \rrbracket$
$\qquad\qquad\qquad\qquad\qquad loop$
$\qquad\qquad\qquad \mathbf{in}\ catchError\ loop\ (\lambda \text{Exit} \rightarrow return\ ())$
$\llbracket s_1 \measuredangle c \diagdown s_2 \rrbracket = ifM\ (gets\ (evalTerm\ c))\ \llbracket s_2 \rrbracket\ \llbracket s_1 \rrbracket$
$\llbracket \mathbf{E} \rrbracket \qquad\qquad = throwError\ \text{Exit}$

To get a runnable IO computation from a specification, we can start the interpreter with an empty environment and ignore both a potential Exit value and the final environment as follows:

$$buildComputation :: \text{Specification} \to \text{IO} \ ()$$
$$buildComputation \ s = void \ (runSemantics \ [\![s]\!] \ (map \ (, [\,]) \ (vars \ s)))$$

Interestingly, and usefully, the interpreter can also be seen as an alternative formulation of the semantics of specifications in the first place: to understand what behavior a specification is representing, understanding either the *accept*-function or the interpreter semantics suffices. For someone already with a good grasp of Haskell and monads, the latter option could be substantially more attractive. That is, the target audience for the interpreter semantics are certainly not our students taking the course, but neither is that the case for the *accept*-function. Consider, though, the situation of handing the job of creating new exercise tasks to teaching assistants, which in our case could be advanced students from previous years. They need to be able to very clearly understand the semantics of the DSL in order to be successful at task creation. The *accept*-function is probably not for them, but they can certainly work informed by $[\![\cdot]\!]$ as given above. The *accept*-function, on the other hand, as the more mathematical and less programmatical foundation, is relevant in the background when extending the overall framework, devising new testing and feedback methods, etc.

These considerations rely on the *accept*-function and the interpreter semantics being equivalent, and obviously just claiming that they are is not very convincing. But fortunately we can formulate a simple, mechanically checkable, property that relates the interpreter to the *accept*-function. This property states that every interpretation of a specification has to lead to a computation that can only produce traces acceptable by that specification. We can capture it thus:

$$prop :: \text{Specification} \to \text{Property}$$
$$prop \ s = buildComputation \ s \ `satisfiesAccept` \ s$$

Of course, it is basically just a play on normal correctness checking of candidate solutions (the candidate now not being a student submission but an interpreter call). In order to check this property automatically, randomly generated specifications (see Sect. 4.1) come in handy again.

Note that the above property covers only the soundness of the interpreter. It does not test whether every valid trace for the given specification can be generated by the interpretation result. Looking at the interpreter's definition as a deterministic definition, the resulting program clearly cannot, in general, produce all traces the specification would accept, since we always choose one particular value to output and discard all other possibilities. In order for the interpreter to act as a semantics alternative to *accept*, we need to view it as containing some form of non-determinism. For example, we can interpret the selection of an element from the set of possible outputs as a random choice or change the definition to ultimately produce a list of all possible combinations of choices. (We have not done any of that yet.)

6   Further Support: Validation and Program Generation

Recall that for each exercise task there are five artifacts that an educator might need to keep consistent (see Sect. 3): the general idea of what the task is to be about, the specification expression used for testing, a task description for students, a sample solution, and additional material like example runs of programs.

In the previous section we have shown how to run a specification as if it were a program. Thus we already have an automated way to create a correctly behaving computation from a given specification and use it to drive example runs. This interpreting of specifications does not yet cover our need for a sample solution, though, since we do not directly get any actual program code that could be shown to students. What we have instead is a way for an educator to validate their own sample solution by comparing it to both the interpreted and the actual specification (via the testing procedure). By doing so, the educator can validate that their idea for the task matches the written specification, since a mismatch between these two might manifest as a mismatch in observed behavior between "solutions".

Now the last artifact (as per Sect. 3, Fig. 2) that is not yet connected to the others in any systematic way is the description of the task as handed to students. Up front, it might seem quite impossible to automatically generate any reasonably formulated task description. But if we shift our focus away from classic verbal descriptions, instead to tasks that require the re-implementation of some (imperative) program with Haskell, then generating task descriptions gets way easier. For example, we might want to pose tasks of the form "Write a Haskell program that has the same behavior as the following Python program …" (building on the students' knowledge from their introductory programming course), and then we just need to be able to automatically generate Python code from a specification expression. Such tasks are not generally what one always wants, but they work well when the goal is to highlight the differences between I/O in Haskell and in languages with mainly ambient effects [2]; concerning type distinctions between pure and impure expressions, syntactic differences like the two relevant forms of binding in Haskell's **do**-blocks, **let** vs. ←, etc.

To actually generate the Python code needed, we can define a translation function similar in structure to our interpreter from the previous section:

$$
\begin{aligned}
[\![0]\!] \quad &= \textbf{pass} \\
[\![s_1 \cdot \ldots \cdot s_n]\!] \quad &= [\![s_1]\!] \\
&\quad\ \ \ldots \\
&\quad\ \ [\![s_n]\!] \\
[\![[\,\triangleright x\,]^\tau]\!] \quad &= x_A \mathrel{+}= [\textbf{int}(\textbf{input}())] \\
[\![\{\varepsilon,\ldots\}\triangleright]\!] \quad &= \textbf{pass} \\
[\![\{t,\ldots\}\triangleright]\!] \quad &= \textbf{print}(\lfloor t \rfloor) \\
[\![s^{\rightarrow \textbf{E}}]\!] \quad &= \textbf{while } \text{True} : \\
&\quad\ \ [\![s]\!] \\
[\![s_1 \angle c \diagdown s_2]\!] \quad &= \textbf{if } \lfloor c \rfloor : \\
&\quad\ \ [\![s_2]\!] \\
&\quad\ \textbf{else} : \\
&\quad\ \ [\![s_1]\!] \\
[\![\textbf{E}]\!] \quad &= \textbf{break}
\end{aligned}
$$

The target domain is now not a type of I/O semantics but actual syntactic program text. Additionally to the program text emitted by the above translation function, we also need to prepend an initialization $x_A = []$ for each variable x used in the specification. Moreover, $\lfloor t \rfloor$ as used above means to replace all variable occurrences of the form x_C in a term t by $x_A[-1]$. Note that in order for the translation to be carried out automatically, we need access to the structure of terms used for outputs and for branching. Otherwise we could not generate textual descriptions, including the replacement of certain variable occurrences via $\lfloor t \rfloor$. Our implementation of the specification language therefore provides an appropriate representation of terms, as mentioned in Sect. 3.

Applying the code generation procedure to our earlier example specification $[\triangleright n]^{\mathbb{N}}([\triangleright x]^{\mathbb{Z}} \angle len(x_A) = n_C \diagdown \mathbf{E})^{\rightarrow^{\mathbf{E}}}[\{sum(x_A)\} \triangleright]$, we obtain the following Python program:

```python
n_A = []
x_A = []

n_A += [int(input())]
while True:
    if len(x_A) == n_A[-1]:
        break
    else:
        x_A += [int(input())]
print(sum(x_A))
```

Even though this program has the intended behavior, it is not an ideal program to hand to students. Due to the compositional nature of the translation, the resulting program code does not generally exploit any information regarding the overall structure of the specification. Thus, we end up with programs that do not necessarily adhere to good programming practice. It is possible to manipulate such programs further or to optimize the process generating them. For example, if for some variable x the operation $\lfloor \cdot \rfloor$ never (throughout the whole processing above) encountered variant x_A, then for that variable we can use a simple version x_C only, without initialization and without altering it in $\lfloor \cdot \rfloor$, and $x_C = \textbf{int}(\textbf{input}())$ instead of $x_A += [\textbf{int}(\textbf{input}())]$ in translations of input operations for it. Doing so for the example used above, we would end up with:

```python
x_A = []

n_C = int(input())
while True:
    if len(x_A) == n_C:
        break
    else:
        x_A += [int(input())]
print(sum(x_A))
```

This program is still not ideal and further improvements are needed before we can use such artifacts for programming education. One of the most obvious improvements would be to detect special cases like "**while** True: **if** ... **break else:** ..." and to transform them into other **while**-loops with an explicit loop condition. We have not done any deeper investigations into this area, as of yet, but definitely plan to do so in the future since we see a lot of potential for automatic task generation based on this approach.

An important difference to the previous section is that the target audience for the generated Python code are indeed the students taking the course. And certainly the code generation approach advocated here is not limited to Python programs. Alternatively to interpreting a specification as a Haskell value in a semantics type as in the previous section, we could also emit the actual program text *there*, given a printable representation of the Terms used by the specification exists. We have not implemented this Haskell version of the code generation yet, but by looking at the definition of the interpreter one could imagine translating the DSL expression

$$readInput \; \texttt{"n"} \; nats <>$$
$$tillExit \; (branch \; (length \; (getAll \; \texttt{"x"}) == getCurrent \; \texttt{"n"})$$
$$(readInput \; \texttt{"x"} \; ints)$$
$$exit) <>$$
$$writeOutput \; [sum \; (getAll \; \texttt{"x"})]$$

to the following program:

```
prog :: Semantics ()
prog = do
  modify ∘ store "n" =≪ readLn
  let loop = do ifM (gets (evalTerm (
                      length (getAll "x") == getCurrent "n")))
                (throwError Exit)
                (modify ∘ store "x" =≪ readLn)
                loop
  catchError loop (λExit → return ())
  print =≪ gets (evalTerm (sum (getAll "x")))
```

In principle, this translation could let an educator automatically generate a correct sample solution. However, in the above form this approach does not lend itself directly for generating sample solutions presentable to students, even less so than for the case of targeting Python. Not only is the usage of the state and exception monads nowhere near an idiomatic solution for such a simple specification; they also make it somewhat difficult to identify the actually interesting part of the computation here. But by inlining the monad transformer operations and simplifying the resulting program, the educator could systematically derive a presentable program. It might even be possible to do this derivation fully automatically with the use of some program analysis and transformations, also including specialized simplification strategies as mentioned for Python above.

Again, we have not done any deeper exploration on such transformations yet, but will do so in the future.

7   Putting It All Together

To summarize, let us once again consider our running example and go through the steps we would take to implement the task inside the presented framework.

The first step is coming up with an idea for what the task should be. For our summation example, the idea might be formulated as follows: *"We want students to realize a simple I/O loop, so they should write a program that reads a number and then as many further numbers and finally prints a sum."* Next, we write a task description, a specification, and a sample solution based on this idea:

"Write a program which first reads a positive integer n from the console, then reads n integers one after the other, and finally outputs their sum."

$[\triangleright n]^{\mathbb{N}}([\triangleright x]^{\mathbb{Z}} \angle len(x_A) = n_C \searcom \mathbf{E})^{\rightarrow \mathbf{E}}$
$[\{sum(x_A)\} \triangleright]$

```
main = do
  n ← readLn
  let loop xs =
    if length xs == n
      then print (sum xs)
      else do
        x ← readLn
        loop (x : xs)
  loop []
```

To verify that these components are consistent with each other and our idea, we now use the different connections shown in Fig. 2 to relate them to each other. First off, we can run both our sample solution and the specification, using the interpreter, on some sample inputs to see if their behavior matches our idea of the task as well as each other. Next, we use the testing procedure to make sure that the sample solution fulfills the specification. If all these checks are successful, we can be confident that the idea, the sample solution, and the specification are indeed consistent. What is left is validating the written task description. Without the ability to automatically generate useful descriptions, or when hand-written descriptions are preferable, this has to be done by the usual careful inspection of the description.

With confidence in the consistency established, we can then generate supporting material; for example, we can give a run of the sample solution on some specific input. For instance, we can add the following line to our task description: *"Example: After reading 2, 7, and 13, your program should print 20."*

We cannot yet report on any concrete experience using this workflow, as we will only start using it in the upcoming iteration of our Haskell course.

One interesting detail to note is the fact that the presented approach is, in principle, not limited to tasks dealing with I/O. Given a suitable specification language and testing framework, the basic idea of (semi-)automatically generating artifacts and cross-validating them against manually created ones, and each other, is certainly applicable in other settings as well.

8 Related Work

As mentioned in Sect. 3, our implementation builds upon an inspectable representation of side-effecting programs [10]. The Haskell IOSpec library[8] implements such representations not only for console I/O but supports also forking processes, mutable references, and software transactional memory. However, it only features a very minimal API. Also, no higher-level abstractions currently exist.

Another tool for testing stateful computations is the state machine version of QuickCheck for Erlang [4,5].[9] Instead of testing specific programs, like we do, it can be used to test stateful APIs. Behavior is specified as a semantic model, given in Erlang, of the API together with pre- and post-conditions for each stateful action. Testing is then done by generating random sequences of actions based on the pre-conditions and checking the result of the actual API calls against the model and post-conditions. Any found sequence of API calls that differs from the semantic model is shrunk to provide a small counterexample.

9 What Next?

We have an implementation of the specification language from earlier work [12] along with supporting components, correctness checkers for both student submissions and the framework itself, and semantics/code generators. Our hope is to benefit from this investment when we grow the specification language, and with it the overall framework, to accommodate further needs on the education side. Being able to safely grow the framework is precisely what the "keeping in check" part of this article's title refers to: when the expressiveness of the underlying DSL is to be extended, different parts of the implementation have to be revisited as well, and we expect that the thoughts and work put in now at the beginning will pay off in the sense of maintainability and certain guarantees. By way of an outlook, let us discuss a concrete extension we have in mind.

At the moment, the specification language does not yet talk about how a program (e.g., a student submission) should cope with possible input errors. For example, in $[\triangleright n\,]^{\mathbb{N}}(\ldots)^{\rightarrow^{*\mathbf{E}}}\ldots$ we expressed that the first number that is read in should not be negative, but what happens otherwise is left completely unspecified. Of course, the *accept*-function is formulated in such a way that a trace starting with a negative input value would be rejected here, but the actual testing of student submissions deliberately only presents inputs that are well-formed according to the specification. From a different perspective, the interpreter given in Sect. 5 (which builds computations that also serve as possible sample solutions; see the second half of that section as well as Sect. 6) completely ignores the τ argument in this line:

---

[8] https://hackage.haskell.org/package/IOSpec.

[9] A Haskell version can be found at http://hackage.haskell.org/package/quickcheck-state-machine.

$$[\![\, [\triangleright x\,]^\tau \,]\!] = modify \circ store\; x \mathrel{=\!\!\ll} readLn$$

If we were to instead write

$$
\begin{aligned}
[\![\, [\triangleright x\,]^\tau \,]\!] = \mathbf{do}\; &v \leftarrow readLn\\
&when\;(v \notin \tau)\;(error\;\texttt{"blow up"})\\
&modify\;(store\; x\; v)
\end{aligned}
$$

then the potential runtime error added there would never actually be triggered during any automatic test runs, simply because a decision was made to not subject student submissions to ill-formed or otherwise undesirable inputs. The rationale for that decision is that students just beginning to learn I/O programming in Haskell should not have to worry about checking inputs for correctness. But what about later? At some point we might want to explicitly require them to do so, that is, to turn the management of expectations about input values from a job of the testing framework into a job of the students. And we might want to be able to be selective about at which input actions such checks are required, and at which not, as well as to retain flexibility concerning how exactly student submissions should deal with incorrect inputs.

Our suggestion now is to extend the specification language by two additional atomic forms: $[\triangleright x\,]_{\underline{\mathbb{I}}}^\tau$ and $[\triangleright x\,]_{\circlearrowleft}^\tau$. The intuitive semantics of the first variant is that if an input outside the set τ is read, the program stops (in a controlled fashion, not via a runtime error), while that of the second variant is that if an input outside the set τ is read, the user is prompted again (and possibly again and again) for an input until the value read is indeed in τ. In the *accept*-function, these new forms would be defined as follows:

$$
accept([\triangleright x\,]_{\underline{\mathbb{I}}}^\tau \cdot s', k)(t, \Delta) =
$$
$$
\begin{cases}
\textsf{True} & \text{, if } t =?v\,\textsf{stop} \wedge v \notin \tau\\
accept(s', k)(t', store(x, v, \Delta)) & \text{, if } t =?v\,t' \wedge v \in \tau\\
\textsf{False} & \text{, otherwise}
\end{cases}
$$

$$
accept([\triangleright x\,]_{\circlearrowleft}^\tau \cdot s', k)(t, \Delta) =
$$
$$
\begin{cases}
accept([\triangleright x\,]_{\circlearrowleft}^\tau \cdot s', k)(t', \Delta) & \text{, if } t =?v\,t' \wedge v \notin \tau\\
accept(s', k)(t', store(x, v, \Delta)) & \text{, if } t =?v\,t' \wedge v \in \tau\\
\textsf{False} & \text{, otherwise}
\end{cases}
$$

and the remaining components of the framework, the checkers, generators, etc., would be extended as well, while relying on existing invariants and established connections/correspondences.

References

1. Claessen, K., Hughes, J.: QuickCheck: a lightweight tool for random testing of Haskell programs. In: International Conference on Functional Programming, Proceedings, pp. 268–279. ACM (2000). https://doi.org/10.1145/351240.351266

2. Filinski, A.: Controlling effects. Ph.D. thesis, Carnegie Mellon University (1996)
3. Gibbons, J., Wu, N.: Folding domain-specific languages: deep and shallow embeddings (Functional Pearl). In: International Conference on Functional Programming, Proceedings, pp. 339–347. ACM (2014). https://doi.org/10.1145/2628136.2628138
4. Hughes, J.: QuickCheck testing for fun and profit. In: Hanus, M. (ed.) PADL 2007. LNCS, vol. 4354, pp. 1–32. Springer, Heidelberg (2006). https://doi.org/10.1007/978-3-540-69611-7_1
5. Hughes, J.: Experiences with QuickCheck: testing the hard stuff and staying sane. In: Lindley, S., McBride, C., Trinder, P., Sannella, D. (eds.) A List of Successes That Can Change the World. LNCS, vol. 9600, pp. 169–186. Springer, Cham (2016). https://doi.org/10.1007/978-3-319-30936-1_9
6. Liang, S., Hudak, P., Jones, M.P.: Monad transformers and modular interpreters. In: Principles of Programming Languages, Proceedings, pp. 333–343. ACM (1995). https://doi.org/10.1145/199448.199528
7. McBride, C., Paterson, R.: Applicative programming with effects. J. Funct. Program. **18**(1), 1–13 (2008). https://doi.org/10.1017/S0956796807006326
8. Peyton Jones, S.L., Wadler, P.: Imperative functional programming. In: Principles of Programming Languages, Proceedings, pp. 71–84. ACM (1993). https://doi.org/10.1145/158511.158524
9. Siegburg, M., Voigtländer, J., Westphal, O.: Automatische Bewertung von Haskell-Programmieraufgaben. In: Proceedings of the Fourth Workshop "Automatische Bewertung von Programmieraufgaben", pp. 19–26. GI (2019). https://doi.org/10.18420/abp2019-3
10. Swierstra, W., Altenkirch, T.: Beauty in the beast – a functional semantics for the awkward squad. In: Haskell Workshop, Proceedings, pp. 25–36. ACM (2007). https://doi.org/10.1145/1291201.1291206
11. Waldmann, J.: Automatische Erzeugung und Bewertung von Aufgaben zu Algorithmen und Datenstrukturen. In: Proceedings of the Third Workshop "Automatische Bewertung von Programmieraufgaben", CEUR Workshop Proceedings, vol. 2015. CEUR-WS.org (2017)
12. Westphal, O., Voigtländer, J.: Describing console I/O behavior for testing student submissions in Haskell. In: Eighth and Ninth International Workshop on Trends in Functional Programming in Education, Proceedings, EPTCS, vol. 321, pp. 19–36. EPTCS (2020). https://doi.org/10.4204/EPTCS.321.2

System Description: Lang-n-Change - A Tool for Transforming Languages

Benjamin Mourad$^{(\boxtimes)}$ and Matteo Cimini

University of Massachusetts Lowell, Lowell, MA 01854, USA
benjamin_mourad@student.uml.edu, matteo_cimini@uml.edu

Abstract. LANG-N-CHANGE is a tool for transforming language definitions into other language definitions. It provides a declarative domain-specific language for expressing algorithms over languages. LANG-N-CHANGE is implemented in OCaml and generates language definitions that can be compiled and executed in λProlog. The tool provides a repository with a number of language definitions and a handful of transformations.

Keywords: Language transformations · Domain-specific languages · Functional languages

1 Overview of Lang-n-Change

1.1 Motivation

Over the years, we have seen much effort in assisting language designers with tool support such as language workbenches [9] and semantics engineering tools [10,16]. In this paper, we describe a tool that addresses an aspect of language evolution that has not received enough attention: Automatically augmenting language definitions with desired programming features. We address this issue for languages defined in operational semantics, one of the widest approaches to the formal semantics of programming languages.

Consider the task of adding pattern matching to a language, a task that language designers frequently undertake. The operational semantics of pattern matching makes use of auxiliary relations to handle matches at compile-time and run-time. For example, one of these relations is the typing of patterns with a judgment of the form $\Gamma \vdash p : T \Rightarrow \Gamma'$. This relation ensures that the pattern is well-formed, and provides an output type environment Γ' with bindings (from variables to types). In a language with lists, we must add the rules below on the right, derived from the typing rules of the language (on the left).

$$\Gamma \vdash \mathtt{nil} : \mathsf{List}\ T \quad \Longrightarrow \quad \Gamma \vdash \mathtt{nil} : \mathsf{List}\ T \Rightarrow \Gamma$$

$$\frac{\Gamma \vdash e_1 : T \qquad \Gamma \vdash e_2 : \mathsf{List}\ T}{\Gamma \vdash \mathtt{cons}\ e_1\ e_2 : \mathsf{List}\ T} \quad \Longrightarrow \quad \frac{\Gamma \vdash p_1 : T \Rightarrow \Gamma_1 \qquad \Gamma \vdash p_2 : \mathsf{List}\ T \Rightarrow \Gamma_2 \qquad \Gamma' = \Gamma_1 \cup \Gamma_2}{\Gamma \vdash \mathtt{cons}\ p_1\ p_2 : \mathsf{List}\ T \Rightarrow \Gamma'}$$

© Springer Nature Switzerland AG 2020
K. Nakano and K. Sagonas (Eds.): FLOPS 2020, LNCS 12073, pp. 198–214, 2020.
https://doi.org/10.1007/978-3-030-59025-3_12

Can we describe this transformation as an algorithm over language definitions? Intuitively, such an algorithm must copy typing rules and insert *ps* in place of *es*. Furthermore, it must lift recursive calls to the shape of the typing judgement for patterns, which entails that we assign a new variable to accommodate the output of the call. Finally, all outputs of the recursive calls must be collected together to form the output of the overall rule. Once this algorithm is defined it can be applied not to just one language but to a variety of languages. LANG-N-CHANGE is a tool for expressing and executing language transformations over language definitions [14]. LANG-N-CHANGE can be used to automatically augment languages with features. This is beneficial to language designers as they can be relieved of the burden of manually modifying their languages, an error prone task.

1.2 Lang-n-Change

The tool pipeline of LANG-N-CHANGE is below.

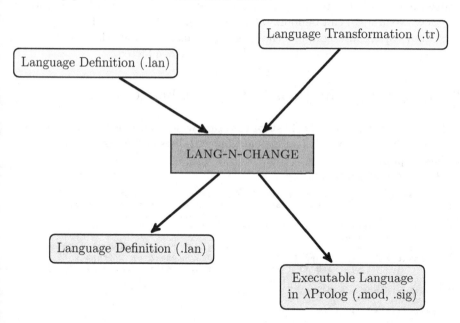

LANG-N-CHANGE takes in input two components: a language definition and a language transformation. A language definition is a `.lan` file and describes the operational semantics using a domain-specific language that is in close correspondence with pen&paper formulations. A language transformation is a `.tr` file and contains an algorithm over language definitions. The algorithm is specified declaratively with a domain-specific language which is applied to the language `.lan` given in input.

LANG-N-CHANGE is a command line tool. Given a language definition file `language.lan` and a transformation file `transformation.tr`, users can call

LANG-N-CHANGE with: `./lnc transformation.tr language.lan`. The result
is a file `language_transformation.lan` that contains the language definition
generated. To test the generated language definitions, LANG-N-CHANGE compiles
`.lan` files into λProlog executables [11]. We have implemented LANG-N-CHANGE
in OCaml. In the rest of the paper, we describe LANG-N-CHANGE as follows.

Roadmap of the Paper. Section 2 shows an example of a language definition in
LANG-N-CHANGE. This will be our running example. Section 3 shows an example of a language transformation in LANG-N-CHANGE. The example is an algorithm for adding pattern matching to functional languages. Section 3.2 applies
the algorithm to our running example, which shows an example of output
of LANG-N-CHANGE. Section 4 describes how languages can be tested through
a compilation to λProlog. This section also shows some queries on the language generated in Sect. 3.2. Section 5 gives details about the implementation
of LANG-N-CHANGE. Section 6 describes the current repository of languages and
transformations of the tool. Section 7 discusses related work and future work.

LANG-N-CHANGE can be found at http://cimini.info/LNC/index.html.

This webpage also contains the language transformations that we have formulated, and the details of the tests that we have conducted.

2   Language Definitions in Lang-n-Change

Below we show the file `stlc_list_pairs.lan`, which contains the language definition of the simply typed lambda-calculus with lists and pairs (`int` serves just
as base type).

file `stlc_list_pairs.lan`:

```
1   Expression e ::= (VAR x) | zero | (abs T (x)e) | (app e e)
2                  | (emptyList T) | (cons e e) | (head e) | (tail e)
3                  | myError | (pair e e) | (fst e) | (snd e)
4   Type T ::= int | (arrow T T) | (list T) | (times T T)
5   Error ::= myError
6   Value v ::= zero | (abs T (x)e) | (emptyList T) | (cons v v) | (pair v v)
7   Context E ::= [] | (app E e) | (app v E) | (cons E e) | (cons v E)
8                | (head E) | (tail E) | (pair E e) | (pair v E)
9                | (fst E) | (snd E)
10  TypeEnv Gamma ::= MAP(x, T)
11
12  member((x => T), Gamma)
13  ------------------------------------
14  Gamma |- x : T
15
16  Gamma |- zero : int
17
18  Gamma, x : T1 |- e : T2
19  ------------------------------------
20  Gamma |- (abs T1 (x)e) : (arrow T1 T2)
21
22  Gamma |- e1 : (arrow T1 T2),
23  Gamma |- e2 : T1
24  ------------------------------------
25  Gamma |- (app e1 e2) : T2
26
27  Gamma |- e1 : T,
28  Gamma |- e2 : (list T)
```

```
29   -------------------------------------
30   Gamma |- (cons e1 e2) : (list T)
31
32   Gamma |- (emptyList T) : (list T)
33
34   Gamma |- e : (list T)
35   -------------------------------------
36   Gamma |- (head e) : T
37
38   Gamma |- e : (list T)
39   -------------------------------------
40   Gamma |- (tail e) : (list T)
41
42   Gamma |- myError : T
43
44   Gamma |- e1 : T1,
45   Gamma |- e2 : T2
46   -------------------------------------
47   Gamma |- (pair e1 e2) : (times T1 T2)
48
49   Gamma |- e : (times T1 T2)
50   -------------------------------------
51   Gamma |- (fst e) : T1
52
53   Gamma |- e : (times T1 T2)
54   -------------------------------------
55   Gamma |- (snd e) : T2
56
57   (app (abs T (x)e) v) --> e[v/x]
58   (head (emptyList T)) --> myError
59   (tail (emptyList T)) --> myError
60   (head (cons v1 v2)) --> v1
61   (tail (cons v1 v2)) --> v2
62   (fst (pair v1 v2)) --> v1
63   (snd (pair v1 v2)) --> v2
```

This definition describes a grammar (lines 1–10) and inference rules (lines 12–63). Inference rules define a type system (lines 12–55), and a dynamic semantics (lines 57–63). The syntax is a textual representation for operational semantics and is in close correspondence with pen&paper formulations. (This is not a novelty. Indeed, our syntax is directly inspired by the Ott specification language [17], which has demonstrated such close correspondence before.) We do not give a complete account of the syntax, but discuss some essential elements. Binding is limited to unary lexical scoping [3]. We express binding with the syntax (x)e, that is, x is bound in e[1]. The term e[v/x] represents the capture-avoiding substitution.

The term (VAR x) can appear as grammar item of a syntactic category, as in line 1. This declares that occurrences of x (including x1, x2, etc.) denote elements of that syntactic category. LANG-N-CHANGE can define maps with MAP. At line 10, MAP(x,T) is a map from variables x to types T. LANG-N-CHANGE, then, offers the predicate member to lookup elements in maps, as used in line 12.

A technical detail of MAP is that it handles the bindings from variables to types as a list of associations, and member retrieves the most recent association that has been inserted (which occurs at the head of the list). Therefore, a variable x can be mapped to multiples types, and member retrieves the first available binding. This

---

[1] This is similar to the directive (+ bind x in e +) in the Ott tool [17]. We prefer our style for binding. We also prefer our constructs MAP and MAP_UNION, therefore we have not adopted Ott.

is a typical design choice to accommodate the shadowing that occurs in lambda-terms such as $\lambda x \texttt{Int}.\lambda y \texttt{Int}.\lambda x : \texttt{Bool}.\ x$, where the high-lighted x refers to last binding and is of boolean type.

None of this is an innovation, as these features are standard in language workbenches. The innovation of LANG-N-CHANGE is in providing a language for expressing language transformations, which we will see next.

3 Language Transformations: Adding Pattern Matching

Language transformations are defined in a domain-specific language. In this section we show an example: automatically adding pattern matching to functional languages.

Pattern matching is a standard feature in modern programming languages. When adding pattern matching to a functional language we augment the language with the typing rule and reduction rules of a pattern matching operator, and also with the definition of two auxiliary predicates. In the introduction we have seen examples of the first auxiliary predicate, which is used for type checking patterns and has a judgement of the form $\Gamma \vdash p : T \Rightarrow \Gamma'$. This judgement says that the pattern p is well-typed, has type T under the assignments in Γ, and returns bindings Γ'. The second auxiliary predicate performs pattern matching at run-time and has the form $pmatch(p, v) = R$, where p is a pattern and v is a value that the pattern is matched against. The result R can be a set of substitutions if the match succeeds or an error if it fails. To make an example, the following rules are some of the definitions for $pmatch$ for lists when pattern matching succeeds.

$$
\begin{array}{c}
\text{(MATCH-VAR)} \\[4pt]
pmatch(x, v) = \{x \mapsto v\}
\end{array}
\qquad
\begin{array}{c}
\text{(MATCH-CONS-OK)} \\[4pt]
\dfrac{pmatch(p_1, v_1) = S_1 \qquad pmatch(p_2, v_2) = S_2}{pmatch((\texttt{cons}\ p_1\ p_2), (\texttt{cons}\ v_1\ v_2)) = S_1 \cup S_2}
\end{array}
$$

The rule on the left matches variables with any value and returns a substitution accordingly. The rule on the right matches a pattern with a value only so long that we encounter the same top level operator $\texttt{cons}$. It also matches arguments recursively.

The language must also include the definition of $pmatch$ for when pattern matching fails. We show only a few rules.

$$
\begin{array}{c}
\text{(CONS-MATCH-ERR-PAIR)} \\[4pt]
pmatch((\texttt{cons}\ p_1\ p_2), (\texttt{pair}\ v_1\ v_2)) = \textbf{error}
\end{array}
$$

$$
\begin{array}{c}
\text{(CONS-MATCH-ERR-EMPTYLIST)} \\[4pt]
pmatch((\texttt{cons}\ p_1\ p_2), (\texttt{emptyList}\ T)) = \textbf{error}
\end{array}
$$

$$
\begin{array}{c}
\text{(CONS-MATCH-ARG-ERR)} \\[4pt]
\dfrac{pmatch(p_1, v_1) = \textbf{error}}{pmatch((\texttt{cons}\ p_1\ p_2), (\texttt{cons}\ v_1\ v_2)) = \textbf{error}}
\end{array}
$$

With the two rules at the top, we compare the cons pattern to every value that is not cons and give an error. With the rule at the bottom, we handle the case for when a recursive match fails. (The rule that handles the second argument is straightforward and omitted).

3.1 Algorithm

We do not give a complete account of the syntax and semantics for transformations, which can be found at [12,13]. Instead we describe the constructs of LANG-N-CHANGE as we encounter them (as frequently done in system description papers).

Below, we show the file pattern_matching.tr, which contains our algorithm for adding pattern matching to functional languages[2].

file pattern_matching.tr:

```
1   Expression e ::= ... | (match [e, MAP(p, e)]);
2   Context E ::= ... | (match [E, MAP(p, e)]);
3   Pattern p ::= Value[(op es)]:
4                     let withPs = es[e]: if e is Value then p else e
5                     in ((op ^ "_p") withPs)
6                   | (var_p x T);
7
8   Rule[GammaR |- (op es) : T]:
9     if not(op is Value) then nothing else
10     let myMapToPs = makeMap(es, es[*]: newvar(p)) in
11     let myMapToGs = makeMap(Premise, Premise[*]: newvar(Gamma)) in
12       myMapToGs[G |- ee : TT]: G |- myMapToPs.[ee]:TT => myMapToGs.[self],
13       GammaRes = MAP_UNION((GammaR @ myMapToGs.values)),
14       listDifference(premises, myPremises)
15       -----------------------------------------------------------------
16       let esToPs = myMapToPs[e]: if e is Expr. then myMapToPs.[e] else e
17       in GammaR |- ((op ^ "_p") esToPs): T => GammaRes
18   ;
19
20   Gamma |- (var_p x T) => MAP_UNION(Gamma, MAP(x, T));
21
22   Value[(op vs)]:
23     let vsToPs = makeMap(vs, vs[e]: if e is Value then newvar(p) else e) in
24     let substitutions = makeMap(vs, vs[*]: newvar(s)) in
25       substitutions[e]: if e is Value
26                         then pmatch vsToPs.[e] e substitutions.[e]
27                         else nothing,
28       S = MAP_UNION_ERR(error, substitutions[e]:
29                         if e is Value then substitutions.[e] else nothing)
30       -----------------------------------------------------------------
31       pmatch ((op ^ "_p") vsToPs.values) (op vs) S
32   ;
33
34   pmatch (var_p x T) v MAP(x,v);
35
36   Pattern[(op1 ps)]:
37     Value[(op2 vs)]:
38       if op1 = (op2 ^ "_p") then nothing else
39         pmatch (op1 ps) (op2 es) error
40
41   ;
42
```

---

[2] LANG-N-CHANGE makes use of brackets { and } rather than indentation, though we use the latter style in the code here for readability.

```
43    Value[(op vs)]:
44      let vsToPs = makeMap(vs, vs[e]: if e is Value then newvar(p) else e) in
45      vs[e]: if not(e is Value) then nothing else
46         pmatch vsToPs.[e] e error
47         ----------------------------
48         pmatch ((op ^ "_p") vsToPs.values) (op vs) error
49
50    ... typing and reduction rules for match ...
```

The algorithm applies to a language definition .lan given in input. For example, we can apply it to stlc_lists_pairs.lan. The first part of the algorithm extends the grammar of the language definition (lines 1–6). Line 1 makes use of the notation Expression e ::= ... | (notice the dots). With this notation, LANG-N-CHANGE extends the existing grammar Expression of the current language. Here, we add the pattern matching operator match e with $\{p_1 \Rightarrow e_1, \ldots, p_n \Rightarrow e_n\}$. Arbitrarily long sequences of branches pattern-body are represented with MAP(p, e). Line 2 extends the category Context with the evaluation context for match.

Lines 3–6 add a new syntactic category Pattern to the language. If this category already exists it is replaced. As pattern matching works on values, patterns must correspond to values. To generate the grammar for patterns, then, we iterate over the values. We do so with the expression Value[(op es)]: *body*, which we call a *selector*. This expression retrieves the grammar items of the category Value and executes *body* for each of them. However, it selects only those with pattern (op es). In this case, the pattern is intentionally the most generic, i.e. a top level operator applied to arguments. Therefore, all values are selected. This pattern, however, has the effect of binding op and es in *body* accordingly for each iteration. For example, when the iteration selects the value (pair v v), op will be bound to pair and es bound to the list [v ; v]. For values that have no arguments such as zero, we have that es is the empty list. Also, despite the use of the name es, which recall expressions, es is just a place holder for any match. For example, in the case of the type annotated emptyList we have that es is the list [T], and in the case of abs we have that es is the list [T ; (x).e], containing a type and a bound term. The body of the iterator (lines 4 and 5) returns a grammar item (op_p withPs) for each (op es). (To avoid confusion, we distinguish the operators that are used for expressions and those that are used for patterns by appending _p to the name of operators.) The variable withPs is a list of arguments that is computed in line 4 as follows. The selector es[e]: ... selects all the elements of the list es (e is, again, a pattern that matches all of them). The body of the selector returns p if the argument is a v and e otherwise. To make an example, (pair v v) is turned into (pair_p p p). If pairs were lazy, i.e., the value were (pair e e) we would return (pair_p e e) because expressions are to be evaluated, and not pattern matched before evaluation. After the selector at line 3 has added these grammar items, line 6 (which is outside of the selector body) adds the pattern for matching variables.

Lines 8–17 add new inference rules to the language. These inference rules define the typing judgement $\Gamma \vdash p : T \Rightarrow \Gamma'$. Line 8 makes use of the selector Rule[GammaR |- (op es) : T]: .... The keyword Rule means that the selector iterates over the inference rules of the language. We select only the rules whose conclusion matches the pattern GammaR |- (op es) : T, that is, all the typing rules. For each of them, we do the following. Since only values are to be pattern matched, we seek only typing rules for values. Line 9 detects whether the operator op belongs to the grammar Value or not. If not, we do not add any new rule (nothing). Otherwise, we execute the code in lines 10–17.

Lines 10 and 11 create some variable bindings that we use later. Line 10 creates a mapping myMapToPs from the arguments of the value (es) to new pattern variables. The operation makeMap takes two lists and performs an operation similar to the functional programming function zip, and results in a map. To create the lists of ps we iterate over the elements of es. The pattern * selects all of them without creating any binding. For each of them we create a new variable for patterns with newvar(p). For example, for the typing rule of (pair e1 e2), we have that myMapToPs contains the map $\{e1 \mapsto p1, e2 \mapsto p2\}$. This map is useful because the conclusion of the matching judgement must be $\Gamma \vdash (pair\ \boxed{p_1}\ \boxed{p_2}) : T_1 \times T_2 \Rightarrow \Gamma'$. Line 11 creates a mapping myMapToGs from each premise of the typing rule to a new type environment variable Γ. This variable is the output for the premises of the pattern matching judgment, that is, for the recursive calls to the arguments. For example, for pairs the premise $\Gamma \vdash e_1 : T_1$ of the first argument is mapped to a new variable Γ_1 so that we later can create the premise $(\#)\ \Gamma \vdash p_1 : T_1 \Rightarrow \boxed{\Gamma_1}$.

Lines 12–17 make the inference rule. The premises are computed with lines 12–14, and the conclusion is computed with lines 16 and 17. Line 12 iterates over the keys of the map myMapToGs, which are premises. We select those with pattern G |- ee : TT. The body of the selector creates the premises such as (#) above. It replaces an e with its corresponding new p (myMapToPs.[ee] performs a look up in the map). It also adds the output type environment to the premise. (Programmers can refer to the current item selected by the selector as self.) After the premises that are generated at line 12, line 13 creates a premise that defines GammaRes. This variable is the final type environment output of the rule, and collects all the output environments of the premises we just created, plus the environment GammaR that the rule begins with (bound at line 8). In this line, the operator @ represents the concatenation of lists. LANG-N-CHANGE does not perform a union immediately with MAP_UNION, but it places a premise that specifies that the typing rule performs the union of maps when applied[3]. The MAP_UNION operation fails if the given associations map a variable to two different types. In that case, the typing rule simply fails to be applied and the program is rejected. Line 14 adds the rest of the premises, i.e. the premises in the typing rule that were not modified. Line 16 creates the list of arguments esToPs. This is a list in which each argument of op is replaced with its corresponding p, but we replace only those arguments that are expression variables. For example, in

---

[3] This is similar to printing out a premise with printf. In printf("T = Γ1, Γ2") we do not perform the concatenation Γ1, Γ2. Instead, we are placing that equation in the typing rule we are creating, and that notation specifies that the typing rule will do the concatenation when applied.

emptyList T we do not replace T with a p. Line 17 provides the conclusion of the rule. It makes use of esToPs as the arguments of op, and of GammaRes as the output of the overall rule. Line 20 adds the typing rule for matching variables.

Lines 22–31 add the inference rules that define the (run-time) pattern matching operation pmatch p v s, where p is a pattern, v is a value and s is the output substitution. These inference rules cover the case for when pattern matching succeeds. Line 22 iterates over all patterns and we create an inference rule for each of them. Line 23 creates a mapping psToVs from each argument of the pattern to a new value variable. For pairs, psToVs would be $\{$p1 $\mapsto$ v1, p2 $\mapsto$ v2$\}$, which we use to create the match between (pair_p p1 p2) and (pair v1 v2). Line 24 creates a mapping substitutions from each argument of the pattern to a new variable for substitutions. This is because we have to recursively match arguments and obtain the substitution from that call. For example, for pairs we will create a premise (#) pmatch p1 v1 $\boxed{\text{s1}}$ for the first argument. Next, lines 25–31 create the rule. Lines 25–27 compute the premises of the rule, and line 31 creates the conclusion. Line 25 iterates over all the keys of the map substitutions and creates a premise such as (#). In particular, the value is obtained from the map psToVs, and the output substitution from substitutions. We create a recursive match call only for those arguments that are patterns (line 25). Lines 28–29 create a premise that define S as the union of all the output substitutions that have been used in the recursive calls. We do so by placing a premise in the typing rule that performs the MAP_UNION_ERR operation. This operation acts like MAP_UNION and performs the union of maps. Differently from MAP_UNION, which simply fails to be applied when we attempt to map a variable to two different values, MAP_UNION_ERR specifies the error that should be returned in that event (error in this case). Line 31 creates the conclusion of the rule by matching the pattern with a version of itself that makes use of value variables. It also sets the output of the overall rule to S. After these rules are added, line 34 adds the match rule for variables.

Lines 36–39 generate the definition for when the pattern matching fails. In particular, it generates rules such as (MATCH-CONS-ERROR) that apply when there is a mismatch in the top level operator between the pattern and the value. We select patterns in Pattern (line 36), and for each of them we iterate over values (line 37). For those values that do not correspond to the top level operator of the pattern we generate a matching rule that outputs an error (lines 38 and 39).

Lines 43–48, too, generate definitions for when pattern matching fails. These rules, however, cover the case for when a recursive call to match an argument fails, such as in rule (MATCH-CONS-ARG-ERR). Lines 43 selects values. Line 44 creates the mapping vsToPs between the arguments of the value and the new arguments, which replaces values with ps. Line 45 iterates over the arguments of the value. For each of them we create an inference rule (lines 46–48) if the argument is a value. The inference rule is such that the premise at line 46 checks whether the recursive call on this argument fails. The conclusion, then, produces the output error for pmatch (line 48).

The rest of **pattern_matching.tr** contains the typing rule and reduction rules for **match**. Since these rules are out of the textbook we omit them.

3.2   Generated Language Definition for stlc_lists_pairs.lan

When we apply **pattern_matching.tr** to **stlc_lists_pairs.lan** we obtain the following language definition.

file stlc_lists_pairs_pattern_matching.lan:

```
 1  Type T ::= ...
 2  Value v ::= ...
 3  Error ::= ...
 4  Expression e ::= ... | (match e MAP(p, e))
 5  Pattern p ::= (abs_p T (x)e) | zero_p | (emptyList_p T) | (cons_p p p)
 6             | (pair_p p p) | (var_p x T)
 7  Context E ::= ... | (match E MAP(p, e))
 8
 9  Gamma, x : T1 |- e : T2
10  ------------------------------------
11  Gamma |- (abs_p T1 (x)e) : (arrow T1 T2) => Gamma
12
13
14  Gamma |- (emptyList_p T) : (list T) => Gamma
15  Gamma |- zero_p : int => Gamma
16
17
18  Gamma |- p1 : T => Gamma1,
19  Gamma |- p2 : (list T) => Gamma2,
20  GammaRes = UNION(Gamma, Gamma1, Gamma2)
21  ------------------------------------
22  Gamma |- (cons_p p1 p2) : (list T) => GammaRes
23
24  Gamma |- p1 : T1 => Gamma1,
25  Gamma |- p2 : T2 => Gamma2,
26  GammaRes = UNION(Gamma, Gamma1, Gamma2)
27  ------------------------------------
28  Gamma |- (pair_p p1 p2) : (times T1 T2) => GammaRes
29
30
31  (pmatch (abs_p T (x)e) (abs T (x)e) [])
32  (pmatch (emptyList_p T) (emptyList T) [])
33  (pmatch zero_p zero [])
34
35  (pmatch p1 v1 s1),
36  (pmatch p2 v2 s2),
37  S = UNION(s1, s2)
38  ------------------------------------
39  (pmatch (cons_p p1 p2) (cons v1 v2) S)
40
41  (pmatch p1 v1 s1),
42  (pmatch p2 v2 s2),
43  S = UNION(s1, s2)
44  ------------------------------------
45  (pmatch (pair_p p1 p2) (cons v1 v2) S)
46
47  (cons p1 p2) =/= e
48  ------------------------------------
49  (pmatch (cons_p p1 p2) e (error.))
50
51  ... the rest of reduction and typing rules ...
```

Above, we have omitted some parts of the grammar with ..., as they come straight from **stlc_lists_pairs.lan**.

4   Testing the Generated Languages

LANG-N-CHANGE compiles language definitions (.lan) into executable λProlog logic programs [11]. These can be used to perform tests on the language definitions generated by LANG-N-CHANGE. λProlog is a statically-typed language. It requires that operators and predicates are declared before they are used. For example, the following pieces of grammar

```
Expression e ::=  (abs T (x)e) | (emptyList T) | (cons e e) |  (head e)
Pattern p ::= (emptyList_p T) | (cons_p p p) | (pair_p p p)
```

and the declaration of the typing judgement and reduction relation are compiled as:

```
type abs typ -> string -> expression -> expression.
type emptyList typ -> expression.
type cons expression -> expression -> expression.
type head expression -> expression.
type emptyList_p typ -> pattern.
type cons_p pattern -> pattern -> pattern.
type pair_p pattern -> pattern -> pattern.
type typeOf typeEnv -> expression -> typ -> prop.
type step expression -> expression -> prop.
```

Variables are modeled with strings and we automatically generate substitutions predicates. The compilation of the inference rules is straightforward. We show some examples of typing rules (cons and pair), reduction rules (head and fst), and pattern matching definitions (cons).

```
typeOf (typeenv Gamma) (cons E1 E2) (list T) :-
    typeOf (typeenv Gamma) E1 T, typeOf (typeenv Gamma) E2 (list T).

typeOf (typeenv Gamma) (pair E1 E2) (times T1 T2) :-
    typeOf (typeenv Gamma) E1 T1, typeOf (typeenv Gamma) E2 T2.

step (head (cons V1 V2)) V1 :- value V1, value V2.
step (fst (pair V1 V2)) V1 :- value V1, value V2.

matchPred (cons_p P1 P2) (cons V1 V2) (matchSubst S) :-
    matchPred P1 V1 (matchSubst S1),
    matchPred P2 V2 (matchSubst S2), internal_union [S1, S2] nil S.
```

(That logic programming can model language definitions well is not a novelty.)

To test the languages we can run queries on the corresponding logic programs. We show two examples with pattern_matching_stlc_lists_pairs.lan. Let us consider the following program, which takes a pair of two lists of integers, swaps the two lists in the pair, and removes the head of each list:

$$\texttt{match } \langle [0,0], [0] \rangle \texttt{ with } \{\langle x :: y, w :: z \rangle \mapsto \langle z, y \rangle\}$$

This program is the following in λProlog, which we refer to as *prg* =

```
(match
 (pair (cons zero (cons zero (emptyList int))) (cons zero (emptyList int)))
 [internal_pair
  (pair_p
   (cons_p (var_p (var "x") int) (var_p (var "y") (list int)))
   (cons_p (var_p (var "w") int) (var_p (var "z") (list int)))
   ) /* this above is the pattern */
   (pair (var "z") (var "y"))] /* this is the body of the clause */
)
```

Here, `internal_pair` internally represents the map from patterns to the body of the their clause. We can type check the program with the following λProlog query.

```
[stlc_lists_pairs_pattern_matching] ?- typeOf (typeenv nil) prg T.
```

```
The answer substitution:
T = times (list int) (list int)
```

We can execute the program with the following query. (The result is the pair $\langle [], [0] \rangle$.)

```
[stlc_lists_pairs_pattern_matching] ?- nstep prg E.
```

```
after a few steps, we obtain
The answer substitution:
E = pair (emptyList int) (cons zero (emptyList int))
```

The fact that users test their languages in a syntax (λProlog) different from that of the language specification is not unusual. To make a notable example, the Ott system, too, generates OCaml code (and other types of code) for tests.

We have conducted several tests on the language generated in Sect. 3.2. Our tests also aimed to check type checking failure and run-time pattern matching failure (i.e., no pattern applies). This gives us some confidence on the correctness of the language generated by our algorithm.

5 Implementation

LANG-N-CHANGE is implemented in OCaml. The major components of the tool are the following:

- *Language Definitions Parser*: We have an OCaml data type called `language`, which models language definitions. This component parses a `.lan` file into this data type. We also provide an API library to interact with this data type. The library includes operations to
  - retrieve all of the grammar items of a syntactic category,
  - add a syntactic category to the grammar of a language,
  - retrieve all of the variables that occur in a given term,
  - retrieve all of the rules whose conclusion makes use of a certain predicate,

  as well as a host of other operations that are useful when manipulating languages.

- *Language Transformations Parser*: We have an OCaml data type called `expression`, which models language transformations. This component parses a `.tr` file into this data type.
- *Transformation Executor*: The language transformation parsed in the data type `expression` is compiled into OCaml code, that is, into an `.ml` file. The generated code includes a function `transform : language → language` that takes a language definition and performs the transformations prescribed. To perform these transformations, the generated code relies on the API library mentioned above. Below we show an example of the code generated at this stage. The Transformation Executor calls `transform` passing the language definition previously parsed into `language`. The result is a value of type `language` that contains the language definition after all transformations.
- *Compiler to Language Definitions*: The result produced by the Transformation Executor is pretty-printed into a `.lan` file.
- *Compiler to λProlog*: The result produced by the Transformation Executor is also compiled into a λProlog program, that is, a pair of files `.mod` and `.sig` that can be executed with a λProlog implementation such as the Teyjus system.

We show an excerpt of the OCaml code that is generated for the transformation `pattern_matching.tr`. We single out the first instruction of that transformation, which is the adding of the operator `match` to the `Expression` grammar category, i.e. Expression e ::= ... | (match [e, MAP(p, e)]).

```
1   let transform lan =
2    let lan' =
3    language_replaceSyntacticCategory lan
4     (SyntacticCategory
5      ( "Expression",
6       "e",
7        syntax_getTermVariable "Expression" lan,
8        (syntax_getTerms "Expression" lan)
9         @ [Constructor
10             ("match",
11              [Var "e" ; TermMap("p", Var "e")])])
12     )
13    )
14  in
15   (* rest of the transformations *)
16   (* last transformation produces lan''''' *)
17   lan'''''
```

The language definition that we have parsed into a `language` data type is passed to the function `transform` as argument `lan`. At line 2, we create `lan'` with the language definition after executing the first transformation instruction (adding `match` to the grammar). `language_replaceSyntacticCategory` is called on line 3, which replaces the existing `Expression` category with a new one that we construct in lines 4–13. Intuitively, we replace `Expression` with what `Expression` already contains augmented with the `match` operator. To do so, we build the category with the same name and meta-variable previously used (lines 5–6). (We postpone explaining line 7). Lines 8–11 construct the grammar items of the new category. First, line 8 calls `syntax_getTerms` to collect the list of existing terms of `Expression`. Lines 9–11 append this list with the `match` operator. Line 7 inherits the *term variable* of the category (if it exists). These are the variables that can be used in programs as placeholders for the grammar items of the category. A notable example is the variable `x` in the `Expression` category of the λ-calculus.

The rest of the code, omitted at lines 15 and 16, makes use of `lan'` rather than `lan` to perform subsequent transformation instructions. Each of these instructions produce a new `lan'` variable to be used in the next instruction. (There is therefore a series of variables `lan'`. `lan''`, `lan'''`, and so on). At the end, `transform` returns the last language variable, which is `lan'''''` in the example above, and which contains the language after all transformations have been performed.

6 Repository

LANG-N-CHANGE comprises a repository with several language definitions `.lan` files and a handful of language transformations `.tr` files.

Our Experiments. Language definitions include λ-calculi with lists, pairs, tuples, if-then-else, options, let-binding, function composition $(g \circ f)(x)$, the recursor on natural numbers, and System F. The repository contains these calculi in both call-by-value and call-by-name versions, as well as lazy evaluation for data types such as pairs and lists. Languages with lists have been defined with the operators filter, map, append, range and reverse.

The repo of LANG-N-CHANGE includes language transformations for

- adding subtyping
- switching from small to big-step semantics
- adding references
- adding objects
- adding gradual typing
- adding pattern matching (presented here).

We have applied all our transformations to all our language definitions, and we have performed several tests on the generated languages. Our tests confirm that the functionalities that our transformations are meant to add are added indeed. The webpage of LANG-N-CHANGE contains the details of all the tests that we have conducted [14].

We have also performed experiments in composing our algorithms, and performed tests on these combinations as well. Some combinations are not possible, as we explain in the next paragraph. The number of composition combinations is large and we omit enumerating them here. The webpage of the tool [14] contains a well-marked section with a table that summarizes our experiments w.r.t. combining our transformations.

Limitations and Errors. The algorithms that we have devised are not capable of transforming *every* language definition. For example, our algorithms are currently tuned to handle functional languages only. This aspect can be seen in the algorithm for pattern matching in Sect. 3 where the selectors look for the explicit pattern `Gamma |- e : T` for typing rules. The algorithm then would not work for language definitions with a different shape for typing rules. In that case, depending on the language at hand, rules may not be selected and the transformation may produce an incomplete language definition. Our current algorithms also do not capture every possible operator within the realm of functional languages. For example, our subtyping algorithm adds subtyping for simple types and system F, but if we applied it to recursive types we would obtain a wrong treatment of subtyping because recursive subtyping has its own particular treatment [1].

As another limitation, the composition of some transformations cannot be performed. For example, the theory of *automatic* gradual typing does not handle references and objects [4,5]. Therefore, if we apply the algorithm to add reference first and that to add gradual typing afterwards we obtain an incorrect language. Also, some combination may not produce attractive languages such as adding references to call-by-name languages. It is also to notice that the composition of transformations is sensitive to the order in which they are applied. For example, if we add subtyping first and add pattern matching afterwards we obtain a language where the arguments of `match` are not subject to subtyping. This observation suggests that it may be worth to explore a principled semantics of language transformations.

LANG-N-CHANGE programmers can also make mistakes and have transformations that output ill-defined languages. For example, some transformations may generate a formula `Gamma |- bool : true`, where `bool` and `true` appear swapped, or generate the term `List bool bool`, where `List` is actually a unary type constructor. These type errors are reported to the user after the language definition is generated. This is thanks to the fact that languages are compiled into λProlog and λProlog is a statically typed language. Therefore, the type checker of λProlog detects these errors.

Just like programmers can write bad programs, LANG-N-CHANGE users can define transformation that do not lead to the languages they intended, or lead to ill-defined languages. Programmers are responsible for the correctness of their output.

7   Related Work and Future Work

The syntax for language transformations (.tr) of LANG-N-CHANGE is inspired by a formal calculus defined in [13]. [13] is a short paper that presents selected parts of the syntax, typing rules and reduction rules of a minimal calculus for language transformations. Our language for .tr is based on such calculus. The short paper [13] does not describe a tool. In contrast, this paper is a system description paper, describes LANG-N-CHANGE in detail together with its implementation details. The algorithm for adding pattern matching is also new in this paper.

LANG-N-CHANGE is mostly related to the work in language workbenches [9]. Language workbenches are specialized tools that support the definition, reuse and composition of domain-specific languages. They provide automated services for generating parsers, AST classes, and assisting in code generation. Some language workbenches go as far as generating evaluators, debuggers and trace management features [2]. Similarly, tools such as K and Redex perform automatic test generation [10,16], and K automatically generates verifiers. To the best of our knowledge, none of the previous works provide features in automatically adding common programming languages features to the languages being defined, such as pattern matching, subtyping, references, objects and gradual typing, which LANG-N-CHANGE does.

Language workbenches also offer operations for manipulating languages. An excellent classification of language transformations has been provided in [8]. Languages can be extended, unified, and restricted, and grammars can be renamed and remapped [18] among other operations. These type of transformations are coarse-grained in nature because they do not access the components of languages with precision. LANG-N-CHANGE, instead, includes operations to scan rules, premises, and terms, and select/manipulate them with precision. In this regard, LANG-N-CHANGE offers low-level language manipulations and a domain-specific language to express them.

Previous works have addressed the automatic transformation of languages. Danvy et al. [7] and Ciobâcă [6] offer a translation from small-step to big-step semantics. Poulsen and Mosses derive a variant of big-step semantics called pretty-big-step semantics [15]. The Gradualizer tool automatically generates gradually typed languages [4,5]. These are but a few examples. The main difference between LANG-N-CHANGE and these works is that the latter works are tools that target just one specific feature. LANG-N-CHANGE, on the contrary, offers a suite of transformations, and programmers can define new language transformations by writing new .tr files. Furthermore, we are not aware of any work that specifically automates the adding of pattern matching, subtyping, references, and objects, which LANG-N-CHANGE does.

LANG-N-CHANGE is an ongoing and long-term effort. For future work we plan to use LANG-N-CHANGE to formulate algorithms for automatically generating type inference procedures in Hindley-Milner style, automatically generating the definitions of logical relations for strong normalization proofs, and adding dependent types. We also plan on compiling language definitions into Ott specifications and benefit from Ott's features of generating OCaml and Coq implementations for free [17]. Furthermore, the work on language workbenches inspires us on developing a comfortable IDE for LANG-N-CHANGE. At the moment, users interact with LANG-N-CHANGE in a command-line fashion.

References

1. Amadio, R.M., Cardelli, L.: Subtyping recursive types. ACM Trans. Program. Lang. Syst. **15**(4), 575–631 (1993). https://doi.org/10.1145/155183.155231
2. Bousse, E., Degueule, T., Vojtisek, D., Mayerhofer, T., Deantoni, J., Combemale, B.: Execution framework of the gemoc studio (tool demo). In: Proceedings of the 2016 ACM SIGPLAN International Conference on Software Language Engineering, SLE 2016, pp. 84–89. ACM (2016)
3. Cheney, J.: Toward a general theory of names: binding and scope. In: Proceedings of the 3rd ACM SIGPLAN Workshop on Mechanized Reasoning About Languages with Variable Binding, pp. 33–40. ACM, New York (2005)
4. Cimini, M., Siek, J.G.: The gradualizer: a methodology and algorithm for generating gradual type systems. In: Symposium on Principles of Programming Languages, POPL, January 2016
5. Cimini, M., Siek, J.G.: Automatically generating the dynamic semantics of gradually typed languages. In: Proceedings of the 44th ACM SIGPLAN Symposium on Principles of Programming Languages, POPL 2017, pp. 789–803. ACM, New York (2017)
6. Ciobâcă, Ş.: From small-step semantics to big-step semantics, automatically. In: Johnsen, E.B., Petre, L. (eds.) IFM 2013. LNCS, vol. 7940, pp. 347–361. Springer, Heidelberg (2013). https://doi.org/10.1007/978-3-642-38613-8_24
7. Danvy, O.: Defunctionalized interpreters for programming languages. In: Proceedings of the 13th ACM SIGPLAN International Conference on Functional Programming, ICFP 2008, pp. 131–142. ACM, New York (2008)
8. Erdweg, S., Giarrusso, P.G., Rendel, T.: Language composition untangled, LDTA 2012, pp. 7:1–7:8. ACM, New York (2012)
9. Erdweg, S., et al.: The state of the art in language workbenches. In: Erwig, M., Paige, R.F., Van Wyk, E. (eds.) SLE 2013. LNCS, vol. 8225, pp. 197–217. Springer, Cham (2013). https://doi.org/10.1007/978-3-319-02654-1_11
10. Felleisen, M., Findler, R.B., Flatt, M.: Semantics Engineering with PLT Redex. MIT Press, Cambridge (2009)
11. Miller, D., Nadathur, G.: Programming with Higher-Order Logic, 1st edn. Cambridge University Press, New York (2012)
12. Mourad, B., Cimini, M.: A calculus for language transformations. Technical report (2019). arXiv:1910.11924 [cs.PL]
13. Mourad, B., Cimini, M.: A calculus for language transformations. In: Chatzigeorgiou, A., et al. (eds.) SOFSEM 2020. LNCS, vol. 12011, pp. 547–555. Springer, Cham (2020). https://doi.org/10.1007/978-3-030-38919-2_44
14. Mourad, B., Cimini, M.: Lang-n-Change. Webpage of the tool (2019). http://cimini.info/LNC/index.html
15. Bach Poulsen, C., Mosses, P.D.: Deriving pretty-big-step semantics from small-step semantics. In: Shao, Z. (ed.) ESOP 2014. LNCS, vol. 8410, pp. 270–289. Springer, Heidelberg (2014). https://doi.org/10.1007/978-3-642-54833-8_15
16. Rosu, G., Şerbănuţă, T.F.: An overview of the K semantic framework. J. Log. Algebraic Program. **79**(6), 397–434 (2010)
17. Sewell, P., et al.: Ott: effective tool support for the working semanticist. In: Proceedings of the 12th ACM SIGPLAN International Conference on Functional Programming, ICFP 2007, pp. 1–12. ACM, New York (2007)
18. Vacchi, E., Cazzola, W.: Neverlang: a framework for feature-oriented language development. Comput. Lang. Syst. Struct. **43**, 1–40 (2015)

An SMT-Based Concolic Testing Tool for Logic Programs

Sophie Fortz[1]([⊠]), Fred Mesnard[2], Etienne Payet[2], Gilles Perrouin[1], Wim Vanhoof[1], and Germán Vidal[3]

[1] Université de Namur, Namur, Belgium
sophie.fortz@unamur.be
[2] LIM - Université de la Réunion, Saint-Denis, France
[3] MiST, VRAIN, Universitat Politècnica de València, Valencia, Spain

Abstract. Concolic testing combines symbolic and concrete execution to generate test cases that achieve a good program coverage. Its benefits have been demonstrated for more than 15 years in the case of imperative programs. In this work, we present a concolic-based test generation tool for logic programs which exploits SMT-solving for constraint resolution.

1 Concolic Testing of Logic Programs

Concolic testing is a well-established validation technique for imperative and object-oriented programs [3,8], but only recently investigated for functional and logic programming languages. Concolic testing for logic programming was initially studied by Vidal [11] and Mesnard *et al.* [4], while Giantsos *et al.* [2] and Tikovsky *et al.* [10] considered concolic testing of functional programs.

Concolic testing performs both concrete and symbolic execution in parallel: given a test case (atomic goal), e.g., $p(a)$, we evaluate both $p(a)$ (the *concrete* goal) and $p(X)$ (the *symbolic* goal), where X is a fresh variable, using a concolic execution extension of SLD resolution. The symbolic goal mimics the steps of the concrete goal but is aimed at gathering constraints that can be later used to produce alternative test cases. In particular, alternative test cases are computed by solving so-called *selective unification* problems [4,6]. The previous algorithm introduced by Mesnard *et al.* [4] does not scale well and does not support negative constraints. By defining selective unification problems as constraints on Herbrand terms and relying on an SMT solver, we address both scalability and completeness issues.

Let us motivate our approach by illustrating one of the problems of the previous framework [4]. Consider the following logic program defining predicates $p/1$ and $q/1$:

$$(\ell_1) \ \ p(a). \qquad\qquad (\ell_3) \ \ q(b).$$
$$(\ell_2) \ \ p(X) \leftarrow q(X).$$

Third author is a research associate at FNRS that also supports this work (O05518F-RG03). The last author is partially supported by the EU (FEDER) and the Spanish MCI/AEI under grants TIN2016-76843-C4-1-R/PID2019-104735RB-C41 and by the *Generalitat Valenciana* under grant Prometeo/2019/098 (DeepTrust).

K. Nakano and K. Sagonas (Eds.): FLOPS 2020, LNCS 12073, pp. 215–219, 2020.
https://doi.org/10.1007/978-3-030-59025-3_13

where ℓ_1, ℓ_2, ℓ_3 are (unique) clause labels. Given an initial call, say $p(a)$, the algorithm considers all possible matching clauses for this call (i.e., all combinations from clauses l_1 and l_2) and produces the sets $\{\}$, $\{p(a)\}$, $\{p(X)\}$, and $\{p(a), p(X)\}$ with the heads of the clauses in each combination.

The considered initial call already covers the last case (i.e., it matches both $p(a)$ and $p(X)$). As for the remaining cases:

- *Matching no clause.* This case is clearly unfeasible, since the head of the second clause, $p(X)$, matches any call.
- *Matching only clause ℓ_1.* This case is unfeasible as well since every atom that unifies with $p(a)$ will also unify with $p(X)$.
- *Matching only clause ℓ_2.* This case is clearly feasible with, e.g., $p(b)$, since $p(b)$ unifies with $p(X)$ but it does not unify with $p(a)$. Thus $p(b)$ is our next initial goal.

In the second iteration, $p(b)$ calls $q(b)$ (using clause ℓ_2) and, then, successfully matches clause ℓ_3. Since we only have one clause defining $q/1$, the only alternative consists in producing an initial call to $p/1$ that i) unifies with clause ℓ_2 but not with clause ℓ_1 and, then, ii) calls $q/1$ but fails. Unfortunately, since the approach of Mesnard et al. [4] cannot represent negative constraints, the algorithm tries to find an instance $p(X)\sigma$ of $p(X)$ such that $q(X)\sigma$ does not unify with $q(b)$. A possible solution is then $p(a)$. Observe that this goal will not achieve the desired result (matching clause ℓ_2 and then fail) since it will match clause ℓ_1 and terminate successfully. Indeed, since $p(a)$ was already considered, the concolic testing algorithm of Mesnard et al. [4] terminates computing the test cases $\{p(a), p(b)\}$, which is unnecessarily incomplete.

For example, if we assume that the domain comprises at least one more constant, say c, then the right set of test cases should be $\{p(a), p(b), p(c)\}$, so that the last test case actually matches clause ℓ_2 and then fails. In this work, we overcome the above problem by introducing constraints, which can represent both positive and negative information. In particular, the search for an instance of $p(X)$ that first unifies with clause ℓ_2 only, and then fails, is represented as follows:

$$p(X) \neq p(a) \wedge (\forall Y \ p(X) \neq p(Y) \vee q(Y) \neq q(b))$$

Solving this constraint (using an SMT solver) would produce the desired test case, $p(c)$, thus achieving a full path coverage.

For this purpose, we have designed a concolic testing tool for logic programs that is based on the following principles:

- As in the approach of Mesnard et al. [4], we instrument a *deterministic* semantics for logic programs (inspired by the linear semantics of Ströder et al. [9]) in order to perform both concrete and symbolic execution in parallel.
- In contrast to previous approaches, our instrumented semantics also considers negative constraints, so that the problems mentioned above can be avoided (i.e., our implemented semantics is complete in more cases).

- Finally, the generated constraints are solved using a state-of-the-art constraint solver, namely the Z3 SMT solver [1]. This allows us to make concolic testing more efficient in practice.

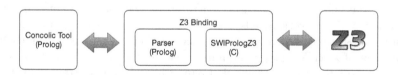

Fig. 1. Implementation workflow.

Table 1. Summary of experimental results

Subject program	size	Initial goal	Ground Args	Max Depth	time concolic	time contest	#TCs concolic	#TCs contest
Nat	2	nat(0)	1	1	0.050	0.0273	3	4
Nat	2	nat(0)	1	5	0.0897	0.1554	7	12
Nat	2	nat(0)	1	50	1.6752	19.5678	52	102
Generator	7	generate(empty,_A,_B)	1	1	1.4517	0.7096	9	9
Generator	7	generate(empty,T,_B)	2	1	1.3255	4.4820	9	9
Generator	7	generate(empty,T,H)	3	1	1.3211	crash	9	N/A
Activities	38	what_to_do_today(sunday, sunny,wash_your_car)	3	2	6.3257	timeout	122	N/A
Cannibals	78	start(config(3,3,0,0))	1	2	0.0535	timeout	2	N/A
Family	48	parent(dicky,X)	1	1	20.0305	64.1838	9	19
Monsters and mazes	113	base_score(will,grace)	2	2	0.2001	0.4701	6	7

2   A Concolic Testing Tool for Prolog

Our prototype is implemented in SWI-Prolog [12] and the Z3 SMT solver [1], as depicted in Fig. 1. Regarding the termination of concolic testing, we impose a maximum term depth for the generated test cases. Since the domain is finite and we do not generate duplicated test cases, termination is trivially ensured.

Let us show some selected results from a preliminary experimental evaluation of our concolic testing tool. We selected six programs from previous benchmarks [4] and from GitHub.[1] We ran concolic testing between 3 and 100 executions on a MacBook Pro hexacore 2,6 Ghz with 16 GB RAM in order to get reliable results. Reported times, in seconds, are the average of these executions. Our results are reported in Table 1. Here, concolic refers to our tool, while contest refers to the tool introduced by Mesnard *et al.* [4]; the size of a subject program is the number of its source lines of code; column Ground Args displays the number of ground arguments in the initial symbolic goal; and #TCs refers to the number

---

[1] https://github.com/Anniepoo/prolog-examples.

of generated test cases. A timeout for contest is set to 1000 1000 s (the crash is an overflow).

Regarding execution times, our new tool exhibits a certain overhead on small programs with a low depth due to the calls to the SMT solver. As program size and/or depth increase, our tool performs up to 10 times faster than contest. We note that the number of test cases generated by the tools are not comparable since our new framework avoids a source of incompleteness (as mentioned in the previous section), but also restricts the number of test cases by forbidding the binding of so-called *output* arguments (which is allowed in contest). More details can be found in the companion paper: http://arxiv.org/abs/2002.07115. The implementation is also publicly available at https://github.com/sfortz/Pl_Concolic_Testing.

3   Conclusion

In this paper, we report our experience in the development of an SMT-based concolic testing tool that is based on the approach of *Mesnard et al.* [4] but adds support for negative constraints, thus overcoming some of the limitations of previous approaches [5,6]. Our preliminary experimental evaluation has shown promising results regarding the scalability of the method.

Recently, concolic testing has been extended to CLP programs [7], so that both positive and negative constraints can be represented in a natural way. As future work, we plan to extend our concolic testing tool to the case of CLP programs.

References

1. de Moura, L., Bjørner, N.: Z3: an efficient SMT solver. In: Ramakrishnan, C.R., Rehof, J. (eds.) TACAS 2008. LNCS, vol. 4963, pp. 337–340. Springer, Heidelberg (2008). https://doi.org/10.1007/978-3-540-78800-3_24
2. Giantsios, A., Papaspyrou, N., Sagonas, K.: Concolic testing for functional languages. Sci. Comput. Program. **147**, 109–134 (2017)
3. Godefroid, P., Klarlund, N., Sen, K.: DART: directed automated random testing. In: Proceedings of PLDI 2005, pp. 213–223. ACM (2005)
4. Mesnard, F., Payet, É., Vidal, G.: Concolic testing in logic programming. TPLP **15**(4–5), 711–725 (2015). https://doi.org/10.1017/S1471068415000332
5. Mesnard, F., Payet, É., Vidal, G.: On the completeness of selective unification in concolic testing of logic programs. In: Hermenegildo, M.V., Lopez-Garcia, P. (eds.) LOPSTR 2016. LNCS, vol. 10184, pp. 205–221. Springer, Cham (2017). https://doi.org/10.1007/978-3-319-63139-4_12
6. Mesnard, F., Payet, É., Vidal, G.: Selective unification in constraint logic programming. In: Vanhoof, W., Pientka, B. (eds.) PPDP, pp. 115–126. ACM (2017)
7. Mesnard, F., Payet, É., Vidal, G.: Concolic Testing in CLP. CoRR abs/2008.00421 (2020). https://arxiv.org/abs/2008.00421
8. Sen, K., Marinov, D., Agha, G.: CUTE: a concolic unit testing engine for C. In: ESEC/ FSE, pp. 263–272. ACM (2005)

9. Ströder, T., Emmes, F., Schneider-Kamp, P., Giesl, J., Fuhs, C.: A linear operational semantics for termination and complexity analysis of ISO Prolog. In: Vidal, G. (ed.) LOPSTR 2011. LNCS, vol. 7225, pp. 237–252. Springer, Heidelberg (2012). https://doi.org/10.1007/978-3-642-32211-2_16

10. Tikovsky, J.R.: Concolic testing of functional logic programs. In: Seipel, D., Hanus, M., Abreu, S. (eds.) WFLP/WLP/INAP -2017. LNCS (LNAI), vol. 10997, pp. 169–186. Springer, Cham (2018). https://doi.org/10.1007/978-3-030-00801-7_11

11. Vidal, G.: Concolic execution and test case generation in prolog. In: Proietti, M., Seki, H. (eds.) LOPSTR 2014. LNCS, vol. 8981, pp. 167–181. Springer, Cham (2015). https://doi.org/10.1007/978-3-319-17822-6_10

12. Wielemaker, J., Schrijvers, T., Triska, M., Lager, T.: SWI-prolog. TPLP **12**(1–2), 67–96 (2012). https://doi.org/10.1017/S1471068411000494

Author Index

Printed in the United States
By Bookmasters